Democracy, Electoral Systems, and Judicial Empowerment in Developing Countries

The power granted to the courts, both in a nation's constitution and in practice, reveals much about the willingness of the legislature and the executive to accept restraints on their own powers. For this reason, an independent judiciary is considered an indication of a nation's level of democracy. In *Democracy, Electoral Systems, and Judicial Empowerment in Developing Countries,* Vineeta Yadav and Bumba Mukherjee use a data set covering 159 developing countries, along with comparative case studies of Brazil and Indonesia, to identify the political conditions under which de jure independence is established. They find that the willingness of political elites to grant the courts authority to review the actions of the other branches of government depends on the capacity of the legislature and expectations regarding the judiciary's assertiveness. Moving next to de facto independence, Yadav and Mukherjee bring together data from 103 democracies in the developing world, complemented by case studies of Brazil, India, and Indonesia. Honing in on the effects of electoral institutions, the authors find that, when faced with short time horizons, governments that operate in personal vote electoral systems are likely to increase de facto judicial independence, whereas governments in party-centered systems are likely to reduce it.

Vineeta Yadav is Assistant Professor of Political Science at Pennsylvania State University.

Bumba Mukherjee is Associate Professor of Political Science at Pennsylvania State University.

NEW COMPARATIVE POLITICS

Series Editor
Michael Laver, New York University

Editorial Board
Ken Benoit, Trinity College, Dublin
Gary Cox, University of California, San Diego
Simon Hix, London School of Economics
John Huber, Columbia University
Herbert Kitschelt, Duke University
G. Bingham Powell, University of Rochester
Kaare Strøm, University of California, San Diego
George Tsebelis, University of Michigan
Leonard Wantchekon, Princeton University

The New Comparative Politics series brings together cutting-edge work on social conflict, political economy, and institutional development. Whatever its substantive focus, each book in the series builds on solid theoretical foundations; uses rigorous empirical analysis; and deals with timely, politically relevant questions.

Curbing Bailouts: Bank Crises and Democratic Accountability in Comparative Perspective
   Guillermo Rosas

The Madisonian Turn: Political Parties and Parliamentary Democracy in Nordic Europe
   Edited by Torbjörn Bergman and Kaare Strøm

Political Survival of Small Parties in Europe
   Jae-Jae Spoon

Veto Power: Institutional Design in the European Union
   Jonathan B. Slapin

Democracy, Dictatorship, and Term Limits
   Alexander Baturo

Democracy, Electoral Systems, and Judicial Empowerment in Developing Countries
   Vineeta Yadav and Bumba Mukherjee

Democracy, Electoral Systems, and Judicial Empowerment in Developing Countries

VINEETA YADAV

and

BUMBA MUKHERJEE

The University of Michigan Press
Ann Arbor

Copyright © by the University of Michigan 2014
All rights reserved

This book may not be reproduced, in whole or in part, including illustrations, in any form (beyond that copying permitted by Sections 107 and 108 of the U.S. Copyright Law and except by reviewers for the public press), without written permission from the publisher.

Published in the United States of America by
The University of Michigan Press
Manufactured in the United States of America
♾ Printed on acid-free paper

2017   2016   2015   2014   4 3 2 1

A CIP catalog record for this book is available from the British Library.

Library of Congress Cataloging-in-Publication Data

Yadav, Vineeta, author.
    Democracy, electoral systems, and judicial empowerment in developing countries / Vineeta Yadav, Bumba Mukherjee.
      pages   cm. — (New comparative politics)
    Includes bibliographical references and index.
    ISBN 978-0-472-11908-0 (alk. paper) — ISBN 978-0-472-02962-4 (ebook)
    1. Judicial independence—Developing countries.   2. Judicial review—Developing countries.   3. New democracies.   4. Brazil—Politics and government.   5. Indonesia—Politics and government.   I. Mukherjee, Bumba, author.   II. Title.
    K3367.Y23   2014
    347'.012091724—dc23

                                                  2013044061

To Biswanath and Usha Mukherjee
   AND
To the "Asha-Gang," who always saw the lotus in the mud
   AND
To the indefatigable and intrepid Reyhan!

CONTENTS

	Acknowledgments	ix
1	Explaining Variation in De Jure and De Facto Judicial Independence	1
2	The Theoretical Framework	32
3	New Democracies and De Jure Judicial Review: The Empirical Evidence	75
4	Democratic Transition and Judicial Review in Indonesia and Brazil	108
5	Empirical Tests for Electoral Particularism and De Facto Judicial Independence	148
6	De Facto Judicial Independence in Particularistic Systems: Brazil and India	180
7	De Facto Judicial Independence in Party-Centered Systems: Post–Suharto Indonesia	227
8	Conclusion	260
	Appendix	277
	Notes	283
	References	315
	Index	353

ACKNOWLEDGMENTS

We would both like to thank our colleagues at the Department of Political Science at Penn State University for providing an intellectually stimulating and convivial environment. Vineeta Yadav would like to gratefully acknowledge the financial support provided by the Kellogg Institute at University of Notre Dame through a faculty grant award during 2009–2010. The grant funded the fieldwork necessary to conduct interviews in these countries.

We would like to thank Frances Rosenbluth, Chris Zorn, Michael Laver, and especially Scott Mainwaring and Timothy Power for sharing their data on the ANC voting for Brazil. At the University of Michigan Press, we would like to thank Melody Herr for her support and patience. We would also like to thank two anonymous reviewers for their comments and encouragement. They helped considerably improve this book. The final errors are, of course, all ours. We also thank J. Naomi Linzer Indexing Services for their excellent work on indexing this book.

Several research assistants were invaluable in carrying out this project. For their outstanding research assistance we would like to thank Sergio Béjar, Chad Evans, and Ben Begozzi. For assistance with field research in Brazil and for translations from Portuguese to English, we thank Chad Evans. For assistance with field research in India we thank Shrey Yadav. We owe a special thanks to the many interviewees in Brazil, India, and Indonesia who were gracious enough to share their expertise and experiences with us.

And to our families and friends—for their support, encouragement, and patience throughout the long process of working on a project of this magnitude. Vineeta would like to thank her parents, Sonu, Meghna, Alison Bruey, Katie Paul, Aleksandra Sznajder, Ravi, and Sonali. Finally, to Reyhan, who made sure we got some exercise in by making us run after him all the time!

CHAPTER 1

Explaining Variation in De Jure and De Facto Judicial Independence

The global movement toward democracy in the developing world during the past 30 years gave birth to many new democracies which raised the political freedom of millions of citizens in these states. Political elites in these new democratic regimes were confronted with a new set of political challenges—how to protect their citizens' rights, "insure" their own political future, and preserve their political hegemony in the new electoral marketplace they found themselves in.[1] Judicial reforms were an important part of the strategies elites adopted in response to these new challenges. The specific judicial institutional forms these political responses took, however, varied considerably across states. Incumbents in some new democracies responded to these challenges by establishing de jure judicial independence through constitutional provisions during the initial post–transition years in their countries.[2] Elites in these countries chose to grant their courts (1) full or partial judicial review, (2) provided judges with guaranteed life or long tenure and financial independence, and (3) established the judiciary as a separate branch.[3] Others, however, chose to deal with these challenges by choosing not to constitutionally empower their judiciaries.

The variation in constitutional judicial empowerment in the initial post–transition years across newly democratized states in the developing world is illustrated in figs. 1.1 and 1.2. Fig. 1.1 reveals that in the first four post–democratic transition years, more than 90 percent of 63 newly democratized states—which are listed in table 1.1[4]—constitutionally guaranteed life or long tenure for judges, allowed courts to control judicial appointments and their budget, and established the judiciary as a separate branch from the executive and the legislature.[5] In contrast, fig. 1.2 shows that in the first four post–transition years, approximately 40 percent of new democracies chose not to provide their courts with constitutional guarantees for full judicial review authority, whereas the others did.[6] Thus, unlike the lack of variation in rules dealing with tenure, budgets, or separation of the judiciary, rules that allow judges to overturn government policies (judicial review) vary significantly across these countries. For example, elites in Brazil and Bulgaria adopted constitutional provisions for judicial review

TABLE 1.1. Democratic Transitions in the Developing World since 1982

Country	Transition Year	Country	Transition Year
Albania	1992	Madagascar	1993
Argentina	1983	Malawi	1994
Armenia	1998	Mali	1992
Bangladesh	1991	Mexico	1997
Benin	1991	Moldova	1994
Bolivia	1982	Mongolia	1992
Brazil	1985	Mozambique	1994
Bulgaria	1990	Nepal	1991
Cape Verde	1991	Nicaragua	1990
Central African Republic	1993	Niger	1999
Chile	1990	Nigeria	1999
Comoros	1990	Pakistan	1988
Croatia	2000	Panama	1994
Czech Republic	1993	Paraguay	1993
Djibouti	1999	Peru	1980
El Salvador	1994	Philippines	1987
Estonia	1991	Poland	1990
Ethiopia	1995	Romania	1990
Georgia	1995	Russia	1993
Grenada	1984	Sap Tome and Principe	1991
Ghana	1996	Senegal	2000
Guatemala	1996	Slovak Republic	1993
Guyana	1992	Slovenia	1992
Haiti	1994	South Africa	1994
Honduras	1982	Suriname	1991
Hungary	1990	Tanzania	1995
Indonesia	1999	Thailand	1992
Korea, South	1988	Turkey	1983
Latvia	1991	Ukraine	1991
Lesotho	1993	Uruguay	1985
Lithuania	1991	Zambia	1991
Macedonia	1991		

Note: The democratic-transition year for each country in this table is identified using the Przeworski, Alvarez, Cheibub, and Limongi 2000 data set and the Polity indicator of the year of democratic transition.

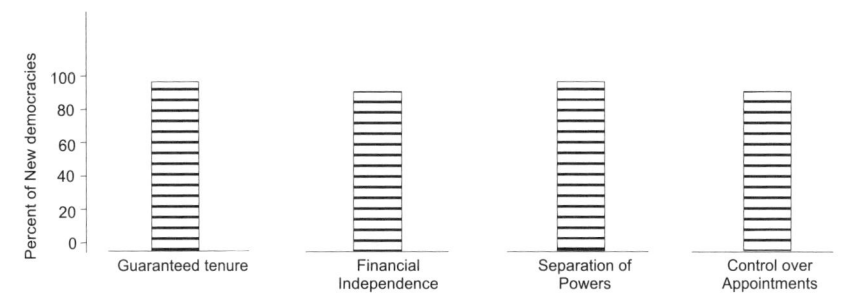

Fig. 1.1. Components of de jure judicial autonomy in new democracies

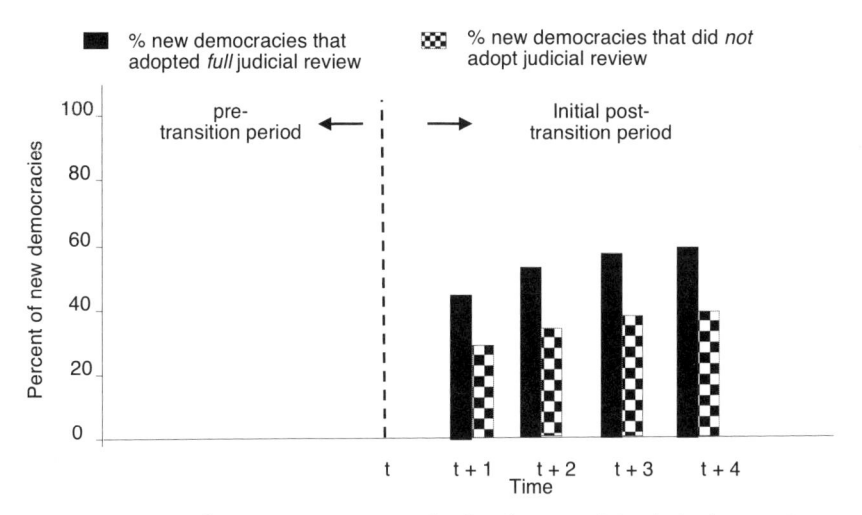

Fig. 1.2. New democratic regimes and judicial review. (The dashed vertical line in the figure indicates the democratic transition year, which is denoted as t. Note that $t + 1$, $t + 2$, $t + 3$, $t + 4$ indicate the first four initial post-democratic-transition years. The data sources employed to generate figs. 1.1 and 1.2 are listed in chapter 3.)

but those in Bangladesh and Romania did not. Fig. 1.2 therefore raises the following important puzzle which is the first question addressed in this book: why are governments in some new democratic regimes, but not in others, less likely to adopt full and explicit judicial review in the initial post–transition years?

Growing literatures in judicial and comparative politics have identified important factors such as political fragmentation (Shapiro 1981; Ackerman 1997; Smithey and Ishiyama 2000; Stephenson 2003; Herron and Randazzo 2003), electoral uncertainty (Ginsburg 2003; Finkel 2001, 2008; Hirschl 2004), and the idea of protecting human rights (Shapiro 1981; Guarnieri and Pederzoli 2002) as being crucial determinants of the decision to adopt judicial review powers. This body of research provides substantively rich predictions that have been empirically assessed in specific regions such as Asia, Eastern Europe, or Latin America.[7] Yet to the best of our knowledge, sufficient attention has not been paid toward explaining the full range of variation in de jure judicial review observed in new democracies across the entire developing world. As such, this motivates us to address the substantively interesting puzzle posited in the preceding paragraph.

Any analysis of judicial empowerment in developing countries however, cannot stop at the study of *de jure* independence alone. As scholars have noted,[8] the challenge of judicial independence in developing states does not end with the constitutional establishment of de jure judicial independence. Instead it continues with respect to maintaining the courts' de facto independence—that is, the independence of the judiciary "in practice"—over time.[9] For example, even though the first post–transition governments in Argentina and the Ukraine constitutionally established key components of de jure judicial independence, successive governments in the two countries interfered in judicial decisions and curtailed their courts' de facto independence once these states evolved into stable democracies.[10] In contrast, successive governments in Brazil and Hungary not only maintained the judiciary's constitutionally granted independence but in fact enhanced their courts' de facto judicial independence as they evolved into full-fledged democracies (Prilliman 2000; Santiso 2003; Taylor 2004; OSI 2002; Sajó 2006). While this distinction is particularly relevant for newly democratized developing states as they evolve into "newly consolidated" democracies, variation in de facto judicial independence is not restricted to new developing democracies alone. Indeed, the map illustrated in fig. 1.3 indicates that the average level of de facto judicial independence (hereafter DFJI) varies significantly across a global sample of 103 newly consolidated and established developing country democracies during the 1985–2004 period.[11]

Scholars have put forth numerous theories to explain this variation in DFJI.[12] Two of the most influential theories in academic research and policy circles argue that DFJI is higher in countries which have separation of powers, and in countries with high levels of political competition. Research

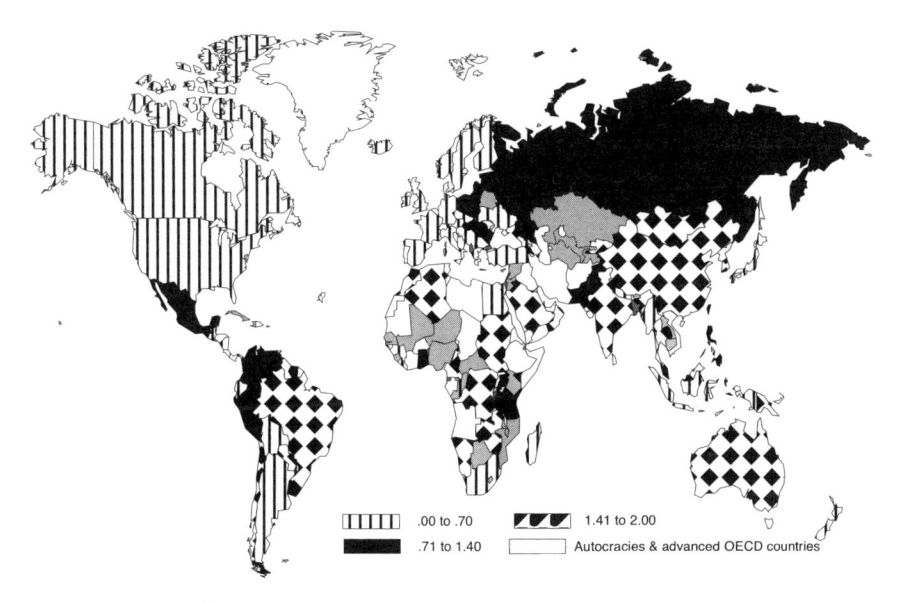

Fig. 1.3. De facto judicial independence in developing country democracies. (Map based on calculating the average level of de facto judicial independence [bounded between 0 and 2] for developing countries that are observed as democracies during the 1985 to 2004 period. Data sources used to compute the mean of de facto judicial independence are listed in chapter 5.)

on separation of powers systems has also emphasized the importance of genuine interbranch political competition found in a divided government as opposed to the low levels of interbranch competition found in a unified government for increasing levels of de facto independence (Rosenberg 1992; Whittington 2003; Iaryczower, Spiller, and Tommasi 2002). Hence, arguments based on political competition have gained increased salience in explaining DFJI.

The argument is that higher political competition creates more political uncertainty regarding the outcomes of elections, which in turn induces political elites to develop strategies to deal with the domestic political challenges it creates.[13] Elites, for instance, devise strategies to insure themselves against future retaliation by the opposition (Ginsburg 2003; Finkel 2001, 2008; Magaloni 2003; Magalhaes 1999), continue their preferred policies (Hirschl 2004; Trochev 2004; Shambayati and Kirdis 2008) or solve time-inconsistency problems for their donors (Landes and Posner 1975). In the context of short time horizons in office, elites respond to such strategic uncertainties by creating a genuinely independent judiciary. In contrast, the longer time horizons associated with low political competition do not present elites with these strategic challenges, scholars argue. In fact, they provide elites with incentives to increase their own power by curtailing judicial independence (Ramseyer 1994; Cooter and Ginsburg 1996; Stephenson 2003; Whittington 2003; Hansen 2004; Beer 2006; McCubbins et al. 2006; Ferejohn et al. 2007). This is a compelling argument, but further study of these countries reveals an intriguing puzzle.

Fig. 1.4 maps the hazard rates of governments (their predicted probability of failure)[14] to proxy for the strategic time horizons of governments for the countries listed in table 1.2 against their DFJI scores. As fig. 1.4 shows, high hazard rate of governments—or equivalently low time horizons—in office are associated with increased de facto judicial independence in 56 percent of these countries as predicted by current political competition theory. However, in the remaining 44 percent of the developing democracies in the sample, contrary to theoretical expectations, shorter time horizons are associated with reduced de facto judicial independence. Why do low time horizons in office provide incentives to governments in some developing country democracies to enhance de facto judicial independence, but induces governments in other developing democracies to curtail de facto judicial independence? This puzzle invites us to reexamine the role that political competition plays in explaining variation in de facto judicial independence and reiterates the original question—why do countries choose to invest in such different levels of judicial independence? This is the second question addressed in this book.

Thus, put together, this book seeks to first study the determinants of constitutional empowerment (or lack thereof) of the judiciary in new democracies by examining the conditions under which judiciaries are given the important de jure power of judicial review. Secondly, it seeks to analyze the politics of maintaining the de facto independence of the judiciary in established and newly consolidated developing country democracies. As described later in this chapter, we answer these puzzles theoretically by analyzing the interaction between the government, the opposition, and the judiciary in the context of different domestic institutional and political conditions. We then assess the empirical validity and generalizability of our theoretical explanations by conducting statistical tests on comprehensive global samples of

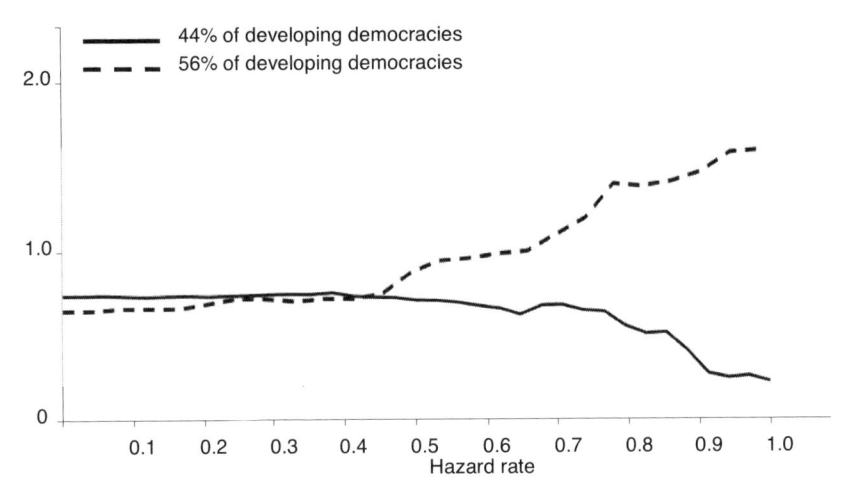

Fig. 1.4. Hazard rate of governments and de facto judicial independence. (Data sources used to construct this figure are listed in chapter 5. A higher hazard rate in office implies lower time horizons in office for incumbents. A lower hazard rate implies higher time horizons in office.)

countries. Finally, we use carefully selected sets of comparative case studies to illustrate the underlying causal dynamics of de jure judicial review adoption and de facto independence in developing country democracies.

The rest of this chapter is divided into six sections. The following section defines the concepts of de jure judicial review and de facto judicial independence as used in this book. The third section describes why studying the politics of de jure and de facto judicial independence is important in the context of developing countries. The fourth section briefly examines existing theoretical explanations for variation in the adoption of de jure judicial review and the observed levels of de facto judicial independence in order to identify key missing elements from these arguments. The fifth section briefly previews the theoretical arguments forwarded in this book to explain de jure review empowerment and de facto independence and presents the specific theoretical hypotheses that are tested in this book. The sixth section then summarizes the logic and design of the multi-methodological approach that we employ to empirically assess our theoretical claims. Finally, we provide a summary of the organization of the rest of this book in the conclusion of this chapter.

Definitions of De Jure Judicial Review and De Facto Independence

Vanberg (2008: 100) defines judicial independence as a concept which, "refers to an abstract, conceptual as well as a formal, institutional dimension. At the broadest level, the ideal of judicial independence expresses the aspiration that judicial decisions should not be influenced in an inappropriate manner by considerations judged to be normatively irrelevant.... The desire to reduce the impact of inappropriate considerations gives rise to a formal, institutional dimension of judicial independence that identifies it with specific institutional safeguards that can serve to insulate judges against these influences." In this book, we follow Vanberg and a host of other scholars as well in making this conceptual distinction between the *institutional rules* intended to create judicial independence and the *actual independent* practice of adjudication explicit by referring to the latter as de facto judicial independence (DFJI) and the former as de jure judicial independence (DJJI).[15]

De jure judicial independence is defined by the extent of formal legal powers assigned by the constitution to the judiciary in order to insulate judges from undue pressures, and to give them the legal authority to undertake various actions.[16] Rules which provide for apolitical appointment processes and provide judiciaries with wider jurisdictions, give them powers of judicial and constitutional review, guarantee long tenures, give them final authority over matters within their competence, and control over judicial budgets, court administration and their internal judicial operations, are believed to be consistent with higher levels of de jure independence.[17]

Judicial review, defined as "the power of a court to invalidate a statute or other action of government because it is in conflict with the constitution" (Shapiro 2002: 149), has been identified by scholars as one of the most important de jure powers courts can have.[18] Following Ferejohn, Rosenbluth, and Shipan (2007) and Carubba et al. (2008), we define "full judicial review" here and throughout this book broadly[19] to include the review by courts (not only constitutional courts) of statutes, constitutional provisions, legislative bills, amendments, and government acts.[20] Since the power of judicial review allows courts to overturn government legislation, executive decrees, and administrative directions, it allows courts to provide a constitutional check on government behaviors and policies.[21]

The ability to freely exercise judicial review powers in practice is a function of the judiciary's de facto independence. Larkins (1996: 611) provides a thorough definition of de facto judicial independence: "Judicial independence refers to the existence of judges who are not manipulated for political gain, who are impartial towards the parties of a dispute, and who form a judicial branch which has the power as an institution to regulate the legality of government behavior, enact "neutral" justice, and determine significant constitutional and legal values." This definition encompasses three key facets of genuine independence. First, independence is typically defined in terms of standards of behavior applied to the judiciary as an institution and to the behavior of individual judges. Second, independent judges issue judgments reflecting their sincere beliefs and preferences but do so in accordance with the laws of the land. Third, it includes the explicit stipulation that judicial decisions must be enforced in practice for the judiciary to be considered independent (World Bank 2003; Cameron 2002).[22] This definition is thus conceptually distinct from the independence judges have been guaranteed formally through constitutional provisions and the laws of the country and requires a very different operationalization.[23]

The relationship between de jure and de facto independence has been a matter of some debate. Some scholars have argued that higher levels of de jure independence lead to higher levels of de facto independence (MacCormick 1999; Russell and O'Brien 2001; Hayo and Voigt 2007). Others, however, have argued that de jure independence is neither necessary nor sufficient for de facto judicial independence (Rosenn 1987; Vyas 1999; Widner 2001; Herron and Randazzo 2003; Chavez 2008; Vanberg 2008). Feld and Voigt (2003) and Rios-Figueroa and Staton (2009) find that the correlation between de jure powers and de facto independence across countries is low. Given this debate and given the two questions we start out with, we do not make any assumptions regarding the necessity of de jure rules for de facto judicial independence. Rather, we consider this an empirical question and ensure that we are controlling for these de jure powers when we examine the determinants of de facto judicial independence in our cross-country analysis as well as our case studies.

Why Analyzing Judicial Independence in Developing Countries is Important

Understanding the relationship between democracy and judicial independence across developing states is not just an important issue of academic significance but also has important implications for policy-making and socioeconomic development. Our book provides valuable insights on how certain domestic political institutions can help promote judicial independence across developing countries and thus help realize the potential of the judiciary to improve national performance in delivering growth, reducing corruption, and increasing respect for human rights in these states. We begin by considering the consequences of these findings for the extensive judicial reform efforts undertaken by various domestic and international actors interested in promoting these outcomes through the establishment of a strong and independent judiciary.

The widely shared belief that greater judicial independence leads to more stable societies and greater respect for property rights, which facilitates economic development (Landes and Posner 1975; Stone Sweet 2000; World Bank 2003; La Porta et al. 2004; Carothers 2006; Scartiscini 2008; Gibler and Randazzo 2011), has led international institutions such as the World Bank, the USAID, Asian Development Bank, Inter-American Development Bank, and advanced industrial governments to invest substantial amounts of aid to promote independent courts in the developing world. For example, the World Bank alone has spent over $7 billion dollars over a 20-year period supporting projects geared at creating and strengthening independent judiciaries in developing nations around the world (World Bank 2003, 2010). Likewise, individual countries such as the United States (Millennium Challenge Corporation 2010: 18) and Denmark (Gloppen and Kanyongolo 2006) have explicitly used their national political influence and foreign aid to support the establishment of independent judicial institutions and respect for politically threatened judges. However, this significant and sustained investment of aid for the judiciary in developing states—often spent on technical training and facilities (e.g., building law schools) to create a professional and independence judicial system—has failed to consistently create independent judiciaries across developing countries (Gloppen et al. 2010; Hammergren 2007a; World Bank 2004; IMF 2004). This has raised a considerable quandary for donors and reformers as to the nature of measures required for successful reform efforts.

The findings in this book suggest (see chapter 8) that while donor aid for creating technical training and facilities to develop independent judiciaries in developing states is vital, it is not in fact sufficient. Rather, our analyses of the determinants of judicial independence suggest that understanding how and when the design of domestic political institutions can foster judicial independence is absolutely vital. In particular, by highlighting the important and contrasting effects electoral institutions can have on de facto independence, our findings suggest that policymakers and donors must take into account the incentives the choice of electoral rules create for political elites to support or undermine the independence of the judiciary in their country when designing judicial reforms. Conversely, the decision to adopt specific electoral rules should account for their potential impact on the country's judicial independence. Reform efforts that take these factors into accounts should significantly increase the chances of successfully reforming the judiciary.

Second, our book provides some lessons about the impact of judicial independence on socioeconomic development in developing nations. Researchers recognize that judicial independence is critical for promoting economic growth,[24] and, arguably, democratic consolidation.[25] Surveys of business elites in developing countries consistently identify the independence of the judiciary as one of the key criteria for investing and doing business in these states as well (WEF 2004; WBES 2007; BEEPS 2005). Yet, some studies find that de facto judicial independence has a positive influence on economic growth, while other researchers find its impact on growth is statistically insignificant.[26] In order to understand these mixed empirical findings, it is important to consider how the political conditions that affect judicial independence, also modify the extent to which an independent judiciary can positively influence mechanisms that drive growth such as property rights and corruption. Our findings regarding the impact of electoral rules on DFJI help spell out a more clear mechanism that elucidates when the judiciary can in fact promote higher economic growth by effectively reducing corruption.

Finally, our analysis of the politics of adopting de jure judicial review and maintaining de facto independence sheds light on why the transition to democracy has arguably failed to improve human rights in numerous developing countries as suggested by some recent studies (see e.g., Sorensen 2007). It does so by identifying the political and social conditions that lead elites to avoid granting constitutional guarantees for de jure judicial review authority to the courts, which in theory (and practice) would allow courts to protect human rights. Our study also identifies the political conditions under which leaders are more likely to respect and maintain de facto judicial autonomy. Identifying these political conditions is vital as—we argue later in this book—that it helps us understand more deeply when governments in new and established democracies in developing states are more likely to implement policies that protect the human rights of their citizens.

A Brief Look at Existing Studies

The academic literature on judicial independence has grown dramatically in recent years.[27] This diverse and rich literature has investigated how variation in many factors including—institutional separation of powers, political competition, judicial behavior, legal systems, public social support for the judiciary, economic policies, culture, and ideas lead to variation in judicial independence observed across countries. Each of these explanations has added more depth and nuance to our understanding of the determinants of DJJI and DFJI. Institutional theories for example are considerably strengthened by understanding how the diffusion of ideas, the actions of social groups, and cultural factors influence the payoffs political and judicial actors receive from their strategic choices. Theories exploring the role of ideas, judicial culture, and social groups are similarly strengthened by an understanding of the manner in which institutional incentives entrench certain practices in a country and make certain ideas more politically appealing than others. Here we briefly analyze some of the most influential political explanations of de jure and de facto judicial independence and discuss how our book fills some gaps in this literature.[28] Subsequent chapters of this book, especially chapter 2, provide further discussions of the many insights these literatures provide.

Current Theories of Judicial Review

A rich body of research in political science and judicial studies analyzes the conditions under which countries adopt constitutional provisions giving their judiciaries the powers of judicial review and, the conditions under which judiciaries exercise these powers. In this section, we are interested in understanding the first phenomenon—the adoption of judicial review. The active impartial exercise of judicial review by the judiciary is one of the facets of judicial independence in practice. Thus, studies explaining the exercise of judicial review will be discussed part of the literature on de facto judicial independence. Influential scholarly theories explain the adoption of judicial review by countries as being driven by the functional need to solve strategic political problems faced regularly by political elites, the global spread of certain ideas, and by key external actors.

Some of the most influential theories explaining the choice to adopt judicial review are strategic models that analyze this decision as the outcome of strategic interactions between rational political elites and courts. In strategic models, political elites choose to adopt judicial review in a country when it is the optimal solution to a functional political problem they are facing. The nature of the political problem that is being solved by judicial review differs among the various models in this set of theories and includes problems relating to political fragmentation, electoral uncertainty, the need to make politically unpopular policy decisions, or the need to gain legitimacy.

Political fragmentation may be the result of institutional choices such as federalism (vertical fragmentation) or presidentialism or mixed systems (horizontal fragmentation), or it may result from high levels of political competition, which creates fragmented legislatures. As Whittington (2005: 594) points out, "Fragmented institutions limit the hegemony of governing coalitions, and as a result limit the ability of political leaders to insure by political means that the status quo reflects their preferences." Under these conditions, political elites find that their ability to perform various tasks such as resolving disputes among different levels and branches of government, implementing their policy agenda via legislation, and reversing policies passed by previous regimes through the legislative process is effectively limited (Shapiro 1981; Stone Sweet 1992; Whittington 2005; Graber 2000). Empowering the judiciary with review powers in such situations enables elites to perform these tasks and pursue their policy preferences through the courts instead of the legislature and to rely on the judiciary to impartially mediate disputes. This suggests that federal (Shapiro 1981; Ackerman 1997) and presidential systems will be more likely to adopt judicial review. However, others have argued that a strong president makes it less likely that judicial review will be adopted because in this case the executive will be strong enough to enforce her own legislative agenda across levels and branches of government (Herron and Randazzo 2003).

When high levels of political competition create fragmented legislatures, ruling and opposition parties will not be able to influence the legislative process in order to legislate their agenda. Faced with this scenario, both may choose to support empowering courts with the power to review legislation and executive decrees and then use them for resolving policy conflicts (Ramseyer 1994; Tate 1995; Stone Sweet 2000; Ferejohn 2002; Stephenson 2003; Dotan and Hofnung 2005). Similarly, when political power is fragmented among members of a large, ideologically disparate governing coalition, parties and politicians may find themselves politically incapable of legislating their preferred agenda due to coalition politics and may adopt judicial review with the goal of using courts to resolve policy differences (Whittington 2005).

Empirical evidence testing the links between these various types of political fragmentation and the choice to adopt judicial review has been mixed. While most early adopters of judicial review powers were in fact federal systems, this has not been the case for countries which have made more recent transitions to democracy (Ginsburg 2008). Many presidential systems have chosen to adopt judicial review while some parliamentary countries have not. While some scholars have found that high political competition and fragmentation positively influence the likelihood that reviews powers will be adopted (Stephenson 2003; Ginsburg 2003), others have found the exact opposite—that high competition can actually reduce the likelihood of review adoption (Ishiyama-Smithey and Ishiyama). Ishiyama-Smithey and Ishiyama (2000: 178) point out why opposing granting the judiciary review powers would be a logical course of action for members in fragmented legislatures.

> When the number of effective parties is higher, it is more difficult to predict which ones will win control of government. In such a fluid situation, party leaders may hold out hope that their groups will gain legislative power or even executive office. As such, they may prefer to leave parliamentary power less rather than more encumbered by judicial power as a sort of hedge against limiting one's own power should one's own party achieve office.

Given that both courses of action seem rational, this mixed evidence linking various types of fragmentation suggest that the effect of fragmentation on the incentives to adopt judicial review may be mediated by factors that are yet unaccounted for in current theories.

Judicial review may also emerge as a solution to the electoral uncertainty faced by elites in countries that are transitioning to democracy or that are stable democracies. If current ruling elites anticipate losing power as a result of elections during the initial transition period when the constitution is being designed, they may choose to insure themselves politically against retaliation by the future winners by adopting judicial review (Ginsburg 2003; Finkel 2001, 2008; Chavez 2004; Magaloni 2006). Here, an impartial court would check any persecution by future winners, as well as protect any rights and protections negotiated by the outgoing elites. Even in countries that are stable democracies, elites who anticipate losing elections may choose to constitutionalize political bargains and rights and give their judiciary review powers to protect these bargains in the future (Hirschl 2004). Thus, the choice to adopt judicial review in response to intertemporal electoral uncertainty could also be motivated by the need for political insurance or hegemonic preservation.

Judicial review as this tool for hegemonic preservation, however, explicitly assumes an environment where the judiciary has an established reputation for being fair and impartial (Hirschl 2004: 44). In this framework, political elites must share the belief that the courts will uphold constitutional bargain in order to make it rational for them to make courts the guardian of their bargains at a time of political weakness. While courts in some developing countries did enjoy such high reputations during transition, this empirical reality does not fit well with that of courts in many other countries in the early stages of democratic transition (Gibson, Caldeira, and Baird 1998; Staats, Bowler, and Hiskey 2001; OSI 2001, 2002, 2003). In these countries, ruling elites would not have had enough confidence in their courts to rely on them as a means of preserving their policy hegemony or as protection against vengeful opposition winners.

Judicial review may also be adopted in response to other problems such as the political need to deflect blame for unpopular policy decisions onto a politically insulated targeted (Fiorina 1986; Weaver 1986; Salzberger 1993), and to enhance the legitimacy of government policy (Ishiyama-Smithey and Smithey 2000; Whittington 2005). As scholars have pointed out, these explanations assume that citizens do not see through this political strategy—an assumption that is empirically unexplored (Stephenson 2003). Additionally, review powers may be adopted for societal or economic reasons such as to provide an impartial referee for resolving disputes between ethnic groups in an ethnically diverse society (Ishiyama-Smithey and Ishiyama 2000) or to constrain the government from making undesirable policy decisions and challenge them during economic downturns or transitions (Tate and Vallinder 1995; Bugaric 2001). On the other hand, the decision to avoid judicial review could be explicitly motivated by the need to create a strong centralized executive who could make unchallenged decisions on ethnically divisive issues (Horowitz 1985) or on tough economic issues (Holmes 1993; Haggard and Kaufman 1995).

Ideational theories stress the importance of two distinct ideas—human rights and limited government. Scholars have argued that the spread of the concept of human rights had a profound impact on the political and public demand for an institution that would check government abuse of individual human rights, and hence, on incentives to adopt constitutional provisions granting judicial review (Shapiro1999: 200). These incentives were seen to be stronger in countries that had seen high levels of human-rights abuses under previous regimes such as the ex-Communist countries in Eastern and Central Europe. Polities that were former English colonies are believed to be more likely to adopt judicial review as well because they would be more likely to share a cultural commitment to limited government (Shapiro 1996, 1999). In these countries, courts with powers of judicial review would be seen as checks on government behavior and a means of holding it accountable. However, some cultures hold the opposite belief due to their historical experiences or social beliefs and assign the state a larger role in social and economic management (Jowitt 1992; Carter 1995). In these countries, there will be considerably less support for judicial review since it will be seen as an undesirable constraint on the state. Cross-country empirical studies have so far not found robust evidence supporting the role of ideas or cultural legacy as being central to the political choice to adopt judicial review in developing country democracies (Ishiyama-Smithey and Ishiyama 2002; Ginsburg 2008). Furthermore, as suggested by Ginsburg (2008), these theories do not sufficiently explain the observed variation in the adoption of judicial review adopted or the timing of their adoption.[29]

Finally, scholars have also analyzed the influence that actors other than political elites and courts may have on the decision to adopt judicial review. International institutions, foreign donors, foreign and domestic businesses, and interest groups may choose to lobby for judicial review powers as a tool to hold governments accountable for policy and prevent abuse of state power (Epp 1998; Vanberg 2001; Boulanger 2003). However, others have pointed out that interest groups may also lobby against the adoption of judicial review because it would give courts the power to strike down any constitutional provisions protecting special privileges interest groups have negotiated during the constitutional process (Ginsburg and Elkins 2010).

The most influential set of theories in this extant literature have been those exploring the role of political fragmentation and electoral uncertainty. These theories posit a link between expected legislative weakness due to fragmentation or high competition and the choice to adopt judicial review as a preemptive measure to deal with the consequences of legislative weakness. Courts are attractive as referees to politicians precisely because they are expected to be neutral. Governments and opposition parties expect courts to issue decisions based on the legal foundation of the constitution rather than according to their partisan preferences or according to any other agenda. This is the assumption that rationalizes the political decision to give courts judicial review powers in order to constitutionalize hegemonic bargains, deflect blame for unpopular policies, or to enhance the legitimacy of government policy. Additionally, for the blame deflection strategy to work in favor of elites the courts must be willing to accept public displeasure and loss of popularity. These theories assume that politicians trust that a judiciary empowered with judicial review powers, which give it the powerful ability to overturn legislative statutes and executive decrees and intervene much more directly in policy-making, nevertheless chooses to exercise these powers in an impartial, constitutional manner—that is, political elites do not fear the strategic use of judicial review powers by the judiciary in line with its own agenda. Yet, a large literature on judicial behavior tells us that courts are in fact strategic and can act to defend their own institutional interests rather than blindly and strictly following the constitution.

Studies on judicial behavior tell us that judges actively cultivate the confidence and trust not just of the political establishment, but also of their citizens. Diffuse support for democratic institutions and specific support for courts among the public provide the judiciary with a political buffer that discourages politicians from manipulating courts and allows judges to resist efforts to undermine the judiciary's independence (Caldeira 1986; Eskridge Jr. 1991; Gibson, Caldeira, and Baird 1998; Vanberg 2000, 2001, 2005; Staton 2004, 2006; Carrubba 2009; Gibson and Caldeira 2009). Such political capital will be especially important in new democracies where the intentions of political elites regarding their support for an independent judiciary may be subject to more uncertainty (Gibson, Caldeira, and Baird 1998; Epstein, Knight, and Shvetsova 2001; Chavez 2004, 2008).

In order to cultivate such support, judges could employ a variety of tools that raise the profile of politically sensitive policy issues at times of their choosing (Epstein, Knight, and Shvetsova 2001; Couso 2003), and frame the decisions in ways that reflect well or poorly on political elites (Vanberg 2001; Hammergren 2007b; Staton 2010). Even more directly, judges could choose to avoid making unpopular decisions (Durr, Martin, and Wolbrecht 2000; McGuire and Stimson 2004; Vanberg 2005) and in fact actively make decisions that are in line with public opinion (Barnum 1985; Caldeira 1986; Marshall 1989; Mishler and Sheehan 1993, 1996) in order to establish their credentials as the peoples' champions. Importantly, they enjoy the advantage that they can employ procedural tactics such as manipulating their dockets, timing their decisions, and framing decisions in terms of constitutional and procedural constraints, which can avoid the public appearance of judicial manipulation or impropriety while allowing them to engage successfully in strategic behaviors (Epstein, Knight, and Shvetsova 2001; Couso 2003).

They could also actively collaborate with social and economic interest groups to build support for their institutions (Epp 1998; Keck and Sikkink 1998: 16–25; Klug 2000; Domingo 2004; Chavez 2004; Sieder 2003) and use the media to present their reasons for making important legal decisions, their views on government policies, and government behavior with respect to the judiciary decisions and how to frame those decisions (Vanberg 2001; Staton 2010). Thus, even without the power to overturn executive and legislative statutes by using judicial review, courts have considerable means to establish their independent identity as an institution.

Importantly, given the uncertainty regarding political support for the judiciary in new democracies, judges will also have incentives to build up and use this capital to establish their independence from the political establishment. This combination of motivation and means points to a potential dilemma for political elites considering whether or not to grant de jure their judiciary judicial review powers. If governments empower courts further by granting them de jure powers, and then get saddled with an activist independent court, they will bear the costs of such an independent, activist, empowered court without necessarily reaping the benefits they had hoped for from judicial review powers. Conversely, if they empower a court which does not proactively engage in its own institutional agenda, political elites will reap the many benefits of courts with judicial review powers without incurring the costs of an activist court. This suggests that the political decision to adopt de jure powers may not be a function of legislative fragmentation alone but also of the beliefs that political elites hold regarding the risk that empowered courts may pose to their agenda and goals.

The question this raises for researcher then is this: how do political elites develop their beliefs about the courts potential for activism and resolve their dilemma regarding the adoption of de jure review? In the theoretical framework we present next, we suggest that politicians use the confidence that the public repose in their judiciary as a measure of the potential risk that courts may act on their own strategic agenda when empowered with judicial review, and use this information to make their decision regarding judicial empowerment through review powers.

Theoretical Framework and the Hypothesis

New Democracies and De Jure Judicial Review

We build on this rich body of existing studies to develop a theoretical framework that explains the likelihood that the government in a new democracy will adopt full judicial review as the outcome of the interaction of two conditions—the legislative concentration of seats that the ruling party (or parties) achieves in the first post–transition elections, and the level of public trust that the judiciary enjoys in the initial post–transition years. The legislative concentration of seats that the post–transition government controls influences whether or not it has the capacity to ensure legislative passage of its policy agenda including the policy to grant or deny de jure judicial review powers to the judiciary and, whether it will find an empowered judiciary with the power to overturn its legislative statues and decrees politically desirable. As discussed earlier, governments with high legislative concentration will find courts with review powers less desirable, while those with low concentration will find them highly attractive.

However, as the literature on judicial behavior suggests, the judiciary has its own institutional interests at stake and it acts strategically in order to protect them. The pursuit of these interests may lead it to ally with the government, opposition groups, or act independently and exercise its review powers to support its own strategy. Therefore, as we pointed out earlier, whether a government with high or low legislative concentration will choose to pursue legislation constitutionalizing judicial review power will also be influenced by the risk political elites perceive that a strategic judiciary empowered with review powers poses for them. A government will only act to adopt judicial review if it rationally expects ex ante that the judiciary will not abuse the power of judicial review ex post for their (the court's) political ends.

The judiciary's ability to pursue its own agenda depends on its institutional powers, as well as the degree of trust and support it enjoys among the public. The higher the levels of specific and diffuse support for the judiciary are during the initial post–transition years, the higher the legitimacy the courts will enjoy—thus the harder it will be for governments to attack courts or to capture them (Helmke and Staton 2010; Helmke 2010), and the higher the leverage that courts will have vis-à-vis the political establishment during the constitutional process. Trusted courts will therefore be in a better position to protect their rights and powers, and to assert their independence through the strategic use of judicial decisions and various apolitical procedural tactics.[30] Hence, highly trusted courts will have higher capacity to challenge the government's policy agenda without undermining their own legitimacy if they are given the important powers of judicial review. Given this potential risk of facing an activist judiciary, we suggest that a post–transition government is more likely to develop the expectation that it will face a less activist judiciary if it empowers the judiciary with review powers if public trust in the judiciary is low during the immediate post–transition years.

Our first hypothesis therefore predicts that governments in new democratic states that enjoy a high concentration of legislative seats and thus control the legislature after the transition election are less likely to adopt judicial review if public trust in the judiciary is high in these states in the immediate post–democratic transition period. Even though they have the capacity to ensure passage of the enabling legislation, they will choose not to risk empowering a popular judiciary with the potential to be activist. A corollary to the hypothesis stated earlier, is that the interaction of low concentration of legislative seats held by the post–transition government and low public trust in the judiciary in the post–transition period that increases the likelihood of adoption of constitutional guarantees for full judicial review authority for the courts in new democracies across the developing world. A weak government, therefore, will only be willing to risk empowering the judiciary when it believes the court does not enjoy enough public support to use review powers to pursue its own agenda. Chapter 2 presents this argument in detail.

Theories of De Facto Judicial Independence

The current literature on judicial independence has investigated how variation in many factors including the degree of genuine political competition, institutional separation of powers, judicial behavior, legal system, public social support for the judiciary, judicial culture, historical legacy, and economic policies lead to variation in the level of de facto judicial independence observed in these countries.[31] These theories broadly fall into two schools—strategic and nonstrategic theories. Theories that primarily focus on the role that culture, historical legacies, and ideas play in judicial empowerment generally tend to fall under the rubric of nonstrategic models.[32] These studies have emphasized the important role that social and judicial culture and a country's history play in influencing the outcomes for judicial independence. Theories that explain judicial outcomes as the product of strategic interactions between political actors such as executives, legislatures, and courts fall under the umbrella of strategic models. Each of these schools has significantly advanced our understanding of the determinants of DFJI and they have successfully drawn on each other's insights to build their analysis.

As Ginsburg (2008: 93) notes, strategic models have "been most successful in explaining the success of courts abroad." Furthermore, many of these strategic models have also integrated insights from nonstrategic models regarding the role of culture and history into their theoretical framework by incorporating their impact on the costs and benefits actors believe different actions might generate.[33] Stephenson (2003: 86), for example, summarizes this approach nicely: "this perspective suggests that political battles over the proper role of the judiciary, often seen as philosophically or ideologically motivated, can be reinterpreted as reflecting the political calculations of different factions." Not only have these strategic theories informed a significant share of comparative judicial research—they have also provided some of the most persuasive empirical evidence.[34] For these reasons, we primarily focus on three strategic political explanations for high levels of DFJI—high levels of political competition, the existence of separation of powers institutional arrangements, and strategic judicial behavior.

Theories based on political competition argue that when political elites are assured that elections will be continued, when they value the future, and when they compete in a highly competitive electoral environment where there is genuine uncertainty regarding the outcome of elections, political elites will be more likely to support DFJI (Ramseyer 1994; Stephenson 2003). High electoral competition creates uncertainty in the minds of political elites regarding the length of their tenure in office and reduces their strategic time horizons. Short time horizons create several incentives for them to increase DFJI. DFJI may emerge as political insurance motivated by fear of retaliation by a victorious opposition (Finkel 2008; Magaloni 2003; Ginsburg 2003; Magalhaes 1999), as a tool for ensuring access to policy-making in opposition (Ramseyer 1994), for consolidating policy preferences for incumbents fearing electoral losses (Hirchl 2004), or as an extension of power by politically strong elites (Trochev 2004; Shambayati and Kirdis 2008). It may be a means of compensating for the time-inconsistent preferences parties and politicians may have across elections in order to deliver credible policies to donors (Landes and Posner 1975) and investors (Klug 2000).

Recall from figure 1.4, however, that in 44 percent of countries, high political competition is actually associated with lower DFJI. Popova (2010) similarly finds that governments in the Ukraine that face more competitive elections than those in Russia, in fact support lower levels of de facto independence for their courts than do Russian governments. These trends suggest that short time horizons are actually creating the opposite incentives for political elites in some countries. This poses a considerable puzzle for the political competition theory. The question thus remains: what can explain this tremendous variation in incentives for supporting DFJI and the resulting outcomes?

A second influential school of thought analyzes the impact separation of powers institutions have on incentives to support DFJI. Classic separation-of-powers theory argues that when different branches of government can draw on independent institutional and political sources of authority, they will act to check court-curbing behavior by each other.[35] The inability of any single political actor to capture the entire legislative process creates incentives for all actors to invest in an impartial arbitrator of disputes. At the same time, the lack of a dominant institutional actor prevents successful capture of the judiciary. Furthermore, the lower capacity of divided governments to retaliate, also allows judges to exercise more discretion in their interpretations and defer less to political preferences (Cooter and Ginsburg 1996). Therefore, whether or not a country has a separation of power institutional system, should allow us to predict its success in achieving DFJI.

The evidence, however, is mixed. Many parliamentary systems such as India and South Africa, which do not have separation of powers systems, nevertheless support an independent judiciary. Hayo and Voigt (2007) find that federalism has no significant effect on the de facto level of judicial independence across 46 countries. Herron and Randazzo (2003) find that presidentialism is associated with lower levels of DFJI. In Argentina (Iaryczower, Spiller and Tommasi 2002) and the United States (Segal and Spaeth 2002; Whittington 2003; Segal and Westerland 2005; Rosenberg 1992), scholars find that the system of checks and balances created by the institutional separation of powers in these countries is effective in protecting DFJI only when different branches are controlled by different parties—that is, when there is genuinely divided government. These findings and examples invite further theoretical exploration of the underlying incentives of political elites in countries with formal separation of powers systems.

One of the missing variables in this discussion is party discipline. As Cooter and Ginsburg (1996: 297) point out:

> Several factors can minimize the salience of institutional vetoes. If parties are disciplined so that individual members seldom defect from bargains, party leadership can control the votes of backbenchers. This means that party leaders in a coalition can bargain on a given proposal with relative certainty that they will be able to deliver on their votes. Once such a bargain is struck, it does not much matter how many legislative vetoes, exist, as long as they are all controlled by the coalition.

Party discipline can allow incumbents to trump the problems of separation of powers because the dominant party will be able to forge collaboration between the executive and the legislature and engage successfully in court curbing to reduce DFJI (McNollgast 1995, 2006). These findings therefore highlight the potential importance of the ability of elected parties to impose discipline on their members in and across different branches of government as a factor influencing the supply and demand for judicial independence. They suggest that the theoretical framework analyzing DFJI in systems with separation of powers needs to be revised to accommodate the potential variation in party discipline found across these systems.

Another important strand of strategic models literature in judicial politics analyzes how judges themselves can be important elements in enhancing or reducing DFJI. By being strategic about the cases they consider (Epstein, Knight and Shvetsova 2001; Couso 2003), the legal decisions they make (Ferejohn 1998: 366; Burbank 2002 McNollgast 1992, 1994; Eskridge and Ferejohn 1992; Gely and Spiller 1992), the timing of these decisions, and by framing judicial decisions and communicating them strategically to the public (Vanberg 2001; Staton 2010), judges can choose whether or not they want to be supportive of the current government. Courts can also constrain the government's ability to implement policies by facilitating or hindering political control of the bureaucracy (McCubbins and Schwartz 1984; Ferejohn and Shipan 1990; Spiller 1996). Importantly, judges can frame the rationale of these actions in procedural and constitutional terms, which allows them to minimize the appearance of strategic behaviors. Thus, they can be strategic without jeopardizing their image as impartial guardians of the constitution in the minds of the public.

Judges can therefore use all of these abilities and tactics to court public support directly and build up a strong foundation of specific and diffuse support for judicial institutions that would raise the political cost of attacking the judiciary considerably for ruling and opposition parties (Caldeira 1986; Eskridge Jr. 1991; Vanberg 2000; Staton 2006, 2010; Carrubba 2009). Furthermore, they can form strong alliances with a variety of domestic and international social and business organizations and international financial institutions in order to put pressure on governments for reform and for compliance with judicial rulings (Epp 1998; Keck and Sikkink 1998; Sieder 2003; Domingo 2003; Chavez 2004). All these judicial options raise the threat independent courts potentially represent to parties and politicians and can invite political repression of courts. By acting strategically and deferring selectively to political preferences, judges can act to reduce political fears of judicial interference and build political support for respecting DFJI.[36] As Stephenson (2003: 75) notes:

> some judicial "bias" in favor of a more powerful political party is not just a by-product of the same social or cultural factors that made that party powerful in the first place, or simply evidence that the judiciary is manipulated or stacked with political appointees. Rather, the model here suggests that such "bias" may be necessary in order for the judiciary to preserve its authority.

The extent to which such deference is exercised voluntarily or indeed must be exercised to ensure survival reflects the judiciary's strategic assessment of the political ability to retaliate.[37] When such coordination is routine, judiciaries may even develop cultures of deference to political elites in response to such strategic fears of repression (Schwartz 1998; Hilbink 1999; Sieder 2003; Scribner 2004). As Staton (2010: 12) notes, "strategic judicial deference is especially likely when the political branches find it relatively easy to coordinate on a response to unfavorable resolutions." Political capacity to coordinate responses and to retaliate against the judiciary is therefore at the heart of the calculus of strategic deference by the judiciary.[38] The degree of judicial deference exhibited should be strongly linked to the ability of parties to implement their preferences through effective legislation. This ability, in turn, will depend strongly on the capacity of party leaders to impose legislative discipline on their legislative delegations. Thus, arguments examining the role that strategic judicial behavior plays in supporting or weakening DFJI also need to account for factors that influence legislative party disciplinary strength in their analysis.

All three schools of argument highlight the importance of the preferences of political elites and their capacity to implement these preferences across different institutional arrangements and, different strategic time horizons in driving DFJI. These explanations implicitly or explicitly discuss the role of party discipline in establishing the legislative capacity to engage in court curbing and the preferences of political elites over de facto independence. However, as of yet, they have not fully incorporated its effects. This suggests that examining the sources of party discipline, and the patterns of elite preferences and behaviors different levels of discipline engender and allow, may help us gain leverage on some of the outstanding puzzles of judicial independence previously discussed.

A rich literature in political institutions argues that party leaders and politicians differ systematically with respect to the tactics they use to get elected and to stay in office if they are operating in more particularistic (i.e., personalist) electoral systems compared to less particularistic (i.e., party-centered) systems.[39] To the extent that judicial actions impact these tactics, this suggests that party leaders and legislators may incur very different costs and derive distinct benefits from DFJI conditional on the degree of particularism produced by electoral rules. Furthermore, the level of electoral particularism also influences the capacity of parties to discipline party delegations and legislate successfully (Hix 2004; Cox and McCubbins 2001; Hicken 2006). This suggests that the capacity of party leaders to implement plans to increase or reduce DFJI through legislation will differ systematically across countries depending on their level of particularism. This in turn could induce judiciaries to engage in very different patterns of deference across electoral systems that exhibit different levels of particularism.

The degree of electoral particularism should therefore influence whether or not in a given developing country democracy: (1) party leaders and politicians will find it in their interest to support DFJI; (2) the extent to which judges find it optimal to defer to incumbents in order to avoid capture; and (3) whether or not parties have the capacity to act in their interests— whether that interest lies in increasing or decreasing the independence of the judiciary. These insights from the institutional literature therefore suggest that differences in the electoral rules countries adopt might give us some analytical leverage for explaining the different levels of judicial independence they support in practice. This is the theoretical lens we employ in order to understand the underpinnings of de facto judicial independence in developing country democracies.

Particularism, Time Horizons of Governments, and De Facto Judicial Independence

As discussed earlier, the influential political competition theory of DFJI has argued that because higher levels of political competition create shorter ex ante time horizons in office for governments, they value the benefits an independent judiciary could provide them during their tenure out of office more highly, and thus invest in independent judiciaries. However, this analysis does not take into account how the strength of the party system in a country changes the incentives short time horizons create for governments, opposition members, and the judiciary. We build on a rich literature in institutions to argue that electoral institutions, because they influence the discipline party leaders can exert over their legislative delegation, create fundamentally different behavioral incentives for political elites to support or oppose DFJI as they become less particularistic (more party centered), and create strong parties compared to when they are more particularistic (personal vote centered) and create weak parties. Through this, they affect how much the judiciary chooses to defer to political elites as well.

In highly particularistic electoral systems, party leaders, even of ruling parties, have little capacity to impose legislative discipline and hence, to assure passage of desired bills (Hix 2004; Cox and McCubbins 2001; Hicken 2006). This inability has the following two important consequences when the ruling party leaders' time horizons in office are low. The first is that it changes their calculus of supporting DFJI as it raises the benefits and lowers the cost of an independent judiciary for ruling party leaders. Second, it lowers the capacity of ruling and opposition elites to punish an uncooperative judiciary. Lacking strong party leadership ability, weak parties and their members need an impartial court to mediate political disputes between branches and levels of government, between ruling and opposition members, between party leaders and rank-and-file members, and finally, to insure themselves against future retaliation and give them access to policy when in opposition. A *de facto independent judiciary* therefore offers both ruling and opposition party elites several advantages that they cannot otherwise gain in highly particularistic electoral systems.

In contrast, in countries where less particularistic electoral systems create party-centered incentives, strong party leaders leading disciplined delegations do not need courts for mediation. In fact when their time horizons in office are low, ruling parties may find impartial courts an obstacle to their attempts to exercise patronage and extract rents from their shorter tenures in office. Such judicial interference with party patronage and rent-seeking activities can reduce party access to policy-making in the future and their ability to insure themselves in opposition, and to raise party funds for future elections. At the same time, strong parties possess the capacity to successfully pass legislation reducing judicial powers if they desire it. A *de facto subservient judiciary* therefore offers ruling party elites several advantages that they cannot otherwise gain in less particularistic electoral systems. Therefore, whether electoral incentives create strong or weak parties fundamentally affects whether ruling and opposition parties and members strategically lose or benefit respectively from an independent judiciary.

Finally, electoral systems will also influence the degree to which a strategic judiciary will choose to defer to the political establishment. Judges realize that when the time horizons of ruling elites in office is low, it increases their (the judges') political leverage vis-à-vis the political establishment since judicial decisions on political issues can in this context have substantial impact on the future political fortunes of both the current government and opposition.[40] However, judges must also take into account the political ability of governments to penalize them for acting against them.

Governments in party-centered systems have higher ability to act cohesively and will be able to successfully use their legislative clout to impose high penalties on an independent judiciary. Hence, judges will choose to defer more to governments in party-centered electoral systems, making it easier for governments to reduce their de facto independence. Conversely, because their legislative discipline is weaker, governments in particularistic systems will have less success in imposing costs on an antagonistic or independent judiciary. Hence, the judiciary will choose to defer less to governments in highly particularistic systems, making it even harder for governments to reduce their independence.

Taken together, we argue that the incentives various electoral systems create for government and opposition members and the judiciary when the government's time horizons in office shrinks lead to the following hypothesis on DFJI: when faced with low time horizons in office, governments that operate in highly *personalistic vote* electoral systems are likely to increase de facto judicial independence. Conversely, the corollary to this hypothesis is that when faced with low time horizons in office, incumbents in democracies characterized by lower levels of electoral particularism (i.e., party-centered systems) are more likely to reduce de facto judicial independence. By accounting for the effects of electoral systems on the incentives of governments, opposition, and the judiciary, our theory disaggregates the predictions about time horizons in office for ruling party leaders from those about party strength.

Research Methodology

We adopt a multi-methodological approach to test the hypotheses and the causal claims presented earlier. We first conduct statistical tests on large-n time-series-cross-sectional (TSCS) data sets for both de jure (chapter 3) and de facto independence (chapter 5), and then use comparative case analysis of two sets of most similar cases to illustrate the mechanisms in practice in selected developing country democracies for de jure (chapter 4) and de facto independence (chapters 6 and 7). The large-n analyses allows us to test the generalizability of our results, whereas the comparative case analyses allow us to directly reconstruct the process of political decision-making and illustrate precisely how the interests and strategic behavior of governments vis-à-vis the opposition and courts across developing country democracies generates variation in the de jure and de facto judicial independence. To enhance the quality and reliability of our qualitative analysis, we conduct *within-case* analysis using a variety of within-country evidence, including interviews with judicial officials, analysis of judicial reform bills, time-series data on judicial independence, and public trust in the judiciary and the hazard rates (i.e., time horizons) of governments in office.

To test hypothesis 1 regarding the effects of legislative concentration and public trust on the adoption of de jure judicial review, we use a TSCS data set of 159 developing countries from 1985 to 2004 in chapter 3 to conduct various statistical tests. The results from this data set statistically corroborate the hypothesis. We then present detailed discussions of the political decision-making processes and behaviors, and judicial behaviors leading up to decisions regarding de jure judicial review adoption in two developing countries—Brazil and Indonesia—in chapter 4. While these countries share several important social, economic, and political characteristics, legislative concentration and public trust in the judiciary were considerably higher in Indonesia than in Brazil during their immediate post-transition years.[41] We use evidence from interviews with key officials and analyze within country data from Indonesia and Brazil to illustrate how these key differences led to judicial review being politically resisted in Indonesia but enthusiastically adopted in Brazil.

To test hypothesis 2 regarding the effects of electoral rules and strategic political time horizons on de facto judicial independence, we use a sample of 103 developing country observed as democracies from 1985 to 2004 defined according to Przeworski et al.'s (2000) criteria for democracy.[42] The statistical results obtained from this data set, presented in chapter 5, strongly support our second hypothesis. In order to illustrate our causal arguments about de facto judicial independence, we then present detailed discussions of the dynamics underlying de facto independence in three developing country democracies—Indonesia, Brazil, and India. As chapters 6 and 7 discuss, these three countries share many historical, social, and political characteristics,[43] and importantly, have remarkably similar hazard rates of governments in office.[44] However, while Brazil and India are both examples of personalistic vote systems, with Brazil using an open-list proportional (PR) electoral rule and India using a pluralistic electoral rule, Indonesia is a party-centered system with closed list PR rules. In chapter 6, we use evidence from interviews with judicial officials, analyze within-country time-series data on the time-horizons of governments, de facto judicial independence, and legislative bills associated with judicial reform for each of the three cases to illustrate how the incentives created by personalistic electoral rules motivated successive governments in Brazil and India to maintain and even promote the de facto independence of their courts when their survival in office was threatened and their time-horizons were thus low. Chapter 7 uses similar evidence from Indonesia to illustrate how the incentives created by the party-centered electoral rules motivated Indonesian governments to actively curtail the de facto independence of their courts when their time horizons in office decreased.

Since the robust results from the quantitative analyses in chapters 3 and 5 assess the empirical generalizability of our hypotheses across countries that differ from our selected cases on many political, institutional, social, and economic features, we can be more confident that specific peculiarities of the selected cases are not driving our results on de jure judicial review or de facto independence. This research strategy of combining large-n analysis and case studies therefore pays rich methodological dividends.

The Book's Roadmap

In chapter 2, we develop the book's central theoretical framework and derive two testable hypotheses linking specific features of a country's institutions to its choice of de jure judicial review and its level of de facto independence. Subsequent chapters test their validity through a variety of large-n and case study techniques. In chapter 3, we present results from statistical tests of the first hypothesis regarding the adoption of a de jure judicial review. We discuss the sample and the operationalization of variables we use for our analysis, discuss the challenge that the selection of countries into democratic regimes poses for estimating the effects of our explanatory variables, and then explain how our estimation strategy addresses it. Finally, we present the main results from our tests, discuss the robustness and generalizability of our findings, and conclude by discussing their broader implications for understanding constitutional choices regarding the judiciary. Chapter 4 presents then presents a detailed comparative case study analysis of Brazil and Indonesia, which illustrates the dynamics of the causal mechanism proposed in hypothesis 1.

In chapter 5, we present results from statistical tests of the second hypothesis discussed in chapter 2 regarding de facto judicial independence.

We discuss the sample used, the operationalization of our variables, and our estimation strategy. We then present our main statistical results on de facto independence and conclude by discussing the main substantive implications of these results. Chapters 6 and 7 then present detailed case studies of Indonesia, Brazil, and India, which illustrate the dynamics of the causal mechanism underlying hypothesis 2. We conclude by discussing how the empirical findings from the large-n analysis in chapter 5 and these case studies complement our understanding of judicial independence and point out some key implications of their combined findings.

In chapter 8 we summarize the theoretical, empirical, and methodological contributions that this study makes to our understanding of judicial independence, and discuss some of its limitations. We then discuss some implications of these findings for judicial reform. The finding that different electoral systems can lead to opposite results despite similar de jure rules has significant repercussions for current judicial reform efforts, which are focused disproportionately on administrative and constitutional changes. Finally, these findings suggest that the debate on the welfare tradeoffs between independence and accountability must be revisited in the context of developing countries where independent judiciaries have imposed significant economic and social costs on society.

CHAPTER 2

The Theoretical Framework

In chapter 1, we presented two empirical trends. These trends demonstrated significant variation in both de jure judicial review (DJJR) across new democracies in the developing world and de facto judicial independence (DFJI) among developing country democracies. The observed variation in DJJR across new democracies leads to the following puzzle: why (and when) are governments in some new democracies in the developing world less likely to constitutionally adopt full judicial review in the initial post–transition years? The first research objective in this chapter is to address this question. We present a theoretical framework that identifies the conditions under which political elites in new democracies across the developing world will choose to empower their courts with de jure judicial review powers.

As numerous scholars have noted however, de jure rules are neither necessary nor sufficient for de facto independence (e.g., Rosenn 1987; Widner 2001; Vanberg 2008; Chavez 2008; Carrubba 2009), and their presence can be poorly correlated (Feld and Voigt 2003; Herron and Randazzo 2003; Rios-Figueroa and Staton 2009). Political incumbents can choose to limit their support for judicial institutions merely to the adoption of "parchment rules" and use the many powers at their disposal to handicap the courts ability to exercise their powers in practice. Scholars have identified the fear of losing office when competition is high as one of the strongest political incentives to support DFJI. Yet, as figure 1.4 shows, this fear was not sufficient to build political support for DFJI in 44 percent of 103 countries examined over 20 years where governments chose instead to reduce judicial independence when their time horizons in office was low. This raises a second puzzle—why do low time horizons in office provide incentives to governments in some developing country democracies to protect and enhance de facto judicial independence, but induces governments in others to curtail de facto judicial autonomy? In this chapter, we also develop and present a theoretical framework to answer this second puzzle. The answers to these questions should help us further our understanding of when (1) incumbents in new democracies in developing states resist the adoption of full judicial review authority,[1] and (2) incumbents in "newly consolidated" and established democracies actually succeed in maintaining judicial independence.

In order to answer these questions, this chapter is organized in the following way. We first build on the detailed discussion of extant studies presented in chapter 1 to identify some key missing elements from current explanations. Next, we discuss how we add to this literature and present our argument that the decision to adopt judicial review powers in new democracies is a function of the degree of legislative concentration and the level of public trust in the judiciary. This argument generates our first hypothesis, which we test in subsequent chapters. We then focus our analysis on de facto judicial independence. We again begin by building on the theoretical foundations of current studies discussed in chapter 1 to identify important missing factors and discuss the additional leverage our theoretical framework brings to this literature. We then present our theoretical argument that incumbents in more particularistic electoral systems increase de facto judicial independence in the context of low time horizons in office, but those in party-centered electoral systems reduce the de facto independence of their courts under similar conditions. We then derive our testable hypothesis and conclude.

Judicial Review in New Democracies: Theoretical Arguments

As discussed in chapter 1, strategic theories of judicial review argue that political elites choose to adopt de jure review powers as the optimal solution to one of many political problems they may face. These political problems could stem from political fragmentation in the legislature (Ramseyer 1994; Stephenson 2003), electoral uncertainty during transition to democracy (Ginsburg 2003; Finkel 2005, 2008; Magaloni 2006) or after it (Hirschl 2004), the need to deflect blame for unpopular policy decisions (Fiorina 1986; Weaver 1986; Salzberger 1993), the need to enhance the political legitimacy of government policy (Ishiyama Smithey and Smithey 2002; Whittington 2005), or the need for political posturing to increase political and electoral attractiveness (Fox and Stephenson 2011). All these theories implicitly assume that politicians trust that a judiciary empowered with judicial review powers that allow it to overturn legislative statutes and executive decrees and intervene much more directly in policy-making, nevertheless chooses to exercise these powers in an impartial, constitutional manner (i.e., political elites do not fear the strategic use of judicial review powers by the judiciary in line with its own agenda).

However a large, empirically robust literature on judicial behavior, discussed in chapter 1, tells us that judges can and do in fact use their constitutional and logistical powers to serve their own institutional agenda—that is, judges in fact behave strategically to protect their institutional interests (Helmke 2003; Staton 2010; Vanberg 2001, 2005). Furthermore, in new democracies where diffuse and specific support for the judiciary and other political institutions are still in their formative stages and political commitment to judicial independence is unclear, judicial incentives to engage in strategic behaviors maybe even stronger (Epstein, Knight, and Shvetsova 2001; Couso 2003; Friedman 2010). The combination of judicial motivation and means this literature identifies poses a serious challenge to the implicit assumption of judicial impartiality that current theories of judicial review make. The potential for strategic judicial behavior creates a serious dilemma for political elites in new democracies in developing states considering whether or not to grant de jure their judiciary judicial review powers—a dilemma which, to our knowledge, has not received adequate attention in existing studies.

If governments empower courts further by granting them de jure powers, and then get saddled with an activist independent court, they will bear the costs of an independent, activist, empowered court without necessarily reaping the benefits they had hoped to gain from judicial review powers. Conversely, if they empower a court that does not proactively engage in its own institutional agenda, political elites will reap the many benefits of courts with judicial review powers without incurring the costs of an activist court. The question this raises then is this: how do political elites develop their ex ante beliefs about the courts ex post potential for activism if empowered with review powers, and how do political elites incorporate these beliefs to resolve their dilemma regarding the adoption of de jure review? We now present a theoretical framework that suggests that politicians use the confidence that the public repose in their judiciary as an ex ante measure of the potential risk that courts may act on their own strategic agenda if empowered with judicial review. Politicians, in fact, condition their decision to adopt judicial reviews powers in light of this threat and of their own legislative capacity to meet it.

We begin our theoretical story by assuming from existing studies that judicial independence in a new democracy is not fully consolidated during the initial years after democratization (see, for example, Weingast 1997; Epstein, Knight, and Shvetsova 2001; Ginsburg 2003; Helmke and Rosenbluth 2009; Helmke and Staton 2011). This story particularly focuses on how the incentives of the government and the judiciary in a new democracy, and the interaction between them in the immediate post–transition period affect the adoption of constitutional provisions for full judicial review after democratization. We explain why the interaction of two conditions—high concentration of legislative seats held by the post–transition government, and high and increasing public trust in the judiciary—discourages incumbents in new democracies from adopting full judicial review authority for the courts after democratization.

The theoretical framework first briefly explores the various incentives that the first post–transition government in a new developing country has to dominate the legislature. We then analyze how courts, through their actions, can potentially affect the goals a legislative dominant government seeks, thus creating incentives for governments to create weak courts with few powers. Building on this, we examine the conditions of public support for the courts under which governments are more likely to act on their desire to create weak courts. Doing so allows us to derive our first testable hypothesis. We then analyze how these incentives change when government can only muster low legislative concentration and face courts with low and decreasing public popularity. Our theoretical framework leverages the insights offered by the judicial behavior literature to understand how decision-making by new post–transition governments with respect to de jure judicial review is altered by the potential threat posed to its goals by a popular judiciary.

Legislative Concentration and "Capture" in a New Democratic Regime

Two main factors increase the likelihood that certain political parties may secure a high concentration of legislative seats after democratization— elections and post–electoral co-optation. As shown by the literature on democratic transitions, elections are typically held almost immediately after make the transition to democracy.[2] These elections determine the initial distribution of seat shares across parties and can result in an outcome where only one or a few political parties win a majority of the legislative seats and enjoy high legislative concentration in the national legislature. The second factor that determines the actual concentration of legislative seats controlled by these parties is the strategy of *co-optation* employed by political parties themselves.

In particular, extant research on new democracies in developing states suggests that if the parties in the new government win a significant share of legislative seats in the first post–authoritarian election, then they have strong incentives to increase their share of seats in the legislature by inducing legislators from the opposition to defect and join their government (see, for example, O'Donnell 1998; Moser 2001). These incentives stem from the fact that legislative concentration through co-optation allows the government to extend its control over the legislature and thus over the legislative process. As we discuss in detail later, such control offers the government numerous political advantages.

First, a high share of legislative seats fosters the belief and the claim that the ruling parties' agenda is the one genuinely legitimate agenda supported by a strong popular mandate. Hence, high legislative concentration boosts the legitimacy of the governments political and policy agenda. Second, since such substantial legitimacy has been earned through vertical accountability via direct and free elections, ruling parties may feel there is less need for them to submit to the forms of horizontal accountability found in democracies—by credible opposition parties in the legislature, and by credible courts (Linz and Stepan 1996; O'Donnell 1998). Thus, high legislative concentration can be used as a mandate to boost the legitimacy of various government actions and tactics. As stated by Case (2011: xii):

> At the same time, with the executive in a new democracy having some legitimacy by submitting to accountability on a vertical front through popular election, he or she is less in need of the legitimacy that is earned on a horizontal plane through legislative scrutiny.

Finally, dominating the legislature allows the executive in a new democracy to implement policies that are closer its ideal point. This consequently provides the post–transition government with an opportunity to engage in agenda setting with respect to policy-making, which facilitates implementation of its partisan political and economic policies (Linz and Stepan 1996; Rakner and Van de Walle 2009; Case 2011). These three advantages offered by legislative hegemony may therefore influence the executive to increase its legislative share of seats by co-optation after elections. Such efforts to increase government hegemony through co-optation in fact occurred widely in the initial post–democratic transition years in developing countries as diverse as Bangladesh, Indonesia, the Philippines, and Malawi.[3]

Such co-optation, if facilitated by the fact that despite their recent elevation to elected office, opposition legislators can also have strong incentives to defect from their party to join the ruling parties. The reasons for doing so are noted by Case (2011: 8), who observes that during the initial post–democratic transition years, opposition party legislators in Indonesia, the Philippines, and Thailand enthusiastically defected from their party and joined the government as they were "scarcely motivated to check the executive in hopes of producing better governance. Rather they sought to collude with the executive in hopes that they might share in state patronage." Rakner and Van De Walle (2009: 115) observe similar behaviors in many new democracies in Africa, where opposition party legislators were successfully co-opted into government because for these legislators, "political positions are often the route to business opportunities such as obtaining licenses of state contracts."

Such mutually beneficial exchanges between the new government and new opposition can allow governments in new democracies to successfully increase their share of legislative seats, and thus their legislative influence, while significantly weakening their political opposition in the legislature. For example, after the ruling Golkar and the PDI-P Party in Indonesia's new democracy co-opted additional opposition party legislative members to join the government in late 1999, the concentration of the ruling coalition headed by these parties increased from 0.57 to 0.73 by early 2000.[4] This substantial increase in its legislative power greatly enhanced its influence in the legislature and created a significant decline in the opposition's legislative capacity.

It is important to note here that governments in new democracies in the developing world often recognize ex ante that they cannot automatically or inevitably exert their hegemony over the legislature ex post, even when they control a fairly high concentration of legislative seats. Political elites recognize that there are other institutional actors in a new democracy that may yet create obstacles in their path. Specifically, they recognize that courts are one of the institutions that may potentially hold the government accountable and prevent it from controlling or using the legislature to implement the government's partisan agenda (Larkins 1998; Magalhaes 1999; Ishiyama Smithey and Ishiyama 2002).[5] As noted by Gloppen et al. (2007: 1), in new democracies, "courts are central to making political power-holders accountable . . . and imposing checks if government officials overstep the boundaries for their power." Importantly however, governments recognize that the extent to which courts can become credible roadblocks to the government's agenda is determined by a number of factors, including the de jure powers the new government-dominated legislature itself chooses to grant the courts. The government's decision regarding whether or not to grant its courts de jure judicial review powers will therefore be strongly influenced by the extent to which the government believes that the courts may in the future use its review powers to become a credible roadblock to the government's agenda.

Next, we argue that governments assess the ex post risk they may face from an empowered court by evaluating the degree of public support courts enjoy. We build on a rich literature studying the relationship between public trust and judicial behavior to argue that the level of public trust in the judiciary in the initial post–transition years determines the ex ante belief that governments hold regarding the potential for judicial activism by an empowered court. This in turn influences the government's decision to grant or avoid granting judicial review authority to courts.

Public Trust and Judicial Behavior

We argue that if courts enjoy high levels of public trust at the time of transition, they begin their institutional life in the new democracy with a reservoir of diffuse support for the judiciary. In this case, governments face a relatively more formidable judiciary, which can potentially appeal to this public support to curb government attempts to curtail or deny its powers. Furthermore, we suggest that increasing public trust in and support for the judiciary in the immediate post–transition period encourages the courts in a new democracy to (1) publicly challenge and confront the government during this period, and (2) to demand more judicial authority. These behaviors, we argue, strengthens the belief among members of the ruling party that the judiciary will act as a serious roadblock against the ruling party's attempt to capture the legislature and implement its political and policy agenda if empowered with review authority. Thus, high public trust will make them less likely to support the adoption of constitutional measures granting courts more de jure powers such as judicial review.

Scholars have understood judicial use of review power in the context of public trust in two contrasting ways. Ginsburg (2003) and Carrubba (2009) argue that judges use review powers to gradually expand judicial power by building public and political support for the exercise of judicial review powers and compliance with its review decisions. They do this by avoiding the use of review powers to challenge governments on significant policy issues or imposing significant political costs on them. In this case, courts empowered with review powers will be benign actors in the view of ruling parties and do not pose a threat to the government's agenda. In contrast, Helmke and Staton (2011) argue that such a conservative strategy can in fact be counterproductive as it encourages the public impression that courts are either unwilling to take on the government or that they are partisan themselves. Thus, a prudential strategy of gradual expansion of judicial powers through the avoidance of outright conflict may damage the courts by undermining public trust in them. In this case, courts will indeed present a significant threat to the government's political and policy agenda as they will be willing to use review powers aggressively to maintain their support with the public.

The political consequences for governments of granting courts de jure review powers may therefore differ drastically as a direct result of the behaviors that courts engage in if granted review powers. Governing parties recognize that either of these contrasting patterns of judicial behaviors may emerge once a judiciary has been granted review powers. The challenge facing governing elites, however, is to identify which of the two behavior patterns—co-operative or activist—empowered courts are more likely to engage in before courts have in fact been given these powers. Our analysis therefore explicitly needs to identify which factors influence the beliefs politicians will hold regarding the likelihood that courts empowered with review powers will be cooperative, as Ginsburg (2008) and Carrubba (2009) argue, or more activist, as Helmke and Staton (2011) argue. We now argue that the level of public trust that courts enjoy at transition and the subsequent increase or decrease in this trust in the initial post–transition period is a key factor in establishing political beliefs regarding future judicial behavior, and, hence, in their decision to adopt or deny courts de jure review powers.

Judiciaries obtain their legitimacy and political support not just from the constitutional provisions that determine their powers but also from the popularity and respect they enjoy among the citizens of a country. For new democracies, the level of public trust that the judiciary enjoys at the time of transition will be influenced by the legacy of trust it carries from the previous regime to the current regime, as well as the trust it develops subsequently in the new democratic regime. The legacy of trust courts inherit will vary across countries, depending on the degree of collusion between courts and previous authoritarian regimes. The higher the level of diffuse and specific support is for the judiciary at the time of transition, the higher the legitimacy the courts will enjoy (Gibson, Caldeira, and Baird 1998; Friedman 2010). Hence, the harder it will be for governments to attack courts or to capture them (Helmke and Staton 2010; Helmke 2010), and the higher the leverage that courts will have vis-à-vis the political establishment during the constitutional process. Trusted courts will be in a better position to protect their rights and powers, and to assert their independence through the strategic use of judicial decisions and various apolitical procedural tactics.[6] We argue that these consequences of high public trust for judicial behavior are critical for understanding de jure empowerment decisions because they influence the courts to engage in more activist and confrontational behaviors rather than in cooperative ones vis-à-vis the governing parties.

As Helmke and Staton (2011: 326) note, "there is evidence that public support empowers courts, that judges believe it, and that they care about influencing it." Similarly, in his study of legislative-judicial relations, Vanberg (2001: 353) points out that "The court becomes less deferential and more powerful as the support it can expect from the public in a confrontation with the legislature increases." Scholars of the American judiciary have similarly argued that high public trust enhances the institutional legitimacy of courts and allows them to serve as a more effective check on the government (Gibson et al. 1998; Gibson 2007; Clark 2009; Friedman 2010).[7] In the context of comparative judicial politics, some scholars find that increasing public trust in the judiciary emboldens Russian courts to pursue their agenda and promote certain causes (e.g., Baird and Javeline 2007), whereas Staton (2004: 41) finds that in Latin America, "public support also can provide the political cover courts require to take on sensitive political conflicts." Building on the insights from these scholars, we suggest that increasing public trust in the judiciary during the post–transition period creates two kinds of incentives for the judiciary during this period to behave in more activist and confrontational, rather than subservient cooperative, ways.

First, it provides the courts in new democratic states in the developing world with a window of opportunity to signal their political autonomy from the executive. It also provides the courts in a new democracy with more leverage to challenge the executive. In fact, in the context of growing public trust in the judiciary, the courts in a new democracy are more likely to confront the executive, rather than being deferential, as challenging the government may help the judiciary to credibly signal its autonomy. Furthermore, it is possible that the courts in a new democracy may believe (rightly or wrongly) that growing public trust in the judiciary could shield them from backlash from the government if they challenge the incumbent. This is because "a decision by elected officials to resist a judicial ruling"[8] or challenges stemming from the courts can be extremely difficult if citizens trust and support the courts. We, therefore, argue that the courts' belief that greater levels of public trust may protect them from executive backlash could also encourage them to confront the government during the post–transition years.

Second, we suggest that growing public trust in the judiciary in the post–transition period induces courts in new democracies to vociferously appeal to the executive to adopt constitutional provisions that explicitly provide the courts with full judicial review authority.[9] This in turn can lead political elites to develop strong beliefs about the potential for an activist judiciary if they were to grant their courts de jure review powers. Increasing public trust and confidence in the judiciary in the post–transition period is likely to enhance the courts' perception of their legitimacy as an autonomous institution (Gibson, Caldeira, and Baird 1998; Gloppen et al. 2004; Trochev 2011). This greater sense of legitimacy could induce the courts in a new democracy to believe that they have the "right" to constitutionally attain full judicial review authority and embolden them to publicly put pressure on the government to provide courts with explicit constitutional guarantees for judicial review authority. Appeals for judicial review by the courts are likely to be construed by governments in new democracies as an attempt by the judiciary to obtain constitutional means to challenge the executive's legislative authority.

Both of these dynamics can be seen in constitutional discussions in many developing countries. For example, in Indonesia's public trust in the judiciary grew from 42 percent to 57 percent during the first two years after

Indonesia's transition to democracy in 1999. As ex-justice from Indonesia's Supreme Court, Dewa Gede Palguna observed, this growing public trust in the judiciary encouraged Indonesian courts to repeatedly challenge certain policies proposed by the Indonesia's first post–transition government under Abdurrahman Wahid.

> Once the public understood what we were doing and the tide of public opinion turned in favor of the judiciary, the country's judges could take the necessary steps and boldly oppose the Wahid government's policies on constitutional grounds.[10]

The link between public trust and judicial behavior, and its consequences were noted by key members from the ruling Golkar Party in Indonesia in 2000 (a year after the country's transition to democracy), who reflected "that public faith in the judiciary and in some honest judges undoubtedly influenced the courts to attack the government . . . and Wahid's cabinet saw such attacks as obstructing its own legitimate power." The ruling coalition therefore concluded in the post–transition period that the courts would block the governing coalition's effort to dominate the legislature and chose to deny it judicial review authority.[11]

Likewise, increasing public trust in the judiciary in Malawi during the immediate post-democratic transition years (i.e., from 1994 to 1996)[12] influenced the courts there to use "favorable public opinion as leverage to challenge the constitutionality of key social and economic policies implemented by the state in the country's new-born democracy" (Ngongola 2001: 104). Many cabinet members in Malawi's first post–transition government believed that the country's prominent judges chose to "boldly stand up against the government's program because they felt that they had enough support from citizens to do so . . . of course, this meant that the government could no longer automatically assume that it could implement the economic policies that it favored."[13] The ruling coalition in Malawi's new democracy thus recognized that growing public trust in the judiciary was encouraging the courts to confront the executive and concluded that the courts would block the governing coalition's effort to dominate the legislature in the post–transition period if empowered further with review powers.[14]

Similarly, the belief that reserves of public support for the judiciary would force governments to pay attention to judicial demands motivated the judicial community in Bulgaria to exploit the window and publicly air their demands for judicial review. As Evgeni Tanchev—a former member of the Bulgarian Constitutional Court—notes, during the initial years after the transition to democracy in Bulgaria (i.e., from 1991 to 1993):

> Growing public faith and confidence in the country's judicial system influenced many scholars and practitioners in Bulgaria's legal community to believe that the government would neither restrain the judiciary nor disregard the legal community's demand for judicial review. . . . public faith in the judiciary was an important factor that inspired many judges to collectively request the government to establish judicial review.[15]

In Indonesia as well, the possibility that courts perceived judicial review as a "right" as political support for the judiciary grew is indicated by the chairman of the National Law Reform Consortium, Firmansyah Arifin, who observed the following.

> Since the Indonesian people have started expressing growing confidence and respect in the judiciary, the legal community in the country justifiably feel that it is the duty of Indonesia's new democratic government to grant the power of judicial review to the judiciary.[16]

As we argue and as these examples suggest, courts will be more likely to believe in the legitimacy of their demand for increased powers, and in their ability to get it during the post–transition period of institutional design if they can draw on deep reserves of public support for their institution. Courts that enjoy high public trust therefore pose a dilemma for governments and opposition groups as empowering such a court may empower an independent actor whose preferences may or may not align with either the government's or the opposition's agenda. Rational elites may therefore observe that empowering such a popular judiciary with formal judicial review powers could consolidate the power courts enjoy vis-à-vis the government, increasing both their ability to block preferred government policies, as well as to further build popular support.

In the minds of the government, granting a trusted court judicial review is more likely to result in activist intervention by the courts in the government's agenda. As a result, it will infer that a judiciary empowered with review powers is more likely to engage in activist rather than co-operative behaviors and prove to be a serious hindrance to its goal of establishing hegemony over the legislature, particularly when public trust in the judiciary increases after democratization. Next, we argue, given the potential of these credible challenges from the judiciary, how favorably the government is able to respond them, depends on the government's ability to control the legislative process. This ability, in turn, is determined by the share of seats it commands in the legislature.

Legislative Concentration and the Government's Response

If the government in a new democracy controls a sufficiently high concentration of legislative seats, it is in a position to ensure passage of bills it favors. Under this condition, it will rationally anticipate that granting full judicial review authority to the courts—when public trust in the judiciary increases—is likely to have the following two costly consequences for the executive. First, providing the courts with constitutional guarantees for full judicial review authority may erode the government's existing policy-making hegemony in the legislature given that growing trust and support for the judiciary by citizens encourages the courts to veto government policies. This will constrain the governments from enacting its desired legislative agenda.

Second, judicial activism stemming from the use of judicial-review provisions if they are granted, may encourage opposition legislators to ally with the judiciary instead of the government on key policy issues. Such an alliance may potentially generate considerable political and public opposition to government policies, and could consequently threaten the political fortunes and the political survival of the government in office. Thus, if public trust in the judiciary grows after the transition to democracy, then the government in a new democracy that seeks to exert its hegemony over the legislature will have low incentives to constitutionally grant full judicial review authority to the courts owing to the reasons previously delineated.

High legislative concentration allows a new government to tailor a response to judicial demands for review powers that minimizes these political costs to the government while ensuring courts do not have the power to challenge government policies. As Helmke and Staton (2009: 2) find that in response to "judges challenging powerful actors" in Latin American democracies, the government can target and attack courts via court packing, impeachment, forced resignations of judges, or institutional dissolution. However, as they note, when public confidence in courts is high, governments are less likely to resort to such direct political attacks. Since courts enjoying public trust command legitimacy, governments must find less visible and less politically costly methods of containing judicial challenges. Legislative hegemony provides governments with the ability to use the legislative process to pass bills and amendments that reduce the judiciary's ability to challenge the government's legislative agenda. As Ferejohn, Rosenbluth, and Shipan (2007: 773) argue, politicians in democracies need to secure adequate support in the legislature to curtail judicial authority. They specifically state that:

> Elected politicians have a variety of tools they can use to influence the actions of court, such as . . . passing legislation that overrides court rulings, or possibly even amending the constitution. But politicians are only able to undertake those measures to the extent that they are sufficiently coherent as a group to amass the legislative votes needed in each case.

Whereas in the absence of sufficient legislative support, Tate (1995: 31) notes that the executive "will find it difficult to develop effective policies with the political . . . support that can sustain them through opposition challenges directed from the judiciary." Governments with high concentration of legislative seats can use their legislative muscle to ensure the passage of bills that deny constitutional guarantees for full judicial review authority to the courts if provisions for judicial review did not exist previously in the country's constitution or to severely restrict its review authority if it was previously granted. Control over the legislative process therefore provides governments with the ability to curb judicial activism ex ante, without resorting to politically costly high-profile tactics. It is important to note that while all governments faced with courts that enjoy high public credibility and trust may recognize the potential threat the courts could represent if they are granted de jure review powers, only a government with a high share of legislative seats will be able to act to contain this threat without attacking the judiciary directly.

The arguments put forth by Tate (1995) and Ferejohn et al. (2007) emphasize that a sufficiently high concentration of legislative seats is critical as it provides the government with the necessary "legislative capacity" to curb the courts' judicial authority in the new democratic state. However, legislative concentration by itself does not allow us to predict whether or not judicial review powers will be adopted by a government. Similarly, high public trust by itself provides motive but not capacity to deny review powers, and therefore does not explain the absence of review powers in a country. Rather, our theoretical story predicts that it is the interaction of these two conditions that reduces the likelihood of adoption of constitutional provisions for judicial review by government in new democracies in the developing world.

To summarize, the first condition is the concentration of legislative seats won by the government in the post–authoritarian election. This condition first motivates the ruling party to capture the legislature. The second condition is growing public trust in the judiciary during the immediate post–transition period. This latter condition encourages the courts to publicly appeal for judicial review authority, which influences the government to perceive the judiciary as a threat to its power. In the context of high public trust, a government with a high concentration of legislative seats then uses the party's majority presence in the legislature to secure sufficient support for bills and amendments that reduce the likelihood that the courts will attain full judicial review authority. Given that it is this interaction of the two conditions that reduces the probability that the government in a new democratic regime will adopt explicit constitutional provisions for full judicial review, our theoretical argument therefore lead to the following testable hypothesis.

Hypothesis 1: *Governments in new democracies in the developing world that control a sufficiently high concentration of legislative seats will be less likely to adopt judicial review if public trust in the judiciary during the immediate post–democratic transition period increases.*

The main causal arguments that lead to the prediction in hypothesis 1 are briefly illustrated in fig. 2.1. At this stage, however, we turn to examine the conditions under which governments in new democracies choose to adopt constitutional provisions for judicial review.

Low Legislative Concentration, Low Public Trust, and Judicial Review

In this section, we argue that it is the interaction of the following two conditions—low concentration of legislative seats held by the immediate post–transition government, and low public trust in the judiciary in the

High concentration of legislative seats held by post-transition governments in new democracies increases their political capacity to implement policies closer to their ideal point

⬇

Post-transition governments in new democracies that control a high concentration of legislative seats, however, fear that courts may curtail their policy-making capacity mentioned above especially if judicial review authority is granted to the judiciary

⬇

This fear described above is exacerbated when public trust in the judiciary increases during the immediate post-transition period in new democracies; this provides incentives for post-transition governments to resist granting judicial review authority to the courts

⬇

Hypothesis 1: Governments in new democracies in the developing world that control a sufficiently high concentration of legislative seats will be less likely to adopt judicial review if public trust in the judiciary increases during the immediate post-transition period in these states.

Fig. 2.1. Summary of causal claim that generates hypothesis 1

post–transition period—that increases the likelihood of adoption of constitutional guarantees for full judicial review authority for the courts in new democracies. This theoretical argument is presented in the following way. We first explain why in new democracies, governments that do not command a legislative majority have political incentives to grant judicial review authority to the courts. To this end, we identify how the nature of these political incentives influences their preferences with respect to judicial review, and how it shapes the post–transition governments' behavior vis-à-vis the judiciary. We then discuss why the ruling party in a new democracy that controls a low concentration of legislative seats will adopt judicial review only if public trust in the judiciary is low during the initial post–transition years.

As mentioned earlier, the first post–transition election in a new democracy determines the share, and thus concentration, of legislative seats won by the ruling party. When the concentration of seats held by the government in the immediate post–democratic transition period is low, it will engender uncertainty about its political future—especially its prospects for surviving in office. The ruling party in the new democracy, which is politically weak in the legislature, may also potentially fear that opposition parties (which could include members from the ancien régime) may change the constitution and thus the "rules of the game" once the ruling party loses office (Hirschl 2003; Linz and Stepan 1996). In particular, if the opposition wins office, then it may change the constitution in ways that politically hurt the current ruling party but are advantageous for the opposition. Furthermore, the lack of majority legislative status for the first post–transition government could also increase the possibility that opposition parties who might win the upcoming election will overturn the post–transition government's policies once they (the opposition parties) assume office (Hirschl 2003, 2004; Garoupa et al. 2011). This will make it difficult for the first post–transition government to develop long-term bargains with different constituencies, which may jeopardize its political future. It may also have an adverse impact on the post–transition government's partisan goals, reputation, and fundraising.

Given that the government's lack of a majority status in the legislature in a new democracy may cause the kind of aforementioned problems, the politically weak government will, we argue, have two strong incentives to adopt judicial review in the initial post–transition years. First, borrowing from the "electoral market logic" of judicial independence,[17] we claim that it is more likely to enhance the political autonomy of the judiciary "to ensure that the *next* ruling party cannot achieve its policy goals through the judiciary" (Hirschl 2003: 2). The logic underlying the argument posited above is nicely summarized by Whittington (2003: 454), who states the following.

> Although a generally friendly but independent court armed with the power of judicial review may impose some unwanted restrictions on the current legislature, those costs may be worth bearing in the expectation that the

same court would impose even greater restrictions on future legislatures controlled by a divergent party.

Granting review powers will therefore provide the courts with the constitutional means to limit the policy-making options, and hence the policy reversing ability of the future ruling party, or, in the words, the current opposition party (or parties). Hence, the ruling party will have incentives to "tie their own (and the opposition parties') hands" by constitutionally granting full judicial review authority to the courts.

Second, following Ginsburg's (2003) study, we argue that the government in a new democracy that controls a low concentration of legislative seats during the post–transition years is more likely to believe that judicial review authority for the courts may provide "insurance" for the constitution that is designed by this government. After all, if the courts have constitutional guarantees for full judicial review authority, then they can credibly challenge attempts by the opposition (once the opposition enters office) to change the constitution in ways that adversely affects the first post–transition government, and society at large. The rationale underlying this claim is emphasized by Ginsburg (2003: 200–201), who states the following.

> Where constitutional designers believe that they may not control the political institutions of government, they are likely to set up a court to serve as an enforcement body protecting the constitutional bargain from encroachment.

Since judicial review provides "insurance" for politically weak post–transition governments, it is thus easy to see why the ruling party in a new that has a low concentration of legislative seats has incentives to constitutionally adopt full judicial review authority for the courts.

However, incentives to design constitutional rules for judicial review driven by low legislative concentration may not necessarily translate to an outcome where full judicial review authority is formally implemented in the constitution. For example, the first post–transition government of Chua Leekpai in Thailand had a weak presence in the legislature during the initial post–transition years as it did not win a majority of the legislative seats in the post–authoritarian election of September 1992 (Baker and Phongpaichit 2005). Despite this legislative weakness, constitutional guarantees for full judicial review authority for the courts were not implemented in the initial post-transition years between 1992 and 1996 (Baker and Phongpaichit 1995, 2005; Bunsuwan 1997). In contrast, the first post-transition governments in Bulgaria and Latvia—which also did not command legislative majorities after the first post-authoritarian election—rapidly implemented constitutional provisions for full judicial review authority after the transition to democracy.[18] These examples suggest that even legislatively weak governments in new democracies do not always adopt constitutional provisions for full judicial review authority. Rather, they provide constitutional guarantees for full judicial review authority for the courts only under certain conditions. We argue that such legislatively weak governments in new democracies will act on their political incentives and adopt full judicial review authority only if public trust in the judiciary in the immediate post-transition period is low.

As discussed in the previous section, if public trust in the judiciary is high, then courts will be able to draw on the legitimacy this support provides them to pursue their own agenda through the use of judicial review powers. Under these conditions of public trust, even if the ruling party controls a low concentration of legislative seats, it might believe that granting courts judicial review powers could have immediate costly consequences for the government. An activist court may choose to pursue its own agenda rather than adjudicating political disputes in a neutral impartial manner. This could provide the worst outcome for the incumbent, legislatively weak government, as an activist court with review powers would impose significant policy costs on the current government during its current tenure in office without necessarily providing the assurance of impartial constitutionally based insurance in the future when the current government may find itself in the opposition benches. This, in turn, might dissuade the ruling party from constitutionally establishing full judicial review, despite having some incentives to do so.

On the other hand, lack of public support would prevent the courts from enjoying the kind of legitimacy with the public that could allow them to pursue their own policy and institutional goals. This would prevent them from disrupting the government's efforts to pass its own legislative agenda. At the same time, low public support would make it more likely that courts would only use any judicial review powers they were granted to adjudicate disputes in an apolitical, impartial manner. This would reassure the current government that courts could in fact provide political insurance to the current government if it were to find itself in the opposition in the future. Under these conditions of low public trust, a legislatively weak government recognizes that is more likely to enjoy the insurance benefits that a court with de jure review powers could provide it with in the future, while minimizing the chances that it could be faced with an activist court that could impose immediate costs. To this end, such governments will put together a minimum-winning coalition on the legislative floor to implement bills or amendments that provide the courts with judicial review.

Thus, as summarized earlier, the causal story discussed in this section suggests that it is the interaction of the following two conditions that will increase the likelihood of adoption of constitutional provisions for full judicial review in new democracies in the developing world: low concentration of legislative seats held by the post-transition government and low public trust in the judiciary during the initial post-transition years. This can be stated more formally as the following.

Corollary to Hypothesis 1: *Governments in new democracies across the developing world that control a low concentration of legislative seats will be more likely to provide the courts with constitutional guarantees for full judicial review authority if public trust in the judiciary in the immediate post-transition period is low.*

We next turn to present our theoretical claims about variation in de facto judicial independence across developing country democracies.

De Facto Judicial Independence: Existing Studies

In chapter 1, we outlined three influential theories that have been used to explain why some countries but not others choose to invest in de facto judicial independence (DFJI). These theories emphasize the importance of robust political competition, separation of power institutions, and strategic judicial behavior. Political competition theories argue that if ruling political elites face genuinely high levels of political competition, they may be motivated to increase their judiciary's independence to ensure continued future access to policy process if they lose office (Ramseyer 1994; Stephenson 2003), to forestall future retaliation by the opposition if it wins office (Ginsburg 2003; Magaloni 2006; Finkel 2007), or to consolidate their policy preferences through constitutionalized bargains (Hirschl 2003; Trochev 2002).

Separation-of-power theorists argue that the inability of political actors to dominate the policy process due to the institutional division of powers raises the demand for an impartial dispute mediator, and this leads political elites to support the judiciary as this neutral arbitrator (Shapiro 1981). Finally, strategic theories of judicial behavior analyze how judges themselves affect the level of DFJI they are able to exercise by choosing to behave in ways that increase or decrease both political and public support for their independence (Epstein, Knight and Shvetsova 2001; Vanberg 2001, 2005; Stephenson 2003; Staton 2010).

Since the level of DFJI emerges in these theories as a result of the tradeoff between the costs and benefits strategic political elites expect to experience under an independent and a dependent judiciary, a first-principles approach suggests identifying factors that directly affect these costs and benefits. We draw on a rich literature in political institutions to suggest that the electoral systems of countries may be one such critical factor. A substantial body of research argues that party leaders and politicians differ systematically with respect to the tactics they use to get elected, to stay in office, to legislate and to delegate powers if they are operating in more particularistic (i.e., personalist) electoral systems compared to less particularistic (that is, party-centered) systems.[19] To the extent that judicial actions impact these tactics, this suggests that party leaders and legislators may incur very different costs and derive distinct benefits from DFJI conditional on the degree of particularism produced by the electoral rules they are operating under. The degree of electoral particularism should, therefore, influence whether or not in a given developing country democracy: (1) party leaders and politicians will find it in their interest to support DFJI; (2) the extent to which judges find it optimal to defer to incumbents in order to avoid capture; and (3) whether or not parties have the capacity to act in their interests—whether that interest lies in increasing or decreasing the independence of the judiciary.

Furthermore, allowing for the distinction in electoral particularism should allow us to analyze whether incumbents have similar or different incentives and capacities to support judicial independence when their time horizons in office are low, or, equivalently, their hazard rate in office is high. Incorporating the effect of electoral particularism on parties and politicians in the context of low time horizons in office may therefore allow us to disaggregate the effects of time horizons from that of party discipline and address many of the questions raised by the observed empirical pattern of variation in DFJI. This is important given that the illustration in chapter 1, fig. 1.4, shows that low time horizon in office cannot by itself provide a clear prediction about variation in DFJI across developing country democracies.

Additionally, current work on judicial independence has not yet explored how DFJI affects an important strategic characteristic of developing country politics—the use of patronage and corruption rents to build political support. Scholars have increasingly noted the importance of patronage and rents rather than policy alone as a source of electoral appeal and a goal of political office in developing country democracies.[20] Furthermore, they have noted that the prevalence of these activities varies across countries as a function of their institutions and party strength.[21] These arguments suggest that in order to understand the variation in DFJI across developing countries' democracies, we should also expand our analysis to consider how the incentives of party leaders and politicians to support DFJI are affected by its impact on their ability to engage in such patronage and rent-seeking activities while in government and in opposition.

In the next section, we present a theoretical framework that applies the insights from the literature on electoral institutions—particularly studies on electoral particularism and corruption—to explain why developing democracies support very different levels of de facto judicial independence for their courts. We build on the existing literature on judicial independence to analyze in detail (1) how the costs and benefits of independent judiciaries for political elites differ systematically across countries due to the given level of electoral particularism, and (2) how the response of political elites to short time horizons in office depends on the degree of particularism, and how (3) judicial elites modify their behavior in response to the political strength of parties, and the time horizons of governments they observe in their country. This allows us to explain the observed variation in DFJI and to explain why politicians in some developing democracies respond to high hazard rates in office by increasing the de facto independence of courts, whereas others respond to it by reducing it.

Particularism, Time Horizons, and De Facto Judicial Independence: The Theoretical Story

In order to understand the determinants of variation in DFJI, we build on the current literature by analyzing a key factor highlighted by scholars in comparative politics—the internal dynamics of parties. In this section, we propose a theoretical framework that explains how the interaction of the following two factors—the time horizons elected officials face in office and the level of electoral particularism—influences DFJI in developing countries' democracies. The rest of this section is organized in the following way. We first briefly discuss extant studies that describe how electoral rules, which create different levels of particularism in democracies, affect the relationships between party leaders and members, and thus intraparty discipline. We then build on this foundation to construct our theoretical story about DFJI in developing countries' democracies.

Electoral Rules and Political Particularism

Electoral rules are widely believed to be one of the most important influences in shaping party systems because they directly influence the degree to which politicians have incentives to cultivate a personal vote, and hence, they influence the degree of intraparty unity.[22] In terms of the policy-making process, this means that electoral rules influence how many political actors sit at the bargaining table in the legislature, how representative their preferences are, and their ability to act on these preferences. Scholars have identified four electoral dimensions that influence the degree to which individual politicians will choose to balance investing in their personal reputation with investing in their party's reputation in order to advance their political careers (Carey and Shugart 1995). These four dimensions include (1) rules that govern whether parties control access to the ballot and candidate's rank on it (ballot), (2) the degree to which a candidate's electoral fate depends on the votes his co-partisans poll (pooling), (3) the number and manner of votes voters can cast (vote), and (4) the number of candidates standing for elections in a given district (district magnitude). These rules yield systems with levels of particularism ranging from completely candidate-centered (high particularism) to completely party-centered (low particularism).

When electoral rules give voters a direct vote for individual candidates, an individual's votes are not pooled with anyone else to determine his seat allocation, and when a single vote is cast for a specific candidate, then the fate of party candidates depends on their personal reputation rather than their party's. In these electoral systems, party members face the strongest incentives to cultivate a personal vote and the degree of electoral particularism is very high. As the number of seats assigned per district goes up, these incentives become even stronger. Japan, the Philippines, and Colombia are examples of countries with high degrees of electoral particularism. The higher the degree of electoral particularism, the stronger the political premium on personal performance and reputation, and the stronger the incentive for individual politicians to make electoral and legislative decisions that favor their personal interests rather than their party's (Carey and Shugart 1995; Cox and McCubbins 2001; Ames 2001). These electoral rules therefore directly affect the extent to which politicians must respond to their party leaders in order to succeed in their careers.

The higher the degree of electoral particularism, the less weight voters place on party reputations, thus creating lower incentives for legislators to follow the directives of their party leaders in the legislature.[23] At the same time, higher particularism reduces the capacity of party leaders to induce compliance with their directives since they do not control access to a valuable party label under these electoral rules. Cox and McCubbins (2001: 39, 45) note the cumulative effect these electoral incentives have on the ability of party leaders to influence policy-making.

> Putting these features together, one gets parties that cannot control legislative decision-making, cannot command the loyalty of their own members, and cannot avoid being torn apart by the competing and unaggregated demands of their own allied interest groups. The ultimate consequence in terms of policy is the aforementioned governmental paralysis.

Hence, as electoral particularism increases, the ability of party leaders to successfully induce legislative discipline among their legislators declines. Consequently, legislators are increasingly empowered to act on their personal preferences regarding policies and party leaders are increasingly unable to exert influence on the policy process or policy outcomes.

As electoral systems give parties increasingly more control over ballot access, pool the votes of co-partisans before seat allocation (as in party lists) and give voters the choice of casting party, rather than candidate-based, votes, voters place increasingly more weight on the reputation and performance of parties, and party leaders gain increasingly more control over the careers of individual party members. Both these factors increase the incentives politicians have to follow the diktat of their party leaders during elections and while in office since their political fate is tied to their party brand,

and party leaders control their access to it (Carey and Shugart 1995; Cox and McCubbins 2001; Jones 2002). The higher the number of seats per district, the harder it will be for candidates to distinguish themselves from their-co-partisans in the eyes of the voters, and the stronger their incentive to comply with party wishes will be. Thus, party leaders are able to successfully impose discipline on their members in less particularistic system. As Gerring and Thacker (2008: 68) point out, for these reasons, low electoral particularism creates a very different political and policy environment in the legislature.

> Leaders of strong parties are better able to bargain effectively with each other, across partisan divides, since they enjoy considerable insulation from their constituents on most issues . . . Moreover, any agreements reached among the parties are likely to hold. Enforceability is likelier and with it a measure of credible commitment. These features at the national level should also alleviate problems of policy coordination within the national government and across different levels of government.

Hence, the lower the level of electoral particularism, the stronger the ability of party leaders to forge and maintain disciplined legislative delegations and influence policy outcomes. In these systems, party leaders are credible negotiators who are able to successfully and reliably deliver policy outcomes to their voters and donors. Countries such as Britain, Spain, and Argentina are examples of countries with very low degrees of electoral particularism where parties exert such policy influence. In contrast, as electoral particularism increases, legislative party discipline decreases, and party leaders are able to exert less and less influence over the policy agenda and the policy-making process.

A substantial body of empirical research supports these predictions regarding the different legislative behaviors of party leaders and legislators under varying degrees of electoral particularism and the impact these differences have on policy outcomes. Scholars have found that the degree of electoral particularism influences the nature of committee assignments and legislative service legislators choose to undertake (Stratmann and Bauer 2002), their propensity to initiate narrow legislation (Crisp et al. 2004), to vote with their party delegation (Carey 2007), and even the direction, timing, and frequency of party switching by legislators (Heller and Mershon 2005; Thames 2007). These studies therefore provide firm empirical evidence of the link between electoral incentives and legislative behavior and suggest they should exert strong policy influence as well. Empirical studies confirm this prediction. Studies have found that more particularistic electoral systems are associated with higher fiscal deficits (Hallerberg and Marier 2004), less efficient education spending (Hicken and Simmons 2008), more protectionist trade policies (Hankla 2006), and higher corruption (Chang and Golden 2007). These studies therefore establish a strong link between the incentives electoral systems create and various policy outcomes.

Despite their focus on political institutions and political competition, scholars of judicial politics have yet to investigate whether judicial independence is one of the outcomes affected by the type of electoral system in place. As discussed earlier, and in chapter 1, judicial scholars have argued that the capacity of ruling and opposition elites to enact policy is an important determinant of political willingness to support DFJI and judicial willingness to defer to governments. A substantial literature on electoral institutions suggests that electoral systems have a direct impact on the ability to implement policy. Together, these insights raise the following question—does the variation in electoral particularism across developing democracies explain the observed variation in de facto judicial independence?

High Electoral Particularism, Time Horizons, and DFJI: The Theoretical Argument

Vanberg (2008: 109) summarizes the crux of the de facto puzzle independence puzzle, "an independent judiciary is created and maintained primarily because it serves the interests of those in a position to undermine it." The actors in the strongest position to undermine courts in any system are the party leaders and politicians of ruling and opposition parties, and the courts themselves. In order to identify why DFJI will be in the best interests of these distinct actors in some countries and why they will be better served by judicial subservience in other countries, we need to understand the tradeoffs all three sets of actors face by choosing different levels of DFJI under different time horizons in office for elected leaders. We therefore analyze the effect shrinking time horizons of elected leaders have on the incentives of courts, as well as party leaders and politicians (from the ruling and opposition parties) first in personalistic electoral systems and then party-centered systems.

To start with, when judges observe that governments are under credible political threat of losing power, they can choose to stay subservient or increase their efforts to gain more autonomy. A strategy of subservience would realize its own set of rewards in the form of perks given to individual judges who have catered to political requests, generous retirement benefits for the judiciary as a whole, and a blind eye toward petty corruption schemes and patronage by judges (Dakolias 1997; Hammergren 2007a; Rose-Ackerman 2007). Judges could also be more assured of their personal safety and more certain that they would not be stripped of their current powers (Helmke 2003; Hammergren 2007a; Finkel 2008). These are substantial benefits. However, judges could also choose to make a bid for more independence at such times. The challenge here is to identify the conditions under which judges will decide that the benefits of taking on the government at a time when it is relatively weak outweigh the potential gains they can make by supporting it during this period.

When governments face higher hazard rates in office or equivalently lower time horizons in office, the incentives that judicial elites face with respect to cooperating (or not) with the government changes considerably. First, the heightened political threat to government survival magnifies the potential impact courts can have in changing political fortunes and increases their political value to elites. As Cox and McCubbins (2001: 33) note, through their legal decisions on government policies, government implementation of policies, oversight, or their conduct in general, courts can have a considerable impact on the governance capacity of elected officials.

> The judiciary's interpretative discretion gives it a limited check on legislative authority. Courts in many countries also have a check on administrative and executive actions. Often special court exist to hear appeals to administrative and executive decisions ... If judges can veto policy, then any legislative project must clear one more hurdle before it becomes law. In principle, the existence of this additional hurdle might translate into gridlock—an inability to pass and sustain legislation.

By overturning executive and legislative statutes (Ferejohn 1998: 366; Burbank 2002), reinterpreting laws to change their original intent (McNollgast 1992, 1994; Eskridge and Ferejohn 1992; Gely and Spiller 1992), and facilitating or hindering political control of the bureaucracy (McCubbins and Schwartz 1984; Ferejohn and Shipan 1990; Spiller 1996), courts could undermine government ability to implement its policy platform and strengthen the hands of the opposition. To the extent that voters and interest groups care about policy, the inability to deliver on electoral promises will affect the image of the current government in the minds of citizens and civil-society groups and reduce its popularity and credibility. Given their low time horizons if office, this will be of great and immediate concern to incumbents. Therefore, judicial ability to influence public opinion regarding the legitimacy of political actors, their policies, and their behaviors have even greater value for ruling and opposition political elites as government time horizons shrink, making judicial actions more valuable bargaining chips for courts.

Alternatively, courts could aid the government and weaken opposition efforts to bring the government down by dismissing opposition challenges to government policy. This would curtail the legitimacy of political challenges raised by opposition against the government. Since even courts lacking full independence can increase the legitimacy of political actions by approving them (Larkins 1998), judges can use this ability as an asset to bargain strategically in order to enhance judicial independence. Courts can also strengthen the government or the opposition by its rulings on cases against important political figures relating to their personal conduct in matters of influence peddling, corruption, or their legal eligibility for office. This can be an especially potent tool for judiciaries in developing countries, where charismatic individual leaders often form the heart and soul of thinly institutionalized parties lacking grassroots organization or support (Popova 2010).

Furthermore, as Helmke (2003) points out in the case of Argentina, if government time horizons in office are shrinking, judges may decide that defecting strategically from the incumbent has a lower cost, while allying with the opposition yields higher benefits. Therefore, they could choose to curry favor with the opposition in hopes of obtaining a better deal for their institutions if and when the opposition wins office. As a result, they may choose to resist further capture by the current government, and issue rulings against the incumbents and in favor of the opposition. Gloppen et al. (2010: 125) find similar evidence of judges behaving with increased independence during periods when governments are perceived to be weak in Malawi and Zambia.

While court rulings are the strongest tools courts can use against political elites, there are several additional tools that they can use to undermine the government, support opposition parties, and to strengthen their position vis-à-vis elected officials. Courts may strategically select their dockets to raise the public profile of certain cases and associate these issues with ruling or opposition parties in the public mind (Epstein, Knight, and Shvetsova 2001), they can maintain the public image of parties by choosing to ignore certain cases (Couso 2003), or they can choose to reject considering cases based on technical form or on substance (Hammergren 2007b). Importantly, judges can engage in these tactics using procedural and constitutional terminology, thus minimizing the appearance of political maneuvering and the cost in public support for courts. This ability to draw public attention to or away from selected cases and for selected reasons at politically sensitive times will also enhance the bargaining power of courts with the government and the opposition. Therefore, strategic judges will recognize that these judicial abilities enhance the strategic opportunity presented by short government tenures, and will judiciously manage their rulings and their docket selection to secure more power and resources for the judiciary in the future.

The second consequence of low time horizons of governments in office for judicial behavior in developing democracies is that by raising the public salience of courts, they offer judges the opportunity to build diffuse public support for an independent judiciary. The legal arena frequently becomes one of the key battlegrounds for ruling and opposition groups as they bid to maintain or gain power, respectively, in a competitive political environment (Ramseyer 1994; Helmke 2003; Stephenson 2003; Vanberg 2005; Hirschl 2004; Finkel 2008; Popova 2010; Staton 2006, 2010). This requires courts to adjudicate politically motivated disputes brought to them by ruling and opposition elites at a time when political brinkmanship is at its height. In addition to the opportunities this provides to cultivate support with ruling and opposition groups as previously discussed, such visible and salient adjudication also provides courts with the opportunity to cultivate the support of the public and civil-society groups for DFJI because it draws public attention to judicial proceedings and decisions, and to the central role of the judiciary in mediating disputes.

Increased public attention gives judges an opportunity to raise public knowledge of political violations of judicial rights, and to enhance the image of courts in the public eye (see, for example, Vanberg 2005; Staton 2006, 2010; Carrubba 2009; Gibson and Caldeira 2009). Thus, courts get the chance to inform their citizens about the behavior of political elites, especially relating to their interference with court functions and resource allocations, and noncompliance with constitutional provisions for de jure independence. Increased public awareness and the resulting monitoring of current political interference with courts, increases the possibility that citizens will punish politicians for further interference, and increases the bargaining power of courts relative to the legislature (Gibson and Caldeira, and Baird 1998; Vanberg 2001, 2005; Staton 2006; Baird and Javeline 2007).

Since public support for the judiciary will be a function of their perceptions of the court as acting in their interests, especially vis-à-vis elected officials (Rogers 2006), judges can also use this window of increased public salience to improve public perception of the courts. Courts can actively build public support for the independence of judicial institutions by proactively using the media "to construct conditions favorable to the exercise of independent judicial power" (Staton 2010: 7). They can strengthen the court's image as a champion of the people by avoiding unpopular decisions (Durr, Martin, and Wolbrecht 2000; McGuire and Stimson 2004; Vanberg 2005) and by making decisions in line with public opinion (Barnum 1985; Caldeira 1986; Marshall 1989; Mishler and Sheehan 1993, 1996) at a time when such behavior is more likely to be noticed. They can also strategically manage compliance with constitutional rulings to build up support among the public for their role as the guardian of the constitution (Carrubba 2009). Indeed, as Staton (2010: 25) points out, the courts "are more likely to exercise their power when they expect the public to learn about and understand their decisions." Scholars have found considerable evidence that courts do in fact try to use the media in developing democracies to build up public support, and where they lack such opportunities, they can pay a price.[24]

Civil-society groups are also important targets of judicial communication and public relations. These groups can be especially useful as allies for the judiciary since they can complement the court's efforts by disseminating relevant information and mobilizing pressure on governments from domestic and international sources (Epp 1998; Keck and Sikkink 1998: 16–25; Klug 2000).[25] Business groups and international institutions will also typically be more concerned about the potential for political instability if governments seem likely to collapse on a regular basis, and hence, will be more likely to pay attention to the political insulation and consolidation of courts. Hence, in a scenario where the expected time horizon of the government in office is low, judges will be more likely to find willing allies among influential international actors such as international financial institutions and foreign-aid donors who have the means to exert considerable pressure on governments to refrain from undermining their courts (Klug 2000; Hammergren 2007b; Chavez 2004, 2008). Hence, using their enhanced public stage to improve the judiciary's image with civil society at large also allows courts to build diffuse support for DFJI in society.

Therefore, as the discussion suggests, by strategically choosing their legal decisions, and by managing the public's knowledge and perception of the courts' role in politics and policy, courts can use the opportunity provided by short time horizons of governments in office to build public support for the judiciary. The more public support courts enjoy, the higher the political cost of challenging their decisions becomes (e.g., Caldeira 1986; Eskridge Jr. 1991; Vanberg 2000; Gibson and Caldeira 2009; Clark 2010; Friedman 2010; Helmke and Staton 2011), the less politically deferential courts have to be (Vanberg 2001), and the more independent political influence they acquire in that country (Hayo and Voigt 2007; Gibler and Randazzo 2011; Baird and Javeline 2007). These reserves of public support that courts build during periods when the hazard rate of the government in a developing democracy shrinks can potentially act as a constraint on attempts by the current and future governments to undermine the courts, and can pay dividends for courts well into the future.

Low time horizons for governments in office therefore offer the judiciary a window of opportunity to consolidate their institutional position by exploiting their enhanced bargaining leverage with political elites to bargain for stronger institutional rights and more resources in exchange for forming an alliance with either of the following two actors: the government (which implies that the courts will end up protecting the government's interests) or the opposition (which implies that the courts may need to act against the current government). Importantly, courts have this capacity to favor either the government or the opposition at a time when such capacity enjoys a high premium. Hence, the lower the expected time horizon of the current government in office, the more credible the threat an uncooperative judiciary could pose to its continued survival. Therefore, we expect that when hazard rates of incumbents in developing country democracies are high, the judiciary will be in a position to threaten governments and opposition groups more strongly and more credibly.

In these circumstances, the judiciary will be a sought after ally for both governing and opposition parties. The tactical choice that the judiciary eventually makes, and hence, the actual outcome of this strategic interaction between judges, government, and opposition groups for DFJI in a specific country, will depend not just on the benefits of these tactical choices for judges but also on the costs they impose on them. These costs will be determined by the tactical choices available to ruling and opposition parties.

The set of political tactics available to ruling and opposition parties and politicians are strongly influenced by the extent to which the electoral system is particularistic. As discussed earlier, the degree of electoral particularism in developing democracies shapes whether or not parties can act as strong unified actors in the legislature. Thus, when the standoff between judicial and ruling elites previously described takes place in a particularistic (i.e., personalist) electoral system, judicial elites will essentially encounter decentralized legislative parties where neither ruling nor opposition party leaders have the party discipline necessary to guarantee passage of bills they prefer. This ensures that the ability of ruling parties to penalize judicial behavior against government preferences through legislation will be low.

On the other hand, when this interaction takes place in less particularistic—in other words, strongly party-centered—electoral systems, judicial elites will be squaring off against strong, centralized parties where party leaders can use disciplined legislative delegations to ensure the passage of any bills they deem necessary. We hypothesize that in party-centered democracies in the developing world, ruling parties will be able to retaliate more successfully against the judiciary by passing suitable legislation. As we argue, this difference in legislative capacity under electoral systems with varying degrees of particularism, will lead ruling parties and politicians facing government collapse to adopt very different strategies towards the judiciary. This in turn results in different levels of DFJI in these countries.

DFJI in Developing Country Democracies with Particularistic Electoral Systems

When ruling parties in more particularistic (that is, personalist) electoral systems face low (high) time horizons (hazard rates) in office, they will essentially have a menu of two choices with respect to dealing with the judiciary. First, they can either try to curb the judiciary by tabling legislation that reduces judicial independence by decreasing the levels of resources the judiciary receives, the autonomy it (the judiciary) has, or by completely denying any resources and autonomy for the courts. For example, they could try to legislate cuts to the judiciary's budget, change the qualifications for judges in order to appoint partisan judges, or legislate parallel courts and tribunals to reduce the judiciary's jurisdiction in important areas. The payoffs of having a subservient court include favorable legal rulings on political and policy matters, more electoral security, and more opportunities to engage in clientelism and raise corruption rents. However, given the inability of party leaders under particularistic electoral rules to induce discipline and make members to vote with party preferences,[26] a strategy based on passing legislation would have low and uncertain chances of success.

Furthermore, many party legislators may in fact have strong preferences for an independent judiciary. Legislators, faced with the need to raise money for their campaigns from donors, will need to convince potential donors that political deals brokered by legislators in their interests will be valuable. While the independence of courts will prevent legislators from guaranteeing preferred outcomes to donors, the inability to capture it makes independence in enforcement the next best option. Given the inability of party leaders to guarantee deals made with other institutional actors, legislators may prefer to support independent courts as the guarantor of impartial enforcement of laws and agreements forged in the legislature and across levels of government (Landes and Posner 1975). Additionally, politically costly policy decisions could also be passed onto the judiciary, thus enabling legislators to deflect blame for these decisions (Salzberger 1993; Whittington 2003; Ura 2006). Independent courts could be used to undo policies enacted by previous administrations that cannot be dismantled via legislative actions (Whittington 2007). Legislators may also want to signal their personal support for rule of law to voters, especially in environments where poverty, discrimination, and unequal access to the justice system make obtaining justice a politically sensitive issue for voters (Gloppen et al. 2010).

A party leader's legislative strategy to reduce DFJI in particularistic systems in developing democracies would therefore be fraught with additional risks since party members with such preferences could be easily persuaded by opposition members to vote against such bills or to denounce them publicly as efforts to weaken judicial independence. In the latter case, such efforts could actually backfire on party leaders and hurt the reputation of the party with voters without realizing any countervailing benefits for them. Not only would ruling parties be more likely to lose cases they favor under this tactic—they would also be more likely to risk being branded by voters as threats to democratic institutions.

The inability to consistently pass legislation in accordance with party wishes in particularistic systems also makes it less likely that the government has successfully captured other state agencies such as the bureaucracy and the police in these systems (Huber 2000; Cox and McCubbins 2001; Huber and Shipan 2002; de Figuerido 2002). Lack of such partisan state capture reduces the ability of governing parties to use informal bureaucratic channels to pressure the judiciary through threats or entice them through inducements. Thus, governments that operate in particularistic electoral systems in developing states will be considerably less likely to successfully threaten or cajole bureaucrats into delaying legitimate payments to the judiciary, framing false corruption charges against them, or undertaking tax raids against uncooperative judges.[27] Nor will they be able to promise individual judges lucrative and desirable postings, extended tenures, and the ability to forge their own patronage networks in exchange for favors since their bureaucrats have no incentives to cooperate with such illegal behaviors and jeopardize their own careers. Therefore, lacking legislative discipline, parties will not be able to use informal tactics to threaten or co-opt the judiciary into subservience either.

Finally, the costs that politicians may incur from mounting an attack on the judiciary under particularistic electoral rules would also be higher. Judicial elites in personalistic electoral systems are aware of the weakness of party leaders and the inability of legislative actors to act cohesively and punish the judiciary. They will therefore have little incentive to show high levels of voluntary deference to the preferences of the incumbents (Stephenson 2003; Andrews and Montinola 2004; Helmke 2005; Rios-Figueroa 2006). This will allow judges to gradually develop a reputation for being more independent of the political establishment and to lay the foundation for developing a strong reserve of public support for judicial institutions. Since public support for the judiciary raises the political cost of attacking judicial institutions (Eskridge Jr. 1991; Clark 2010; Friedman 2010; Helmke and Staton 2011), this is an important asset. Civil-society groups will also be more willing to organize and fight to protect the independence of the judiciary, if it has a prior record of being less deferential to government wishes.[28] Therefore, as a consequence of lack of legislative capacity, the strategy of preventing potential judicial bids for more independence through the ex ante passage of retaliatory legislation becomes a high-cost, high-risk choice for ruling parties in personalistic electoral systems when governments are faced with short terms in office and fighting to survive opposition challenges.

The second strategy that governments in particularistic systems in the developing world could employ when facing high hazard rates in office is to co-opt the judiciary by preemptively increasing its de facto independence. This would reduce judicial incentives to publicly oppose the government or to ally with the opposition in the first place. This would entail the opportunity costs of using the judiciary to enact their preferred legislative agenda and to weaken the opposition's electoral performance, and the ability to prevent or squash legal challenges to the governments' patronage and rent practices. On the other hand, it would increase the legitimacy and popularity of the government as a champion of democratic institutions (Ferejohn 1998; Burbank 2002), endow government policies that do surmount legal challenges with considerable legitimacy (Larkins 1998; Ginsburg 2003), increase the value of legislative policy outcomes for interest groups (Landes and Posner 1975), and prevent the opposition from successfully co-opting the courts.

The immediate benefits of this strategy given the government's low time horizons in office are threefold. First, it would prevent opposition groups from using the courts unfairly in their effort to hasten the fall of the current government or to weaken its electoral attractiveness. Second, it would guarantee that conflicts were resolved impartially and deals enforced evenly by a neutral referee. Third, it would allow ruling parties and politicians to raise campaign finance from their business-interest-group supporters. Therefore, while this strategy does entail high opportunity costs of lost court manipulation, these losses would be offset by immediate benefits in the form of higher legitimacy, lower chances of a hostile alliance between courts and opposition groups, and opportunities to extract political finance from business donors.

We suggest that opposition groups that operate in particularistic electoral systems in developing country democracies also receive similar benefits from supporting the judiciary. By supporting increased independence for courts, they can also demonstrate their goodwill toward the judiciary and prevent anti-opposition alliances between the government and grateful courts from forming. The assurance of a politically neutral court allows them to challenge government policies and conduct with the expectation of a fair and nonhostile hearing. Such reassurance can be critical for opposition groups when the expected time horizon (hazard rate) of the government in office is fairly low (high).[29]

Importantly, the benefits of impartial arbitration are not restricted to election periods alone. When hazard rates of governments increase during its term in office due to party switching, votes of confidence, or party splits and mergers, independent courts ensure both governments and opposition of politically unbiased arbitration. For example, courts have frequently been used in India (which is characterized by high levels of electoral particularism)[30] to challenge the rulings of partisan congressional speakers regarding the recognition of party mergers and splits, and the expulsion of party members for switching parties at various points during their legislative terms (Kashyap 2006). Governments have often formed and fallen based on these rulings in India. Thus, all parties have benefited from neutral adjudication of such decisions at various times. Since no party knows ex ante where the next such threat to their term may rise from, at any given point in time government and opposition parties have an incentive to maintain the court's neutrality. Similarly, in Malawi, when President Mutharika formed a new party after elections and took a significant share of MPs with him to his new party, the courts were critical in peacefully and constitutionally mediating the ensuing battle between his old party, the UDF, and his new party, the DPP (Gloppen et al. 2010: 103–4). Independent courts therefore allow both governing and opposition parties to appeal to an impartial arbitrator whenever government survival is threatened during elections or during its term in office.

The impartiality of courts also allows them to reassure donors that the chances that courts will side with future governments and reverse current policy gains will be minimized, and thus to raise valuable political funds. Moreover, since neither the ruling nor the opposition parties have the legislative discipline necessary to overturn the court's independence, this tactic has lower risks of being reversed by co-partisans or opposition members for both government and opposition party leaders.

This analysis suggests that while high hazard rates in office clearly provide governing parties with some motive to capture the judiciary, in particularistic electoral systems, ruling parties lack the capacity to do so. Given this handicap, party leaders and rank-and-file legislators from ruling parties will find that supporting a genuinely independent judiciary better serves their interests than trying to undermine it. It offers greater net benefits, as well as lower risks. Since politicians and party leaders from opposition parties face similar challenges in capturing the judiciary through legislation or informal channels, they will also find supporting DFJI to be their optimal strategy.

Under these conditions, both ruling and opposition elites will support increasing the de facto independence of the judiciary and legislation extending DFJI will pass successfully in the legislature. Given the strong political support for neutrality, judges will find it strategically optimal to adjudicate in accordance with their own legal philosophies, and the legal merits of the cases under consideration. Hence, under these conditions, all three sets of actors will find it in their best interests to maintain and strengthen an independent judicial system, and we should expect to see higher levels of de facto judicial independence. This leads to the following testable hypothesis.

> **Hypothesis 2:** *In the context of high hazard rates (or equivalently low time horizons) in office, incumbents in particularistic electoral systems in the developing world are more likely to increase the de facto independence of the judiciary.*

The main causal argument that leads to hypothesis 2 are summarized in the flowchart in fig. 2.2. We now turn to discuss the politics of DFJI in electoral systems that exhibit low levels of particularism.

DFJI in Electoral Systems Characterized by Low Particularism

Similar to particularistic democracies, we theorize that when governments in less particularistic—that is, party-centered—electoral systems in the developing world face high hazard rates in office, it provides an opportunity for the judiciary to credibly challenge the parties, including the ruling party. The judiciary's strategic rationale for doing so was described earlier, and hence will not be discussed here to avoid repetition. When governments in party-centered systems face low (high) time horizons (hazard rates) in office, they can also choose to either enhance judicial independence or reduce it by capturing the judiciary. Unlike politicians in personalist systems, however, we argue that incumbents in party-centered systems will optimally choose to curb the courts' de facto autonomy when their time horizon in office is low (hazard rate in office is high).

To see why, first recall from the earlier discussion on electoral particularism, that political parties operating under party-centered electoral rules are strong, centralized units that display considerable discipline in the legislature. The ability to exercise party discipline allows party leaders to identify policies that serve the best interests of the party as a whole and to suc-

High concentration of legislative seats held by post-transition governments in new democracies incresaes their political capacity to implement policies closer to their ideal point

⬇

Post-transition governments in new democracies that control a high concentration of legislative seats, however, fear that courts may curtail their policy-making capacity mentioned above especially if judicial review authority is granted to the judiciary

⬇

This fear described above is exacerbated when public trust in the judiciary increases during the immediate post-transition period in new democracies; this provides incentives for post-transition governments to resist granting judicial review authority to the courts

⬇

Hypothesis 1: Governments in new democracies in the developing world that control a sufficiently high concentration of legislative seats will be less likely to adopt judicial review if public trust in the judiciary increases during the immediate post-transition period in these states

Fig. 2.2. Summary of causal claim that generates hypothesis 2

cessfully implement them through the legislative process. Furthermore, strong legislative capacity also allows ruling parties to capture other state agencies, including the bureaucracy, the police, and various oversight and regulatory agencies (Epstein and O'Halloran 1996; Huber and Shipan 2002). This enables parties to use these state institutions, as well to put pressure on the judiciary (McNollgast 1987, 1989).

This implies that extra-legislative actions such as delayed budgetary disbursements to the judiciary and noncompliance with judicial rulings, for example, could be used to put effective pressure on individual judges, and to make the judiciary impotent as an effective agent of change. Similarly, the framing of corruption charges against judges by the police could be used to undermine public perception of the judiciary's integrity and to harass uncooperative judges individually. These informal measures could augment formal legislative measures and effectively hobble an uncooperative judiciary. As a direct consequence of high legislative capacity, therefore, the costs and benefits of the same strategic choices for parties and politicians in party-centered electoral systems will be very different from those in particularistic systems.

Consider the first strategic option ruling parties have—to reduce the judiciary's de facto independence. A *dependent* judiciary offers ruling parties many important electoral and political benefits. They can provide parties with the ability to ensure that their policy programs are implemented, and that any legal challenges by opposition parties, or social or economic groups are dismissed in court. This will allow ruling parties to enact their policy agenda and boost the credibility of their policy promises to voters and interest groups (Cooter and Ginsburg 1996). The shorter the time horizons governments face in office in party-centered systems, the more valuable the ability to shepherd legislation quickly and earn credibility with voters will be for ruling parties since elections will be imminent, rather than in the future.

Reducing DFJI offers the added benefit that subservient courts could be used to maximize the incumbents' electoral chances by reducing the electoral competitiveness of elections, and undermining the credibility of their opposition (Popova 2010). For example, courts could be used to challenge the electoral eligibility of key opposition figures the fundraising practices of important opposition financial donors, and even by challenging unfavorable electoral results at different levels of government (Popova 2010; Transparency International 2007).[31] A subservient judiciary will also allow party leaders in party-centered systems in the developing world to successfully raise funds from interest groups and donors in exchange for promising policy favors.

Since there are no guarantees that consecutive legislatures will respect the judiciary's independence (Boudreaux and Pritchard 1994) or that they will interpret statutes according to the intent of the legislature responsible for its passage (Epstein 1990), the creation of an independent court does not necessarily solve the problem of time-inconsistent preference that interest groups face. This is especially true in party-centered developing democracies where even if judiciaries rule entirely according to legislative statutes, bureaucracies under political pressure can simply choose not to comply with judicial decisions not favored by their current political principals. A disciplined ruling coalition can provide such policy guarantees by using its legislative discipline to ensure that both the judiciary and bureaucracy are subservient to its interests and support its influence-peddling efforts. In fact, dependent courts can help facilitate political control over the bureaucracy as well (McCubbins and Rodriguez 2008: 277; Rodriguez 1994). Thus, in party-centered systems, donors will find legislative promises more credible when the government can assure them that a compliant judiciary will issue friendly rulings. A compliant bureaucracy will, in turn, implement them, and the judiciary cannot be used to overturn favorable government decisions because it is subject to partisan capture.

Furthermore, considerable evidence shows that business lobbying is frequently motivated not by policy goals but by rent-seeking goals in developing states (Bhagwati 1987; Hellman and Kaufmann 2001; Open Society Institute 2003; Yadav 2011). These maybe realized by short-term policy initiatives such as subsidies, tax exemptions, or special licenses whose benefits are not conditional on the long term. Such quid pro quos do not require multiple terms or an impartial court to be delivered. In fact, a strong neutral external referee might actually pose a challenge to the ability of disciplined parties to raise funds from their donors on this basis. Given the short time horizons of many business interests in developing countries (Hellman 2000), state capture as a guarantor of policy value will be preferred by many business groups to DFJI even if parties do not expect to dominate power for long periods.[32] Thus, unlike particularistic systems, where courts were needed to deliver policy credibility to donors, intraparty discipline in party-centered developing democracies provides the same reassurance with the additional guarantee that courts cannot be used to undermine such promises. Donors will therefore value government promises more and be more willing to provide financial support for parties in exchange for influence peddling through subservient courts.[33]

To summarize these advantages, when the time horizons of governments in office in party-centered developing countries' democracies shrink, the funding needs of the ruling party will be to finance elections and to buy off opposition figures will be direr. Furthermore, as mentioned earlier, the government's high hazard rate in office will induce the judiciary to challenge the ruling party. Dire need for funding and opposition stemming from the judiciary will give the ruling party incentives to curtail the autonomy of the courts and control the courts. Doing so will influence donors (owing to reasons previously delineated) to provide much-needed funding to the ruling party in the party-centered developing countries' democracy.

Finally, note that when the hazard rate of the government in a party-centered democracy is sufficiently high, the opposition will recognize that it can expect to extract rents and to extend patronage benefits through a dependent judiciary in the near future if and when it gains office. If the current opposition pushes for an independent judiciary, however, it loses this future opportunity. Under an independent judiciary, both ruling and opposition parties will be constrained in their efforts to milk office for benefits and neither will be able to maximize the patronage and rent benefits of holding office. If the time horizons of governments are low on average, then this is an important opportunity cost for the opposition as well. An independent judiciary, therefore, imposes rent and patronage losses on both ruling and opposition parties since both can expect to hold office with some confidence and both require these resources. Compared to this, a subservient judiciary allows all parties to maximize the expected benefits from their tenures in office.

Given that parties (including the ruling party) in party-centered developing democracies reap benefits from having a dependent judiciary, the government in such democracies will have incentives to reduce de facto judicial independence in the context of low (high) time horizons (hazard rates) in office. Note, however, that incentives alone are not enough. Rather, we suggest that since party-centered systems engender strong parties with high levels of intraparty unity, ruling party leaders in this system will be able to exercise their leverage over individual party members effectively in order to successfully pass legislation that reduces DFJI when their time horizon in office is low. Therefore, to summarize, the arguments presented in this subsection lead to the following corollary.

Corollary to hypothesis 2: *When faced with high hazard rates (that is, low time horizons) in office, incumbents in developing democracies characterized by low levels of electoral particularism (party-centered systems) will curtail the courts' de facto autonomy.*

Conclusion

We started this chapter with the objective of explaining two puzzles in the developing world: Why during the initial post–transition years do governments in some new democracies, but not in others, constitutionally deny or restrict full judicial review authority for the courts? And why does high political competition resulting in low time horizons in office provide incentives to governments in some developing country democracies to protect and enhance de facto judicial independence, but induces governments in others to curtail de facto judicial autonomy? An extensive and rich literature in comparative judicial politics analyzes de jure and je facto independence as the outcomes of strategic interactions between key rational actors as they work to resolve various political challenges they face in gaining and maintaining office. In this chapter, we build on these theories and develop a distinct theoretical story to address each of the two questions.

In the institutional landscape of the immediate post–transition period in new democracies, the relative strength and public legitimacy of various institutions is still in the process of being established. Thus, the strategic behavior of courts and judges can have long-term consequences for political actors and is of profound concern to them. Hence, decisions regarding judicial empowerment are made by ruling elites not just with an eye to containing opposition threats to power but also of assessing and addressing the political threat the judiciary may pose to the government. Our first hypothesis predicts that governments in new democratic states that enjoy a sufficiently high concentration of legislative seats after the first post–authoritarian transition election are less likely to adopt judicial review if public trust in the judiciary is high and increases in these states in the immediate post–democratic transition period.

The corollary to this hypothesis posits that governments that do not gain enough legislative seats to control the legislature immediately after democratization will be more likely to adopt judicial review if public trust in the judiciary is low and decreases during the immediate post–transition period. The political decision to adopt review powers is therefore a function of the legislative power of governments in new democracies, but is tempered by the degree of public trust (or lack thereof) in the judiciary. By explicitly incorporating the institutional challenge that judiciaries represent in this uncertain environment, and the manner in which political elites assess this risk before making decisions, our theoretical story presents a more nuanced picture of the decision-making process regarding judicial empowerment in these countries.

Our second hypothesis addressed the second puzzle regarding the variation observed in de facto judicial independence across countries. We incorporate insights from the rich institutional literature that highlights the effects of electoral institutions on the nature of political competition to argue that the strategic responses of political and judicial elites regarding de facto judicial independence are conditioned by the incentives created by the electoral system. We posit that in the context of low (high) time horizons (hazard rates) in office, governments in more particularistic electoral systems will maintain and enhance de facto judicial independence. Conversely, as the corollary states, when faced with high hazard rates in office, governments in party-centered systems in the developing world will choose to reduce de facto judicial independence. Thus, in the context of low time horizons in office, the behavior of governments with respect to the judiciary in developing countries' democracies is influenced by the level of electoral particularism.

In order to assess the validity of these theoretical predictions, we need a research design that allows us to empirically test these hypotheses as robustly and precisely as possible. In order to accomplish the former, we will apply large-n statistical analysis techniques to comprehensive datasets covering global samples of countries. Chapter 3 begins the empirical analysis by testing hypothesis 1 and the corollary to this hypothesis in a sample of 159 developing countries from 1985 to 2004. Chapter 4 then presents two case studies of Indonesia and Brazil to illustrate the causal mechanism for de jure judicial review. Chapter 5 tests hypothesis 2 and its corollary in a sample of 103 developing country democracies for the 1985–2004 period. Chapters 6 and 7 then analyze the cases of Brazil, India, and Indonesia, respectively, in order to illustrate the causal mechanism for de facto judicial independence.

CHAPTER 3

New Democracies and De Jure Judicial Review
The Empirical Evidence

The first half of the theoretical story in chapter 2 explored how political contestation between parties during the immediate years following a democratic transition—that is, in new democratic regimes—affects the design of constitutional provisions for de jure judicial review in developing countries. This story produced the following prediction, which is labeled as hypothesis 1: governments in new democracies in the developing world that control a high concentration of legislative seats in the initial post–transition years will be less likely to adopt judicial review if public trust in the judiciary during the immediate post–democratic transition period is sufficiently high. The corollary to this hypothesis suggests that incumbents in new democracies will be more inclined to constitutionally grant the authority of judicial review to the courts if the concentration of legislative seats held by the ruling party and public trust in the judiciary in the immediate post–transition period is low.

Does the data provide statistical support for the prediction in hypothesis 1? In this chapter, we statistically test this hypothesis on a comprehensive time-series cross-sectional (TSCS) data set of de jure judicial review across 159 developing countries from 1985 to 2004. We also briefly evaluate whether the corollary to this hypothesis finds support in the data. Our sample and the statistical tests allow us to evaluate the hypothesis mentioned earlier while explicitly controlling for other factors that may potentially influence the probability with which incumbents adopt judicial review. However, one limitation of the quantitative analysis conducted in this chapter is that it is insufficient for testing the underlying causal mechanisms of the causal story that lead to hypothesis 1. Hence, in the following case-study chapter (i.e., chapter 4), we use a combination of case-study research and analysis of within-country data to test more directly the causal mechanism that leads to the theoretical predictions summarized in the preceding paragraph.

The rest of this chapter is organized as follows. We first describe the sample and the dependent variable that is employed to test hypothesis 1. We then discuss the operationalization of the independent and control variables that are included in the specification for the statistical tests. This is followed by a brief description of the statistical model that we use to test our hypothesis about judicial review. Section five presents the results obtained from the statistical tests of this hypothesis. Section six consists of the conclusion, in which we summarize the empirical findings and discuss the implications of the findings in this chapter. The tables and the figures that report the statistical results are presented in the appendix.

Sample and Dependent Variable

Since hypothesis 1 applies to developing countries, we conduct our statistical analysis on a comprehensive time-series cross-sectional (TSCS) data set of 159 developing countries from 1985 to 2004; these countries are listed in table 3.1. Our sample starts from 1985 since systematic and reliable data to operationalize particularly the dependent variable for testing hypothesis 1 (this is described later) is only available for a truly global sample of developing states from 1985 onward.[1] That said, the comprehensive cross-sectional size and temporal range of our sample allows us to obtain more efficient estimates. It also enhances the generalizability of the empirical findings.

The dependent variable of interest in hypothesis 1 is the extent to which constitutional rules provide courts with full and explicit de jure judicial review. Following extant research on the review of legislative and executive decisions by the courts, we employ an ordinal measure of de jure judicial review developed from several sources.[2] The operationalization of this measure, which is labeled as *judicial review*, is drawn from Finkel et al. (2007), who have documented the existence of constitutional provisions that allow for judicial review of legislative and executive decisions. More specifically, following Finkel et al. (2007: 42), we operationalize *judicial review* as a discrete ordinal scale where:

TABLE 3.1. Developing Countries in the Data

Afghanistan	Costa Rica	Korea, South	Poland	Ukraine
Albania	Croatia	Kuwait	Qatar	Uruguay
Algeria	Cuba	Kyrgyzstan	Romania	Uzbekistan
Andorra	Côte d'Ivoire	Laos	Russia	Vanuatu
Angola	Cyprus	Latvia	Rwanda	Venezuela
Antigua and Barbuda	Czechoslovakia	Lebanon	Samoa	Vietman
Argentina	Czech Republic	Lesotho	San Marino	Yemen
Armenia	Djibouti	Libya	Saudi Arabia	Zambia
Azerbaijan	Dominica	Liberia	Serbia	Zanzibar
Bahamas	Dominican Republic	Lithuania	St. Kitts	Zimbabwe
Bahrain	Ecuador	Macedonia	St. Lucia	
Bangladesh	Egypt	Madagascar	St. Vincents	
Barbados	El Salvador	Malawi	Senegal	
Belarus	Ethiopia	Malaysia	Seychelles	
Belize	Estonia	Maldives	Sierra Leone	
Benin	Fiji	Mali	Singapore	
Bhutan	Gabon	Malta	Slovakia	
Bolivia	Georgia	Mauritania	Slovenia	
Bosnia and Herzegovina	Gambia	Mauritius	Taiwan	
Botswana	Ghana	Mexico	Somalia	
Brazil	Grenada	Mongolia	South Africa	
Brunei	Guatemala	Moldova	Sri Lanka	
Bulgaria	Guinea	Morocco	Sudan	
Burkina Faso	Guinea Bissau	Mozambique	Suriname	
Burundi	Guyana	Myanmar	Swaziland	
Cambodia	Haiti	Nauru	Syria	
Cameroon	Honduras	Namibia	Tajikistan	
Cape Verde	Hungary	Nepal	Tanzania	
Central African Republic	India	Nicaragua	Thailand	
Chad	Indonesia	Niger	Togo	
Chile	Iran	Nigeria	Tonga	
China	Iraq	Oman	Trinidad and Tobago	
Colombia	Jamaica	Pakistan	Turkmenistan	
Comoros	Jordan	Panama	Tunisia	
Congo, Republic	Kazakhstan	Papua New Guinea	Turkey	
Congo, D.R.	Kenya	Paraguay	United Arab Emirates	
	Kiribati	Peru	Uganda	
	Korea, North	Philippines		

- −1 indicates that the constitution gives the power of constitutional (judicial) review to another branch of government such as the executive or the legislature
- 0 operationalizes a situation where the constitution does not provide for judicial (constitutional) review for the judiciary
- 1 indicates that the constitution provides for judicial review for the judiciary somewhat or provides for it vaguely but not fully and
- 2 indicates that the constitution provides for judicial review fully and explicitly for the judiciary

The measure described just now shows that an increase in the ordinal scale of *judicial review* from its lowest value to its maximum value captures a shift from a situation where the constitution grants the authority of constitutional review to the executive or legislature to an outcome where constitutional rules explicitly provide the courts with the power of full-fledged judicial review. The key advantage of the *judicial review* measure is that it directly operationalizes our theoretical definition of judicial review in the previous chapter. Thus our *judicial review* measure permits us to carefully test the theoretical prediction in hypothesis 1.

Data to operationalize the *de jure judicial review* measure described above is drawn from numerous primary and secondary sources. The secondary sources that have been employed to operationalize *judicial review* include Keith (2002), the Democracy Assistance Project at the University of Pittsburgh compiled by Finkel et al. (2007),[3] and Apodaca (2004). The primary sources that we employed include Blaustein and Flanzeds (1971–), *Constitutions of Countries of the World;* Blaustein (1993), *World Constitutions Illustrated: Contemporary and Historical Documents and Resources;*[4] *Constitution Finder* at the University of Richmond School of Law; Maddex (1995); and Wolfrum and Grote (1971–).

Independent Variables

Hypothesis 1 posits an interactive effect since it suggests that the concentration of legislative seats controlled by governments during the initial post–transition years will decrease the probability of adoption of *judicial review* conditional on the degree of public trust in the judiciary during the post–transition period in new democracies. To test the prediction in hypothesis

1, we thus need to interact two independent variables: (1) a variable that measures the concentration of legislative seats controlled by the government in new democratic regimes in the initial post-transition years; and (2) a continuous measure that operationalizes the citizens' trust in the judiciary in new democracies in the post–transition period as well.

To operationalize each independent variable mentioned earlier, we need to first identify the countries in our sample that made a transition to democracy and the initial post–transition years during which these countries are both observed and are (hence) classified as "new democratic regimes." We do so by using several primary and secondary sources to identify precisely the year in which democratic transitions occurred in the countries in our data and the initial post–transition years in these countries.[5] Specifically, following recent research on democratic transitions,[6] we identify each episode of democratic transition in our data at the timing of the first international deemed "free and fair elections" and the adoption of a new democratic constitution after a prolonged period of autocratic rule.[7] Based on these criteria and the sources previously mentioned, we find that 63 developing countries have made a transition to democracy—in other words, there are 63 episodes of democratic transition in our data—during the 1985 to 2004 time period.

Table 3.2 lists each of these 63 developing countries that experienced a transition to democracy (column 1), the year in which a democratic transition occurred in these countries (column 2), and a brief description of each transition event (column 3). Lastly, column 4 in table 3.2 lists the year (t) in which a democratic transition occurred in each country in column 1 and the subsequent four post–transition years ($t + 4$) for each of the 63 developing countries that experienced a democratic transition. Thus, following the procedure used by Rodrik and Wacziarg (2005) to code countries as "new democracies," we classify the countries listed in table 3.2, column 1, as a "new democratic regime" for the year in which they experienced a transition to democracy and the immediate four post–transition years (this amounts to a total of five years).[8]

After identifying the countries in our sample and the years in which they are observed as new democratic regimes, we operationalize our first independent variable mentioned earlier the concentration of seats in the legislature held by the government in new democracies during the initial post-transition years, which we label as *concentration*. The *concentration* variable—following existing studies[9]—is operationalized as the Hirschman-

TABLE 3.2. Democratic Transition Episodes in Data

(I) Country	(II) Democratic Transition Year	(III) Brief Description of Democratic Transition Episode	(IV) Observed as New Democratic Regime in Data From...
Albania	1992	Subsequent (in 1991 and 1992) elections marked the ending of the communist rule	1992–96
Argentina	1983	First free and fair elections after a prolonged period of military dictatorship	1985 (rather than 1983) to 1987 since our sample of de jure judicial review for developing states starts from 1985
Armenia	1998	The first internationally deemed free and fair elections were held in 1998	1998–2002
Bangladesh	1991	First postindependence (1971) free and fair elections	1991–95
Benin	1991	Adoption of new democratic constitution; free and fair elections	1991–95
Bolivia	1982	Return to civilian rule. Military steps down. Reconvention of 1980 democratic constitution.	1985 (rather than 1982) to 1986 since our sample of de jure judicial review for developing states starts from 1985
Brazil	1985	Return to civilian rule. Military steps down. Reconvention of 1980 democratic constitution.	1985–89
Bulgaria	1990	First internationally deemed fair and free elections after a more than two-decade-long military rule	1990–94
Cape Verde	1991	First postcommunism free and fair general assembly elections	1991–95
Central African Republic	1993	First free election after the oppressive Bokassa rule. The 1996 presidential elections were deemed free but marked by fraud.	1993–97

TABLE 3.2.—*Continued*

(I) Country	(II) Democratic Transition Year	(III) Brief Description of Democratic Transition Episode	(IV) Observed as New Democratic Regime in Data From . . .
Chile	1990	First free and fair presidential elections; ending of two-decade-long military rule of Augusto Pinochet	1990–94
Comoros	1990	First postindependence (1975) free and fair elections	1990–94
Croatia	2000	First free and fair legislative and presidential elections since independence and the ending of the Bosnian War	2000–2004
Czech Republic	1993	Independence from Czechoslovakia. First postcommunism constitution came into effect.	1993–97
Djibouti	1999	First postindependence internationally declared free and fair elections	1999–2003
El Salvador	1994	First free and fair elections after the end of a long-lasting civil war and military rule	1994–98
Estonia	1991	Independence from USSR. Ratification of old (1938) constitution.	1991–95
Ethiopia	1995	First multiparty elections after a long-lived communist era	1995–99
Georgia	1995	First internationally deemed free and fair presidential and legislative elections were held in 1995	1995–99
Ghana	1996	Internationally deemed free and fair elections	1996–2000
Grenada	1984	First free and fair elections held	1985–89 since our sample of de jure judicial review for developing states starts from 1985
Guatemala	1996	End of civil war; return to civilian rule	1996–2000

(*continues*)

TABLE 3.2.—*Continued*

(I) Country	(II) Democratic Transition Year	(III) Brief Description of Democratic Transition Episode	(IV) Observed as New Democratic Regime in Data From...
Guyana	1992	First postindependence (1966) free and fair elections	1992–96
Haiti	1994	A US intervention brought into power the winner of the 1990 elections	1994–99
Honduras	1982	Adoption of new democratic constitution after a prolonged period of oppressive rule. First democratically elected president takes office.	1985–86 since our sample of de jure judicial review for developing states starts from 1985
Hungary	1990	First postcommunist free and fair presidential elections	1990–94
Indonesia	1999	First multiparty elections after the collapse of the Suharto regime	1999–2003
Korea, Republic of	1988	Democratically elected government resumes office. Adoption of new democratic constitution.	1988–92
Latvia	1991	Independence from USSR. Ratification of old (1922) democratic constitution.	1991–95
Lesotho	1993	Military abandons power and internationally deemed free and fair elections mark. The return to civilian rule.	1993–97
Lithuania	1991	Independence from USSR	1991–95
Macedonia	1991	Independence from former Yugoslavia. First constitution approved. National Unity government formed.	1991–95
Madagascar	1993	Presidential elections after a twenty-year-long military junta	1993–97
Malawi	1994	First postindependence, free and fair parliamentary and presidential elections	1994–98

TABLE 3.2.—*Continued*

(I) Country	(II) Democratic Transition Year	(III) Brief Description of Democratic Transition Episode	(IV) Observed as New Democratic Regime in Data From...
Mali	1992	New democratic constitution established a multiparty. Fair and free legislative and presidential elections followed.	1992–96
Mexico	1997	For the first time since 1929 the Institutional Revolutionary party (PRI) lost absolute power in the lower house after the 1997 legislative elections	1997–2001
Moldova	1994	First internationally deemed free and fair presidential and legislative elections were held in 1994	1994–98
Mongolia	1992	New democratic constitution established a multiparty system	1992–96
Mozambique	1994	First postindependence parliamentary and presidential elections	1994–98
Nepal	1991	First free and fair elections since the early sixties	1991–95
Nicaragua	1990	Free and fair elections after the Somosa dictatorship and the Santinistas revolution	1990–94
Niger	1999	Transition to civilian rule in 1999, which was followed by first internationally deemed free and fair election in the same year	1999–2003
Nigeria	1999	After consecutive coups and military interventions, internationally declared free and fair elections mark the return to civilian rule	1999–2003
Pakistan	1988	Legislative elections were held; restoration of the 1985 democratic constitution. In spite of fair and free elections in the nineties, the military coup of 1999 blocked democratization.	1988–92

(*continues*)

TABLE 3.2.—*Continued*

(I) Country	(II) Democratic Transition Year	(III) Brief Description of Democratic Transition Episode	(IV) Observed as New Democratic Regime in Data From ...
Panama	1994	Free and fair presidential and legislative elections after the US intervention	1994–98
Paraguay	1993	First presidential elections after decades of military rule	1993–97
Philippines	1987	Adoption of new democratic constitution; free and fair elections led to the overthrow of Marcos' regime	1987–91
Poland	1990	First postcommunist, free and fair, presidential, legislative, and local elections. Adoption of new democratic constitution.	1990–94
Romania	1990	First postcommunist free and fair elections	1990–94
Russia	1993	Adoption of first postcommunist constitution; free and fair Duma elections	1993–97
Sao Tome and Principe	1991	First internationally deemed free and fair elections	1991–95
Senegal	2000	First postindependence internationally deemed fair and free elections	2000–2004
Serbia	2000	First internationally deemed free and fair elections were held in 2000	2000–2004
Slovak Republic	1993	Independence from Czechoslovakia. First postcommunism elections; a new democratic constitution came into effect. Coded as *new democracy* from 1993 to 1997.	2000–2004
Slovenia	1992	First since gaining independence from Yugoslavia, free presidential and legislative elections. Adoption of a new democratic constitution.	1992–96

TABLE 3.2.—*Continued*

(I) Country	(II) Democratic Transition Year	(III) Brief Description of Democratic Transition Episode	(IV) Observed as New Democratic Regime in Data From ...
South Africa	1994	First free elections with universal participation, brought into power Nelson Mandela and ended the Apartheid regime	1994–98
Suriname	1991	Return to civilian government after a one-party regime; free and fair elections	1991–95
Tanzania	1995	First postindependence, internationally deemed free and fair elections	1995–99
Thailand	1992	Military was forced to step down. Free legislative elections followed.	1992–96
Turkey	1983	First free and fair legislative elections after a military dictatorship. Developing states starts from 1985.	1985–87 since our sample of de jure judicial review for developing states starts from 1985
Ukraine	1991	Independence from USSR. Legislative elections followed.	1991–95
Uruguay	1985	Army returned the power to the democratically elected president	1985–89
Zambia	1991	First postindependence, free and fair elections. New democratic constitution came into effect.	1991–95

Note: Table 3.2 reports the country, the timing, and a brief description of the democratization event in each case. The table lists full incidents of democratic transitions. That is, in these countries democratic institutions became fully consolidated (according both to the Polity and Freedom House indicators) in the five years after they made a transition to democracy. Note that table 3.2 lists democracy transition episodes for developing countries for which data on de jure judicial review is available. Finally, observe that since our sample starts in 1985, developing countries that experienced a transition to democracy at or before 1980 and remained democratic till 1985 (and beyond) are *not* observed as "new democracy" in the data even though they are included in the sample. This is because by 1985—the first/initial year in our sample—the aforementioned countries had evolved into consolidated and stable democracies and are thus not strictly observed as new democratic states from 1985 with respect to our definition of new democratic regimes.

Herfindahl index of the concentration of legislative seats held by the ruling government[10] in the lower chamber of the national legislature in new democracies during the immediate post-transition period. The Hirschman-Herfindahl index of the concentration of the government's legislative seats is computed as the sum of squared seat shares held by the parties in the government in the national legislature.[11] This index ranges from a minimum value of 0 to a maximum value of 1. Summary statistics for the *concentration* measure indicates that there exists significant variation in this variable in our sample.[12] The sources employed to operationalize this legislative concentration measure are listed in table 3.3.

Next, we operationalize the second independent variable required to test hypothesis 1: the degree of public trust in the judiciary in new democratic states in the initial post-transition years. We operationalize this variable in two steps. We first identify the new democratic regimes based on the procedure described in the preceding paragraph. These new democracies, as previously mentioned, are listed in table 3.2. Second, we operationalize the degree of public trust in the judiciary in these new democracies. To do so, we employ the measure of public trust in the judiciary measure from the Democracy Assistance Project database compiled by Finkel et al. (2007). They operationalize the degree of public trust in the justice system for each country by calculating the average response from survey respondents in each country to the following question: "I am going to name a number of organizations. For each one, could you tell me how much confidence you have in them: Is it a great deal of confidence, quite a lot of confidence, not very much confidence or none at all? The justice system."[13] Note that the aforementioned measure of public trust in the judiciary—which is available for each of the 68 newly democratized states in table 3.2—has been compiled by Finkel et al. (2007) and several additional sources listed in table 3.3.[14] We thus use their measure, which is available for each new democratic regime in table 3.2, to operationalize the level of public trust in the judiciary in each of these new democratic states during the immediate post-transition period. We denote this variable as *trust*. The *trust* measure ranges from a minimum value of −20.86 to a maximum value of 48.44 in the developing countries sample. The mean level of *trust* in the sample is −.257, while the standard deviation of this variable is 25.02. This implies that there exists substantial variation in this measure in our sample.

To test the interactive effect posited in hypothesis 1, we interact the *concentration* variable with the *trust* measure and introduce *concentration* ×

TABLE 3.3. Data Sources for Variables

Independent Variables	Data Sources
Concentration	Banks 2003; Inter-Parliamentary Union (various years, Geneva); World Bank (2008) *Database of Political Institutions*
Trust	Finkel, Pérez-Liñán, and Seligson 2007; World Values Survey (various years); Barrett 2005; Justice Studies Center of the Americas (CEJA-JSCA); Latin American Public Opinion Project (LAPOP); Afrobarometer; Asian Barometer

Control Variables	Data Sources
Economic controls	
log GDP per capita, foreign aid, FDI flows, trade openness	IMF (2009), *Government Financial Statistics* (CD-Rom); World Bank 2006
Political controls	
Competition (PARCOMP)	Polity IV database
Presidential	Golder 2005; World Bank (2008), *Database of Political Institutions*
Democracy level (polity)	Polity IV database
Separation of powers	Finkel, Pérez-Liñán, and Seligson 2007; Blaustein and Flanz 1971; Blaustein 1993; *World Constitutions Illustrated: Contemporary and Historical Documents and Resources*; Maddex 1995
Legislative concentration	Banks 2003; Inter-Parliamentary Union (various years, Geneva); World Bank (2008), *Database of Political Institutions*
Federal	World Bank (2008), *Database of Political Institutions*
Press freedom	Freedom House (various years)
elf	Fearon and Laitin 2003. The Fearon and Laitin elf measure is calculated for all the developing states in our sample and is updated through 2004.
Public trust	Finkel, Pérez-Liñán, and Seligson 2007; World Values Survey (various years); Barrett 2005; Justice Studies Center of the Americas (CEJA-JSCA); Latin American Public Opinion Project (LAPOP); Afrobarometer; Asian Barometer
Democracy age	Computed from Przeworski, Alvarez, Cheibub, and Limongi 2000; Cheibub and Gandhi 2004; Polity IV
Data used to identify list of new democratic regimes in table 3.2	*Freedom in the World: Political Rights and Liberties 1972–2005* (New York: Freedom House); Polity IV Index; Country Studies/ US Library of Congress (http://memory.loc.gov/frd/cs/); U.S. Department of State, "Background Country Notes" (http://www.state.gov/r/pa/ei/bgn/)

trust as well as the individual components of this interaction term in the specification where the dependent variable is *de jure judicial review*. Based on the prediction in hypothesis 1, we anticipate that the effect of *concentration* × *trust* in new democratic regimes on *judicial review* will be negative.

Control Variables

We include several political and economic control variables in the empirical model that have been identified by scholars as important determinants of de jure judicial review across countries (see, for example, Vanberg 2000, 2005, 2008; Stephenson 2003; Chavez 2004, 2008; Widner 2001; Ginsburg 2003; Herron and Randazzo 2003; Hirschl 2008; Rios-Figueroa 2007).[15] Introducing these control variables in the empirical model is important as it helps to account for the alternative explanations presented by researchers that may account for variation in de jure judicial review. Extant studies suggest that the following political factors influence the initial establishment of de jure judicial review.

First, Stephenson (2003: 79) and other scholars[16] claim that greater domestic political competition within states increases the likelihood that judicial independence will be enhanced via adoption of constitutional provisions that provide courts with the authority of judicial review. There are a number of different ways of measuring the extent of political competition within countries. A common proxy that researchers use to operationalize political competition is the competitiveness of participation (PARCOMP) variable drawn from the Polity IV data set.[17] PARCOMP measures the extent to which nonelites are able to access institutional structures for political expression: the greater the extent of the franchise and the more that alternative preferences for policies and leadership can be pursued in the political arena, the higher the PARCOMP score and thus the higher the degree of political competition. The PARCOMP measure ranges from 0 (unregulated) to 5 (fully competitive), with 5 indicating fully open competition for political leadership.[18] We include the PARCOMP measure, labeled as *competition*, in the empirical specification as a proxy for political competition. Stephenson (2003: 80) also posits that a longer history of continuous institutionalized democracy leads to higher levels of de jure judicial independence including judicial review. We therefore incorporate the count variable *democracy age* that operationalizes the number of years in which countries are observed as full-fledged democracies according to the Cheibub et al. (2010) criteria for a democratic regime.[19] The data sources that have been used to operationalize the *competition* and *democracy age,* as well as the remaining controls mentioned later are listed in table 3.3.

Numerous scholars have suggested that separation of powers fosters the adoption of constitutional rules that increase judicial independence by providing authority to the courts to conduct judicial review (e.g., Vanberg 2000; Whittington 2003; Friedman 2004; Shapiro 1981). To account for this, we control for *separation of powers* using a 0–2 ordinal measure, which documents the existence of constitutional provisions stating that the courts are housed in a separate branch from the executive and legislative powers. This ordinal *separation of powers* measure is operationalized as follows: a score of 0 indicates that the constitution does not provide for separation of powers; a score of 1 indicates that the constitution provides for separation of powers somewhat or provides for it vaguely but not fully; and finally a score of 2 indicates that the constitution provides for separation of powers fully and explicitly.

Existing studies also hypothesize that higher levels of democracy ensures continuity and repetition of elections and that this, in turn, promotes the design of constitutional rules that provide courts with the authority of judicial review (Stephenson 2003; Hirschl 2004, 2008; Chavez 2004; Ramseyer and Rosenbluth 1993; Ramseyer 1994; Finkel 2008). We thus add the Polity measure, which operationalizes the level of democracy, labeled as *democracy level,* from a −10 (fully autocratic) to a +10 (fully democratic) scale to the specification.[20] Some researchers suggest that presidential systems encourages the constitutionalization of judicial review (e.g., Shaprio 1981; Vanberg 2008), while others make the opposite argument.[21] Notwithstanding the lack of scholarly consensus over this issue, we incorporate the dummy variable *presidential* that is coded as 1 for countries with a presidential system and is coded as 0 otherwise.

In addition to the political controls just listed, we follow existing studies and add numerous economic control variables to the specification as well. With respect to economic controls, we first include *log GDP per capita.* This is because higher levels of per capita income may increase the citizens' interest in an impartial and independent judiciary and consequently induce the government to establish an independent judiciary by adopting judicial review (Stephenson 2003; Hayo and Voigt 2007; Keith 2002; Barrett 2005; Abbasi 2007; Rios-Figueroa and Staton 2009). Some studies claim that governments in the developing world that obtain foreign aid are more likely to respond to pressure from donor states or international development agencies that advocate greater judicial autonomy by adopting judicial review (Chavez 2008; Hirschl 2003). To account for this phenomenon, we incorporate the variable *foreign aid* in the empirical model; *foreign aid* is measured as the level of foreign aid flows (in millions of U.S. dollars) into the developing countries in our sample that have received such aid flows.[22]

It has also been suggested that foreign direct investment flows from international investors to developing countries may provide these investors with leverage over governments of developing states that receive foreign direct investment. Investors may use this leverage to pressure states to adopt an independent judiciary that provides greater protection of property rights and industries set up by foreign investors in developing states (Chavez 2003, 2008; Hirschl 2003; Klerman 2006; Klerman and Mahoney 2005). We thus control for *FDI flows,* which is operationalized as annual net FDI inflows in millions of U.S. dollars for each country year.[23] Some policy analysts have claimed that greater exposure to economic globalization—which is often measured by a country's level of trade openness[24]—may induce governments in the developing world to establish an independent judiciary (Wolf 1997; Bjornskov 2006; Berggren 2003). We thus add *trade openness,* which is operationalized as the ratio of the sum of exports and imports to GDP for each country year. Summary statistics for the dependent variable, the independent and the control variables previously discussed are reported in table 3.4

Statistical Methodology

The dependent variable in hypothesis 1, *judicial review,* is an ordinal measure. We therefore test hypothesis 1 by using an ordered probit model that is estimated with cluster-adjusted robust standard errors that account for within-country correlation and heteroskedasticity. Since we employ a time-series-cross-sectional (TSCS) data set, we estimate the ordered probit (OP) model with random effects,[25] and, moreover, we include year (i.e., time) dummies in the specification as well. We also present below the results obtained in the OP models that are estimated without random effects and year dummies.[26]

We conduct a battery of robustness tests to assess the consistency of our results. First, we conducted a series of specification robustness tests to check if our key results hold when we change the main specification by incorporating additional control variables. Second, we checked whether our estimates remain robust when we account for a potential econometric problem that may lead to inconsistent results—namely, the problem of selection bias. In this regard, note that it is plausible that factors that influence a nonrandom phenomenon such as the probability with which democracy emerges may also explain the choice of *de jure judicial review* by governments in new democracies.[27] If we do not account for the nonrandomness of democratic regimes in the estimation process when testing our hypothesis, then the estimated results may suffer from selection bias.

Researchers typically employ the Heckman selection or the bivariate probit model to account for selection bias (e.g., Przeworski et al. 2000; Przeworski and Vreeland 2003). However, since the dependent variable that we employ (*judicial review*) is ordinal, we cannot use a standard Heckman selection model to address the issue of selection bias. Rather, we use a sample-selected ordered probit model (denoted as S-OP model) to evaluate whether or not the results reported in the standard order probit model remain robust after accounting for selection bias. The S-OP statistical model, which has been developed and analyzed by Greene and Hensher (2009, 2010),

TABLE 3.4. Summary Statistics of Main Variables

Variables	Mean	Standard Deviation	Minimum	Maximum
log GDP per capita	7.104	1.274	3.914	11.236
Foreign aid	2.95e+08	4.56e+08	−9.44e+08	5.43e+09
FDI flows	8.27e+08	3.49e+09	−4.55e+09	7.23e+10
Trade openness	81.72	48.14	.85	427.88
Competition	−2.13	19.26	−88	5
Legislative concentration	.236	.196	0	.980
Trust	−.257	25.02	−20.86	48.44
Democracy level (polity)	−4.480	19.856	−88	10
Democracy age	3.667	5.972	0	21
Press freedom	48.332	9.512	24.957	64.596
Presidential	.540	.498	0	1
Separation of powers	1.20	.939	0	2
elf	.517	.247	.001	1
New democracy	.080	.272	0	1
Federal	.162	.369	0	1
Judicial review	.795	.966	−1	2

consists of two stages. The first stage of the S-OP model is a selection equation (estimated via probit) in which we estimate the impact of covariates on the likelihood that democracy may emerge. This selection equation is defined more formally (after dropping subscript t for time for notational convenience) as:

$$d_i^* = \alpha' z_i + u_i \tag{3.1}$$

$$d_i = \begin{cases} 1 & \text{if } d_i^* > 0 \\ 0 & \text{otherwise} \end{cases}$$

where the dichotomous dependent variable d_i is coded as 1 for a *democratic regime* and is 0 otherwise.[28]

In the selection equation (3.1), we explicitly account for the factors that influence the probability that democracy may emerge. In particular, following extant studies that identify various factors that influence the likelihood that democracies may occur,[29] we incorporate the following variables in the selection equation of the statistical model where *democratic regime* is the dependent variable: *log GDP per capita*, an index of *religious fractionalization, elf,* the total number of democracies in the world per year (*total democracy*), a dummy variable that operationalizes the collapse of democratic regimes (*dem breakdown*), the percentage of *Catholics, Protestants,* and *Muslims* in the population for each country year, a dummy for former British colonies (*colony*), and the lag of the *democratic regime* dummy. The second stage of the S-OP model—that is, the outcome equation—follows the usual ordered probit specification in which we estimate the effect of *concentration × trust* in new democracies, the constitutive components of this interaction term, and the control variables listed earlier on the ordered dependent variable, *judicial review.* The ordered probit outcome equation of the S-OP model is defined (after dropping subscript t for time) as:

$$y_i^* = \beta' x_i + \varepsilon_i \tag{3.2}$$

$$y_i = j \text{ if } \mu_{j-1} < y_i^* \leq \mu_j$$

where y_i^* is the ordered dependent variable, *judicial review.* The error term for the selection equation (ε_i) and the outcome equation (u_i) are correlated and are assumed to be bivariate normal distributed with correlation coefficient ρ.[30] The technical details and the log likelihood function of the sample-selected ordered probit model are provided in the appendix. The procedure that we use to estimate the S-OP statistical model is also described in the appendix.[31] We estimate the sample-selected ordered probit model with random effects and year dummies; however, the results in the S-OP model do not alter substantively and significantly (in the statistical sense) when the model is estimated without random effects and year dummies. We turn now to discuss the results from the statistical tests.

Results

Fig. 3.1 employs data from episodes of democratic transition in our sample to illustrate the trend in *de jure judicial review* during the immediate post–democratic transition period for two cases. For the first case, the solid line in this figure shows the moving average of *judicial review* for the set of new democracies in our sample where the following two conditions are met: the (1) Herfindahl index of concentration of the legislative seats held by the government in the initial post–transition years is higher than 0.6 on the 0–1 scale of this index; and (2) level of public trust in the judiciary in immediate post–transition period is higher than 25 on the −20 (lowest value) to 50 (highest value) range of the judiciary trust measure in the sample. For the second case, the dashed line in the figure reveals the moving average of *de jure judicial review* across the new democracies in our sample where the Herfindahl concentration of the legislative seats held by the ruling party in the post–transition period is lower than 0.3 (and is thus low) and public trust in the judiciary in the post–transition years is lower than −5 on the range of the judiciary trust measure mentioned earlier.

The dashed line in the figure shows that the level of judicial review increases during the initial post–transition years in new democracies where the ruling party does not dominate the legislature and if public trust in the judiciary is low. However, the solid line in fig. 3.1 reveals that the moving average of the *de jure judicial review* measure decreases across new democratic regimes in which the government controls the legislature and where public trust for the courts is relatively high. The negative slope of the solid line previously mentioned provides preliminary support for our first hypothesis. But it is clearly insufficient for statistical inference. In order to

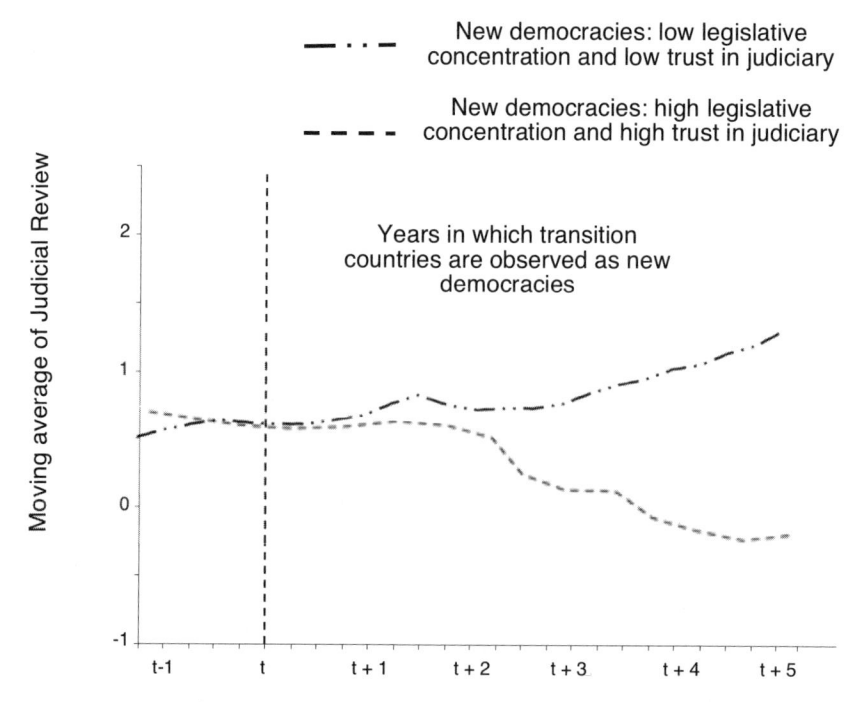

Fig. 3.1. Legislative concentration, trust in judiciary, and *judicial review* in new democracies. (Note that t denotes democratic transition year; $t - 1$ denotes the year prior to the democratic transition year, and $t + 1$ to $t + 5$ denote the first five post-transition years.)

evaluate our hypothesis more systematically, we therefore present the statistical results obtained from a standard ordered probit model and from the outcome equation of the sample-selection ordered probit model (S-OP) model.

Columns 1 and 2 in table 3.5 report the results from testing the effect of *concentration × trust* in new democratic regimes on *de jure judicial review* in the estimated ordered probit model. The ordered probit specification in column 1 is estimated without random effects, while the specification in column 2 is estimated with random effects. The estimate of *concentration × trust* in new democracies is negative and highly significant at the 1 percent level in columns 1 and 2. Moreover, the coefficient of each of the two individual components of the interaction term mentioned earlier—that is, *concentration* and *trust*, respectively—are each statistically insignificant in the

TABLE 3.5. Results for *de jure judicial review*

	Ordered Probit		Outcome Equation of S-OP Model	Ordered Probit		Outcome Equation of S-OP Model
	Column 1	Column 2	Column 3	Column 4	Column 5	Column 6
log GDP per capita	.038	.035	.039	.031	.021	.018
	(.069)	(.077)	(.125)	(.114)	(.119)	(.125)
Foreign aid	−1.31**	−1.26**	−.712**	−.540**	−.394**	−.205
	(.525)	(.537)	(.354)	(.272)	(.217)	(.188)
FDI flows	−2.18**	−2.15**	−.516*	−1.41**	−1.023**	−.212
	(1.04)	(1.04)	(.277)	(.626)	(.619)	(.559)
Trade openness	−.000	−.000	−.000	−.000	−.000	−.000
	(.000)	(.000)	(.021)	(.000)	(.000)	(.026)
New democracy	.989	.974	.809	.677	.618	.344
	(.793)	(.826)	(.635)	(.732)	(.714)	(.493)
Concentration × trust	−.147***	−.125***	−.084***	−.103***	−.093***	−.065**
	(.032)	(.039)	(.021)	(.035)	(.031)	(.033)
Concentration	−.070	−.067	−.012	−.023	−.018	−.006
	(.145)	(.139)	(.028)	(.384)	(.477)	(.039)
Trust	.049	.043	.043	.075	.019	.025
	(.154)	(.173)	(.173)	(.159)	(.184)	(.211)
Competition	.022**	.019**	.015**	.011*	.007*	.010*
	(.010)	(.009)	(.007)	(.006)	(.004)	(.006)
Presidential	.065	.062	.053	.040	.029	.027
	(.140)	(.134)	(.174)	(.188)	(.164)	(.183)
Separation of powers	.652***	.637***	.920***	.855***	.724**	.687***
	(.096)	(.093)	(.217)	(.194)	(.186)	(.132)
Democracy level (polity)	.010	.008	.006	.004	.001	.003
	(.026)	(.025)	(.043)	(.047)	(.066)	(.049)
Democracy age	.011	.012	.023	.019	.010	.011
	(.019)	(.026)	(.035)	(.030)	(.022)	(.036)
elf				−.006	−.002	.001
				(.125)	(.154)	(.236)
Press freedom				.062*	.042	.037*
				(.034)	(.039)	(.021)
Federal				.024*	.009	.006
				(.014)	(.017)	(.045)
Democracy transition sum					.021*	.019*
					(.011)	(.010)
Authoritarian transition sum					−.034	−.081
					(.056)	(.094)
Bicameralism					.012	.010
					(.029)	(.024)
Veto players					.025	.011
					(.136)	(.143)

(*continues*)

TABLE 3.5.—Continued

	Ordered Probit	Outcome Equation of S-OP Model		Ordered Probit		Outcome Equation of S-OP Model
	Column 1	Column 2	Column 3	Column 4	Column 5	Column 6
Judicial review emulation					.146	.095
					(.390)	(.721)
British legal origin					.039	.026
					(.075)	(.081)
French legal origin					.011	.006
					(.042)	(.053)
Legislative concentration					−.010	−.006
					(.062)	(.128)
Judiciary trust					.030	.026
					(.094)	(.112)
μ_1	−.746*	−.916*	−.123	−.118	−.081	−.093
	(.419)	(.540)	(.207)	(.252)	(.255)	(.212)
μ_2	.875**	1.12***	.904**	.631**	.304**	.612**
	(.393)	(.356)	(.451)	(.312)	(.153)	(.307)
μ_3	.377	.510	.624	.409	.409	.248
	(.622)	(.489)	(.571)	(.472)	(.741)	(.792)
ρ			.179**			.112**
			(.083)			(.063)
Wald χ_2	523.41	592.68	814.71	767.52	728.11	933.40
Random effects	no	yes	yes	yes	yes	yes
Time dummies	no	yes	yes	yes	yes	yes
N	2,086	1,979	1,867	1,593	1,086	1,086
Log-likelihood	−901.62	−921.05	−1,165.41	−1,072.51	−1,355.02	−1,641.15

Note: Each model is estimated with cluster-adjusted robust standard errors (reported in parentheses) that account for within-country correlation and heteroskedasticity.

***, ** and * denotes significance at the 1%, 5%, and 10% level, respectively.

two columns. This indicates that it is indeed the interaction of these two independent variables rather than each variable individually that has a negative and statistically significant effect on *de jure judicial review*. This result, therefore, supports the prediction in hypothesis 1. Yet we need to statistically check the marginal effect of *concentration × trust* in new democracies on *de jure judicial review* to thoroughly evaluate the empirical validity of hypothesis 1.

To this end, we derive the two illustrations from the estimates in table 3.5, column 2, by using the formula for computing the marginal effect of interaction terms and the statistical significance (or lack thereof) of this ef-

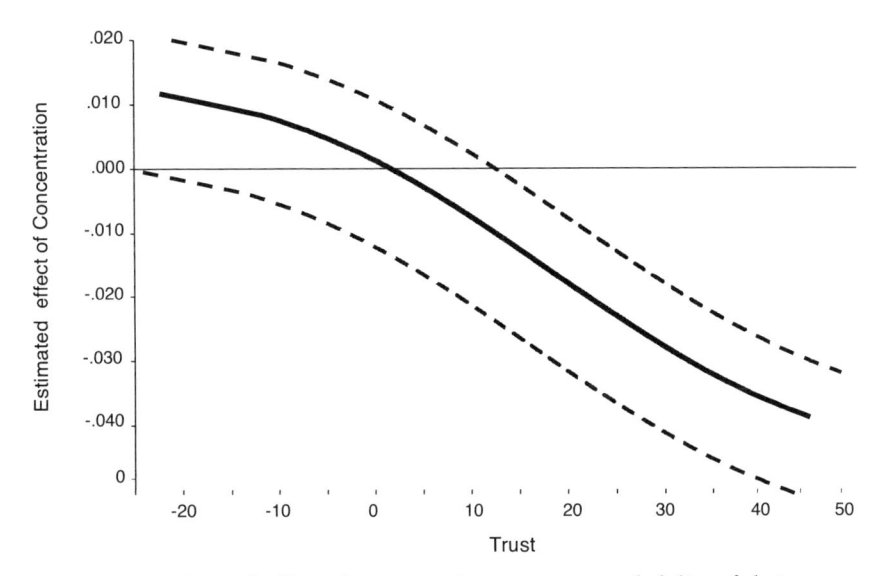

Fig. 3.2. Marginal effect of *concentration* × *trust* on probability of *de jure judicial review* being equal to 1. (Dashed lines indicate 95% confidence intervals.)

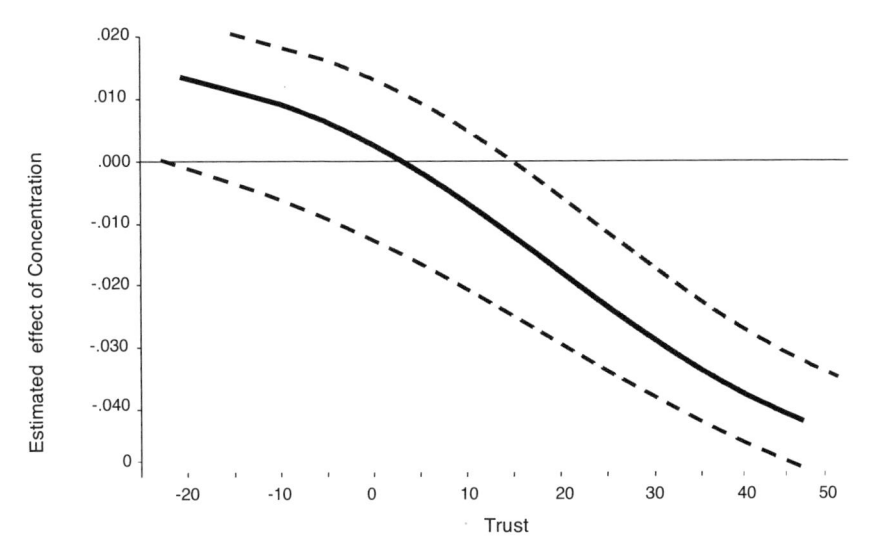

Fig. 3.3. Marginal effect of *concentration* × *trust* on probability of *de jure judicial review* being equal to 2. (Dashed lines indicate 95% confidence intervals.)

fect in ordered probit models; this formula is described formally in the appendix. We proceed in several steps. First, from the estimates in column 2, we illustrate the marginal effect and statistical significance of the legislative *concentration* variable over the entire range of values of the judiciary *trust* measure on the probability of each of the following two categories of the dependent variable: when *de jure judicial review* is equal to 1, which indicates that the constitution provides for judicial review for the judiciary somewhat or vaguely but not fully (see fig. 3.2); and 2, which indicates that the constitution provides for judicial review fully and explicitly for the judiciary (see fig. 3.3).

Note that the solid sloping line in these two figures shows how the value of the estimated causal effect of the legislative *concentration* measure (for new democracies) changes across the full range of the relevant modifying variable, judiciary *trust* (in new democracies). One can check whether these conditional coefficients are statistically significant by considering the 95 percent confidence intervals (dashed lines) that are drawn around them.[32] Keeping this in mind, one can clearly see from these two figures that *concentration* has a statistically significant negative effect on the probability of each of the two highest categories of the *de jure judicial review* when *trust* increases by one standard deviation above its mean. This provides statistical support for the prediction in hypothesis 1.

We also report the precise substantive impact of *concentration* × *trust* on the predicted probability of judicial review from column 2. In this regard, table 3.6 presents the estimated effect of the legislative *concentration* measure on the predicted probability of the two highest categories of the *judicial review* measure when its modifying variable (judiciary) *trust* is increased by one standard deviation above the mean, while other variables in the model are held at their mean in the sample. Panel A in this table shows that when *concentration* shifts from a low of 0.3 to a high of 0.7, increasing *trust* by one standard deviation above its mean—while holding other variables at their mean—increases the probability with which incumbents in new democracies adopt partial de jure judicial review from 0.30 to 0.41, which amounts to 36.7 percent.

The results in panel B of the table reveals that when *concentration* shifts from 0.3 to 0.7, increasing *trust* by one standard deviation above its mean—while holding other variables at their mean—increases the probability with which governments adopt full de jure judicial review from 0.33 to 0.45, which is equal to 36.3 percent. The effects reported above in panels A and B are thus substantial. They are also, as shown in the table, statistically significant at the 95 percent confidence level. In short, the results reported in table 3.6 and the marginal effect figures described above provide strong statistical and substantive support for hypothesis 1.

We turn to an example to show more intuitively the impact of this interaction term on judicial review. Consider the experience of Bangladesh, for instance. With respect to this example, first note that the concentration of the legislative seats controlled by the ruling BNP party in Bangladesh in the initial post–democratic transition years (1991–95) was 0.67 on a 0 to 1 scale, which is quite high. The level of public trust in the judiciary in newly democratic Bangladesh increased during the 1991–1995 period and furthermore lies at the 95th percentile level in the sample in this time period. We thus anticipate from hypothesis 1 that *de jure judicial review* will be low in Bangladesh between 1991 and 1995 as the country is characterized by high legislative concentration of the ruling party and high public trust in the judiciary. The data confirms this prediction as we find in our sample that the moving average of *judicial review* in Bangladesh during the 1991 to 1995 time period (in which Bangladesh is observed as a new democracy) is equal to the lowest value of 0. We also show in the first case-study chapter—that is, chapter 5—that in the initial post–democratic transition years, Indonesia's leaders resisted the adoption of judicial review because of the high

TABLE 3.6. Substantive Effect of Independent Variables on *de jure judicial review*

	Effect of Shift of *concentration* from 0.3 to 0.65 when *trust* Is At . . .	
	Mean	Plus 1 Std. Dev.
Predicted probability of *de jure judicial review* being equal to 1	0.30 (0.16, 0.43)	0.41 (0.29, 0.57)
Difference in predicted probability		0.11 (0.01, 0.26)
Percentage change in predicted probability		36.7 (25.2, 48.1)
Predicted probability of *de jure judicial review* being equal to 2	0.33 (0.17, 0.46)	0.45 (0.19, 0.54)
Difference in predicted probability		0.12 (0.01, 0.26)
Percentage change in predicted probability		36.3 (21.4, 49.2)

Note: Numbers in parentheses correspond to the lower and upper bounds, respectively, of the 95 percent confidence intervals of the estimated probabilities.

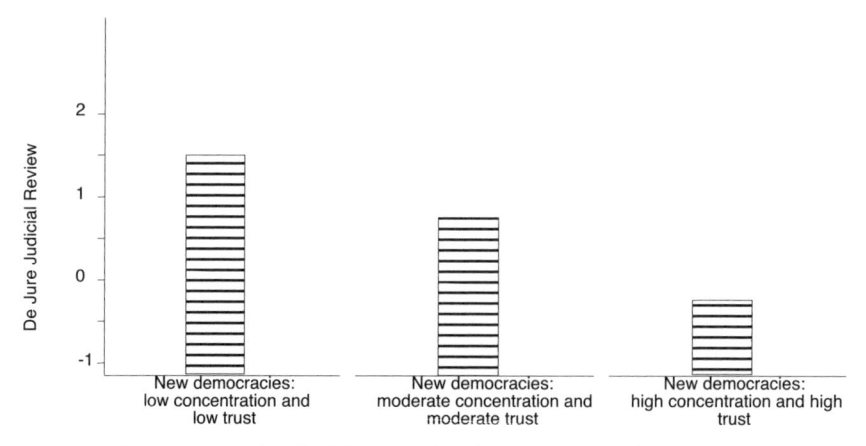

Fig. 3.4. Mean level of *de jure judicial review* in new democracies

concentration of legislative seats held by the ruling party and a slow but steady growth in public support for the courts during this period.

Before doing so, however, we briefly evaluate the probability of adoption of constitutional provisions for full and explicit judicial review in new democracies where the concentration of legislative seats held by the ruling party and public trust in the judiciary in the immediate post-transition period is low. To this end, we derived the bar graphs illustrated in fig. 3.4 from our data. These bar graphs show that the mean of *de jure judicial review* in new democracies characterized by both low public trust in judges and low legislative concentration of the ruling party is substantially higher than the mean of *judicial review* in new democracies in which the ruling party dominates the legislature but where public trust in the judiciary is high.[33] This is confirmed by a difference-of-means test ($p = 0.00$). This descriptive result empirically corroborates the corollary to hypothesis 1, which suggests that ruling parties in new democracies that do not control the legislative are more likely to adopt partial or full judicial review if public trust in the juidicary is low.

The results reported above are undoubtedly encouraging. Yet, it is worth noting here that the estimates reported in the standard ordered probit model in columns 1 and 2 do not account for the potential selection bias problem described earlier. Hence, as a preliminary robustness test, we report in table 3.5, column 3, the effect that our main interaction term of interest has on *judicial review* in the outcome equation of the sample-selection ordered probit (S-OP) model (estimated with random effects), which accounts for selection bias. The selection equation estimates of this S-OP model, in which the democracy dummy is the dependent variable, is reported in table 3.7, column A. We first briefly present the results from the selection equation and then discuss in detail the key estimates in the outcome equation.

As indicated in table 3.7, column A, the specification for the selection equation performs well, correctly predicting above 89 percent of all observations in the sample. As expected, the lag of the *democratic regime* dummy is the best predictor of the likelihood of democratic regimes in the selection equation. Other factors with statistically significant effects include the

TABLE 3.7. Selection Equation Results for S-OP model

	Column A	Column B
	Dependent Variable: *democratic regime*	Dependent Variable: *democratic regime*
	Selection Equation for Outcome Equation in Column 3, Table 3.5	Selection Equation for Outcome Equation in Column 6, Table 3.5
log GDP per capita	.037***	.035***
	(.010)	(.011)
lag democratic regime	.165***	.160***
	(.041)	(.043)
Colony	.023	.020
	(.084)	(.083)
Religious fractionalization	.009	.010
	(.012)	(.011)
Total democracy	.026***	.022**
	(.009)	(.010)
Dem breakdown	−.051***	−.051**
	(.020)	(.025)
Protestants	.019	.017
	(.077)	(.074)
Catholics	.017	.016
	(.048)	(.044)
Muslims	−.029	−.026
	(.062)	(.065)
Constant	−.316***	−.310***
	(.078)	(.071)
% correctly predicted	89.2%	89.6%
Prob > χ^2	0.000	0.000

***, **, * denote 1%, 5%, and 10% levels of significance.

number of democratic breakdowns suffered by each country in previous years, the *total democracy* variable, and the coefficient of *log GDP per capita* that is positive and highly significant.

Keeping aside the selection equation results, it is more important to note here that the estimated coefficient of *concentration* × *trust* in the outcome equation in table 3.5, column 3, is negative and statistically significant at the 1 percent level. Additionally, the estimated coefficient of each of the two individual components of the aforementioned interaction term—that is, the estimate of *concentration* and *trust,* respectively—are each statistically insignificant in column 3. As before, this suggests that it is the interaction of the two variables previously mentioned rather than each variable individually that has a negative and statistically significant effect on *judicial review.* Thus we find statistical support for the prediction in hypothesis 1 in the S-OP model that explicitly corrects for selection bias.

There is mixed empirical support for the political and economic control variables in the specifications reported in table 3.5, columns 1–3. For instance, the respective coefficient for *democracy level, democracy age,* and *presidential* is statistically insignificant in these two columns. The coefficient of *competition* is positive and significant in columns 1–3. The estimate of *separation of powers* is positive and significant at the 1 percent level in all the specifications as well. Thus separation of powers also fosters the adoption of full-fledged judicial review in developing states (Shapiro 1981; Vanberg 2000; Whittington 2003; Friedman 2004). With respect to the economic controls, we find that the log of GDP per capita is positive but insignificant in the specifications in columns 1 and 2, respectively. The estimated coefficient of *FDI flows* and *foreign aid* are surprisingly negative and highly significant in the specifications, while the estimate of *trade openness* is negative and significant in column 1 but insignificant in columns 2 and 3. We turn now to assess the robustness of the results reported earlier.

Robustness Tests

We conduct a battery of specification robustness tests and diagnostic checks. With respect to specification robustness tests, we first added the following additional controls to the ordered probit specification in table 3.5, column 1, where the dependent variable is *judicial review:* ethno-linguistic fractionalization (*elf*), *press freedom,* and *federal.* Hayo and Voigt (2007: 277) suggest that higher levels of ethnolinguistic fractionalization exacerbate collective action problems between citizens, and, therefore, make it more difficult for them to collectively pressure their respective governments to enhance the independence of the judiciary via adoption of judicial review for instance. We thus add a measure of ethnolinguistic fractionalization (*elf*), which is drawn from Fearon and Laitin (2003),[34] to the empirical model.

Researchers have also suggested that the presence of a free press is conducive to de jure (and de facto) judicial independence, which may include adoption of constitutional provisions for granting judicial review authority to the courts. This is because the presence of a free press can make it politically costly for governments to stifle the autonomy of the judiciary (Vanberg 2001; Hayo and Voigt 2007; Heckelman 2010). We thus include the Freedom House measure of press freedom (labeled as *free press*), which is coded on a continuous scale. Some studies have hypothesized that countries with federal systems tend to have a higher degree of judicial independence (Shapiro 1981; Vanberg 2008; Hayo and Voigt 2007; Rodriguez and McCubbins 2008). We thus add the dummy variable *federal*, which is coded as 1 for countries with a federal system and is coded as 0 otherwise.

It is also theoretically plausible that countries that have experienced more frequent transitions to democracy—and have thus experienced a longer history of democratic governance—may be more positively predisposed toward greater judicial autonomy. Such states may therefore be more likely to adopt de jure judicial review.[35] We account for this possibility by controlling for *democracy transition sum*, which operationalizes the sum of past transitions to democracy (as defined by Cheibub et al.'s [2010] definition of democracy) in a country. On the other side, states that have frequently experienced democratic failures and thus repeated transitions to authoritarian rule may be less likely to adopt judicial review. We therefore control for *authoritarian transition sum*, which opertionalizes the sum of past transitions to authoritarian rule (as defined by Przeworski et al.'s [2000] definition of an authoritarian regime)[36] in a country.[37] Finally some studies hypothesize that the legal system—the British common law and the French civil law system—inherited by developing countries from their colonial past could also affect de jure judicial autonomy, including judicial review, in these states. We therefore incorporate in the specification the dummy variable: (1) *British common law*, which is coded as 1 for countries that employ this legal system (0 otherwise); and (2) *French civil law*, which is coded as 1 for countries that employ this legal system (0 otherwise).[38]

Table 3.5, column 4, reports the results from the augmented ordered probit model (estimated with random effects), which includes the three additional control variables previously mentioned. *Concentration × trust* remains negative and statistically significant in the outcome equation in column 4. The coefficient for *elf* in this specification is insignificant, but *federal* and *free press* are each positive and weakly significant at the 10 percent level. The estimate of the remaining control variables that were added to the specification and were listed above are each statistically insignificant. We added some more controls to the empirical model in column 4. These controls include a dummy variable for *bicameralism*,[39] a measure for *veto players*,[40] and the lag of *judicial review*. We also control for the concentration of legislative seats held by the government in the countries in our sample that are not new democracies (labeled *legislative concentration*). Likewise, we include another variable that controls for the extent of public trust in the judiciary in developing countries that are not classified as new democracies in our data (denoted as *judiciary trust*).

Lastly, some scholars have explicitly or implicitly postulated a regional diffusion effect as they claim that developing states in particular tend to emulate judicial reforms and the degree of de jure judicial independence (including judicial review) adopted by neighboring nations.[41] We account for these dynamics in the outcome equation where *judicial review* is the dependent variable by controlling for the gap between the lag of the maximum level of *judicial review* in each region and the lag of each country's extent of de jure judicial review, which we label as *judicial review emulation*. The results from the specification that includes the latter set of additional controls listed in this and the preceding paragraph are reported respectively in (1) column 5 (ordered probit model), and (2) column 6 (outcome equation of S-OP model)[42] in table 3.5. As before, the estimate of *concentration × trust* is negative and statistically significant at the 1 percent level in columns 5 and 6. This indicates that the results that support hypothesis 1 remain robust to changes in the specification. Interestingly, the coefficient for bicameralism is positive and weakly significant in column 5, while lag judicial review is positive and highly significant in these two columns. The estimate of *veto players, judicial review emulation,* the concentration of the government's legislative seats, and trust in the judiciary in countries that are not new democracies in the sample are, however, each statistically insignificant in columns 5 and 6.

We conduct a series of diagnostic tests to further check the econometric validity of our results. First, we implemented Hurlin and Venet's (2003) granger causality test for panel data to assess whether there exists a potential endogenous relationship between the dependent variable, *judicial review,* and each of the two independent variables: *trust* and *concentration* in new democracies. F-statistics from the Hurlin and Venet (2003) tests conducted in our developing countries sample indicates that there is no endogeneity problem between *judicial review* and the two independent variables mentioned earlier. The effect of the contemporaneous measure and the lag of *judicial review* on *trust* and *concentration* are statistically insignificant in pooled regression models estimated with panel-corrected standard errors and fixed effects. These results further indicate that the dependent variable *judicial review* is indeed not endogenous to the independent variables. Finally, diagnostic tests reveal that none of the reported empirical models suffer from severe multicollinearity, serial correlation, or omitted variable bias, and that the residuals are normally distributed.[43]

Conclusion

A growing body of research on comparative judicial politics suggests that democratic politics may influence the likelihood with which politicians adopt constitutional provisions that allow for explicit judicial independence (Ginsburg 2003, 2008; Hirschl 2004; Vanberg 2005, 2008; Helmke and Rosenbluth 2009; Staton 2010). We certainly subscribe to the view that democratic politics and institutions shape the extent to which governments in developing states have incentives to adopt constitutional provisions that, for example, grant courts the authority to conduct judicial review. Building on extant research and the theoretical story presented in chapter 2, the analysis in this empirical chapter explores how politics in what we term *new democratic regimes*—that is, politics during the immediate years following a democratic transition—affects the probability of adoption of constitutional rules that provide judges with explicit authority to employ judicial review. Our theoretical story predicts, as stated in hypothesis 1, that governments in new democracies in the developing world that control a high concentration of legislative seats after the transition election are less likely to adopt judicial review if public trust in the judiciary is sufficiently high in these states. The extensive statistical analysis presented earlier in this chapter statistically corroborates this claim. The data also reveals that incumbents in new democracies are more likely to constitutionally grant courts with judicial review authority if the concentration of legislative seats held by the first post–transition ruling party and public trust in the judiciary is low.

The empirical estimates presented in this chapter have two key substantive implications. First, numerous studies have recently suggested that the transition to democracy in developing states increases the prospects for the constitutional design of an independent and politically autonomous judiciary (e.g., Larkins 1996). This claim is undoubtedly insightful. While we use the aforementioned claim as a starting point for our analysis, our theoretical arguments in chapter 2 and the empirical results presented earlier show that the effect of democratic transitions on the adoption of independent judicial institutions is much more nuanced. In fact, we found here that the likelihood with which elites in new democracies in the developing world may constitutionally grant courts with the authority to conduct judicial review *depends* on two factors: (1) the concentration and thus control of legislative seats by governments in the immediate post–transition period; and (2) degree of public trust in the judiciary. Hence, our results suggest that to fully understand how democratic transitions affect de jure judicial independence (including judicial review), it may be worthwhile for scholars to explore which specific political and social dynamics within new democracies in the initial post–democratic transition years influences judicial politics.

Second, studies on democratization and empowerment of the judiciary politics often focus on just the effect of the "supply-side"—namely, the impact of political institutions including the transition to democracy—on de jure judicial independence in developing countries.[44] Doing so is necessary in order to develop parsimonious theories on how and when political institutions may constitutionally enhance the de jure autonomy of the courts. Yet, the empirical analysis presented here reveals that it is the interaction between the supply side—for example, legislative capture by governments in new democracies, and the demand-side—for instance, the degree of public trust in the justice system, that affects whether or not incumbents may adopt judicial review. We find quite interestingly that when governments in new democracies in developing states control a substantial amount of legislative seats and when public trust in the legal system increases, then these governments are less likely to adopt judicial review. This serves to curtail the political autonomy of the judiciary. Thus an important conclusion that emerges from our analysis is that researchers may develop potentially interesting insights on judicial politics by further exploring how supply-side factors (e.g., democratic institutions) interact with demand-side variables (e.g., public trust in the judiciary) to affect the design of autonomous judicial institutions.

Put together, the results presented in this chapter strongly support our claims about judicial review. In the following case-study chapter, we shift our focus from the large-N analysis to an in-depth analysis of how politics in the initial post–transition years in Indonesia and Brazil influenced the constitutional design of de jure judicial review in these two prominent developing states. These case studies allow us to move beyond the correlations and associations established in this chapter towards empirically identifying whether the causal mechanisms described in chapter 2 in fact lead to the prediction in hypothesis 1 and the corollary to this hypothesis.

CHAPTER 4
Democratic Transition and Judicial Review in Indonesia and Brazil

The theoretical analysis in chapter 2 explores how certain political dynamics in new democratic regimes affects the constitutional design of de jure judicial review during the immediate post–democratic transition period. As stated in hypothesis 1, our theory predicts that in new democracies, governments that control a sufficiently high concentration of legislative seats, are less likely to adopt full and explicit judicial review if during the immediate post–transition period public trust in the judiciary increases. Conversely, the corollary to hypothesis 1 suggests that if the concentration of legislative seats held by the ruling party in new democracies is low, then the executive will be more likely to adopt full and explicit judicial review, provided that public trust in the judiciary is also low and falling. Thus, we claimed that it is the interaction of the two factors—the degree of concentration of the legislative seats held by the first post–transition government in new democracies and the level of public trust in the judiciary during the initial post–transition years—that help explain when incumbents in new democracies across the developing world are less (or more) likely to constitutionally adopt judicial review for their courts.

The two aforementioned predictions were statistically tested on a comprehensive time-series cross-sectional data set of 159 developing countries in the previous chapter. The statistical results provide robust empirical support for these claims and show that our predictions are empirically generalizable across a large set of developing countries. In this chapter, we use evidence from two case studies—Brazil and Indonesia—to illustrate the causal arguments that lead to the predictions in hypothesis 1 and its corollary. We analyze how politics in the immediate post–democratic transition period in Brazil and Indonesia influenced the design (or lack thereof) of constitutional provisions associated with de jure judicial review in these countries.

We focus on Indonesia and Brazil because of two main reasons. First, the choice of Indonesia and Brazil for assessing our claims is dictated by certain methodological reasons that are discussed in the next section. In particular, as emphasized shortly, these two cases provide an opportunity to employ the most similar case-selection design for our comparative analysis of the political determinants of de jure judicial review in new developing country democracies during the immediate post–transition years. Second, from a substantive viewpoint, it is important to note that both Indonesia and Brazil recently experienced transitions to being full-fledged democracies. Indonesia made a transition to democracy in 1999, while Brazil's transition to democracy occurred in 1986.[1] Notwithstanding the recent transition to democracy, the extent of the courts' constitutional authority to conduct judicial review varies significantly across these two countries.

Brazil's political elite adopted constitutional rules that provided the courts with substantial and explicit judicial review authority almost immediately after the transition to democracy (see, for example, Howard 1995; Ballard 1999). In sharp contrast, in the immediate post–democratic transition period in Indonesia—specifically from 1999 to 2003—leaders in Indonesia's new democracy did not provide the courts with constitutional guarantees for full and explicit judicial review (Asshiddiquie 2004; Pompe 2005; Stockmann 2007; Harman 2006). Indonesian elites finally established the Constitutional Court (*Mahkamah Konstitusi*) with significant delay—specifically, four years—after the country's formal transition to democracy (Stockmann 2007; Butt 2007; Omara 2008). More importantly, as discussed later, the *Mahkamah Konstitusi*, as well as other courts in Indonesia, were constitutionally allowed to merely conduct a limited form of constitutional review and the judiciary's authority to exercise judicial review of legislation approved by the legislature (DPR) was (and is) severely restricted.[2]

Why do we observe the remarkable difference in the decision to adopt judicial review powers between Indonesia and Brazil? As we will see, the causal story that leads to the prediction in hypothesis 1 accurately explains why Indonesia's leaders in the post–transition period opted to first deny and then severely restrict the judiciary's authority to conduct judicial review. Furthermore, the casual claims that produce the corollary to hypothesis 1 explain why leaders in Brazil during the immediate post–democratic transition period had incentives to provide the courts with substantial judicial review power.

In this chapter, we present our analysis of the Indonesia and Brazil cases. For each of these two countries, we begin by providing a brief description of the democratic transition process, the structure of the country's judicial system, and the extent to which the constitution provides guarantees for judicial review to the courts. This is followed by a discussion of within-country data and figures that provide information about the (1) concentration of legislative seats held by the first post–transition government in Indonesia and Brazil, and (2) degree of public trust in the judiciary during the initial post–transition years in these two countries. We then use the aforementioned information to explain why Indonesia's leaders first denied and then restricted constitutional guarantees for judicial review for Indonesian courts during the post–transition period, while incumbents in Brazil constitutionally granted full and explicit judicial review authority to the courts after democratization. We end the chapter with a brief conclusion.

Case Selection Strategy

In this book the selected case studies primarily serve to illustrate the causal dynamics of the causal arguments underlying hypotheses 1 and 2. The use of a most similar design for case selection requires cases that are representative of the theoretically relevant category of cases, represent the key independent variables at their most contrasting values, and control variables at their most similar values. Such a strategy optimizes our ability to focus on the causal arguments linking independent variables to the outcomes of interest when while minimizing differences due to other factors. Brazil and Indonesia fit these criteria well.

Since Indonesia transitioned from autocratic rule to democracy in 1999, and Brazil made a similar transition in 1986, these two cases are representative of the theoretically relevant categories in our universe of cases. They share many socioeconomic and political similarities since both countries were colonized, are geographically large, have ethnically diverse populations, have multiple political parties in their polity, and are federal democracies.[3] Furthermore, both countries are, according to the World Bank, large emerging markets in the G20 group that have each experienced high growth rates in recent years (World Bank 2008). Thus, these two cases make for good comparisons because they share many common features that are not critical to our causal mechanism.

Finally, Brazil (low legislative concentration, low public trust in judiciary) and Indonesia (high concentration, high public trust in judiciary) offer contrasting cases that differ the most on the theoretically relevant factors—legislative concentration and public trust in the judiciary. These cases therefore provide the most different values on the independent variables. Given our prediction in hypothesis 1, therefore, Brazil should choose to adopt extensive powers of judicial review in the first five years of transition, while Indonesia should choose not to grant its judiciary review powers at all as a new democracy.

Indonesia: Background on Democratic Transition and Judicial System

Indonesia is a prominent developing country with the largest economy in Southeast Asia. As a developing country, Indonesia's economy is characterized by a division of labor between formal and informal sectors, and an uneven distribution of wealth and income (World Bank 2008; IMF 2009). The size of Indonesia's economy in nominal GDP terms is U.S. $560 billion (IMF 2009). Indonesia's economic size is therefore smaller than Brazil's economy in nominal GDP terms.[4] However, similar to Brazil, Indonesia has experienced high economic growth rates in recent years and as mentioned earlier, it is an important emerging market in the developing world (Guebbert 2009).

While Indonesia's economy has grown steadily, the country has had a tumultuous political history. Indonesian nationalists under Sukarno and Hatta successfully fought the country's colonial power—the Netherlands—for independence, which it gained in December 1949 (Uhlin 1997; Tomsa 2008). After obtaining independence, Indonesian leaders implemented a new constitution in 1950 that mandated a parliamentary system of democratic government (Honna 2003; Tomsa 2008). Unfortunately, the nascent steps taken toward democratization in Indonesia failed in the 1950s.

By 1956, Sukarno—the first president of independent Indonesia—was openly criticizing democracy, stating that it is inherently based on conflict (Feith 2006; Tomsa 2008). Soon, with the support of the military, he abrogated the 1950 constitution by a decree dissolving the Constitutional Assembly and replacing it with one appointed by, and subject to the will of, the president (Honna 2003; Tomsa 2008). Sukarno's actions, therefore, led to the collapse of democracy in Indonesia, and the country was effectively ruled by a single-party dictatorship—which was supported by the military—from the late 1950s to the 1990s (Uhlin 1997; Honna 2003; Tomsa 2008). During the early 1990s, the single-party dictatorial state was headed by Suharto.

By the late 1990s, however, Suharto's grip on office became fragile due to the dire consequences of the East Asian financial crisis for the Indonesian economy and society, and his own presidency (Liddle 2001; Haris 2002; Bhakti 2004). Suharto attempted to salvage the situation by implementing austerity measures, which sparked popular protests against his rule. Despite these protests, Suharto refused to step down from office, and, in fact, took steps to further prolong his tenure in office (Forrester and May 1998; Haris 2002). Suharto's attempt to prolong his dictatorial rule engendered violent protests and riots throughout the country in 1998 (Liddle 2000, 2001; Tomsa 2008). Dissent within the ranks of his Golkar Party and the military finally weakened Suharto, and on May 21, 1998, he stood down from power. He was replaced by his deputy Jusuf Habibie.

Unlike his predecessor, Habibie moved quickly to establish democracy and lift controls on freedom of speech and association. As a result, Indonesia's single-party dictatorial state finally collapsed in 1999, and the first free and fair democratic elections for the national, provincial, and subprovincial parliaments were held on June 7, 1999 (Liddle 2001; Dhakidae 2001). The elections allowed Indonesia to make a transition to a full-fledged democratic regime in 1999 (Haris 2002; Bhakti 2004). By October 1999, Indonesia's first democratic government was formed, which was headed by President Abdurrahman Wahid and Vice President Megawati Sukarnoputri. Thus, in terms of its recent political history and the coding procedure that we employed to identify "new democratic regimes" in the data presented in chapter 3, Indonesia is observed as a "new democracy" from 1999 to around 2004. During this period, Indonesia successfully made the transition to a full-fledged new democratic regime without any threat of reversal to autocratic rule (Von Luebke 2004; Tomsa 2008).

Under Suharto's single-party dictatorial regime, Indonesia's judiciary was controlled by the state and judicial review was prohibited (Lindsey 2002: 261). Indeed, during Suharto's reign, the state passed the Basic Law on Judicial Power (no. 14/1970), which specifically prohibited the exercise of judicial review authority by the courts. Indonesia's successful transition to democracy provided its leaders with an opportunity to introduce amendments to the national constitution that affected the country's judicial system. Before discussing how constitutional amendments adopted by Indonesia's political elite in the post–transition period affected the judiciary, we provide a brief background of the structure of the judicial system in Indonesia's new democracy.

Stated broadly, Indonesia's judicial system consists of the Supreme Court (*Mahkamah Agung*), which is the highest level of the judicial branch. Below the Supreme Court lie the high courts, and finally the district courts. The country's legal system also includes religious courts; however, the decisions taken by the religious courts can only be enforced by the Supreme Court, the high courts, and (on some occasions) the district courts (Lev 2000; Bey 2006). Therefore, the secular courts (i.e., the Supreme Court, the high courts, and the district courts) dominate the country's judicial landscape (Lev 2000; Assegaf 2007). Indonesia inherited a career judiciary with a closed system of recruitment from the Dutch. However, during the military regime of Suharto, military officers were appointed exclusively to the top positions in the judiciary. This trend was reversed starting in the 1990s, and the judiciary has been staffed largely by career judges under the new democratic regime (Pompe 2005). Judges are recruited into the judiciary straight out of law school and move up the ranks based on a combination of merit, seniority, and connections. Most judges are Javanese and belong to elite families, share strong class, regional, and even family ties through blood and intermarriage, and attend a small number of colleges for their training (Pompe 2005: 390–91). Along with the closed recruitment system, such a shared background has fostered a strong shared sense of community and common identification among Indonesian judges.[5]

After the transition to democracy in 1999, numerous articles were added to Indonesia's constitution to rationalize and strengthen the country's judicial system. Some of these articles were ostensibly directed toward enhancing judicial autonomy (Bedner 2003; Assegaf 2005, 2007). Yet, as suggested by various scholars of the Indonesia judicial system, key components of de jure judicial independence were not constitutionally granted to the courts in the immediate post–democratic transition period in Indonesia.[6] Consequently, the degree of the judiciary's political autonomy in Indonesia remains low even after democratization (Clarke 2003; Kumaraswamy 2006).

More importantly, for the purpose of this chapter, observe that during the initial three–four post–democratic transition years, Indonesia's political did not take steps to make the Basic Law on Judicial Power null and void and did not provide the courts with full and explicit constitutional guarantees for judicial review (Stockmann 2007; Mahfud 2007, 2009). In fact, as we discuss in detail in the next section, a brief examination of the political history of judicial review in Indonesia during the initial years after democratization reveals the extent to which country's new democratic leaders were reluctant to grant the power of judicial review to the country's judiciary, including the Supreme Court, and acted to curtail its powers. Furthermore, as mentioned earlier, a Constitutional Court (*Mahkamah Konstitusi*) was established in Indonesia with a significant delay (i.e., four years) after the country's transition to democracy.[7] Hence, it is not surprising that the moving average of the −1 to +2 ordinal de jure *judicial review* measure (described in chapter 3)[8] is (1) merely 0.1 in Indonesia, and is thus (2) substantially lower than the moving average level of 1.3 for de jure *judicial review* in Brazil.

Why did Indonesia's political elite initially refuse after the country's transition to democracy in 1999 to constitutionally grant the courts the authority to conduct judicial review to the country's courts? Additionally, after Wahid's impeachment in 2001, why did the post–transition government choose to restrict the judicial review authority of the courts? We show in the next section that the causal arguments in chapter two that produce the prediction in hypothesis 1 (stated earlier) can help us answer both these questions.

Legislative Control, Trust in Judiciary, and Judicial Review in Indonesia

Recall that our theoretical arguments in the first half of chapter 2 posits an interactive effect between two conditions that produced the following prediction in hypothesis 1: in new democracies, governments that control a sufficiently high concentration of legislative seats in the initial post–transition years will be less likely to constitutionally adopt full and explicit judicial review if public trust in the judiciary increases during the immediate post–democratic transition period. We proposed a simple three-step causal argument in chapter 2 that led to this prediction. For the first step, we claimed that if the first post-transition government succeeds in controlling a fairly high concentration of legislative seats, it will seek to further consolidate its seat share in the legislature by co-opting the opposition. Consolidation of its seat share in the legislature will also encourage the new democratic government to impose its partisan agenda.

Building on this, the second step of the argument suggests that the post-transition government that commands a legislative majority will recognize that the judiciary may block its effort to control the legislature particularly if the level of public trust in the judiciary is high and increases during the immediate post-transition years. This is because increased public trust in the judiciary induces the courts to both challenge the government and publicly appeal to the executive to provide the judiciary with constitutional guarantees for full judicial review authority. Consequently, for the third step of the causal argument, we claimed that the post-transition government will use the sufficiently high share of legislative seats that it controls to secure legislative support for constitutional amendments that deny or seriously limit the courts' judicial review authority. The two conditions previously identified—sufficiently high concentration of legislative seats controlled by the post-transition government, and increasing public trust in the judiciary—were both present in post-transition Indonesia. Thus, as we discuss next, the three-step causal argument allows us to explain the pattern of initial denial and subsequent restriction of judicial review observed there.

Let us start by examining the first condition listed earlier—sufficiently high concentration of legislative seats controlled by the post-transition government. Almost immediately after Indonesia made a transition to democracy in 1999, several new political parties emerged. A large number of these parties (48 parties, to be precise) subsequently participated in Indonesia's first post-authoritarian national election, which was held in June 1999 (Johnson Tan 2006: 91). However, as shown in table 4.1, only the following 5 out of these 48 parties emerged as the most significant players in Indonesia's new democracy: the Partai Demokrasi Indonesia-Perjuangan (Indonesian Democracy Party-Struggle, or PDI-P), Partai Golkar (Functional Group Party, or Golkar), Partai Kebangkitan Bangsa (National Awakening Party, or PKB), Partai Persatuan Pembangunan (United Development Party, or PPP), and the Partai Amanat Nasional (National Mandate Party, or PAN). These five parties collectively won 416 out of a total of 500 seats in the *Dewan Perwakilan Rakyat*. More specifically, the "PDI-P won

34 percent of the national vote and 153 seats in the Parliament; Golkar, 22 percent and 120 seats; PKB, 12 percent and 51 seats; PPP, 10 percent and 58 seats; and PAN, with 7 percent of the vote and 34 seats" (Liddle 2000: 393). Thus the PDI-P and the Golkar emerged as the two largest parties in the legislature after Indonesia's first post–authoritarian election, which was held in June 1999.

That said, none of the major aforementioned parties won, as a single party, a majority of the seats in the legislature. Therefore a multiparty coalition government was formed by four of these five parties—the Golkar Party, the PDI-P, the PAN, and the PKB (Liddle 2000: 396). Abdurrahman Wahid successfully emerged as the leader of this multiparty coalition government and thus became Indonesia's first president after the June election of 1999; Megawati Sukarnopoutri (who headed the PDI-P) emerged as the second-in-command of this coalition and thus became the vice president of Indonesia in 1999 (Liddle 2000; Johnson-Tan 2004). Importantly for the theoretical argument, one can easily observe from the data reported in table 4.1 that the four aforementioned parties in the government collectively controlled 358 out of a total of 500 seats—or, in other words 75 percent of the seats in the legislature.

As a result, the concentration of the legislative seats (calculated from the

TABLE 4.1. Results from the First Postauthoritarian (June 1999) Election in Indonesia

Political Parties	Number of Legislative (DPR) Seats	Percentage of Legislative (DPR) Seats	Vote Share (%)
PDI-P	153	33.1	33.7
Golkar	120	26	22.4
PKB	51	11	12.6
PPP	58	12.6	10.7
PKS	7	1.5	1.4
PAN	34	7.4	7
PBB	13	2.8	1.9
PKPI	4	0.9	1

Source: Data from Electionworld.org, "Elections in Indonesia," http://www.electionworld.org/indonesia.htm and "Perhitungan Perolehan Kursi DPR RI, KPU Indonesia, http://www.kpu.go.id/dprkursi.php.

Note: The full names of the parties are as follows: Golkar = Partai Golkar; PDI-P = Partai Demokrasi Indonesia-Perjuangan; PKB = Partai Kebangkitan Bangsa; PPP = Partai Persatuan Pembangunan; PKS = Partai Keadilan Sejahtera; PAN = Partai Amanat Nasional; PBB = Partai Bulan Bintang; PKPI = Partai Kesatuan dan Persatuan Indonesia. The abbreviation DPR denotes Dewan Perwakilan Rakyat and is the lower house of Indonesia's national legislature.

Hirschman-Herfindahl index of legislative concentration) controlled by Indonesia's ruling parties after the transition to democracy was approximately 0.73 out of a maximum of 1; this is a substantially high.[9] Moreover, this value of 0.73 is significantly higher than the moving average level of 0.45 for the concentration of legislative seats controlled by Brazil's first post–democratic transition government from 1986 to 1992.[10] The government's control of a significant share of the legislative seats in the immediate post–democratic transition period in Indonesia had two main effects. The first effect, as predicted by our causal story, was that it encouraged the leaders of the two largest parties in the governing coalition (the Golkar and the PDI-P Party) to invest a significant amount of time and effort to induce a key opposition party, the PPP,[11] to join the government.[12] They did so because they believed that adding key opposition parties to the governing coalition would allow the government to further extend its political hegemony in the *Dewan Perwakilan Rakyat* (the lower house of the legislature), as well as exert greater control over the policy-making process in the legislature. This particular rationale for co-opting the opposition was candidly admitted by Laksamana Susardi, a prominent member of the PDI-P Party from 1999 to 2003, who stated the following.

> It was necessary to bring some more opposition parties into the government as early as possible . . . this would help to increase the government's majority status in the parliament and make the government more stable.[13]

The time and effort invested by the leaders of the Golkar and PDI-P parties paid off since by October 1999, the PPP Party also decided to join the governing coalition.[14] Consequently, by October 1999, Indonesia's first post–transition government, which was headed by Abdurrahman Wahid, controlled a staggering 85 percent of all the legislative seats in the *Dewan Perwakilan Rakyat*. This, in turn, helped the government to enhance and consolidate its political power in the legislature.

Second, once the Wahid-led government strengthened its control over the legislature by co-opting the opposition, party leaders in the government realized that political control of the legislature provided them with an opportunity to implement policies that were compatible with their preferences (Kingsbury and Budiman 2001; Fallakh 2002). This was emphasized by Theo Sambuaga, a cabinet member in Wahid's government, who stated the following.

> Since the Wahid government led by Gus Dur (Abdurrahman Wahid) has a clear legislative majority and has been legitimately elected, it has precedence over and above other institutions to develop and implement policies that are in the interests of the Indonesian people . . . it is appropriate for Indonesia's first truly democratically government to use its majority legislative mandate to achieve its socio-economic objectives and implement policies that meet the interests of Indonesia.[15]

Likewise, Permadi, a member of the PDI-P Party in the Wahid government, also mentioned that "after democratization, the Indonesian government considered it necessary to preserve its parliamentary power and implement the economic, political and social policies that it promised to deliver."[16]

Other social and economic actors, including civil society groups, academics, and prominent political observers/journalists, also noted the commanding position the ruling parties in Indonesia's polity enjoyed due to their substantial control over the legislature and voiced their concern about the potential adverse consequences that occur (or may occur) as a result of this legislative concentration.[17] For example the editorial page of the *Suara Pembaruan*—a prominent daily newspaper—suggested in December 1999 that the Wahid government's majority status in the legislature allowed his administration to extend its political and policy-making power in ways that may not be beneficial.

> Although different parties constitute Gus Dur's cabinet, the truth is that his government's comfortable majority in the parliament has given it the chance to do exactly what its interests dictate . . . this may not augur well for Indonesia's new democracy.

In a similar tone, a report published by a prominent nongovernmental organization (NGO) in Indonesia, the *Koalisi Ornop untuk Konstitusi Baru* (KOKB),[18] pointed out in 2001 that

> The ministers in Indonesia's new democratic government want to further expand the power of the government . . . they feel that politically capturing the legislature is necessary as it would facilitate the implementation of the government's preferred policies.[19]

Put together, the aforementioned claims by members in Indonesia's first post–transition government and in newspapers indicate that the high concentration of the legislative seats held by this government influenced it to further consolidate its control over the legislature and promote its partisan agenda, as suggested by our theoretical story.

Once the Wahid-led coalition government consolidated its control of the legislature after the transition to democracy, it turned its attention to the judiciary. Indonesian citizens have generally believed that the judges in Indonesia are corrupt.[20] But interestingly, during the initial post–transition years in Indonesia (i.e., 1999–2002), Indonesian citizens progressively developed an increasingly positive attitude (over time) toward the country's courts and this led to more trust in the judiciary. For instance, a poll conducted by the Partnership for Governance Reform (PEGR) in Indonesia four months after Indonesia' formal transition to democracy—that is, in February 2000—revealed that just 39 percent of the citizens that were surveyed trusted the judiciary.[21] However, a similar poll that was conducted by the same organization in August 2001—that is, 22 months after Indonesia's transition to democracy—showed that 55 percent of the surveyed citizens expressed "trust and faith" in the country's judiciary.[22]

The aforementioned numbers are consistent with those reported in other surveys about trust in the judiciary in Indonesia during the post–transition period. For instance, in separate polls conducted in early 2000 by the Global Integrity Report (GIR) and Asian Development Bank Institutional Assessment Survey (ADBIAS), the percent of respondents in Indonesia that expressed either "a great deal of trust" or "quite a lot of trust" in the judiciary were 41 percent (GIR survey) and 42 percent (ADIA survey), respectively.[23] By 2002, however, this increased to 57 percent in both the GIR survey and the ADIA surveys. Similarly, both the World Bank Enterprise Survey in 2003 (WBES) and the World Values Survey (WVS) in 2002 reported that 59 percent (WBES) and 58 percent (WVS) of the surveyed citizens in Indonesia expressed high trust in the Indonesian judiciary.[24] These figures clearly indicate that public trust in the judiciary was indeed growing during the initial post–transition years in Indonesia.

Indonesia's first post–transition government recognized that despite allegations of corruption against some judges, public trust in the country's courts was steadily increasing during the post–transition period (this was discussed in detail earlier).[25] The multiparty coalition government also realized that a politically powerful and autonomous judiciary could potentially hinder their ability to use the government's legislative power to secure approval for policies that suit their preferences (Djawamaku 2001; Indrayana 2002; Lindsey 2002). This particular concern was emphasized by a cabinet member in Wahid's government, Theo Sambuaga, who claimed the following.

> There is no doubt that an independent judiciary is important for Indonesia's democracy. But an excessively powerful judiciary, which may become a "superbody", could block the socio-economic goals and policies of the democratically elected Wahid government.[26]

Sambuaga's statement, in fact, reflected the opinion held by most cabinet members (and other prominent politicians) from the ruling coalition who also felt that the judiciary should be institutionally subservient to the executive in Indonesia's new democracy (Wang 2001; Kansil et al. 2001). At the same time, however, the ruling coalition faced some international pressure to adopt judicial reforms to enhance judicial autonomy in the country (Cumaraswamy 2006; Indrayana 2008). The post–transition coalition government responded to this pressure and its own preference of maintaining a subservient judiciary by implementing a series of "contradictory" policies related to the country's judicial system.

On the one hand, the governing coalition took some relatively minor steps to increase the administrative efficiency by adopting the "one roof," or *satu atap,* reforms in 1999. The *satu atap* reforms, according to Butt (2009: 183), "appear to have achieved . . . improved judicial independence from the government." On the other hand, however, the ruling parties also took steps during the immediate post–democratic transition period to exert direct control over the judiciary. For instance, the parties in the post–transition government designed and subsequently implemented Article 24(b)(1) to the first amendment to Indonesia's constitution, which states that Indonesia's Judicial Commission—a government-controlled body whose members are selected by the president and the *Dewan Perwakilan Rakyat*[27]—has the constitutional

> authority to propose candidates for appointment as justices of the Supreme Court and possesses further authority to maintain and ensure the honour, dignity and behavior of judges.[28]

Article 24(b)(1) thus ensured that the Supreme Court was, in effect, controlled by the executive as the authority to appoint judges to the Supreme Court is granted to the Judicial Commission, which was a government organization.

Since politicians from the ruling coalition in Indonesia's new democracy believed that increasing public trust in the judiciary may induce the courts to use judicial review as a tool against the government, steps were taken by the coalition to first constitutionally deny and then sharply limit the courts' judicial review authority. The Wahid-led coalition government openly rejected the idea of granting judicial review to the country's judiciary. This preference was manifested clearly in the government's legislative agenda when it introduced the first amendment to Indonesia's constitution, which incorporated many provision regarding the judiciary and its powers but explicitly did not contain explicit constitutional provisions that provided the courts with full judicial review authority (Clarke 2003; Omara 2008; Indrayana 2008). The reason for this omission as Stockmann (2007: 14) points out, was that the Wahid administration recognized that

> Judicial review authority ... would clearly have strengthened the principle of separation of powers; the very idea, however, did not fit into the government's integralist concept of the state.

This particular amendment was introduced on the legislative floor of the *Dewan Perwakilan Rakyat* for ratification on October 19, 1999 (Asshiddiqie 2005; Indrayana 2008: 119). Out of a total of 500 legislators, 403 voted in favor of this first amendment in the *Dewan Perwakilan Rakyat* in October 1999.[29] In other words, almost 81 percent of all legislators in Indonesia voted for the first amendment four months after the country's transition to democracy. A careful examination of the 403 legislators that voted in favor of the first amendment further reveals that 92 percent of these legislators were legislative members from the four main parties in the post–transition coalition government headed by Wahid—namely, the PDI-P, the Golkar Party, the PAN, and the PKB.[30] Hence, as suggested by the third step of our causal argument, driven by the potential specter of an independent activist judiciary, the Wahid-led coalition government used its "legislative muscle"—which resulted from the high concentration of legislative seats controlled by this government—to secure legislative support for the first amendment that lacked constitutional guarantees for judicial review for the courts.

The government's decision to deny the judiciary review powers drew strong protests from the judiciary. As discussed earlier, these early post–transition years were marked by increasing public trust in the judiciary in Indonesia. As suggested in the second step of our causal argument, these increasing levels of public trust emboldened the judiciary to become more proactive and challenge the ruling coalition's attempt to restrict the courts' autonomy. More specifically, higher levels of public trust encouraged judges, lawyers, the National Law Reform Commission (NLRC), and the KOKB to openly protest against the Wahid government's decision to not include constitutional provisions for judicial review in the first amendment to Indonesia's constitution in 1999 (Lanti 2001; Mahfud 2005). This is suggested by Slamet Effendi Yusuf, who mentioned the following.

> When the legal community and the NLRC realized by early 2001 that public faith and confidence in the judicial system was progressively increasing, they felt that they had sufficient support from citizens to voice their demands . . . including their demand for judicial review.[31]

Similarly, after realizing that Indonesian citizens view the judiciary in a more positive light than before, the chairman of the National Law Reform Consortium, Firmansyah Arifin, publicly emphasized to the media the following.

> To exclude judicial review in the Constitution will clearly only take away the right of the people to obtain constitutional protection. If so, what is the meaning of the constitution, if it can't be a place of protection for all components of society.[32]

Increasing levels of public trust in the judiciary encouraged the judiciary to become even more proactive by the spring of 2001 (Tobing 2001; Kawamura 2003). In particular, from early 2001 onwards, justices from different courts across the country repeatedly condemned legislation passed by the *Dewan Perwakilan Rakyat* and the new amendments that were added to Indonesia's Constitution by Indonesia's first post–transition government.[33]

Moreover, after June 2001, as evidence that public faith and confidence in the country's judicial system was steadily increasing became more public, the judiciary and the NLRC used the media to challenge the constitutional validity of the first constitutional amendment developed and implemented by the Wahid administration in late 1999. It did so by publicly declaring in July 2001 that the first constitutional amendment "neither satisfied the principles of a true democracy nor protected the constitutional rights of Indonesian citizens."[34] Furthermore, the Supreme Court made a formal request in September 2001 to the multiparty coalition government to "restore judicial independence in Indonesia to the highest possible level"[35] and allow Indonesian courts to check the "constitutional appropriateness of laws approved by the *Dewan Perwakilan Rakyat* in recent years."[36]

The fact that higher levels of public trust in the judiciary induced the courts in Indonesia to publicly question the validity of some constitutional amendments introduced by the executive after the transition to democracy was keenly understood by the country's first post–transition (coalition) government. Key cabinet members in the ruling coalition dominated by the Golkar and the PDI-P Party not only recognized in 2001 that domestic public trust in Indonesian courts had steadily increased in the post–transition period but also believed that growing faith in the justice system among citizens would lead to a "hyperactive" judiciary.[37] According to these cabinet members, a hyperactive judiciary would challenge the government's extensive control over the legislature. Ruling government elites believed that a politically active judiciary would repeatedly check the constitutional appropriateness of bills passed by the legislature and challenge the government's agenda, especially if constitutional guarantees for judicial review were provided to the courts. This concern was emphasized by Amien Rais, who stated the following.

> At the time, we were worried that increasing public popularity of some judges in Indonesia would lead to a hyperactive judiciary . . . this would have encouraged some Supreme Court justices to adopt tactics to weaken our control of the legislature . . . If we adopted constitutional rules that would permit the courts to review legislation, then I have no doubt in my mind that the courts in Indonesia would take advantage of these rules as well as populist support to obstruct the functioning of the legislature. This would have led to chaos and political instability at a critical juncture of Indonesia's political history.[38]

Furthermore, as anticipated by our theoretical claims, the post–transition government also feared that higher levels of public trust in the judiciary could induce judges in Indonesia to believe that they had the "moral right" to intervene in the policy-making process on the legislative floor (Asshiddiqie 2005; Mahfud 2007). Consequently, key members in the Golkar and the PDI-P Party (the largest party in the ruling coalition) felt that the courts in Indonesia would use constitutional guarantees for judicial review—provided these guarantees existed—to block critical socioeconomic policies that the government hoped to implement. They feared that this would hinder the government's ability to achieve its partisan economic goals and seriously hurt the government's credibility among its constituents. As stated by Alex Litaay, who was the secretary general of the PDI-P from 1999–2003:

> The country's problems does not come from the Constitution itself but from its inconsistent application . . . it is therefore not necessary to amend the Constitution by introducing rules that let the courts review all legislation . . . this will make it impossible for the government to generate and distribute the benefits of economic development to society.[39]

Litaay's viewpoint simply reflected the official PDI-P party line on the issue of judicial review. After all, Megawati Sukarnoputri, chairman of the PDI-P Party and president of Indonesia, suggested that granting full and explicit judicial review to the courts would provide the judiciary with "excessive power" that would make it difficult for the PDI-P to "safeguard our national life from attempts to alter the basic philosophy of our country in a direction that . . . implants a whole new ideology that does not conform with the interests of an independent Indonesia."[40]

In addition, many legislators from the first post–transition government also claimed that judges in Indonesia were not "elected" by Indonesian citizens (Yusuf and Basalim 2000; Kansil et al. 2001). These legislators, therefore, argued that the courts should not be granted the privilege to conduct review of all legislation approved by the *Dewan Perwakilan Rakyat* as the judiciary is "not a legitimately elected body"[41] that represented the views of Indonesian citizens. Therefore, as suggested by our three-step causal argument, Indonesia's post–transition government perceived increasing trust in the judiciary and the courts' attempt to leverage this trust to demand for more judicial review authority as a threat to the executive's political power in the legislature, and as we discuss later, proceeded accordingly to curtail its potential for independent activism via review.

In 2001, the post–transition coalition government developed and introduced the third amendment to Indonesia's constitution. The government's lack of sincerity in designing a truly independent Constitutional Court became quickly apparent with the introduction of various "contradictory" constitutional provisions in this amendment, which directly and indirectly restricted the *Mahkamah Konstitusi's* political autonomy, including review powers. The post–transition government endorsed Article 24(1) and the *Mahkamah Konstitusi* law Article 10(1)—added to the third amendment to Indonesia's constitution—that allowed the Constitutional Court to "review the constitutionality of statutes . . . that is, determining whether the legislation enacted by *Dewan Perwakilan Rakyat* is consistent with the principles [in] the new Bill of Rights in chapter XA" (Butt and Lindsey 2009: 3).

This was an important step forward with respect to establishing de jure judicial autonomy because the judiciary (specifically the *Mahkamah Konstitusi*) was constitutionally granted the right to conduct constitutional review in Indonesia's new democratic regime. Yet, this positive proved to be deceptive since the ruling parties in the governing coalition simultaneously also adopted constitutional rules, which ensured that the Constitutional Court's authority to review the *Dewan Perwakilan Rakyat's* legislation would be severely limited.

First, the new rules added to the third amendment by Indonesia's first post–transition government confirms that "the *Mahkamah Konstitusi* cannot . . . review other types of laws below the level of statute (*undang-undang*), such as government, ministerial and presidential regulations (*peraturan*)" (Butt and Lindsey 2009: 3). The Constitutional Court's "jurisdiction also does not extend to decrees of the People's Consultative Assembly,"[42] which is the upper house of the Indonesian legislature. This, in turn, ensures that many bills, legislation, and laws passed by both the *Dewan Perwakilan Rakyat* (lower house of the legislature) and the upper house cannot be reviewed by the Constitutional Court. Moreover, it provides an opportunity for the government to "issue regulations rather than statutes as one way to avoid the *Mahkamah Konstitusi's* intervention in its legislative program" (Butt and Lindsey 2009: 3).

Second, as stated by Stockmann (2007), the new constitutional provisions that were incorporated in the immediate post–transition period by the ruling parties also ensure that "the judicial review authority of the (Constitutional) court is limited to laws passed after the First Constitutional Amendment of October 19th, 1999" (Stockmann 2007: 16). Hence, the Constitutional Court cannot review legislation that potentially violates provisions in Indonesia's constitution that were designed and approved before 1999. This dramatically reduces the jurisdiction of the *Mahkamah Konstitusi's* review authority to a very limited set of constitutional rules as the vast majority of the provisions in Indonesia's constitution were designed and approved prior to 1999. Third, similar to the Constitutional Court, the development and approval of Decree III/2000 by the post–transition government in 2000 substantially restricted the judicial review authority of the country's Supreme Court as well (Clarke 2003: 26). As these provisions make clear, this amendment therefore reflected the government's preferences for a feeble judiciary, which would not be able to threaten the legislative agenda or credibility of the ruling parties despite enjoying public support.

The third amendment was introduced on the legislative floor of the *Dewan Perwakilan Rakyat* for ratification in November 2001. In behavior similar to the voting on the first amendment, 411 out of 500 legislators (that is, 82.2 percent) voted in favor of the third amendment in the *Dewan Perwakilan Rakyat* on November 9, 2001.[43] As many as 94 percent of the legislators that voted for the third amendment were legislative members from the four main parties (mentioned earlier) in Indonesia's first post–transition government.[44] Thus, the Indonesian government was again able to successfully employ its enhanced legislative power (acquired from controlling a high concentration of legislative seats) to critically limit the judicial review authority of the courts, and essentially deny it the political power stemming from the exercise of these powers. Once again, they used their legislative muscle to neutralize the political threat the courts posed to them in the face of public trust and maximized their ability to control and implement their political and policy agenda.

The judiciary was unhappy and disappointed with the actions taken by the post–transition government with respect to judicial review. This disappointment is clearly reflected in the following statement by a prominent lawyer, Mochtar Pabottingi.

> The legal community in the country strongly believed that the emergence of democracy in Indonesia would facilitate judicial independence. We had high expectations that after democratization, President Wahid's cabinet would adopt constitutional reforms that strengthens the judiciary. . . . despite our aspirations, the government did little to address some basic concerns such as the judiciary's right to exercise judicial review across the board.[45]

Repeated appeals were made to the government by the KOKB, the National Law Reform Consortium, and the judiciary to undertake judicial reforms that would enhance the courts' judicial review authority (Lindsey 2002;

Mahfud 2005, 2007; Omara 2008). These appeals were consistently ignored by both the Ministry of Justice and the government throughout the 1999 to 2004 period.

The evidence discussed here therefore corroborates our theoretical claim that high legislative concentration in the context of high public trust will lead post-transition governments in new democracies to avoid strengthening their judiciaries by granting them full and explicit powers of judicial review. Having analyzed the Indonesia case in detail, we now turn to examine below the politics of de jure judicial review in Brazil after the country made a transition to democracy. To preview, our analysis of the Brazil case supports the claim in the corollary to hypothesis 1, which was mentioned earlier.

Introducing the Brazil Case

We provide a brief background of the history of democratization in Brazil and the structure of the judicial system in the country before analyzing the politics of judicial review in the post–democratic transition period in the country. Brazil possesses a diversified industrial and agricultural sector, vast natural resources, and in terms of nominal GDP, it is the tenth largest economy in the world.[46] About 81 percent of its 170 million inhabitants lived in urban areas in 2003 (World Bank 2003, 2004). Politically, Brazil has experienced several spells of democratic and authoritarian regimes in the twentieth century (Fausto 1999; Levine 1999). The transition we focus on here is its most recent transition from a military dictatorship, which lasted from 1964 to 1984, to democracy.

This transition to democracy is held by scholars to have begun on January 15, 1985, when Tancredo Neves of the PMDB was elected president, and Jose Sarney of the PFL was elected vice president on a joint ticket by an electoral college composed of all legislators.[47] In 1986, the first congressional elections were held under democratic auspices. Hence, with respect to its recent political history and the coding procedure that we employed to identify "new democratic regimes" in the data presented in chapter 3, Brazil constitutes a new democracy from 1986 to 1990. It was during this period that its constitution was drafted by a cohort of 559 congressmen who had been elected to serve regular terms as legislators in the Brazilian congress in 1986. From February 1, 1987, to October 5, 1988, these congressmen also served as members of its constitutional assembly.[48] Brazil's political structure after the transition to democracy is partly similar to Indonesia in that it is a presidential democracy with multiple political parties. It is also a federal system, and presidents in Brazil are limited to two terms. The structure of the judicial system in Brazil, however, is slightly different from Indonesia's judicial system.

In particular, Brazil's judicial system is organized into federal and state branches. The apex is the Federal Supreme Court (called the *Supremo Tribunal Federal*), which acts as the guardian of the constitution and the final court of appeals for all five regional appellate courts. Below the Federal Supreme Court lies the Superior Court of Justice, five regional federal courts, and finally state-level courts that include trial courts and justice tribunals. Judges are typically recruited through rigorous exams and personal interviews and move up in the judiciary on the basis of merit and seniority (Brinks 2005). However, a high number of judges are appointed to the judiciary after having served in some capacity in the executive or the legislature (Ros 2010). While regional and collegial backgrounds are shared across the judiciary, these ties are especially strong for those who make it to the apex courts. Judges from the states of São Paolo, Rio, Minas Gerais, and Pernambuco have dominated appointments to both apex courts, and almost 85 percent of judges have trained in the same four law schools (Ros 2010). Thus, like Indonesia, the closed recruitment system and the shared social background of judges tend to create a strong shared bond among judges in Brazil.

The Choice of De Jure Judicial Review in Brazil

Recall that the corollary to hypothesis 1 posits that if governments in new democracies control a low concentration of legislative seats in the initial post–transition years, then they are more likely to grant constitutional guarantees for full judicial review to the courts, provided that public trust in the judiciary during the post–transition period is also low and decreasing. The causal argument underlying this corollary can be summarized as follows. In the immediate post–transition period, governments that have a low concentration of legislative seats will worry about the possibility that future opposition-led governments could overturn their policies and even change the constitution to favor their own interests. Judicial review powers allow current incumbents to credibly insure against such adverse future actions by an incumbent opposition by providing them with the means to limit the policy-making options of the future ruling party through legal constitutional challenges in courts. Hence, incumbents with low concentrations of legislative seats will have strong incentives to adopt de jure judicial review powers.

Importantly, however, we argued that they would act on this incentive only if the judiciary itself is not in a position to become a source of policy threats because it lacks the social capital necessary to challenge government policies in its current term. As scholars have noted, such necessary social capital is provided by high levels of public confidence and support for courts. Therefore, we hypothesized that in new democracy, a government that has a low concentration of seats will be more inclined to adopt constitutional guarantees for full judicial review authority only if courts suffer from low decreasing public confidence in that country.

We now discuss the case of Brazil and analyze the trends in legislative concentration and trust in the judiciary to see if these political dynamics did indeed influence the post-transition government there to grant de jure judicial review powers to the courts. As we discuss in detail shortly, constitutional choices of the Brazilian legislature were made in the context of low levels of legislative concentration and low public trust in the judiciary. The entire 21-month period of constitutional deliberations, as well as the subsequent post-transition years, were characterized by a lack of legislative concentration of the government causing ruling parties to experience high levels of political uncertainty regarding their survival and political strength throughout this period. Furthermore, when the transition to democracy started in 1986, the judiciary, which already suffered from low levels of public trust, saw public support for courts fall even further during the early years of Brazil's democracy. Given the lack of legislative concentration in Brazil during this immediate post-transition period, our theory suggests that this lack of public trust should have encouraged political elites to grant their judiciary extensive powers of judicial review of executive and legislative laws. As our analysis illustrates, as predicted, political elites did in fact choose to adopt constitutional provisions granting the judiciary extensive powers of judicial review for these reasons.

This analysis is organized as follows. In the next subsection, we discuss the state of partisan concentration in the legislature, its effect on the political uncertainty faced by ruling parties, and the incentives it created regarding judicial review in the immediate post-transition years. This is followed by a discussion of the state of public trust in the judiciary over this entire period. These two subsections reveal that Brazil is indeed a case where both conditions—low concentration of legislative seats held by the post-transition governments and low public trust in the judiciary—were present during the immediate post-democratic transition period from 1985 to 1990. Based on the discussion in the two aforementioned subsections, we then illustrate in the final section how these incentives to adopt judicial review did in fact lead elites to do so in the context of low public trust in the Brazilian judiciary.

Legislative Concentration and the Constitutional Process in Brazil

The transition to democracy in Brazil was led by an alliance between the the *Partido da Frente Liberal* (PFL) and the *Partido do Movimento Democrático Brasileiro* (PMDB). The PFL was a new party, which was created in January 1985 by members of the pro-regime *Partido Democrático Social* (PDS) party, who wanted to vote for the PMDB's presidential candidate, Tancredo Neves, in the upcoming presidential elections (Power 2000: 67–69). Jose Sarney, the new head of the PFL, had in fact served as the leader of the regime's PDS party as recently as June 1984 (Prilliman 2000: 79). In exchange for the PFL's support for Neves's candidacy, Sarney was subsequently made the vice presidential candidate on Neves's ticket (Power 2000, 68).

Ideologically, the PFL was a conservative party that shared many of the outgoing military regime's institutional and policy preferences. Its institutional preferences included maintaining the presidential form of government and revising the 1967 constitution promulgated under the military regime to formulate a new constitution for democratic rule rather than convoking a new constitutional assembly to do so (Reich 2007: 187). In terms of policy, the PFL firmly believed in minimizing the role of the state in the economy and stressed the importance of property rights and governance that would allow individuals and firms to function without active state interference (Power 2000; Rosenn 1998; Reich 2007). As we discuss later, this put it at the opposite end of the ideological spectrum from the PMDB and required it to cater to constituencies such as the business sector, the military, and large farmers in order to maintain its political support. Unfortunately for the PFL, the president had little direct authority over the constitutional process (Mainwaring and Pérez-Linán 1997: 21). Therefore, the

PFL had to depend on its legislative delegation in order to influence the constitutional process and the substance of the constitution itself.

The PMDB, on the other hand, was a liberal progressive party that had been the backbone of the opposition to the military regime. Its ideological and institutional preferences were very different from the conservatives in the legislature. The party believed in charting a development path for Brazil that was centered around the state and led by it. Thus, it believed that it was the state's right to take care of poorer marginalized sections of society and ensure that the excesses of free markets and foreign competition were minimized. Many members of the PMDB also supported changing to a parliamentary form of government from the presidential form Brazil currently had. Ideological preferences and factions within the PMDB ranged from moderates to very left-leaning members who voted frequently with the Communist and Socialist parties in Congress (Mainwaring and Pérez-Liñán 1997: 8; Reich 2007: 186). All these factions shared an acute suspicion of the PFL, its loyalties, and its agenda.

After the 1986 congressional elections, these two parties collectively held over 64 percent of the seats in Brazil's Chamber of Deputies (Santos and Vilarouca 2008, 62; Mainwaring and Pérez-Liñán 1997: 5).[49] This seemingly strength of the ruling coalition between the PMDB and the PFL, however, rapidly deteriorated during the immediate post–transition period, and this, in turn, sharply reduced the coalition's control of the legislature. This unlikely alliance was put to the test immediately when Neves died on the eve of assuming power and Sarney unexpectedly ascended to the presidency. While the PMDB accepted Sarney as president in the interests of consolidating the transition to democracy, they had little in common with Sarney, his agenda, or with his party's agenda (Power 2000: 66). Conversely, the PFL delegation in the legislature and the president himself did not share the ideological, policy, or institutional agenda of the PMDB. The alliance was therefore inherently fragile.

Soon, the strong ideological and policy differences that existed between the two parties, and between factions within the PMDB led to splits and defections, which reduced their seat shares considerably. Therefore, the concentration of the legislative seats (calculated from the Hirschman-Herfindahl index of legislative concentration) controlled by Brazil's ruling parties after the transition to democracy declined from approximately 0.63 in 1986 to approximately 0.4 by the end of 1987, and finally to less than 0.35

in 1988.[50] This ensured that the two ruling parties did not collectively command a majority of legislative votes in the initial post-transition years. The low concentration of legislative seats held by Brazil's ruling coalition by 1987–1989 is in sharp contrast to the high concentration of legislative seats that were held by Indonesia's first post-transition government from 1999 to 2004. Thus, the first post-transition government in Brazil was characterized at the outset by a high level of political uncertainty regarding the political and legislative support the governing parties would be able to command for their constitutional and legislative agendas and their ability to consolidate their political power for the future.

This uncertainty was heightened by the high levels of partisan fragmentation in the legislature. In addition to the PFL and the PMDB, 11 parties spanning the ideological spectrum were represented in Congress, with seat shares ranging from 1 to 37.[51] These ranged from regime-friendly parties such as the PDS (37 seats) and the *Partido Liberal* (PL, 7 seats) to left-leaning anti-regime parties such as the *Partido Comunista do Brasil* (PC-doB, 3 seats), and the *Partido dos Trabalhadores* (PT, 16 seats). Thus both the PFL and the PMDB were faced with the possibility that the other party in the ruling coalition could align with these outside parties in order to achieve its preferred legislative goals (Power 2000: 177). As we discuss later, this lack of legislative concentration in the government provoked deep-seated fears among the conservative and progressive factions of the ruling coalition regarding their current and future political prospects, which, in turn, directly affected their preferences over key components of de jure judicial autonomy, including judicial review.

First, lack of legislative concentration undermined the ability of both ruling parties to claim the unchallenged mandate of the people and to secure their grip on power. This made both parties vulnerable to power plays by the other and exposed them to the risk of losing their immediate strength in office. Additionally, given the disputes that inevitably rose regarding government policy and tactics in such a weak government, it also brought home the necessity and advantages of an impartial referee who could resolve contested governance related disputes to both parties. This realization was brought home to both ruling parties most strongly by the dispute regarding the constitutional process itself.

The PFL and Sarney had wanted to revise the 1967 constitution approved under the military regime to serve as the new constitution for a democratic Brazil. This was opposed by the PMDB, who wanted to convene a dedicated constitutional assembly to draft an entirely new constitution. However, both Sarney and the outgoing regime opposed this option and ensured that the bill to authorize it was defeated in 1985 (Skidmore 1988: 258; Power 2000: 20; Reich 2007: 187). The compromise that emerged allowed Sarney to appoint a committee of experts to draft a new constitution, which would then become the working draft of the newly elected congress, which would also serve as the constitutional assembly. However, the expert draft was denounced as too leftist and state-centered by the conservative and the constitutional assembly, the *Assembléia Nacional Constituinte* (ANC) began work from scratch when they were sworn in on February 1, 1987.

The initial drafting was to be done by 24 thematic subcommittees whose drafts would then be integrated into a single draft by a 93-member Integration Committee (*Comissão de Sistematização*) with party proportional membership.[52] The Integration Committees draft would then submit the final draft to the full ANC. The entire constitutional assembly was then supposed to debate, modify, and vote on this draft in time to approve it for promulgation by November 15, 1987. This entire process, however, was torn apart by partisan disagreements between the progressive and conservative factions.

Committee drafts reflected the partisanship of their committee reporters, and hence were fiercely contested once they reached the Integration Committee deliberations. Since most committee reporters were from the progressive wing, the conservatives soon found that their preferences were not being reflected in the drafts being submitted to the Integration Committee (Martinez-Lara 1996: 98–99). The partisan fight soon erupted into a full rebellion by conservatives (Reich 2007: 188; Martinez-Lara 1996: 100; Mainwaring and Pérez-Liñán 1997). The conservatives criticized the draft as too state-centered and liberal (Brazil Report, September 17, 1987; Ames and Power 1990: 2). Their position gained further support from President Sarney, who described it as being hijacked by "radical opportunists" (*Veja*, November 4, 1987, 48). The army chief, who opposed the proposed loss of military cabinet positions, among other issues, declared an early Integration Committee draft "unacceptable" and warned that the ANC was ignoring its "moderate majority" (Brazil Report, September 17, 1987, 2). Soon, the conservatives formed a caucus of 100 members called the Centrao and lobbied the public, interest groups, and the media, among others, to back their demands for a more inclusive constitutional process. Eventually, the progressive wing agreed to change the procedures substantially and allowed a new conservative draft of the constitution to be introduced for consideration as well.

This led to a fierce reaction by the left. The left factions did not consider the draft liberal enough and wanted to amend it further in this regard (Power 2000: 161–66). Afonso Arinos, who had headed Sarney's committee of experts, warned that the *Centrao* was just "an agglomeration of the right" that was undemocratically attempting to "reverse what had already been voted" (Barroso 1993: 172). A legislator from the Communist Party of Brazil (PCdoB) legislator issued an even more dire response warning that "if the right runs over us, many Constituent assembly members will not sign the Charter" (Barroso 1993: 172). Finally, in reaction to the demands of the conservatives and the compromises being made by the PMDB to placate them, in July 1988, the left wing of the PMDB split off and formed the third largest party in the legislature the *Partido da Social Democracia Brasileira* (PSDB). The PFL (22.4 percent of seats in July 1988) and the PSDB were now the leaders of the conservative and left wings in the ANC with the PMDB (42 percent seats in July 1988) situated in the middle (Mainwaring and Pérez-Līnán 1997: 6) and a total of 14 parties represented in the legislature. Fully 62 legislators, or 11 percent of the assembly, had switched parties during this time in a manner that further strengthened the ideological divisions in the Brazilian legislature (Mainwaring and Pérez-Līnán 1997: 6). Thus, when the final round of voting on the final draft, Project B, took place, the concentration of the legislative seats held by the ruling coalition dropped to as low as 0.32 on the 0–1 Hirschman-Herfindahl scale of legislative concentration. Finally, after thousands of amendments, the full draft of the constitution was voted on by the entire assembly and the constitution was approved on October 1, 1988—a full year behind schedule.

The intense patterns of partisan contestation over the substance and process of the constitution were instrumental in establishing the realization among parties that they needed a dispute mechanism that would prevent them from deteriorating into such a political morass again. The inability to resolve disputes almost derailed the entire constitutional process. Reich (2007: 191) describes the dire state of political uncertainty these unresolved partisan battles created: "By the time the integration committee finished its final draft, conflict over the draft and the internal rules had brought the Assembly to a precipice . . ." This crisis brought home to all parties the high political cost that they had paid for the inability to resolve their disputes.

Both the PFL and the PMDB lost significant numbers of legislative members to other parties and suffered serious declines in the eyes of the public. Thus, they were unable to maintain their legislative strength, and, hence, their grip on office to the extent that they had started with. This realization, therefore—that the inability to resolve disputes due lack of legislative concentration had crippled both parties in their efforts to consolidate power and policy in their current term—was crucial in establishing support for the creation of an impartial and politically insulated judiciary, which could act as an impartial referee of political disputes in the future among both ruling parties.

Second, lack of legislative concentration made it more likely that the ruling coalition parties would not be able to pass legislation that would allow them to consolidate their political support among the constituencies vital for their individual support for their future. As mentioned earlier, the PFL and the PMDB had won office based on the votes of very different constituencies—this required them to deliver policy and build credibility with different sets of voters. While the PFL would need to cater to the interests of businesses, military establishment, and big farmers, the PMDB would need to cater to the urban and rural poor, public and blue-collar workers, and the small farmers and landless peasants (Power 2000; Prillaman 2000). The interests of these different constituencies were directly opposed and the support of one could frequently be purchased only at the expense of the other.

For example, while firms wanted flexible labor laws that would allow them to fire workers in line with the needs of the firms, workers wanted employment guarantees against exactly these find of dismissals (Santiso 2003; Reich 2007). Property rights presented another bitter division as the conservative commitment to their voters to ensure inviolate property rights was challenged directly by the demands for land reform and redistribution that the PMDB faced from its voters (Santiso 2003; Zimmerman 2008). The battles fought in the ANC were, therefore, largely fought between wings trying to constitutionalize their preferences along these ideological lines. As Reich (2007: 189) observed:

> The stand-off between supporters and opponents of the draft constitution (and the proposed procedural reforms), revealed two contrasting ideological positions that were central to Brazilian politics throughout the Cold War-era. These contrasting positions revolved around the role of the state

in addressing Brazil's chronic socioeconomic inequality. On one side were those who preferred to maintain the inviolability of private property and enshrine existing property rights in the constitution; on the other side was a group committed to using the constitution to expand the state's power to redistribute land and wealth.

Lacking the necessary legislative concentration, neither side was able to dominate the constitutional process and prevent the opposition from inserting its preferred provisions into the constitution. The initial gatekeeping advantages that the left had enjoyed in the ANC committees were subsequently neutralized after the *Centrao* successfully introduced its own conservative-leaning draft and as a result of the thousands of amendments that were considered during the final rounds of voting. The result was an extensive and comprehensive constitution that contained constitutional provisions on almost any issue that either of the ruling parties considered could be important for their future political prospects.

Thus Reich (2007: 194) similarly comments that "Combined with the other factors that defied constitutional engineering, the final document became a schizophrenic mix of conservative and progressive planks." Rosenn (1998: 21) notes that "The constitutional text in many places contains specific rules normally found only in codes or regulations. . . . Virtually nothing is outside its global scope." Ballard (1999: 247) similarly comments that, "The drafters followed a directed (dirigiste) model in creating a constitution that does more than organize power; it prescribes a program intended to produce profound political economic and social transformation."

The immediate consequence of lack of legislative concentration, therefore, was that the conservative and progressive wings of the government were unable to conclusively secure their preferred provisions, deny the opposition undesirable ones, and unequivocally consolidate their political support among their supporters for future elections through the constitutional process. The final constitution contained provisions that jeopardized the political credibility of the promises that both conservative and progressive parties could make to their voters and could successfully deliver on. Thus, they directly affected their ability to win future elections.

In order to maintain the support of their constituencies, it was therefore essential that facing political uncertainty, parties in government today could access the policy process and challenge government actions in the future if they were to lose the next elections. Both parties also had a strong interest in ensuring that any constitutional concessions they had won in the ANC could be protected via judicial action if a future opposition-led government chose to challenge it from a position of legislative strength (i.e., they had in interest in insuring against future government attacks on their politically salient constitutional provisions). Giving judicial review powers to the courts, therefore, would be an effective way of ensuring that parties would have these capabilities no matter their electoral performance. Thus, they would be able to ensure their future political survival.

Third, lack of legislative capacity and the inability to impose a dominant preferred constitution resulted in "widespread dissatisfaction with the 1988 Constitution" Reich (2007: 195) among all political factions due to all the ideological, institutional, and policy compromises that it embodied. Thus, it seemed clear to all participants that the constitution itself would be subject to many attempts to modify it to favor the parties in a position to sway the legislative votes in the future. The policy dissatisfaction that could motivate such attempts has already been discussed. However, disputes regarding political institutions were also of concern to political parties. The PMDB and some other leftist parties had favored changing the regime to a parliamentary form of government. This had been vehemently opposed by the conservatives led by the PFL and the military establishment, who had fought to maintain the presidential form of government. In the end, the right had won this fight. This had left the progressive wing with an urgent need to provide for other constitutional mechanisms that could act as checks on the executive and prevent unrestrained executive despotism in the future. For the conservatives, it also held out the possibility that progressives could raise the issue of switching to a parliamentary system again in the future when they were in a position to sway the votes. Therefore, both sides feared not just policy challenges by future opposition led governments, but also challenges that could change the nature of the institutional structure of the political system in important ways.

Therefore, as this discussion shows, lack of legislative concentration created high levels of political uncertainty among ruling parties in government regarding their most basic fears—their ability to maintain their power in their current term, their ability to implement policy agendas that would allow them to build political support for the future, and their ability to insure against the opposition making unfavorable changes to the constitution that would handicap their political future. These political fears could be addressed successfully by granting a judiciary extensive judicial review powers that would allow it to overturn any legislative statutes or executive decrees that were inconsistent with the current political compromises as embodied in the current constitution. Therefore, lack of legislative concentration in the Brazilian legislatures created strong incentives for parties and legislators to support the adoption of judicial review powers in Brazil. However, as we argued in chapter 2, while these incentives are necessary, they are not sufficient to ensure that de jure review powers are in fact adopted in a country.

Adoption also requires that elected legislators believe that they are not creating a new political problem by empowering a judiciary that would use its review powers to become an independent policy-making center and challenge the agenda of governments. We argued that ruling parties use the confidence that citizens repose in the courts as a means to judge the potential for the courts to become activist. Therefore, in order to understand whether the incentives created by lack of legislative concentration actually led to the adoption of judicial review powers in Brazil, we need to first assess the level of public trust enjoyed by the Brazilian judiciary during the immediate post–transition years.

Public Trust in the Brazilian Judiciary

Brazilians' perceptions of the judiciary at the beginning of the transition period were shaped by the long history of collaboration between the judiciary and the military regime during the military's rule from 1964 to 1985 (Prilliman 2000: 78; Pereira 2000, 2005). Over this period, the judiciary had been gradually co-opted into the military regime's governance structure and had been actively used as an instrument of the regime's consolidation and control (Pereira 2005: 229; Weschler 1998; Skidmore 1988; Prilliman 2000; Zimmerman 2010). While some elements of the legal system such as the Bar Association and a few individual lawyers and judges had continuously challenged the regime's practices and defended the civil rights of those unfairly prosecuted, the judiciary in general had helped consolidate the military regime's grip on power and policy (Calleros 2009, 2005; Fowraker and Krznaric 2002; Skidmore 1988). Thus, opposition leaders, trade-union activists, civil-rights leaders, among others, who had been prosecuted in the courts for crimes deemed to be against the national interest for taking actions against the regime were motivated to create a politically insulated and empowered judiciary (Hammergren 2007b: 172; Pereira 2005: 140–47; Fowraker and Krznaric 2002: 36, 42; Skidmore 1988: 56–58).

For the same aforementioned reasons, people did not have high levels of confidence in the judiciary's ability to adjudicate disputes in an independent and fair manner when the transition began. This was most clearly illustrated in a poll carried out in 1984, which revealed that fully 57 percent of Brazilians expressed no confidence in the judiciary.[53] Thus, when transition to democracy began in 1985, the judiciary could not draw on any substantial level of public support. Hence, as an institution, it did not pose any significant level of political threat to the political establishment and its agenda.

This image was marred further when the courts supported a controversial amnesty that had been granted to perpetrators of torture against civilians during the military regime.[54] Pereira (2000: 225) notes the importance this issue assumed for framing the subsequent image of the judiciary in the mind of Brazilian citizens.

> The issue was the initial test of a legal system and a judiciary that had been seriously compromised by authoritarian rule, one that was not unwilling to investigate or protest massive and systematic human rights violations. Some retroactive justice, if only to atone for past wrongdoings and to restore the possibility of the rule of law was necessary.

These cases were highly public and actively supported by many respected influential religious and civil society organizations (Weschler 1998; Pereira 2003).[55] Thus, when the courts ruled in favor of respecting the amnesty for the military, they hurt their credibility with the public and with NGOs as defenders of their civil and human rights (Calleros 2009: 119; Pereira 2000: 225–26; Weschler 1998: 76).

Several additional factors caused public trust in the Brazilian judiciary to plummet even further in the next few years. These included the failure of courts to check human-rights abuses by state agencies engaged in violence against citizens (Weschler 1998: 89; Skidmore 1988: 305–6), and the inaccessibility of courts to many segments of society due to high levels of petty judicial corruption and cronyism (Calleros 2009: 169; Pereira 2003: 6–7; Prilliman 2000: 18, 87, 93; Ratliff and Buscaglia 1997: 63).[56] The cumulative effect of these various trends was to lead to a steady downward spiral in the faith and trust Brazilians reposed in the judiciary as an institution over this entire period. As Linz and Stepan (2001: 176) observe of the post–transition period:

> Study after study reveals that the over-riding majority of Brazil's citizens do not believe that the state attempts to enforce laws on all its citizens impartially. In particular, citizens believe that the justice system fundamentally exists to protect the powerful and that the police are not to be trusted.

Similarly, Santiso (2003: 8) observes that in the immediate post–transition, inefficiencies and persistent delays in Brazil's legal system had the effect of "undermining popular trust in the justice system" and eroded the legitimacy of the judiciary.

Hence, not surprisingly, by 1989, polls showed that faith in the judiciary had declined to abysmal levels in Brazil. Of the 3,600 people polled in that year, 58 percent agreed completely with the statement that the judiciary served only the interests of the powerful, and another 26 percent agreed with this statement partially.[57] Thus, an appalling 84 percent of the population did not see the judiciary as an institution that could be trusted to protect their civil and human rights. The situation therefore worsened during the immediate post–transition period and the judiciary commanded much less respect by 1990 than it had at the beginning of the transition to democracy. As Prilliman (2000: 76) notes, "At the state and federal levels, Brazil demonstrated declining confidence in the courts." The trends in public trust in the judiciary worsened considerably over this period.

> Polls taken throughout the 1990s reflected a cynicism that far exceeded the dissatisfaction of the 1980s ... the level of cynicism is now so great that the public appears to have given up on the courts altogether ... (Prilliman 2000: 94–95)

While there was an immense demand among people for an independent, fair, and impartial judiciary staffed by fearless judges who would throw the book at any violators of constitutional rules and rights, the reality of the judicial system they lived with did not comport with this ideal in their minds. Thus, the judiciary as an institution commanded little public support. This then was the state of the judiciary that political elites had to contend with in the immediate post–transition period in Brazil. Therefore, from 1986 to 1990, Brazil had both low legislative concentration and low public trust in the judiciary.

Importantly, political elites were clearly aware of the general lack of confidence the public reposed in the judiciary. For example, during the constitutional deliberations process, Plinio Arruda Sampaiao, relator of the judiciary committee stated during the committee's deliberations, stated the following.

> Today, the Power of the Judiciary—I say this with great sadness to my colleagues who are on the Table, because I am a man of the Judiciary, the son of a man of the Judiciary—is a power discredited by the Brazilian population.[58]

Given these low levels of trust in the judiciary, political elites could be reasonably certain that excessive judiciary interference with political decision-making would not be seen as legitimate by a distrusting public. Hence, if given the power of judicial review, it seemed less likely to elites that the judiciary would abuse it to challenge the agenda of the government of the day. In these circumstances, granting the judiciary extensive powers to overturn executive and legislative laws for being unconstitutional seemed to afford the important strategic advantage of constraining governments formed by the opposition from overturning the current governments programs without invoking the risk of an independent activist judiciary which would interfere with political agendas. According to the corollary to hypothesis 1, given these conditions, we should expect political elites in Brazil to grant extensive powers of judicial review to their judicial. This is indeed the case. As the following discussion shows, both the considerations identified by our theoretical framework played a prominent role in persuading ANC members that adopting de jure judicial review rules would be in their strategic interests.

The Adoption of Judicial Review Powers in Brazil

The Brazilian judiciary has a long history of judicial review. But it had lost these judicial review powers under the military regime (Sato 2003: 10; Ballard 1999: 230). Political elites were therefore very conscious of the benefits of having an independent judiciary that could rein in the excesses of the executive. They were, however, also aware of the strong tradition of judicial review prior to the military regime, which had proved challenging for civilian governments (Sato 2003: 8–9). The benefits of granting judicial review had to be weighed against the risk of creating a judiciary that could become aggressively activist and interfere with the legislative agenda of the government of the day. As discussed earlier, given the lack of trust the Brazilian public reposed in the judiciary politicians were less concerned about this latter possibility in 1987–1988. Hence, the constitutional process and debate was related to defining the parameters of judicial review in a manner that allowed the judiciary to check unconstitutional behavior without giving it the powers to interfere in politically expensive ways. This can be seen most clearly in the constitutional process for judicial review as it unfolded in the ANC.

The ANC convened a thematic subcommittee to draft provisions relating to the judiciary. This subcommittee proceeded to discuss the adoption of various facets of judicial review early on in its deliberations.[59] The constitutional provisions which granted the STF the power to declare laws unconstitutional was introduced into the constitutional draft at the subcommittee stage itself and was retained through the many versions drafted by the integration committee.[60] Some of these dimensions were amended by the initial floor consideration of project A and through the final voting on project B. However all amendments supported the principle to grant the judiciary extensive review powers. Unlike the partisan bickering that led to split votes and frequent defeats of other policy or institutional provisions, relevant articles on de jure judicial review were consistently supported throughout the assembly and both ruling and opposition parties voted in favor of it at every stage.

Article 102 in the Brazilian constitution defines the various dimensions of review powers that were given to the judiciary in the 1988 constitution. These include the ability to overturn laws issued by the executive and the legislature through challenges of unconstitutionality (Article 102.1.a), to mediate disputes between the union and state governments (Article 102.1.f), conflicts of power between federal and state courts (Article 102.1.n), to decide petitions for provisional remedy in direct actions of unconstitutionality (Article 102.1.o), issue writs of injunctions requiring the executive and the legislature to adopt enabling constitutional rights (Article 102.1.p), and rights of habeas corpus and habeas data (Article 102.2.a), among others. The set of actors given the standing to ask for constitutional review is one of the largest in the world and includes political representatives of federal and state assemblies, the president and state governors, party leaders of all parties represented in Congress, the bar association, as well as civic groups such as trade unions and professional associations.

Importantly, these institutional choices were strategic and driven by the perceived need to solve the political problems of insurance in the light of future political uncertainty. Thus, Rios-Figueroa and Taylor (2006: 739) note that the expansive set of actors who have legal standing to request judicial review offers political elites considerable advantages since powers that "privileged standing therefore guarantees these groups considerable potential policy leverage." Furthermore, as Howell (1995: 10–11) points out, judicial review powers

> allowed parties or interest groups whose interests have been defeated in the legislature to 'transpose a political conflict directly into a constitutional one'... [P]olitical parties with only five percent representation in Congress, unable to forge a successful coalition to defeat a legislative act, can use the STF as a means to continue the legislative battle.

Thus, judicial review allowed parties to insure that they had access to the policy process even if they were not in power at the moment and this ability allowed them to cater to the interests of their political and electoral constituencies. Similarly, the decision not to enforce binding precedent on lower courts was made in order to allow the set of privileged actors with legal standing to request judicial review, the freedom to challenge government decisions at multiple venues, especially sympathetic ones, in order to maximize their strategic leverage. Thus, Santiso (2003: 4) notes the following.

> There are many legal and political reasons why Brazil ignores the principle of precedent. It strengthens the independence of individual judges and the autonomy of individual courts vis-à-vis their hierarchies. Politically, it gives politicians more means of legal recourse against the government's decisions.

On the hand, de jure aspects of review that allowed the judiciary to determine the extent of the exact price that governments would pay in case of constitutionality were more politically ambiguous in terms of the additional benefits they yielded in terms of insurance. Therefore, these powers were more heavily debated and some were discarded. For example, the power to issue provisional remedy after a declaration of unconstitutionality was seen to be politically important (Rosenn 2000: 306) and potentially dangerous in the hands of an activist judiciary. The provision to give the judiciary this power was introduced in the Integration Committee, and was subsequently heavily debated and amended at every stage of the process.[61] The abysmal lack of public trust in the judiciary, however, was eventually seen as a sufficient constraint on judicial abuse of this power and legislators were finally convinced to approve this measure on September 14, 1988. Parties therefore united in their effort to limit the political consequences of judicial review powers, but not the fundamental principle of full and explicit judicial review authority granted by the constitution to Brazil's judiciary (this partly explains why the moving average of the ordinal judicial review measure in Brazil is high).

Therefore, the sum of all the constitutional provisions defining de jure judicial review powers in Brazil was to provide "unprecedented power extended to the judicial branch" (Howell 1995).[62] The STF was granted the powers of abstract and concrete review, while lower courts also exercised concrete review powers. As a result as (2003: 5–6) Santiso notes the following.

> The 1988 Constitution undeniably extended unprecedented power and independence to the judicial branch . . . The Constitution grants extensive prerogatives to the courts in the review of the acts of the executive and the legislature.

Similarly, Ballard (1999: 247) observes that

> Under the new Constitution, the judiciary is in a pivotal position to ensure that the Constitution's plans and programs are implemented. To trigger exercise of judicial power, the Constitution outlines broad remedies with liberal standing rules. The Constitution empowers individual citizens, unions, political parties, and other association to initiate law suits against the government with relative ease.

Thus, she notes, "The new constitutional scheme places the judiciary in a prominent position to protect the nascent democratic system."

As a result, it is not surprising that the moving average of the degree to which Brazil's constitution explicitly grants the power of judicial review to the country's courts—(i.e., the ordinal judicial review measure described in chapter 3)[63]—is as high as 1.3 on the ordinal −1 to +2 scale. Furthermore, the moving average of judicial review in Brazil is much higher than the moving average of the same measure for Indonesia's judiciary during each country's immediate post–transition period.

To summarize, the lack of legislative concentration created strong incentives for both ruling parties, the PFL and the PMBD in Brazil, to support granting judicial review powers to the judiciary. The decision to do so, however, was clinched by the fact that the judiciary suffered from such abysmally low public support. Under these conditions, the ruling parties felt reassured that the judiciary would be loath to challenge the government since it did not command the social capital necessary to directly challenge the government of the day in order to establish itself as an independent policy power in the emerging political landscape in Brazil. Therefore, ruling parties chose to adopt de jure judicial review powers during the constitutional assembly itself. Subsequent events have shown the extensive use political parties in Brazil have made of these powers to push for their own agendas, to challenge the government, and to contain the executive (Rosenn 1998; Santiso 2003; Rios-Figueroa and Taylor 2006; Taylor 2008; Zimmerman 2008).

Conclusion

The two cases examined in this chapter provided us with a unique opportunity to evaluate our causal arguments about the politics of de jure judicial review during the immediate post–democratic transition period in developing countries. The Indonesian case revealed that the executive in the first post–democratic transition government in a new democratic state had low (or perhaps no) incentives to provide the courts with constitutional guarantees for full and explicit judicial review when the concentration of legislative seats held by his government is sufficiently high. The Brazil case, in contrast, shows that incumbents are more likely to provide the judiciary with constitutional guarantees for full and explicit judicial review in the immediate post–democratic transition period if the concentration of legislative seats held by the post–transition government is low. That said, we found that the government's control (or lack thereof) of the legislature in a new democracy is a necessary, but not sufficient, condition that affects the probability with which the executive may constitutionally empower courts to review bills or policies passed by the national legislature.

Indeed, the two cases showed that the extent to which citizens trust the judiciary influences the decision by governments in new democracies to adopt constitutional provisions for full and explicit judicial review. The Indonesia case illustrates how increasing public trust in the judiciary influenced the government during the immediate post–transition period to protect its hegemony in the legislature by first denying constitutional guarantees for full judicial review to the courts and then severely restricting judicial review authority for the courts. Conversely, falling public trust in the Brazilian judiciary encouraged Brazil's first post–transition governments from 1987 to 1991, all of which had weak control of the legislature, to constitutionally adopt full and explicit judicial review to restrain the potential political power of future incumbents.

Put together, the analysis of the two cases in this chapter generates at least two main substantive implications for our study. First, as suggested by some studies,[64] we learn from this chapter (especially the Brazil case) that democratization in developing states can indeed promote critical components of de jure judicial autonomy such as judicial review authority for the courts. However, this possibility is only realized under certain conditions. Building on these studies, the analysis in this chapter provides a more nuanced conclusion in that it shows that the transition to democracy fosters the adoption of constitutional guarantees for de jure judicial review in developing countries only if the first post–transition government does not succeed in controlling the national legislature after the first post-authoritarian election. Weak control of the legislature in the immediate post–transition period dampens the political elite's incentives to restrict the courts' judicial review authority.

Second, we found that higher levels of public trust in the judiciary in new democratic states can have both positive and negative consequences. On the positive side, increasing trust in the judicial system by citizens can induce the judiciary to become proactive and credibly restrict the executive's attempt to political hegemony in the legislature in new democracies. This may help to promote democratic accountability in the post–transition period in developing states. On the negative side, however, increasing public trust in the judicial system encourages governments in new democracies— especially governments that have majority control of the legislature—to avoid adopting constitutional rules that provide courts with the power of complete judicial review. Hence, even though some studies claim that greater public trust in the judiciary can strengthen the judicial branch,[65] this chapter broadly suggests that the effect of such trust on the design of constitutional rules that affect the judiciary in new democracies is more complex than suggested by these studies. Whether or not our analysis on the politics of judicial review applies to other cases is a matter for future research.

The in-depth analysis of the Brazil and Indonesia case in this chapter is useful for our analysis about the probability with which incumbents in new democracies constitutionally adopt de jure judicial review authority for domestic court. However, it does not address the issue of whether judges in these countries were able to actually exercise their judicial review powers and have them respected by the political establishment. Such ability falls under the theoretical rubric of de facto judicial independence. In chapter 2 we presented an argument that posited that the interaction between political particularism and the time horizons faced by governments affects de facto judicial independence in "newly consolidated" as well as established democracies across the developing world. Therefore, in the next three chapters, we turn to statistically evaluate our predictions about de facto judicial independence and to illustrate the causal mechanism we presented through comparative case studies.

CHAPTER 5

Empirical Tests for Electoral Particularism and De Facto Judicial Independence

In the introduction, we emphasized the distinction between de jure and de facto judicial independence. Incumbents in new democracies in the developing world may favor the creation of an independent judiciary and thus adopt constitutional provisions that allow for a high degree of de jure judicial independence. But this does not mean that these incumbents or their successors will respect the political autonomy of the judiciary across time. Indeed, the "time inconsistent" preferences of policymakers in developing states may induce them to interfere with the decisions of judges and actively curtail the de facto independence of the courts. Building on this distinction between de jure and de facto judicial independence, we developed a second theoretical story in the latter half of chapter 2. This story explored how domestic political institutions and the time horizons of governments in office—which is given by their predicted probability of failure—influence de facto judicial independence in democratic developing countries.

The testable hypothesis that emerges from this story, which we label as hypothesis 2, posits that in the context of high hazard rates (i.e., low time horizons) in office, incumbents in particularistic electoral systems are more likely to increase the de facto independence of the judiciary.[1] The corollary to this hypothesis states that when faced with high hazard rates in office, incumbents in democracies characterized by lower levels of electoral particularism (i.e., party-centered systems)[2] will curtail the courts' de facto autonomy. In this chapter, we employ a comprehensive pooled sample of 103 democracies from the developing world to primarily focus on statistically testing hypothesis 2 and then broadly evaluate the corollary to this hypothesis.

The rest of this chapter is organized as follows. We first provide a detailed description of the sample. This is followed by a discussion of the operationalization of the dependent and independent variables that are employed for testing hypothesis 2, and the control variables included in the specification. We then describe the statistical model that is used for the tests presented in this chapter. In section five, we report the results from the statistical tests of hypothesis 2 and from extensive robustness tests. The chapter concludes summarizing our results and highlighting the contributions made by the chapter's empirical analysis.

Sample and Dependent Variable

The prediction in hypothesis 2 focuses on de facto independence of the judiciary in *democracies* across the developing world. We thus need a sample of democratic country years from the developing world to test this hypothesis. We compile a time-series cross-sectional (TSCS) sample of 103 developing countries that are observed as democracies—according to the Przeworski et al. (2000) criteria—anytime during the 1985 to 2004 period to test our hypothesis. The democracies in our sample satisfy Przeworski et al.'s (2000) criteria for a democracy which are: (1) the chief executive and legislature must be directly elected; (2) there must be more than one party in the legislature; and (3) incumbents must allow a lawful alternation of office if defeated in elections. The 103 developing countries in the sample that are observed as democracies and the years in which they are observed as democracies are listed in table 5.1.

The size and temporal range of our sample is comprehensive as it includes all democracies in the developing world observed during the 1985 to 2004 time period (based on the Przeworski et al. criteria) for which data to operationalize the dependent and independent variables (described later) are available. This allows us to make more generalizable claims if we find empirical support for our hypothesis. The results reported shortly remain robust when we use the Polity measure of democracy to construct our sample of developing democracies.[3] To save space, however, we focus on reporting the results that we obtain from our country-year sample of developing democracies based on Przeworski et al.'s (2000) criteria for a democracy.

We now turn to describe the operationalization of the dependent variable in hypothesis 2: de facto judicial independence. Recent empirical studies have measured de facto judicial independence across countries as an ordinal variable.[4] Given that our prediction in hypothesis 2 is in terms of

TABLE 5.1. Developing Democracy Country-Years in Sample

Country	Period	Country	Period	Country	Period
Albania	1992–2004	Georgia	1995–2004	Papua New Guinea	1985–2004
Andorra	1986–2004	Ghana	1996–2004		
Antigua and Barbuda	1985–2004	Grenada	1985–2004	Paraguay	1993–2004
		Guatemala	1996–2004	Peru	1985–2004
Argentina	1985–2004	Guinea Bissau	2000–2004	Philippines	1987–2004
Armenia	1998–2004	Guyana	1992–2004	Poland	1990–2004
Bahamas	1985–2004	Haiti	1994–2004	Romania	1990–2004
Bangladesh	1991–2004	Honduras	1985–2004	Russia	1993–2004
Barbados	1985–2004	Hungary	1990–2004	Rwanda	1996–2004
Benin	1991–2004	India	1985–2004	San Marino	1985–2004
Belize	1985–2004	Indonesia	1999–2004	Sao Tome and Principe	1991–2004
Bolivia	1985–2004	Jamaica	1985–2004		
Bosnia and Herzegovinia	1993–2004	Kenya	2002–4	Senegal	2000–2004
		Kiribati	1985–2004	Serbia	2000–2004
Botswana	2003–4	Korea, South	1988–2004	Sierra Leone	1996–2004
Brazil	1985–2004	Latvia	1991–2004	Slovak Republic	1993–2004
Bulgaria	1990–2004	Lithuania	1991–2004	Slovenia	1992–2004
Burkina Faso	1993–2004	Macedonia	1993–2004	Solomon Islands	1985–2004
Cape Verde	1991–2004	Madagascar	1993–2004	South Africa	1994–2004
Central African Republic	1993–2004	Malawi	1994–2004	Sri Lanka	1990–2004
		Mali	1992–2004	St. Kitts and Nevis	1985–2004
Chile	1990–2004	Marshall Islands	1985–2004	St. Vincent	1985–2004
Colombia	1985–2004	Mauritius	1985–2004	Seychelles	1985–2004
Comoros	1990–94	Mexico	2000–2004	Sudan	1986–88
Congo	1992–96	Micronesia	1985–2004	Suriname	1991–2004
Côte d'Ivoire	2000–2004	Mongolia	1992–2004	Taiwan	1985–2004
Costa Rica	1985–2004	Moldova	1985–2004	Timor-Leste	1985–2004
Croatia	2000–2004	Mozambique	1994–2004	Thailand	1992–2004
Cyprus	1985–2004	Namibia	1990–2004	Trinidad and Tobago	1985–2004
Czech Republic	1990–2004	Nauru	1985–2004		
Djibouti	1999–2004	Nepal	1991–2001	Turkey	1985–2004
Dominica	1985–2004	Nicaragua	1990–2004	Ukraine	1991–2004
Dominican Republic	1985–2004	Niger	1999–2004	Uruguay	1985–2004
		Nigeria	1999–2004	Vanuatu	1984–2004
Ecuador	1985–2004	Palau	1985–2004	Venezuela	1985–99
El Salvador	1994–2004	Pakistan	1988–97	Zambia	1991–2004
Estonia	1991–2004	Panama	1994–2004		

Note: The time periods in the columns indicate the years in which each country is observed as a democracy according to the Przeworski, Alvarez, Cheibub, and Limongi 2000 criteria for a democratic regime. Note that countries that are listed above as democracies from 1985 to 2004 are essentially observed as democratic regimes (according to the Przeworski, Alvarez, Cheibub, and Limongi 2000 criteria) for the entire time period in the sample since the sample starts in 1985 and ends in 2004).

support for various degrees of de facto judicial independence (DFJI), an ordinal measure of DFJI is eminently suited to testing it. Therefore, we follow extant studies and also employ an ordinal measure of DFJI as the dependent variable for testing hypothesis 2. The main measure that we use for the dependent variable has been developed by Tate and Keith (2007), who construct their de facto measure of judicial independence from the *Annual Human Rights Reports* of the United States Department of State (Bureau of Democracy, Human Rights, and Labor). Their measure is operationalized on a 0 to 2 scale as follows:

- 0 indicates a de facto nonindependent judiciary. In this case, the judiciary is described as nonindependent, as having significant levels of executive influence or interference, or as having high levels of corruption.
- 1 indicates a somewhat independent judiciary in de facto terms. This implies that the judiciary is described as somewhat independent, with pressure from the executive branch "at times," or with occasional reports of corruption.
- 2 denotes a de facto independent judiciary. The judiciary in this case is described as "generally independent" or as independent in practice with no mention of corruption or outside influences.

We follow Tate and Keith (2007) and operationalize our measure of our dependent variable, DFJI, based on the same 0–2 ordinal scale. We label this measure as *de facto judicial independence*. The data to operationalize it is drawn from several primary and secondary sources including Tate and Keith (2007); Finkel et al. (2007); Rosenn (1987); *Annual Human Rights Reports* of the U.S. Department of State; Cross (1999); and Blais and Cingnarelli (1996).[5]

The key advantage of the *de facto judicial independence* measure we use is that, as required for hypothesis 2, it operationalizes the extent to which the judiciary is factually independent *in practice* rather than merely on paper. An increase in the ordinal scale of *de facto judicial independence* from 0 to 2 captures a shift from a situation where the extent to which governments actually respect the de facto independence of the judiciary is virtually nonexistent to an outcome in which the judicial system is in de facto terms highly independent and politically autonomous. For example, Russia, Bolivia, and Mali are coded as 0 in most years implying their judiciaries enjoyed no DFJI in those years. Mexico, Bangladesh, and Slovakia are coded as 1, suggesting that their judiciaries have some but not high levels of DFJI, whereas Costa Rica, Hungary, and Malawi are coded as 2 in most years, indicating that their judiciaries enjoyed high levels of de facto independence in those years. The scores of DFJI for these countries are consistent with the levels of DFJI scholars have generally ascribed to them making us more confident in their ability to measure the necessary concept.[6]

In addition to the main measure just described, we also use an alternative measure of the dependent variable, Cingranelli's and Richards's (2008) de facto judicial independence variable, which has been used by some studies, for robustness tests.[7] Cingranelli and Richards (2008) conceptualize de facto judicial independence as an outcome where judges are free from control by the government or military and code it on an ordinal 0 to 2 scale where:

- A score of 0 indicates that there are "active and widespread constraints on the judiciary"—in particular, active government interference in cases or judicial dismissals for political reasons.
- A score of 1 implies that there are structural limitations on judicial independence where (1) the chief executive or minister of justice has the ability to appoint and dismiss judges at will, even if they do not actually do so in the particular year being coded, and (2) there is limited corruption or intimidation of the judiciary.
- Finally a state receives a score of 2 (i.e., full de facto independent judiciary) if it satisfies the following criteria: the courts have the right to rule on the constitutionality of legislative acts and executive decrees, judges at the highest level of courts have a minimum of seven-year tenure, the president or minister of justice cannot directly appoint or remove judges and the removal of judges is restricted (e.g., allowed for criminal misconduct), the actions of the executive and legislative branch can be challenged in the courts, all court hearings are public, and judgeships are held by professionals.

We follow Cingranelli and Richards (2008) and operationalize our alternative measure of de facto judicial independence labeled *de facto judicial autonomy* based on the same 0 to 2 criteria described earlier. As required for hypothesis 2, this measure also empirically captures the degree to which the judicial system is factually independent in practice on a consistent basis rather than merely on paper. The data to operationalize this measure is drawn from several primary and secondary sources, including Cingranelli and Richards (2008); Finkel et al. (2007); Tate and Keith (2007); *Annual Human Rights Reports* of the U.S. Department of State (various years); Cross (1999); and Blais and Cingranelli (1996).

Independent Variables

Hypothesis 2 predicts that the interaction of the following two independent variables affects DFJI in developing democracies: the time horizons of governments (or, equivalently, their hazard rate) in office, and the degree of electoral particularism. Thus, in order to test this hypothesis, we interact a continuous variable that operationalizes the hazard rate of governments in our sample per country year, and an index of political particularism for developing democracies. We first describe below the procedure we employed to operationalize the hazard rate of governments and then discuss in detail the operationalization of the index of political particularism.

Operationalizing the ex ante hazard rate of governments in office is not straightforward. Existing studies typically use the mean turnover rate of governments or the number of changes in the chief executive as a proxy for the hazard rate of governments.[8] Although useful, these two measures are primarily an ex post rather than an ex ante measure for the hazard rate of governments. They thus fail to capture the ex ante hazard rate governments face in office and are thus inadequate for testing our theoretical prediction. They also lack temporal variation, which limits their empirical leverage. To avoid these drawbacks, we therefore depart from existing studies and develop a measure that carefully captures the ex ante hazard rate of each government in office in the data, which provides an accurate proxy for the strategic time horizons of each government each year. Specifically, we derived the predicted probability of government failure in office for each year for each government in our sample.[9] We did so in several steps.

First, we estimated some discrete time hazard models with a logit specification to derive the predicted probability of failure of each government in our sample. We use the discrete time-hazard model to examine the duration (in months) of all governments in our sample of developing democracies over the period January 1985 to December 2004. We only include governments that began on or after January 1985 because our TSCS sample of developing democracies (listed in table 5.1) begins in 1985, and governments that did not end before December 31, 2004, are right censored. More formally, the discrete time-hazard model with a logit specification (see Beck, Katz, and Tucker 1998) is defined as:

$$P(y_{i,t}=1) = h(t\,|\,\mathbf{x}_{i,t}) = \frac{1}{1+\exp-(\mathbf{x}_{i,t}\beta' + k_{t-t0})} \tag{5.1}$$

where i denotes each government in the sample, $\mathbf{x}_{i,t}$ denotes the vector of independent variables in the hazard model, and the temporal dummies k_{t-t0} capture the length of the time that each government has been in office from t_0 until the time period t at which the government collapses.[10] The hazard rate in this model, therefore, represents the probability that a government will end at a particular time given that the government has survived to that point. The dependent variable in this model, *failed*, is a dummy variable coded 1 for each instance of government dissolution in democracies, which occurs either due to elections or to a change in the composition of parties, no-confidence votes, or voluntary resignations.

We include the following variables in the discrete time hazard model, which according to several studies,[11] directly influence the probability of government failure in democracies: government polarization,[12] the effective number of legislative parties (ENLP),[13] a count variable for the number of attempts to form the government, a measure of electoral volatility,[14] a continuous 0–1 measure of electoral risk,[15] a dummy for parliamentary democracies and a dummy for minority governments in the sample,[16] and time splines to control for duration dependence.[17] We do not report the estimates from the discrete time-hazard model to conserve space, although the model does a good job in predicting when a government is going to end in the sample (92 percent of the cases).

Importantly, given that we have data on the month of entry into and exit from office of every government in our sample during the entire 1985 to 2004 period, we are able to use the estimates from the estimated discrete time-hazard model to calculate the predicted probability of government failure—that is, the hazard rate, of each government for every year. In more technical terms, the predicted probability of failure in office—that is, the hazard rate for each government is computed from the following formula:

$$\hat{P}(y_{i,t}=1) = \frac{1}{1+\exp-(\mathbf{x}_{i,t}\hat{\beta}' + \hat{k}_{t-t0})} \tag{5.2}$$

where $\hat{\beta}'$ is the estimated log hazard odds ratio for each government given $\mathbf{x}_{i,t}$ and $\hat{k}_{t-t0}$ captures how long each government has been at risk via the estimated baseline hazard probability $h_0(t)$. We denote this predicted probability of failure in office of each government, which is derived from formula in equation 5.2, as their *hazard rate*.

The *hazard rate* variable is bounded between 0 and 1. This measure has four main advantages compared to existing measures of this variable. First, it directly operationalizes the ex ante hazard rate of each government in office, which allows us to closely test the prediction in hypothesis 2. Second, it serves as a powerful and accurate proxy for each government's time horizon in office. This is true because higher values of the *hazard rate* measure empirically operationalize the fact that the government's ex ante time horizon in office is low, while low values of the hazard rate variable indicates that the government's ex ante time horizon in office is high. Third, the mean of the hazard rate measure in our sample is .517, while the standard deviation is .233. This indicates that there is substantial variation in the *hazard rate* variable in our sample.

Fourth, there exists significant *temporal* variation in our hazard rate variable because we compute the hazard rate for each government within each country in our sample. To see this, consider the example in fig. 5.1, which illustrates the hazard rate of governments in office in two prominent developing democracies in the sample: India (from 1985 to 2004) and South Africa (from 1994 to 2004, since South Africa experienced a transition to full-fledged democracy in 1994).[18] The figure shows that in India, the hazard rate of the government was low and stable from 1985 to 1989. This is not surprising given that a stable, single-party majority government—specifically, the Congress-I government headed by Prime Minister Rajiv Gandhi—was in office during the 1985 to 1989 period. However, as shown in the figure, the hazard rate of governments increased dramatically between (1) 1989 and 1991, and then (2) 1996 and 1999, when India was governed by a series of unstable multiparty coalitions or minority governments that did not have adequate legislative support from opposition parties and were thus extremely vulnerable to being removed from office via a no-confidence motion.[19]

As fig. 5.1 shows, unlike India in the 1990s, the hazard rate of the government in South Africa was low and stable from 1994 to 1998 and from 2000 to 2003. This is because South Africa was governed by the single-party majority African National Congress (ANC) government in these two time

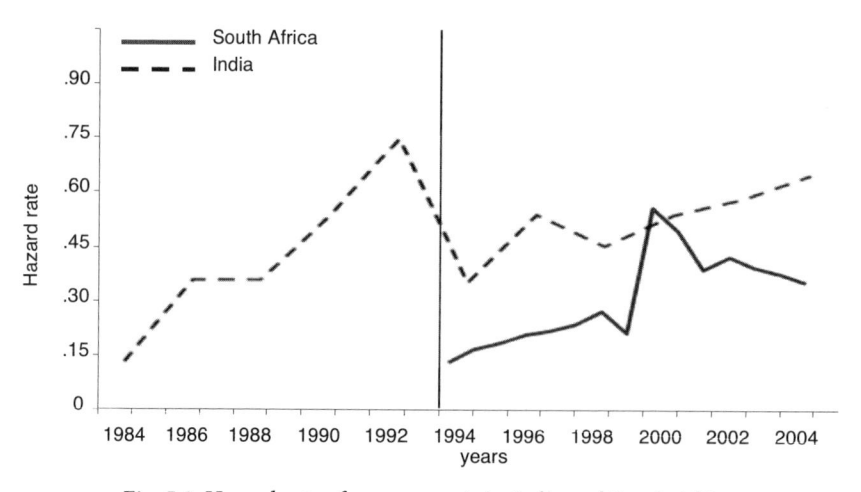

Fig. 5.1. Hazard rate of governments in India and South Africa

periods. We do, however, observe an increase in the government's hazard rate in the two elections years in South Africa: 1999 and 2004. This is consistent with the views that were held by numerous pollsters, journalists, and scholars during these two election years that the ruling ANC party may lose its majority in the legislature or perhaps even lose the upcoming election.[20]

Put together, then, the presence of both cross-sectional and temporal variation in our hazard rate measure, therefore, provides us with an opportunity to directly test the prediction in hypothesis 2. The data that we used to compute the *hazard rate* measure described earlier is drawn from the following sources: Bank's (2005) CNTS data archive; Inter-Parliamentary Union (various years, Geneva); the World Bank's (2010) *Database of Political Institutions;* Przeworski et al. (2000); Chiozza and Goemans (2004).

The second independent variable is the extent to which the electoral system is particularistic in developing democracies. We use Johnson and Wallack's (2007) measure of the personal vote incentives of a country's most dominant or populous legislative tier to operationalize electoral particularism (labeled here as *particularism*). This personal vote ranking is based on coding schemes developed by Carey and Shugart (1995) and specifically operationalizes the extent to which political settings place a premium on personal-vote cultivation by politicians. The ranking has three components: (1) ballot; (2) pool; and (3) vote, with higher values on each denoting greater incentives to cultivate a personal vote, and, therefore, higher levels of particularism. Johnson and Wallack aggregate these components into a 1–13 country-level ordinal scale of personal vote incentives. This 1–13 index records higher values for democracies in our sample that exhibit higher levels of electoral particularism, and thereby serves as our measure of *particularism*.

As mentioned earlier, hypothesis 2 predicts that in developing democracies the interactive effect of the hazard rate of governments and electoral particularism on will be positive. To test the interactive effect posited in this hypothesis, we thus interact the *hazard rate* measure with the *particularism* variable and introduce *hazard rate* × *particularism*, as well as the individual components of this interaction term in the empirical models where the dependent variable are de facto (1) *judicial independence*, and (2) *judicial autonomy*. From hypothesis 2, we anticipate that the effect of *hazard rate* × *particularism* on de *facto judicial independence* and *de facto judicial autonomy* will be positive.

Control Variables

We explicitly account for alternative explanations for de facto independence of the judiciary in our empirical model when testing hypothesis 2. We do so by incorporating various control variables in the specification that account for factors that have been identified by scholars as critical determinants of de facto judicial independence. These are discussed in detail later. In this regard, observe that some of the control variables that influence de jure judicial review, and which were listed in chapter 2, also affect de facto judicial independence according to some scholars.[21] We therefore list this common set of control variables that are believed to affect both de jure and de facto judicial independence and include these variables in our models. Since they were described in chapter 3, we briefly list, rather than discuss in detail, the operationalization of these controls.

We first include the following economic controls in our models for de facto judicial independence, which are drawn from the main empirical specification presented in chapter 3: *log GDP per capita, foreign aid, trade openness,* and *FDI flows*. We control for *log GDP per capita* as researchers have shown that governments in wealthier societies have more incentives to respect and maintain the de facto independence of the judiciary (Stephenson 2003; Hayo and Voigt 2007; Abbasi 2007). We include *foreign aid* and *FDI flows* since some scholars claim that the material benefits realized from foreign aid and FDI flows induce governments to increase DFJI as donor states (that provide aid) and foreign investors (who are a critical source for FDI) typically have strong preferences for an independent judiciary (Klug 2000; Boulanger 2003; Chavez 2003, 2008; Hirschl 2003; Klerman and Mahoney 2005). Higher levels of economic globalization that lead to more exposure to international trade flows may encourage governments in developing states to both establish and maintain or enhance judicial independence over time.[22] We account for this by adding the *trade openness* variable to the model.

We include the following political controls, also described in the previous chapter, in our specification as well: *competition, separation of powers, judiciary trust, legislative concentration, press freedom,* and the *presidential* dummy. We incorporate *competition,* which operationalizes the degree of political competition in countries given by the PARCOMP measure in the Polity IV dataset,[23] as recent studies have suggested that greater political competition increases the likelihood that governments will respect the de facto independence of the judiciary (Ramseyer 1994; Stephenson 2003; Whittington 2003). We add the 0–2 ordinal measure of *separation of powers* since the existence of separation of powers reduces the political leverage that incumbents may potentially have to reduce the de facto autonomy of the judiciary (Vanberg 2000, 2008; Whittington 2003; Friedman 2004; Shapiro 1981). We incorporate the *presidential* dummy as some studies suggest that presidential systems are less conducive for de facto judicial independence (e.g., Herron and Randazzo 2003). We include the *judiciary trust* variable in the specification, which was described in chapter 3, as some scholars have claimed that higher public trust in the justice system increases the likelihood that the government may enhance or at least maintain the de facto independence of the judicial system (Hayo and Voigt 2007; Abbasi 2007).

We add the Herfindahl index of the legislative concentration of seats held by the government, labeled as *legislative concentration* (the operationalization of this variable was discussed in chapter 3). This is because it is plausible that greater control of the legislature by the ruling party may encourage the government to restrict the de facto independence of the judiciary as it may perceive independent courts as a threat to its political hegemony in the legislature (Hirschl 2004, 2008; Durant et al. 2004). We also emphasized in the empirical analysis in chapter 3 that researchers usually hypothesize that the presence of a free press makes it politically costly for the government to stifle the political autonomy of the judiciary (Vanberg 2001, 2005; Hayo and Voigt 2007; Heckelman 2010). We thus include the variable *free press;* the operationalization of this variable was discussed in chapter 3. In addition to the political controls previously listed, we include four more variables in the empirical models for de facto judicial independence that were not included in the models for de jure judicial review in chapter 3. For instance, we include the Pedersen (1983) measure of electoral volatility in the specification, which is defined as:

$$\text{electoral volatility} = \frac{\sum_{i=1}^{n} |p_{it} - p_{i(t+1)}|}{2} \qquad (5.3)$$

where n is number of parties (in each country in the sample), p_{it} and $p_{i(t+1)}$ represents the percentage of votes received by that party in time periods t and $t + 1$, respectively. We incorporate electoral volatility in the specification since higher electoral volatility may induce the ruling party to "tie the hands" of future governments by enhancing the courts' de facto autonomy (Ramseyer 1994; Stephenson 2003; Ginsburg 2003; Hirschl 2004).

In contrast to the predicted effect of electoral volatility mentioned earlier, studies are divided on the issue of whether or not the degree of de jure judicial independence influences de facto independence of the judiciary. Herron and Randazzo (2003); Hayo and Voigt (2007); Rios-Figueroa (2006) suggest that the presence of formal de jure judicial independence provides judges with more room to assert themselves, which, in turn, may promote the de facto independence of the judiciary. Woods and Hilbink (2009: 746), however, are more skeptical about the idea that de jure judicial independence enhances de facto judicial independence. To account for this, we introduce as a control a composite index of *de jure judicial independence,* which is drawn from Finkel et al. (2007). This particular composite index is a first principal component factor score for a factor analysis of the following components of the degree of de jure judicial independence that is guaranteed by the constitution in each country: guaranteed terms for judges, finality of judicial decisions, exclusive judicial authority, enumerated judicial qualifications, and judicial review.[24] The de jure judicial independence index has a factor score with mean 0 and standard deviation equal to 1 in the sample. Table 5.2 in the appendix provides a list of the data sources that have been used to operationalize the control variables mentioned above.

TABLE 5.2. Data Sources for Control Variables

List of Control Variables	Data Sources
Economic controls	
log GDP per capita, foreign aid, FDI flows, trade openness	IMF 2009; World Bank 2006
Political controls	
Competition (PARCOMP)	Polity IV database
Presidential	Golder 2005; World Bank, *Database of Political Institutions* (2008)
Separation of powers	Finkel, Pérez-Liñán, and Seligson 2007; Blaustein and Flanz 1971; Blaustein 1993; *World Constitutions Illustrated: Contemporary and Historical Documents and Resources*; Maddex 1995
Judiciary trust	Finkel, Pérez-Liñán, and Seligson 2007; World Values Survey (various years); Barrett 2005; Justice Studies Center of the Americas (CEJA-JSCA); Latin American Public Opinion Project (LAPOP); Afrobarometer; Asian Barometer
De jure judicial independence (index)	Finkel, Pérez-Liñán, and Seligson 2007; Blaustein and Flanz 1971; Blaustein 1993; Maddex 1995
Lag of judicial review	Data sources for this variable listed in the text of chapter 3
Federal	World Bank (2008), *Database of Political Institutions*
Press freedom	Freedom House (various years)
Electoral volatility	World Bank (2008), *Database of Political Institutions*; Mainwaring and Zoco 2007; Katz and Crotty 2006
elf	Fearon and Laitin 2003, updated by the authors to 2004
Bicameralism	Wallack et al. 2003; World Bank (2008), *Database of Political Institutions*
Veto players	World Bank (2008), *Database of Political Institutions*

TABLE 5.3. Summary Statistics of Main Variables

Variables	Mean	Standard Deviation	Minimum	Maximum
log GDP per capita	7.485	1.180	4.542	11.236
Foreign aid	2.70e+08	4.12e+08	−8.21e+08	3.79e+09
FDI flows	9.25e+08	2.79e+09	−9.44e+08	3.79e+09
Trade openness	83.36	42.01	3.96	253.88
Competition	2.65	9.72	−88	5
Concentration	.220	.197	0	.970
Trust	9.775	24.377	−20.868	47.465
Hazard rate	.517	.233	0	.986
Particularism	5.96	4.06	1	13
Press freedom	54.663	6.95	28.87	64.59
Presidential	.309	.462	0	1
Separation of powers	1.351	.896	0	2
elf	.463	.228	.003	1
De facto judicial independence	1.27	.802	0	2
Federal	.090	.287	0	1
Veto players	3.477	1.609	1	18

Table 5.3 reports the summary statistics for the dependent, independent, and control variables previously discussed.

Statistical Model

The dependent variable that we employ for testing hypothesis 2—*de facto judicial independence* (and *de facto judicial autonomy*) is an ordinal measure. Hence, we test this hypothesis by using an ordered probit model that is estimated with cluster-adjusted robust standard errors that account for within-country correlation and heteroskedasticity. We estimate the ordered probit model with random effects[25] and year dummies in the specification since the model is estimated for a TSCS dataset.[26] We also present the results obtained in the OP models that are estimated without random effects and year dummies.

Following the empirical exercise conducted in the previous chapter, we conduct robustness tests to evaluate the consistency of our results. First, we assess whether our key results hold when we change the main specification by incorporating additional control variables. Second, as done in chapter 3, we check whether our results remain robust after accounting for a potential selection bias problem that may occur from estimating the impact of an institutional variable like *particularism* on the de facto judicial autonomy. After all, it is plausible that factors that influence a *nonrandom* phenomenon such as the choice of electoral institutions that exhibit a higher (or lower) degree of particularism by political elites in developing democracies may also affect their incentives to respect the de facto independence of the judiciary. If we do not account for the nonrandom occurrence of the extent to which electoral systems are particularistic in democracies when testing the effect of *particularism* and the hazard rate of governments on de facto judicial independence, then the obtained results may suffer from selection bias.

Correcting for potential selection bias when estimating the effect of institutional factors like particularism on de facto judicial independence, is econometrically challenging. This is because the dependent variable of interest *de facto judicial independence* is ordinal, and, moreover, the measure of political *particularism* employed here (described earlier) is an ordinal index. Hence, we can neither use standard Heckman selection (or Heckit) model, nor the sample-selected ordered probit model described in chapter 3 to address the selection bias problem in this case. Instead, we use a bivariate ordered probit model to evaluate whether the results reported in the standard ordered probit model remain robust after correcting for selection bias. The bivariate ordered probit model (labeled as BVOP model), which has been used and analyzed by numerous economists,[27] consists of two stages.

The first stage of the bivariate ordered probit model (see equation 5.4) is the selection equation (estimated via ordered probit) in which the dependent variable $y_{i,1}$ is given by the ordinal index of *particularism* described earlier. This selection equation is formally defined (after dropping subscript t for time for notational convenience) as:

$$y_{i,1}^* = \beta_1' \mathbf{x}_{i,1} + \varepsilon_{i,1} \tag{5.4}$$

$$y_{i,1} = j \text{ if } \mu_{j-1} < y_{i,1}^* \leq \mu_j, \; j=0,...,J_1$$

In the selection equation (5.4), we explicitly account for the factors that influence the likelihood that developing democracies may be characterized by a higher level of *particularism*. To this end, we turn to some extant theoretical studies that have suggested a litany of factors that influence when democratic states are more (or less) likely to adopt electoral systems that are more particularistic (i.e., personalist) in nature.[28] Some of these studies suggest that countries with higher (lower) income[29] and democracies that use the closed-list PR electoral rule[30] are less likely to be characterized by more particularistic (i.e., personalistic) systems. Hence, we include *log GDP per capita* and a dummy variable for developing democracies that have a *closed-list PR* system[31] in the selection equation of the bivariate ordered probit model where *particularism* is the dependent variable.

Conversely, scholars suggest that the following electoral institutions generate higher levels of electoral particularism: developing democracies that use the single-transferable vote system (labeled as *stv*) and single-member district plurality systems with open ballots (denoted as *smd ballot*).[32] We thus control for the aforementioned variables in the selection equation as well. Some researchers hypothesize that developing democracies that have experienced a civil war are less likely to have personalisitic parties;[33] thus we include the lag of the *civil war* dummy in the selection equation, which is coded as 1 when countries in the sample suffer from a civil war, and is coded as 0 otherwise. Lastly, we add the lag of the particularism measure in the selection equation.

The second stage of the bivariate ordered probit model (see equation 5.5) is the outcome equation (also estimated via ordered probit) in which we estimate the effect of the *hazard rate × particularism*, the constitutive components of this interaction term, and the control variables listed earlier on the ordered dependent variable, *de facto judicial independence*. This second stage (ordered probit) outcome equation is defined (after dropping subscript *t* for time) is defined as:

$$y^*_{i,2} = \beta'_2 x_{i,2} + \varepsilon_{i,2} \tag{5.5}$$

$$y_{i,2} = j \text{ if } \delta_{j-1} < y^*_{i,2} \leq \delta_j, \ j = 0,...,J_2$$

where $y^*_{i,2}$ is the ordered dependent variable, *de facto judicial independence*. Note that the error term from the selection equation (5.4) (that is, $\varepsilon_{i,1}$) and the outcome equation ($\varepsilon_{i,2}$) are assumed to be bivariate normal distributed with correlation coefficient.[34] The log likelihood function of the bivariate ordered probit model and the procedure that we employ to estimate this statistical model are both described in the appendix. We estimate this statistical model with random effects and year dummies. The results from this estimator, however, do not alter substantively and significantly when the model is estimated without random effects and year dummies. The empirical estimates from the statistical tests are discussed in the following two sections.

Results

The illustration in fig. 5.2 plots the level of the ordinal *de facto judicial independence* for each country year in the sample over the range of values of the *particularism* and the *hazard rate* measure. This figure suggests broadly that the DFJI of the judiciary is relatively high for observations in which both the level of *particularism* and the *hazard rate* measure are high. It also indicates that de facto judicial independence increases when the hazard rate of governments and the degree of particularism increase (see quadrant I in fig. 5.2).Conversely, the figure also reveals that de facto judicial autonomy decreases in developing democracies characterized by low levels of electoral particularism (that is, party-centered democracies) even when the hazard rate of incumbents in these states increase. This provides preliminary support for hypothesis 2 and the corollary to this hypothesis. While useful, the illustration described above is insufficient for statistical inference. Thus we turn to discuss the results that we obtain from estimating the ordered probit model and the bivariate ordered probit model in our sample of developing country democracies.

Table 5.4, columns 1 and 2, report the results from testing the effect of *hazard rate × particularism* on *de facto judicial independence* in the standard ordered probit model. The ordered probit specification in column 1 is estimated without random effects, while the model in column 2 is estimated with random effects. The estimate of *hazard rate × particularism* is positive and highly significant at the 1 percent level in columns 1 and 2. The coefficient of each of the two individual components of the aforementioned interaction term—that is *particularism* and *hazard rate,* respectively—are each statistically insignificant in the two columns. Hence, it is indeed the interaction of the two variables mentioned earlier—rather than each variable individually—that has a positive and statistically significant effect on *de facto judicial independence*. This result is encouraging as it supports the second hypothesis in chapter 2.

We next turn to discuss two figures that are derived from the estimates

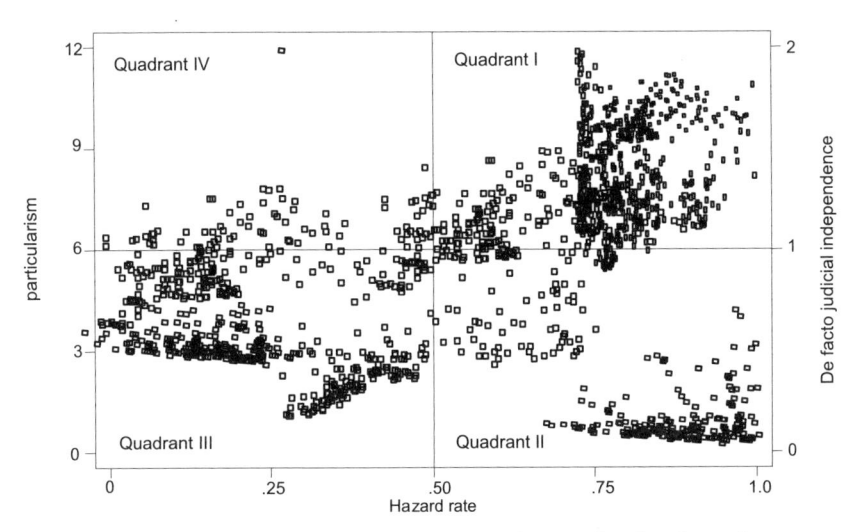

Fig. 5.2. Particularism, hazard rate, and de facto judicial independence. (Plot of *de facto judicial independence* over the range of *particularism* and *hazard rate* in developing country democracies. Each point represents one country-year for which both variables are observed.)

in column table 5.4, column 2, and the formula for computing the marginal effect of interaction terms in ordered probit models (described formally in the appendix of chapter 3). These figures illustrate the marginal effect and statistical significance of the *hazard rate* variable—for the entire range of values of the *particularism* index—on the probability that *de facto judicial independence* is equal to: (1) 1, which implies that the judiciary is "somewhat" (that is, partially) independent in de facto terms (see fig. 5.3); and (2) 2, which indicates that the courts are "generally" and thus fully independent in de facto terms (see fig. 5.4).

The solid sloping lines in these two figures indicate how the value of the estimated effect of the hazard rate measure changes across the full range of the relevant modifying variable, *particularism*. One can check whether these conditional coefficients are statistically significant by considering the 95 percent confidence intervals (dashed lines) that are drawn around them.[35] One can clearly see from these two figures that *hazard rate* has a statistically significant positive effect on the probability of each category of *de facto judicial independence* when *particularism* increases by one standard

TABLE 5.4. Main Results for *de facto judicial independence*

	Dependent Variable: *de facto judicial independence*		
	Ordered Probit Model		Outcome Equation of BVOP Model
	Column 1	Column 2	Column 3
log GDP per capita	.257***	.203**	.183**
	(.043)	(.040)	(.091)
Foreign aid	−.186	−.155	−.109
	(.164)	(.134)	(.097)
FDI flows	−.198	−.165	−.114
	(.178)	(.170)	(.298)
Trade openness	.030	.027	.060
	(.078)	(.087)	(.103)
Competition	.061***	.048**	.020**
	(.020)	(.024)	(.010)
Particularism	.081	.070	.054
	(.073)	(.067)	(.060)
Hazard rate × particularism	.375***	.362***	.284***
	(.038)	(.078)	(.064)
Hazard rate	.197	.189	.150
	(.186)	(.190)	(.140)
Presidential	−.036*	−.029**	−.018
	(.017)	(.015)	(.016)
Judiciary trust	−.094	−.086	−.077
	(.103)	(.090)	(.065)
Separation of powers	.179***	.152***	.088***
	(.061)	(.040)	(.027)
Electoral volatility	.040	.022	.019
	(.026)	(.018)	(.019)
de jure independence	.047*	.032*	.024
	(.025)	(.018)	(.098)
Press freedom	.044**	.031**	.024**
	(.017)	(.015)	(.010)
Legislative concentration	−.048	−.042	−.023
	(.080)	(.051)	(.033)
μ_1	.721***	.508***	.430***
	(.106)	(.102)	(.0118)
μ_2	.194**	.196**	.117**
	(.018)	(.015)	(.043)
ρ			.164**
			(.077)
Wald χ^2	482.25	397.19	254.23
N	1,494	1,494	1,425
Random effects	no	yes	yes
Time dummies	no	yes	yes
log likelihood	−823.2	−777.3	−842.1

Note: Each model is estimated with cluster-adjusted robust standard errors (in parentheses) that account for within-country correlation and heteroskedasticity.

***, **, and * denote significance at the 1%, 5%, and 10% level, respectively.

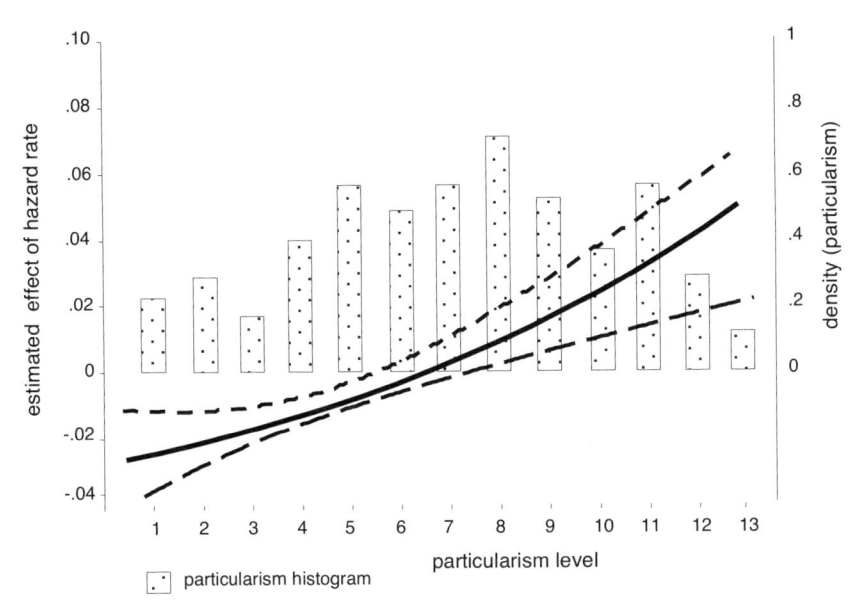

Fig. 5.3. Marginal effect of *hazard rate* × *particularism* on probability that *de facto judicial independence* = 1. (Dashed lines indicate 95% confidence intervals.)

deviation above its mean in the sample. This statistically corroborates the theoretical prediction in hypothesis 2. We also learn from these two figures that when *particularism* is low (that is, between 0 and 4 on 13-point ordinal *particularism* scale), the estimated causal effect of *hazard rate* on the probability of each of the two highest categories of the *de facto judicial independence* measure is negative. This supports the corollary to hypothesis 2, which posits that incumbents in party-centered democracies (where the level of electoral particularism is low) are more likely to curtail the de facto independence of the judiciary when their time horizons in office shrink.

We conduct an additional exercise to assess the substantive impact of the *hazard rate* × *particularism* more precisely. For this exercise, we report in table 5.5 the estimated effect of the hazard rate measure on the predicted probability of the two highest categories of *de facto judicial independence* when (1) its modifying variable *particularism* is increased by one standard deviation above the mean, and (2) other variables in the specification are held at their mean in the sample. Panel A in this table shows that when *hazard rate* shifts from a low value of 0.2 to a high of 0.7, increasing *particu-*

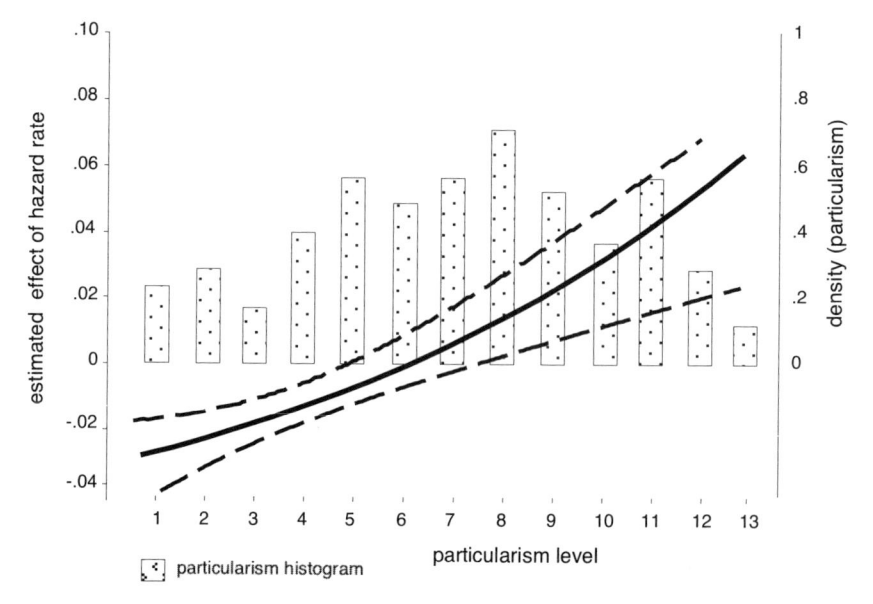

Fig. 5.4. Marginal effect of *hazard rate* × *particularism* on probability that *de facto judicial independence* = 2. (Dashed lines indicate 95% confidence intervals.)

larism by one standard deviation above its mean—while holding other variables at their mean—increases the probability with which governments enhance *partial* DFJI from 0.21 to 0.32, or, in other words, by 52 percent.

Likewise, panel B shows that when *hazard rate* shifts from 0.2 to 0.7, increasing *particularism* by one standard deviation above its mean—while holding other variables at their mean—increases the probability with which governments respect and enhance *full* DFJI from 0.28 to 0.40, or, equivalently, by almost 43 percent. The effects reported in panels A and B are not only substantial but also, as shown in the table, statistically significant at the 95 percent confidence level. Thus the results illustrated in the marginal effect figures and reported in table 5.5 provide strong statistical and substantive support for hypothesis 2.

What is the impact of the hazard rate of governments on DFJI in more party-centered developing democracies where the level of political particularism is low? To answer this question more comprehensively, we derived another figure from the estimated model in column 2. The illustration in this figure (see fig. 5.5) plots the predicted probability of the *de facto judicial independence* measure being equal to 2 (this implies complete de facto independence) over the entire range of the *hazard rate* measure for democracies in which the within-country *particularism* level lies between 1 and 5 in the 1–13 index and is therefore low. Observe that democracies where the within-country level of particularism lies between 1 and 5 strictly includes party-centered democracies. We find that the probability of the *de facto judicial independence* measure is low (less than 0.3) across the entire range of the *hazard rate* variable in fig. 5.5. This figure thus shows that governments in party-centered democracies curtail the de facto independence of the courts even when their hazard rate is high or equivalently their time horizons in office are low. As such, fig. 5.5 corroborates the corollary to the second hypothesis in chapter 2 and shows that short time horizons by themselves do not provide political agents incentives for increasing DFJI.

These substantive effects provide a broad picture of how the time horizons of politicians in office and the extent to which the system in which they operate is particularistic affects the de facto independence of courts in developing country democracies. Specific examples illustrate the distinct impact that different levels of particularism have on de facto judicial inde-

TABLE 5.5. Substantive Effect of Independent Variables on *de facto judicial independence*

	Effect of Shift in *Hazard Rate* from 0.3 to 0.7 when *particularism* Is At...	
	Mean	Plus 1 Std. Dev.
Predicted probability of *de facto judicial independence* being equal to 1	0.21 (0.10, 0.36)	0.32 (0.17, 0.50)
Difference in predicted probability		0.11 (0.01, 0.23)
Percentage change in predicted probability		52.3 (37.6, 68.2)
Predicted probability of *de facto judicial independence* being equal to 2	0.28 (0.19, 0.42)	0.40 (0.24, 0.53)
Difference in predicted probability		0.12 (0.04, 0.25)
Percentage change in predicted probability		42.8 (30.9, 53.7)

Note: Numbers in parentheses correspond to the lower and upper bounds, respectively, of the 95 percent confidence intervals of the estimated probabilities.

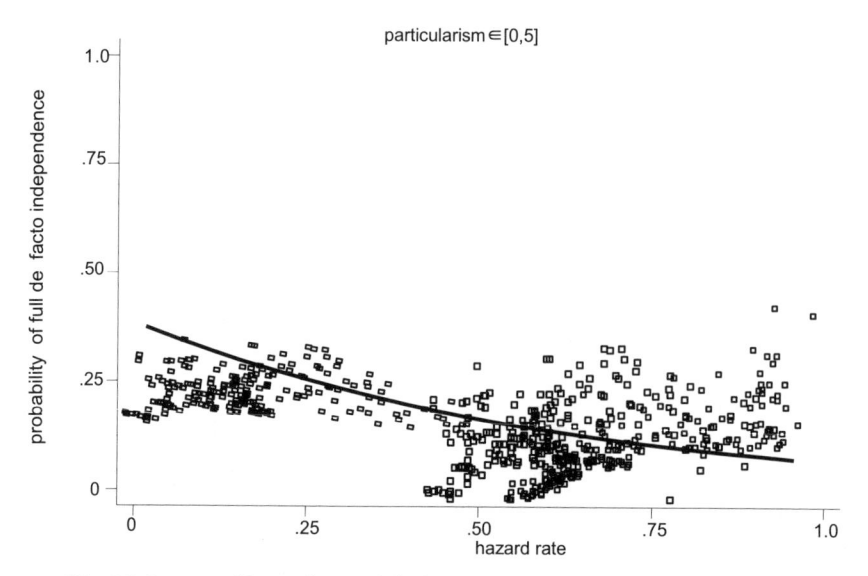

Fig. 5.5. Impact of *hazard rate* on de facto judicial independence for *particularism* ∈ [0,5]. (The figure illustrates the effect of hazard rate on the predicted probability of full de facto judicial independence [$y = 2$] for democratic country-years in which the level of *particularism* lies between 0 and 5.)

pendence in developing democracies given the hazard rate of governments in these states even more clearly. Consider these dynamics in two sets of developing democracies in our sample which are characterized by high hazard rates but different levels of electoral particularism. Brazil and India both have high levels of electoral particularism.[36] The mean of the hazard rate of governments in office in Brazil is .65; in India, it is .62, indicating that it is fairly high in these two countries. Hypothesis 2 therefore leads us to expect that increased hazard rates should lead to increases in DFJI. The data corroborates the hypothesis for these two cases. This is because the data reveals that when the hazard rate of incumbents increases from a low of 0.3 to a high of 0.75 in Brazil and India, incumbents are likely to increase DFJI by almost 55 percent in Brazil and 40 percent in India.

In contrast, Romania and Benin both exhibit low levels of electoral particularism.[37] The mean hazard rate of governments in office is higher than 0.5 in Benin and Romania, which suggests that it is quite high in these countries as well. The corollary to hypothesis 2 therefore suggests that we should expect to see DFJI suffer as the hazard rate increases in these countries. The data supports this corollary as it shows that when the hazard rate of incumbents increases from a low of 0.3 to a high of 0.75 in party-centered Benin and Romania, then incumbents are likely to reduce the de facto independence of the judiciary by 46 percent in Benin and 61 percent in Romania.

We now present the results from a key robustness test. Recall that the estimates in the standard ordered probit model reported in columns 1 and 2 do not account for the potential selection bias problem discussed earlier. Hence, in table 5.4, column 3, we report the effect that our main interaction term of interest has on *de facto judicial independence* in the outcome equation of the bivariate ordered probit (BVOP) model (estimated with random effects), which accounts for selection bias. The selection equation estimates of this model where the *particularism* is the dependent variable is reported in table 5.6, column A. We first briefly present the results from the selection equation and then discuss in detail the key estimates in the outcome equation.

TABLE 5.6. Selection Equation Results for Bivariate Ordered Probit (BVOP) Model

	Column A	Column B
	Dependent Variable: *particularism*	Dependent Variable: *particularism*
	Selection Equation for Outcome Equation in Column 3, Table 5.4	Selection Equation for Outcome Equation in Column 6, Table 5.7
log GDP per capita	−.033	−.034
	(.045)	(.047)
lag particularism	.109***	.111***
	(.030)	(.030)
Closed-list PR	−.043**	−.045**
	(.018)	(.020)
stv	.011**	.010**
	(.005)	(.005)
smd ballot	.020**	.022**
	(.010)	(.011)
Civil war	−.015	−.014
	(.082)	(.080)
Constant	−.615***	−.624***
	(.087)	(.091)
% correctly predicted	87.2%	87%
Prob > χ^2	0.000	0.000

***, **, * denote 1%, 5%, and 10% level of significance, respectively.

As indicated in table 5.6, column A, the specification for the selection equation performs well, correctly predicting approximately 87 percent of all observations in the sample. Not surprisingly, the lag of the *particularism* measure is positive and highly significant in the selection equation. The estimated coefficient of *log GDP per capita* and the *civil war* dummy are each statistically insignificant in column A. However, the estimate of the *closed-list PR* dummy has the predicted negative sign and is statistically significant, while *STV* and *SMD ballot* have the predicted positive sign and are each statistically significant as well. Moving away from the selection equation results, it is worth noting here that the estimate of *hazard rate × particularism* remains positive and significant at the 1 percent level in the outcome equation in table 5.4, columns 3 and 4, while the estimates of the two individual components of this interaction are insignificant. This indicates that statistical support for hypothesis 2 remains robust in the outcome equation of the BVOP model, which explicitly corrects for selection bias.

We next turn to report the estimates for some of the control variables that were described earlier. We find mixed empirical support for these control variables. The political controls *electoral volatility* and *judicial trust* are each statistically insignificant in all the specifications in table 5.4. The *presidential* dummy is negative and statistically significant in some but not all of the specifications. However, the competition measure is positive and significant at either the 5 or 10 percent level in all the specifications. The coefficient of *press freedom* is positive and statistically significant in the models. This indicates that greater media freedom induces governments in developing democracies to maintain and even increase DFJI, as suggested in some studies (e.g., Hayo and Voigt 2007; Chavez 2008). Similarly, the coefficient for *separation of powers* is positive and highly significant at the 1 percent level in all the specifications in table 5.3. This empirically supports the claim that separation of powers increases the prospects that democratic governments will respect the de facto independence of the judiciary (see Vanberg 2000; Whittington 2003; Friedman 2004). The estimate of the *de jure judicial independence* index is, however, statistically insignificant in each specification.

With respect to the economic controls, we find that the coefficient of both *FDI flows* and *foreign aid* is negative but statistically insignificant in the models. However, *log GDP per capita* is positive and consistently significant. The coefficient for *trade openness* is positive in the specifications; however, it is statistically insignificant in each specification. We check and discuss in the next section the robustness of the estimated results reported earlier.

Robustness Test Results

We conduct several robustness tests, which are similar to the robustness checks reported in chapter 3. First, we check whether the results reported above for hypothesis 2 remain robust when we use the 0–2 ordinal index of *de facto judicial autonomy,* which serves as the alternative measure of the dependent variable. Table 5.7, columns 5 and 6, report the results from the specification in which *de facto judicial autonomy* is the dependent variable. The specification in column 5 is estimated via a standard probit model, while the specification in column 6 constitutes the outcome equation of the BVOP model. The estimated coefficient of *particularism* × *hazard rate* has the predicted positive sign and is statistically significant at the 1 percent level in columns 5 and 6.

Second, we conducted some specification robustness tests by incorporating the following additional controls in the relevant models in table 5.5 where the dependent variable is *de facto judicial independence*: ethnolinguistic fractionalization (*elf*), *federal,* and *political instability.* We include *elf* since Hayo and Voigt (2007: 277) suggest that higher levels of ethnolinguistic fractionalization makes it harder for citizens to collectively pressure their respective governments to respect the de facto independence of the judiciary over time.[38] Some scholars claim that governments in democracies with a federal system are more likely to respect and adhere to higher levels of de facto judicial independence since they need an impartial mediator to settle disputes between different levels of government (Hayo and Voigt 2007; Herron and Randazzo 2003; Bednar 2001; Shapiro 1981). Therefore, we include the dummy variable *federal,* which is coded as 1 for countries with a federal system and is coded as 0 otherwise.

Since Hayo and Voigt (2003: 26) argue that greater political instability—measured by the number of violent demonstrations involving the use of physical forces—is correlated with higher levels of DFJI, we incorporate the *political instability* variable as well. Some researchers hypothesize that if courts are constitutionally granted with the power to conduct full and explicit judicial review in developing states, then governments in these countries may find it much harder to reduce the de facto independence of the courts.[39] To account for this, we control for the ordinal measure of *judicial review* that was described in chapter 3. We also include the lag of the dependent variable (lag de facto independence) in the specification. In chapter 3, we pointed out that developing states that have experienced more frequent transitions to democracy may be more likely to favor greater judicial autonomy. This could translate to greater de facto judicial independence as well. We therefore control for *democracy transition sum;* this variable was described in chapter 3. We also control for *authoritarian transition sum* since it is plausible that countries that have experienced more frequent transitions to authoritarian rule may be less likely to favor de facto independence of the judiciary. Lastly, the legal system inherited by developing states from their colonial past could also affect de facto judicial autonomy. We include two dummy variables—*British common law* and *French civil law* (the operationalization of these dummy variables is described in chapter 3)—to account for this possibility.[40]

Columns 7 (ordered probit specification) and 8 (outcome equation of the BVOP model) in table 5.7 report the results from the specification in which we include the additional control variables mentioned earlier and where the dependent variable is *de facto judicial independence*.[41] The estimates of *hazard rate × particularism* remain positive and highly significant in the augmented empirical specifications in these two columns. Hence, the results reported in the preceding section remain robust when we add more controls to the main specification. The additional controls in the specification are, however, consistently insignificant.

We added some more controls to the models. These controls include a dummy variable for *bicameralism*,[42] the *veto players* variable,[43] and the lag of the relevant dependent variable. Furthermore, similar to the spread of de jure judicial independence across developing states, scholars have also postulated a regional diffusion effect with respect to de facto judicial independence in that they claim that governments in developing democracies tend to emulate the level of DFJI adopted by neighboring nations.[44] We thus account for this particular dynamic in the specification where *de facto judicial independence* is the dependent variable by controlling for a variable that operationalizes the gap between the lag of the maximum level of *de facto judicial independence* in each region and the lag of each country's extent of

TABLE 5.7. Robustness Tests

	de facto judicial autonomy		de facto judicial independence	
	Ordered Probit	Outcome Equation of BVOP Model	Ordered Probit	Outcome Equation of BVOP Model
	column 5	column 6	column 7	column 8
lag de facto judicial independence			.201*** (.065)	.123** (.052)
log GDP per capita	.212** (.041)	.190** (.094)	.105* (.060)	.111 (.079)
Foreign aid	−.147 (.129)	−.112 (.101)	−.071 (.140)	−.033 (.109)
FDI flows	−.161 (.172)	−.109 (.290)	−.052 (.096)	−.038 (.054)
Trade openness	.028 (.080)	.073 (.118)	.010 (.031)	.037 (.039)
Competition	.050** (.026)	.021** (.010)	.025** (.012)	.017* (.010)
Particularism	.077 (.059)	.048 (.063)	.036 (.043)	.021 (.032)
Hazard rate × particularism	.345*** (.071)	.293*** (.057)	.205*** (.063)	.184** (.075)
Hazard rate	.127 (.145)	.148 (.163)	.093 (.212)	.147 (.180)
Presidential	−.032** (.014)	−.010 (.011)	−.011 (.010)	−.08 (.05)
Judiciary trust	−.090 (.111)	−.081 (.093)	−.040 (.065)	−.037 (.059)
Separation of powers	.162*** (.054)	.147*** (.033)	.087** (.042)	.051** (.024)
Electoral volatility	.043 (.025)	.026 (.017)	.010 (.079)	.018 (.046)
de jure independence	.045* (.024)	.030* (.017)	.037 (.023)	.022 (.055)
Press freedom	.040** (.019)	.032** (.014)	.029** (.015)	.020* (.012)
Legislative concentration	−.037 (.089)	−.031 (.054)	−.017 (.085)	−.011 (.032)
Judicial review			.042 (.065)	.033 (.112)
elf			.012 (.053)	.014 (.072)
British legal origin			.054 (.062)	.019 (.040)

(continues)

TABLE 5.7.—Continued

	de facto judicial autonomy		de facto judicial independence	
	Ordered Probit	Outcome Equation of BVOP Model	Ordered Probit	Outcome Equation of BVOP Model
	column 5	column 6	column 7	column 8
French legal origin			.083	.046
			(.121)	(.059)
Democracy transition sum			.036**	.030*
			(.017)	(.018)
Authoritarian transition sum			−.051*	−.066
			(.028)	(.102)
Political instability			.012	.006
			(.049)	(.030)
Federal			.040	.032
			(.038)	(.025)
μ_1	.635***	.477***	.403***	.390***
	(.134)	(.155)	(.126)	(.067)
μ_2	.171**	.147**	.084**	.092**
	(.029)	(.020)	(.041)	(.045)
ρ		−.030**		−.020**
		(.015)		(.010)
Wald χ^2	414.2	393.5	399.01	328.31
N	1,392	1,371	916	916
Random effects	yes	yes	yes	yes
Time dummies	yes	yes	yes	yes
log likelihood	−829.1	−916.3	−1,286.1	−1,140.2

Note: Each model is estimated with cluster-adjusted robust standard errors (reported in the parentheses) that account for within-country correlation and heteroskedasticity.
***, ** and * denote significance at the 1%, 5%, and 10% level, respectively.

de facto judicial independence; this variable is labeled as *judicial independence emulation*. To save space, we do not report the results obtained after including these additional controls. However, our main results were unchanged even after adding the several new controls listed earlier.

We conducted two additional diagnostic tests to check the econometric validity of our results. First, we implemented Hurlin and Venet's (2003) granger causality test for panel data to assess whether there exists a potentially endogenous relationship between the main dependent variable of interest—*de facto judicial independence*—and each of the two independent variables: *particularism* and *hazard rate*. F-statistics from the Hurlin and Venet (2003) tests conducted in our sample of developing democracies indicates that there is no endogeneity problem between *de facto judicial independence* and each of the two independent variables: *particularism* and the *hazard rate* measure.

Additionally, the effect of the contemporaneous and the lag of *de facto judicial independence* on *hazard rate* is statistically insignificant in Prais-Winsten models estimated with panel-corrected standard errors and fixed effects. Likewise, the effect of the contemporaneous and the lag of *de facto judicial independence* on *political particularism* is statistically insignificant in ordered probit models estimated with or without random effects. This further indicates that the dependent variable that we employ—*de facto judicial independence*—is not endogenous to the independent variables. The second set of diagnostic tests reveal that none of the empirical models discussed earlier suffer from severe multicollinearity, serial correlation, or omitted variable bias, and that the residuals are normally distributed.[45]

Conclusion

In chapter 2, we argued that variation in DFJI across developing country democracies could be explained by the manner in which the electoral system moderates the effect of the time horizons (hazard rate) of governments in these states on their incentive to support the de facto autonomy of the judiciary. The central prediction that emerged from our theoretical claims is that in the context of high hazard rates in office, incumbents in more particularistic electoral systems will be more likely to increase de facto independence of the judiciary. Conversely, when faced with high hazard rates in office, incumbents in party-centered systems will curb de facto judicial independence. In this chapter, we employed a comprehensive TSCS data of 103 developing countries that are observed as democracies anytime during the 1985 to 2004 time period order to statistically assess these claims.

The statistical results in this chapter corroborate our claims and remain robust when we control for alternative explanations, employ different estimation techniques, and use different measures of de facto judicial independence. These empirical results have two main substantive implications. First, scholars have long recognized that "judicial independence cannot be taken for granted . . . [as] . . . maintaining a system of effective judicial checks and balances depends on the right external circumstances" (Vanberg 2008: 116). Researchers have made substantial progress in terms of analyzing how the strategic calculations of politicians affect their decision to maintain or curb the de facto independence of the judiciary (e.g., Vanberg 2005, 2008; Finkel 2008; Hirschl 2004; Ginsburg 2003; Whittington 2003; Stephenson 2003).

Building on this research, we focus more strongly with respect to understanding and evaluating statistically how a key factor that shapes the strategic political environment politicians operate in—the degree of electoral particularism—influences their decision to constrain or enhance the de facto political independence of the courts. Therefore, the results presented in this chapter are among the first to provide systematic statistical evidence on how the institutional context of electoral particularism affects political decisions to respect (or curtail) the de facto independence of the judiciary in developing democracies. As such, the analysis of the large-n quantitative results presented here may provide a basic foundation for researchers to further explore how electoral systems affect the interaction between incumbents and the courts in both developed and developing democracies.

Second, numerous scholars have suggested either explicitly or implicitly that the time horizons of governments in office determines whether or not they will maintain the de facto political autonomy of the courts (Ramseyer 1994; Stephenson 2003; Whittington 2003; Ginsburg 2003). Following extant research, we also believe that the time horizons of governments, given by their hazard rate in office, affects their political incentives and their decision to maintain or curb judicial autonomy. We refine the analysis of its effects by developing a more detailed measure of time horizons, which has the virtues of being a more conceptually accurate measure of strategic ex ante time horizon—that is, the hazard rate—of each government in office, and one that varies across space and time. The hazard rate measure that we employed for our tests is therefore likely to be useful for scholars of judicial politics who may directly evaluate the effect of the time horizons of incumbents on judicial autonomy in large-n data sets.

The statistical analysis presented earlier evaluates the empirical generalizability of our theoretical claims. However, they do not reveal the causal logic that drives governments in more particularistic systems to enhance de facto judicial independence when their time horizons in office shrink but leaders in more party-centered democracies to curtail DFJI when their hazard rate in office is high. Thus, in chapters 6 and 7 we analyze the politics of DFJI in three prominent developing country democracies—Brazil, India, and Indonesia—to illustrate the causal logic of these arguments. In chapter 6, we use the analyses of Brazil and India to illustrate the causal arguments that lead to the prediction that in the context of high hazard rates in office, governments in more particularistic systems will enhance DFJI. In chapter 7, we examine the Indonesia case in substantial depth as this case helps us to examine why incumbents in party-centered (less particularistic) democracies will rationally choose to curb the de facto independence of the judiciary when faced with low time horizons in office.

CHAPTER 6

De Facto Judicial Independence in Particularistic Systems

Brazil and India

We emphasized earlier in this book that the challenge of judicial independence in developing countries' democracies does not merely end with attempts to constitutionally empower the judiciary. Rather, maintaining the de facto autonomy of the courts poses an important strategic challenge for leaders in these countries. In chapter 1, we analyzed some data that revealed that incumbents in some democratic developing countries, but not others, curtail the de facto independence of the judiciary when their ex ante likelihood of political survival, and thus their time horizons in office, is low. In the latter half of chapter 2, we developed a theory to explain this variation. The central prediction from this theory is that in the context of high hazard rates in office, incumbents in highly personalist (that is, particularistic) systems will increase the de facto autonomy of the courts. The corollary to this prediction posits that when faced with high hazard rates in office, governments in party-centered developing democracies—which, by construction, are characterized by low levels of particularism—will curtail de facto judicial independence. These claims were subjected to rigorous large-n empirical tests in chapter 5.

In this chapter and the next, we move away from the large-n econometric tests on de facto judicial independence undertaken in chapter 5 to directly examine supporting evidence for the causal arguments that led to hypothesis 2 and its corollary. We do so in this chapter by analyzing in detail the politics of de facto judicial independence in two developing countries' democracies characterized by high levels of particularism—Brazil and India. According to hypothesis 2, we should expect to find that political elites in Brazil and India enhance de facto judicial independence when they are faced with high hazard rates or equivalently low time horizons in office. Chapter 7 offers a parallel account of the politics of de facto judicial autonomy in a developing countries' democracy that exhibits a low level of particularism and a high hazard rate—Indonesia. The Indonesia case is employed here to illustrate the causal arguments that produce the corollary to hypothesis 2, which posits that governments in party-centered democracies will reduce the judiciary's de facto autonomy when their hazard rates in office are high. As discussed later, these three cases allow us to effectively implement the most similar case-selection design for our comparative analysis and illustrate the explanatory power of our theoretical framework in explaining the politics of de facto judicial autonomy in developing democracies.

This chapter is organized as follows. We begin with a brief discussion of the methodological criteria that determines the choice of Brazil, India, and Indonesia for our case-study analysis of de facto judicial independence across developing democracies. In the rest of the chapter, we present our analysis of the Brazil and India cases. For each country, we first analyze how electoral rules produce a candidate-centered system in their respective polities, and discuss the observed hazard rates of governments in office. We then analyze the manner in which the context of a candidate-centered system affects how the hazard rates of governments in each country influence the behavior of the ruling and opposition parties when interacting with the judiciary. We use multiple types of evidence from political and policy events, descriptive analysis of within-country data on constitutional amendments and statutory bills, as well as interviews with judicial and political actors in these countries to conduct our analysis. Our study indicates that the candidate-centered nature of Brazil and India's electoral system drives governments in these two countries to maintain and promote the judiciary's de facto autonomy in the context of high hazard rates of incumbents in office in these states. We conclude by discussing the implications of these findings.

Case Selection: Comparing Brazil, India, and Indonesia

For the methodological reasons we discuss here, the comparative analysis of Brazil, India, and Indonesia allows us to illustrate the causal mechanisms underlying the theoretical predictions regarding de facto judicial independence in chapter 2. The decision to employ the Brazil, India, and Indonesian cases for our case-study analysis of de facto judicial autonomy is determined by three main case-selection criteria suggested in Mill's (1834) "most-similar" design. Recall from chapter 4, to fit this research design the selected cases must be representative of their underlying theoretical categories within a well-defined universe of cases, must offer the clearest contrast on the key independent variable of interest, and must match closely on other features and factors, which are irrelevant to the theoretical mechanism we want to test. In our study of de facto judicial independence, this key independent variable is whether each selected case is a party or candidate-centered democracy.

With respect to our hypothesis on de facto judicial independence (hypothesis 2) and the corollary to this hypothesis, our universe of cases consists of developing countries observed as democracies which, in turn, can be divided into two theoretically relevant categories—developing countries' democracies that are candidate-centered (hence, characterized by high levels of particularism), and those that are party-centered (characterized by low particularism). Brazil has used the open-list PR rule to elect legislators, while India employs the single-member district (SMD) plurality rule. As suggested by studies on party-systems, both the open-list PR system and the SMD plurality rule (where party leaders do not control ballots or rank) produce candidate-centered systems which, by definition, are characterized by a high level of political particularism.[1] Hence, by virtue of the electoral rule that they employ, Brazil and India are representative of candidate-centered democracies that exhibit high levels of particularism. In contrast, after making a transition to democracy, Indonesia employed the closed-list PR rule to elect legislators.[2] Because the closed-list PR rule generates a party-centered democracy, Indonesia is representative of developing democracies that are party-centered and which, therefore, exhibit low levels of particularism. Thus, the three developing democracies that we use for analysis are representative of the two theoretically relevant categories in our universe of cases.

Second, Brazil, India, and Indonesia are useful cases to compare since they share many common features that are not critical to the underlying causal mechanism. All three developing countries are federal democracies with multiparty systems, all three were colonized, are geographically large, and have ethnically diverse populations.[3] Furthermore, the size of the Brazilian and Indian economy is largely similar in nominal terms,[4] and all three countries are, according to the World Bank, large emerging markets in the G20 group that have each experienced high growth rates in recent years (International Monetary Fund 2008; World Bank 2008). Importantly, in terms of our case-selection strategy, the moving average of the hazard rate (i.e., time horizons) of governments in office across these three developing democracies is remarkably similar.

Our data, in fact, reveals that the mean hazard rate of the governments in office is 0.61 in Indonesia between 1999 and 2004 (the years in which Indonesia is strictly observed as a party-centered democracy), 0.65 in Brazil from 1986 to 2004,[5] and .62 in India between 1984 and 2004.[6] Homogeneity on this dimension is critical to the suitability of these cases since our theory argues that high hazard rates of incumbents by themselves are not the causal mechanism driving political behavior. Rather, it is the incentive structure created by whether their electoral system is party or candidate-centered that causes incumbents to behave in different ways when dealing with the judiciary in the context of their hazard rate in office. Hence, the hazard rates must be similar across our cases to provide a suitable test of the electoral mechanism.

Third, as previously discussed, the selected cases offer the clearest contrast on the key independent variable of interest in our study of de facto judicial independence: the party or candidate-centered nature of the electoral system. To understand how the personalist nature of (or lack thereof) electoral systems affect political incentives to give judiciaries de facto independence, we need cases where we can compare the behaviors of political elites under different electoral systems, but similar hazard rates of office. Since the hazard rates of governments across these three countries are similar, and Indonesia is a party-centered democracy that exhibits low levels of particularism whereas Brazil and India are candidate-centered democracies that exhibit high levels of particularism, Brazil, India, and Indonesia satisfy this criterion well.

The aforementioned case selection therefore fits the most similar research design well and should allow us to assess our causal claims about variation in de facto judicial independence across developing country democracies. Specifically, given the causal arguments that generate the prediction in hypothesis 2 and its corollary, we anticipate while incumbents in Brazil and India will enhance de facto independence when faced with short time horizons (high hazard rates) in office, incumbents in Indonesia will act to curtail de facto judicial autonomy under similar time horizons. In the remainder of this chapter, we examine various types of evidence from Brazil and India to illustrate the causal mechanism that leads to the outcome of high DFJI in both these countries.

Brazil: Candidate-Centered System and the Hazard Rate of Incumbents

As described in chapter 4, Brazil made a formal transition to democracy in 1986 (Stepan 1989; Skidmore 1998; Power 2000). After the transition to a full-fledged democracy, Brazil adopted an open-list proportional representation system to elect deputies to the lower house of the national legislature (Carey and Shugart 1995; Samuels 1999; Norris 2002). As discussed in detail in chapter 2, extant research on electoral systems suggests that since open-list PR electoral system leads voters to vote directly for candidates, party members operating under this system have incentives to engage in actions that cultivate their personal reputations rather than their party's. As a result, open-list PR systems create weak political parties where party leaders (1) do not have control over the ballot, and (2) have little or no leverage in managing the political behavior of their rank-and-file party members.[7]

The level of political particularism in Brazil—as operationalized in the Carey and Shugart and Wallack et al. ordinal scale of particularism—is fairly high, and is thus classified as a candidate-centered system.[8] Therefore, we would expect Brazilian parties to be weak with party leadership able to exert little control over their rank-and-file members. Scholars have indeed found that Brazil suffers from both of these consequences (Lamounier 1986; Geddes and Neto 1992; Samuels 1996, 2004; Mainwaring 1999; Weyland 2006; Ames, Baker and Renno 2008).[9] For instance, Mainwaring (1999: 23) concludes the following.

> The Brazilian electoral system offers a number of incentives to antiparty behavior on the part of individual representatives. Foremost among these incentives is a peculiar system of proportional representation, which gives the electorate exceptional choice in choosing individual candidates and weakens party control over candidates.

The result, he notes, is that

They (parties) exercise weak control over individual politicians; they are not highly disciplined; they play a secondary role in most political campaigns; they have comparatively little control over who becomes a member, what politicians do, and who gets elected." (Mainwaring 1999: 173)

Ames and Power similarly observe that, "regardless of the regime of the day, political parties have generally not been strong, autonomous actors in the Brazilian polity" (2007: 184), and go on to identify the open-list PR electoral system as "the single most powerful explanatory factor in accounting for the unique weakness of Brazilian parties" (2007: 191).

These incentives are reflected in various facets of party member and voter behaviors. For example, candidates for elected office in Brazil rarely rely on using party-oriented campaign tactics (Mainwaring 1999; Samuels 2001; Hagopian 2009) and court voters, as well as donors on their own account (Mainwaring 1999; Samuels 2001; Ames and Power 2007). Popular candidates who command their own loyal vote banks are therefore worth much more to parties than parties are to them. Voters do not identify strongly with political parties (Mainwaring 1999; Samuels 2006; Nicolau 2007), and routinely cast their votes based on the personal characteristics of candidates rather than that of their parties (ESEB 2002; Kinzo and Carreirão 2004).[10] As a result of the political dynamics previously described, party members in Brazil attribute their electoral success to their personal efforts and thus do not feel obliged to support the political or policy agenda of their party leaderships when in office (Mainwaring 1999; Power 2000; Ames and Power 2007).

Faced with such politically independent legislators interested primarily in building their own reputations through their legislative actions, parties are unable to utilize their tenure in office to enact their own agendas. We assess below how this inability of party leaders to discipline their party members helps to promote the de facto independence of the judicial system in a candidate-centered democracy such as Brazil's when government time horizons in office shrink.

The second political feature of Brazilian politics key to our theoretical argument is that Brazilian governments have consistently had short (high) time-horizons (hazard rates) in office. This is illustrated by the hazard rate of successive governments in Brazil from 1986 to 2004 in fig. 6.1, which is derived from calculating the predicted probability of failure of these gov-

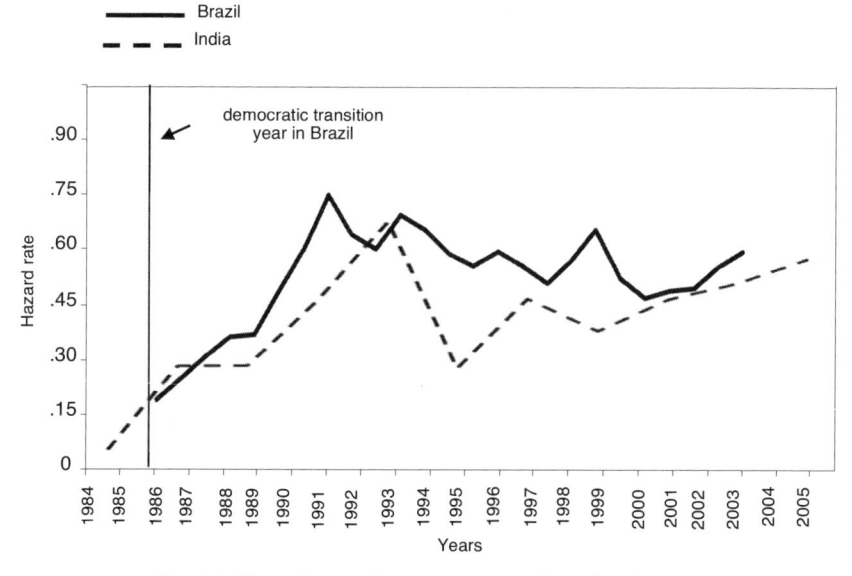

Fig. 6.1. Hazard rate of governments in Brazil and India

ernments.[11] We learn from fig. 6.1 that the moving average of the hazard rate of governments in Brazil between 1986 and 2004 is 0.65, which is almost as high as Indonesia's. The effect of specific political developments on time horizons can be seen clearly in this figure. For instance, the figure indicates a sharp increase in the hazard rate of the (1) Sarney administration from 1989 to late 1990, and (2) Cardoso government from late 2001 to early 2002. This is not surprising given that the Sarney and the Cardoso administrations had become deeply unpopular in the electorate in their penultimate year—(i.e., 1990 in the case of the Sarney administration, and 2002 for the Cardoso government)—in office. The figure also shows that the hazard rate of the executive in Brazil increased quite dramatically in 1992. This occurred because the incumbent at the time, President Ferdinand Collor, was embroiled in a serious financial scandal that eventually led to his impeachment from office (Keck 2002; Fernando 2007).

The high hazard rate of Brazilian governments partly results from the fact that Brazil has been consistently governed by shaky and unstable coalition governments, particularly from 1990 onwards (Pereira et al. 2008; Samuels 2000). These governing coalitions have been in a constant state of flux—changing in composition and size almost every year, which has engendered instability within these multiparty ruling coalitions (Kingstone 1999; Santos and Vilarouca 2008; Simmons 2008). Furthermore, the effective number of legislative parties in Brazil increased considerably from 1.9 in 1986 to 6.2 in 2004.[12] Consequently, the number of potential targets for coalition building by both ruling and opposition parties has gone up dramatically. This has not only created more room for "opportunism" for coalition partners in successive governments in Brazil but has also increased the likelihood of "party-switching" and defection by party members from the ruling coalition to the opposition (Machado 2006). Despite the presence of a presidential system, these dynamics have posed constant threats to the executive and his party's governments. Greater room for opportunism has therefore served to further increase the instability of multiparty coalitions, and thus the likelihood of government dissolution in Brazil. This, in turn, has contributed to the relatively high hazard rate of Brazilian governments.

In chapter 2, we hypothesized that incumbents in candidate-centered democracies (which, by construction, are characterized by a high degree of particularism) are more likely to respect and increase the de facto judicial independence when the hazard rate of governments in office in these systems become high. Is this prediction, as well as the causal logic underlying this prediction, valid for Brazil, given that (1) it is candidate-centered, and (2) the hazard rate (time horizons) of successive governments in the country has been high after the country emerged as a full-fledged consolidated democracy? We turn to address this question in the next section.

The Politics of De Facto Judicial Independence in Brazil

We proposed the following causal argument in chapter 2 to explain why governments in candidate-centered developing democracies such as Brazil's are more likely to maintain and increase de facto judicial independence in the context of high hazard rates or equivalently low time horizons in office. To start with, we suggested that due to the highly particularistic electoral system, party leaders in the government would be unable to influence the preferences and voting behavior of members on the legislative floor regarding judicial independence. As a result of this lack of political and legislative capacity, when faced with instability and shrinking time horizons, these governments would be unable to restrict the judiciary's autonomy to prevent courts from challenging the executive or prevent the opposition from using the courts for their own political ends. In the context of this electoral system, the judiciary will therefore be in a strong position to credibly challenge political parties—especially the ruling party—when its time horizons start falling.

Given these constraints, we argue that the ruling coalition will, much like the opposition parties, have tactical reasons to invest in and rely on the use of an independent judiciary. It will strategically seek to obtain the judiciary's support for its policies to (1) neutralize the judiciary's challenge, (3) preempt the opposition from successfully coalescing with or using the judiciary for their political ends, and (3) to bolster the credibility of its own tactics in the eyes of the electorate. Thus, it has strong incentives to maintain and enhance the de facto independence of the judiciary. In the following two subsections, we demonstrate these causal dynamics at work in Brazil by first presenting a detailed analysis of the events of the 2001 energy crisis, and then moving beyond this specific example by presenting broader evidence showing that incumbents in Brazil typically solicit the courts' support by enhancing their de facto autonomy rather than choosing to restrain judicial independence whenever their time horizons in office shrink.

The Role of the Judiciary in the 2001 Energy Crisis

The 2001 energy crisis in Brazil was a severe, high-profile public crisis, whose potential for impact on the political fortunes of ruling and opposition parties became clear to all these players early in the crisis. As such, it motivated considerable political strategizing by all parties. Thus, it provides an excellent example to study the interactions that typically emerge between ruling and opposition political parties and the courts during political battles and their consequences for de facto judicial independence. We first briefly discuss the nature of the crisis and then provide a detailed discussion of the political context (i.e., the high hazard rate of the Cardoso government) in which the interaction between the three aforementioned actors took place. Finally, we discuss how the judiciary strengthened its independence from the political establishment as a consequence of the political battles related to this crisis.

In early April 2001, after four consecutive years of poor rainfall and quasi-rationing, it was clear that Brazil would face a massive shortfall in electrical power over the coming months.[13] At this time, Cardoso was serving his second term as president at the head of a shaky coalition. In order to articulate and manage a policy for the crisis, he constituted a high-level body—the Chamber for the Administration of the Energy Crisis (CGE)—and in a move signifying its political importance, appointed his chief civilian advisor, Pedro Parente, as its head (Taylor 2008). The government and the CGE soon formulated and announced *Energia Brasil*—a program that would employ a mix of compulsory rationing, increased price tariffs, penalties for excessive use, bonuses for frugal consumers, and blackouts to try to reduce consumption by 20 percent. When the program was implemented on June 1, 2001, Cardoso went on television in what would be the first of a series of speeches to justify and defend the government's plan (*BBC News*, June 5, 2001). Over the next few months, the program would evolve into a significant political and policy battle between the government and the opposition.

At the time of the crisis, Cardoso and his coalition government were struggling to survive politically. While Cardoso's presidential term was assured, his ability to legislate and to enact his party's policy agenda were under severe threat. Cardoso's government had started with six parties, but by April 2001 this had fallen to only four parties—the center-left *Partido da Social Democracia Brasileira* (PSDB), headed by Cardoso; the centrist *Partido do Movimento Democrático Brasileiro* (PMDB); the center-right *Partido da Frente Liberal* (PFL); and the *Partido Progressita Brasileiro* (PPB)[14] (Santos and Vilaroucas 2008: 68). Steady desertions by parties from the ruling coalition had weakened the government and the high level of intense infighting among the remaining parties promised more desertions (Santos and Vilaroucas 2008).

By May, various scandals had forced the resignations of senior coalition party leaders such as Antonio Carlos Magalhaes of the PFL amid acrimonious circumstances, and the PFL began to publicly voice its threats to withdraw from the coalition. The continued support of the PFL was especially critical since it had enough congressional seats to block any government proposal in Congress and held several critical cabinet posts as well. This fragility was intensified by disagreements between the PFL and the PMDB, the other major ally in the ruling coalition (*BBC News*, May 3, 2001). Ideological disagreements between the three parties, political positioning for the upcoming 2002 presidential elections, and jockeying among the various party leaders for key institutional positions such as the Senate presidency had all combined to create a situation where the legislative strength and the stability of the government were fairly unpredictable at any moment in time. These coalition dynamics also damaged the ruling party's image, and Cardoso's personal approval ratings took a nosedive as well (Goertzel 2003: 4; Taylor 2008: 68). The government was therefore fragile, and faced a high hazard rate in office at this time.

A critical input into the political strategies adopted by the governing and opposition parties was the role the courts would play in the unfolding tussle. Various judges at local and regional courts, and the STF had publicly voiced their views on the government's role in creating this crisis and on rationing as a solution to it (Taylor 2008: 66). While some judges favored the government's position, others were against it. The courts therefore seemed to provide potential allies for both the government and the opposition. Even before June 1, the official date of implementation, the legal battle was begun by both the government and the opposition.

The government had two strategic options regarding the judiciary in this political battle. Option one—at the cost of alienating the judges, it could choose to curb the judiciary by reducing its powers through legislative or executive actions. This would guarantee that legal decisions on rationing went in its favor. Or, option two—it could choose to turn the judiciary into friendly allies, or at least prevent them from allying with the opposition by not antagonizing them via adoption of policies that restrict the courts' (including the Supreme Court's) autonomy. Although President Cardoso could potentially implement option one, this option required the ruling coalition to successfully muster the votes necessary to pass legislation curbing judicial powers through Congress. As discussed earlier, at this time, the government was too politically fragmented and weak to mount any such legislative effort successfully. This left them with the option of using a presidential decree to bypass Congress in order to restrict judicial powers. However, in 1990, as Collor's finance minister, Cardoso had directly witnessed the high political cost Collor had paid for taking executive actions against the courts in his fight to contain inflation.[15] He therefore did not want to risk a similar political debacle by using executive decrees to curb the court's abilities to act against the government's policies.

It is important to note here, however, that it was not merely the lessons learnt from Collor's failed attempt to control the judiciary that discouraged President Cardoso from implementing executive decrees against the courts' autonomy. Rather, the opposition parties' political tactic of soliciting the judiciary's support for their stand against the government's proposed rationing policy also played a critical role in influencing the Cardoso government to avoid adopting executive decrees against the judiciary.

Recall that the Cardoso administration's decision to adopt a rationing policy during the energy crisis came at a time of high and rising hazard rates for Cardoso's government.[16] The opposition parties led by the *Partido dos Trabalhadores* (the PT, led by Lula) therefore realized that the government's proposed rationing policy was weakening Cardoso's grip on office, and saw the crisis as a window of opportunity to politically challenge the Cardoso government and position themselves for the upcoming 2002 election. As suggested by our theoretical arguments, they chose to make legal challenges one of the mainstays of their strategy for accomplishing both these goals. They did so by publicly endorsing the judiciary's credibility and centrality in resolving this policy dispute, and then using courts to challenge the government's policy.

The PT, the *Partido Comunista do Brasil* (the PCdoB), and the *Partido Democrático Trabalhista* (the PDT), proceeded to file two cases challenging the constitutionality of the rationing policy (Taylor 2008: 67). It also collaborated with unions, firms, and consumer groups to file injunctions challenging specific provisions of its implementation. These legal challenges were then used by opposition leaders during antigovernment demonstrations and public rallies to signal their position on rationing to their supporters. This strategy of making the status of the rationing policy legally precarious bought the opposition two important political advantages—it sabotaged the long-term success of rationing by undermining its immediate implementation, and it created serious political rifts among an already weak alliance since many coalition allies were unwilling to implement or be associated with a potentially unconstitutional policy (Monken 2001).[17] Given the high hazard rate the Cardoso government already faced, this was a serious threat to its political survival in office.

In response to these opposition tactics, the Cardoso government chose not to restrict any of the judiciary's powers in order to prevent them from passing antigovernment judgments on rationing that Cardoso would be forced to implement. Instead, it adopted a three-pronged approach to deal with the challenges on implementation and the constitutionality of the rationing policy. First, as predicted by our theoretical story, the Cardoso government preemptively initiated its own legal strategy, which involved lobbying judges for their support for the rationing policy. While the policy was still in its planning stages, the government began its "judicial charm offensive" by sending its chief advisor, Pedro Parante, to present its case personally to the Federal Supreme Court judges on May 24 (Taylor 2008: 67). It also solicited a diverse range of legal opinions and modified important aspects of the initial draft in response to legal concerns. For example, when public prosecutors and a federal judge criticized a proposal to restrict consumers' ability to use the Consumer's Defense Code to challenge the rationing policy as going too far, the government dropped this provision from their subsequent draft (Taylor 2008: 68). Second, in order to deal with the injunctions, the government mobilized hundreds of public lawyers to fight the cases in the lower courts—again, respecting the legal route rather than trying to curb the ability of lower courts to act on government policy.

Third, in response to the opposition's constitutional challenges, on June 11, 2001, the Cardoso government requested that the court rule on the constitutionality of the rationing policy by filing a Declaration of Constitutionality (denoted as ADC) case in the Supreme Court. The ADC effectively ensured that the judiciary would be the final arbiter on the rationing policy issue since if the courts found even a single provision of the policy to be unconstitutional, then it could rule against the entire policy. Given the legal differences of opinion in the judiciary as evidenced by the many injunctions that had been granted against rationing, and the ideological divisions as evidenced by the public statements by a few individual judges, it was by no means certain ex ante that the judiciary would rule in the government's favor. Notwithstanding this ex ante uncertainty, however, the Cardoso government in Brazil's candidate-centered democracy still chose to file the ADC. This action therefore enhanced the courts' role in resolving this dispute and raised its status as it made the court the final arbiter over the rationing policy issue. Thus, as suggested by our theory, instead of curbing the court's powers, the government invested in and relied on the court's power and its potential to exercise this power impartially at a time when the Cardoso government's hazard rate in office was high.

This strategy was a winning rational strategy for the government because it offered four key advantages. First, by making the courts the final arbiter of an urgent and politically critical decision, the government demonstrated its good faith regarding the judiciary to the judges. This ensured that the courts did not feel threatened, and hence, had no motive to ally with the opposition. They could therefore stay impartial in their outlook to the government's legal appeal. Second, it reduced the credibility of the opposition parties' declaration of the rationing policy as unconstitutional, and also weakened the legitimacy of their (the opposition's) tactic of using the judiciary for their political goals. Third, if the Supreme Court did rule in the government's favor, then the government would be able to settle all challenges to the policy in one stroke since the ruling would set a binding precedent for lower courts (Sato 2003; Zimmerman 2008). Fourth, it would reassure government allies and ensure that they wholeheartedly implemented the policy and publicly gave it their full political backing.

Furthermore, given the credibility the courts enjoyed, such a decision would be considered legitimate by ordinary Brazilians and would increase citizen compliance with rationing, therein boosting the effectiveness of the rationing policy. Finally, whether or not the decision favored the government, the government's use of institutional means to resolve an important policy dispute rather than to undermine the institution itself would buy it public support as a guardian of Brazil's democratic institutions and practices. The Cardoso government's political strategy of turning to the judiciary for support on the rationing policy issue paid off since in June 2001, the Supreme Court ruled 8–2 in the government's favor. The injunctions that had been granted were all squashed, and further challenges disallowed. The rationing policy was finally implemented in its entirety across the country. And in February 2002 it was concluded amidst considerable success.

It is worth noting here that throughout this political battle, the judiciary as an institution benefitted tremendously through its position as the only impartial and nonpartisan arbiter of a grim political dispute between ruling and opposition parties. By ruling in line with impartial legal criteria rather than short-term interests, it proved its political value to both the government and the opposition. It also signaled clearly to both sides that it could not be taken for granted on ideological or policy grounds. Hence, it created an incentive for all sides to ensure that the judiciary was supported as an institution so that they could be assured of its goodwill, if not its political support. In this case, that meant supporting its independence as an institution. Moreover, by maintaining its neutrality and choosing not to collaborate with the current government, the judiciary did not make enemies with the future government. This was especially crucial in Brazil since the short (high) time horizons (hazard rate) of government created great uncertainty about the precise composition and power of the ruling and opposition coalitions at any given time. Additionally, its image as an apolitical institution increased public respect and support for the judiciary, which further boosted its political capital and made politicians wary of interfering with it. Hence, impartial adjudication through the various legal cases during the energy crisis served to further enhance the de facto independence that the judiciary enjoys in Brazil.

Put together, then, the politics of the rationing policy during the energy crisis clearly illustrate our causal arguments explaining why governments in Brazil's highly particularistic candidate-centered democracy have incentives to tie their hands to the courts and enhance the latter's de facto autonomy when their hazard rate in office is high. In the next subsection, we show that the causal arguments that we proposed to account for the politics of de facto judicial independence in a candidate-centered system like Brazil is supported more generally as a matter of common practice. The energy crisis, in fact, represents typical interactions between the government, the opposition, and the judiciary in Brazil.

Political Capacity, Opposition Parties, and Judicial Autonomy

The first part of our theoretical story on de facto judicial independence suggests that when the time horizons of governments in candidate-centered systems shrink, opposition parties tend to solicit the courts' support to politically challenge the ruling party or parties. Extant research on judicial politics in Brazil's candidate-centered democracy, as well as examples of when the opposition tends to use the judiciary for their political ends, corroborate the causal claim posited earlier. To start with, recall that the hazard rates of governments in office in Brazil have often been high. As a result, ruling parties in Brazil have faced short time horizons in office. Researchers have pointed out that opposition political parties frequently challenge the government under these conditions by actively seeking the judiciary's support for the stands that they take against the ruling party. This strategy offers various tactical benefits such as allowing the opposition to undermine the legitimacy of the government's policies, obstruct the implementation of government policy and undermine its performance, and to burnish the legitimacy of the opposition's position. For instance, Taylor (2008: 159) notes that opposition political parties in Brazil have been aggressive

> in using the courts to voice their opposition, political actors also sought to impose costs on their opponents, by exposing the pitfalls of policy, high-

lighting their opposition, or delaying and calling into question the final implementation of policy.

Likewise, Werneck Vianna et al. observe that when the ruling party's grip on office becomes tenuous, opposition parties use an independent judiciary for

> establishing a position against the majority (represented by the ruling party) and expressing to . . . adherents and the public in general the party's disposition to exhaust, in the institutional environment, all the possibilities open for interventions.[18]

The tactical use of the courts by opposition parties in Brazil along the aforementioned lines can be seen most clearly in the copious use of various legal instruments such as ADINs and the *acao popular* by political parties, as well as by politicians at various levels.[19] Between 1988 and 2002, for example, a significant portion of the 1,000 constitutional challenges against proposed government policies that were filed in the courts by opposition have been done through the use of ADINs (Taylor 2008: 81).[20] The timing of these challenges is worth noting here since the opposition's filing of ADINs in courts were undertaken significantly more frequently in situations when the government's grip on power became tenuous. In addition, almost half a million cases have been brought against government actions through lower courts every year in the same period (Arantes 2005: 237). These numbers show that opposition parties across the ideological spectrum in Brazil believe that contesting the government's politics through the courts provides some political value. Their belief is supported by the fact that 200 of the 1,000 constitutional challenges did, in fact, force governments to make changes in their proposals (Taylor 2008: 67).

Additionally, when the hazard rate of governments in Brazil rises significantly, opposition parties tend to file ADINs to the court against government policies in order to draw the public's attention to the government's poor performance, to further their own issue agendas, and to raise their political profiles (Taylor 2008; Rios-Figueroa and Taylor 2006; Santiso 2003; Prilliman 2000). For example, in the energy crisis case discussed earlier, opposition parties and politicians used their legal challenges to signal their opposition to the specific rationing policy, as well as to the government's entire reform agenda. Thus, Anthony Garotinho, who was governor of Rio in 2001, first threatened to sue the federal government unless it reduced the power tariffs it was imposing on citizens during the crisis (Taylor 2008; BBC News, December 3, 2001), and then subsequently used the rhetoric of this public threat to establish his policy credentials as the anti-IMF candidate for the 2002 presidential race. PT party leaders similarly used the constitutional challenges and injunctions they filed against the *Energia Brasil* policy as evidence to signal their sincere opposition to this policy to voters (Reuters, June 28, 2001).

Ruling parties implement their own strategy regarding courts in anticipation of and in reaction to such opposition tactics. Our theoretical arguments predict that in candidate-centered democracies, government strategy will be predicated on the government's knowledge that they lack the political capacity to enact legislation curbing the judiciary's power and autonomy. Lacking legislative capacity, governments in such systems will choose instead to invest in the judiciary as an institution and then use it to serve their goals of obtaining policy legitimacy through judicial endorsements and to prevent the opposition from allying with the courts. The awareness of governments regarding their legislative weakness and the tactics they adopt as a result of this weakness can be observed very clearly in the behavior of various governments in Brazil and beyond the specific example of the energy crisis.

As discussed earlier, Brazil's open-list PR system creates parties where leaders exercise little legislative leverage over their delegations (Mainwaring 1999; Samuels 2004; Ames and Power 2007). President Cardoso articulated exactly this problem in 1996 when he pointed out that "Weak parties make changes twice as hard to achieve. Gathering a majority for a bill becomes a case-by-case exercise" (1996: 12). In the case of many judicial powers, the legislative challenge is even stronger since changes require a constitutional amendment, which requires three-fifth majorities in both houses in two separate votes. Leaders from the ruling parties and the opposition are thus aware that they cannot influence their party members to support legislation that would effectively undermine the judiciary either by reducing its authority, jurisdiction, or review powers, or by politicizing its administrative and financial apparatus in order to implement an agenda of weakening judicial independence.

Even in situations when the opposition parties solicit the courts' support to challenge the government, the inability of leaders from the ruling parties to influence their party members to vote for preferred legislative bills makes it extremely difficult for the executive to pass legislation to undermine judicial independence. Consider President Cardoso's attempt to pass and implement a pension-reform provision in the legislature in 1996. This pension reform was openly opposed by the opposition political parties and important civil-society groups, who requested the courts to support their stand against it (Alston 2005: 103; Silver Martins 1996). The opposition tactic worked, as the judiciary in Brazil declared Cardoso's pension-reform provision as unconstitutional.

In response to this declaration, Cardoso actively threatened to roll back judicial powers (Santiso 2003: 118; Alston et al. 2009). Ultimately, however, he could not deliver on these threats because he lacked the capacity to influence members from his own party and from other parties in the ruling coalition to vote for the legislative measures that would have curbed the powers and autonomy of the courts.[21] Not surprisingly, he eventually gave up on the idea of curtailing the judiciary's power, and as discussed later, proceeded to pursue an alternative strategy that reaffirmed and strengthened the independence of the judiciary. In 1998, in constitutional amendment 19, Cardoso's government instead affirmed many important powers of the judiciary, including its power to control internal promotions, and restated its support for the principle that judicial salaries could not be reduced (Taylor 2008; Ríos-Figueroa and Taylor 2006).

Even though successive Brazilian governments led by different parties have been frustrated in their policy-making by an uncooperative judiciary, to date, none of the occasional legislative attempts to curb DFJI has actually succeeded (Alston et al. 2009). Thus, a congressional committee that was formed in 1995 under the chairmanship of the PFL to articulate policy bills to restrain the judiciary's "excessive independence" consistently failed to agree on the substance of the exact reforms proposed in 1996 (Santiso 2003: 122–23). Various drafts could not even be put to a committee vote due to serious disagreements between committee members, and the committee never generated a bill that was then considered by the entire floor. In 1998, the commission was finally disbanded after it failed to produce any substantial legislation or even draft proposals that could form the foundation for future proposals or bills. This is confirmed by Abramo, who emphasized in a recent interview that he was "not aware of any bills that proposed to reduce the political independence of the judiciary"[22] in Brazil.

Conversely, as suggested by our causal claims, the incumbent's inability to constrain the courts in Brazil has instead encouraged successive governments in the country to cultivate the courts' autonomy and legitimacy in order to exploit the political benefits these provide, and to prevent them from forming alliances with the opposition. To this end, the government has strengthened court authority, increased their perks, and increased their institutional prestige and legitimacy by appealing to courts to resolve important political disputes, and then respecting their decisions in practice.

For example, in 2003, Lula's government succeeded in passing and implementing a pension-reform policy that was very similar to the failed Cardoso proposal after the new proposal specifically excluded judicial officials from the purview of this new law (Alston and Mueller 2006; Alston et al. 2009). Rather than trying to capture the judiciary, the ruling alliance led by Lula—which faced a high hazard rate in office in 2003[23]—chose instead to sweeten the deal and attract the judiciary to their side of the issue. This prevented the opposition from allying with the judiciary to defeat this bill yet again, and the PT was finally able to pass this contentious decade-old bill. Another example illustrates the government's investment in building judicial legitimacy and prestige as a political strategy to handle threats to its survival. In 2008, the Lula government lost a key constitutional challenge on a financial tax, which then created a 10 percent hole in the government budget. Rather than working on bills to preemptively reduce judicial ability to rule against the government or ignoring the court's decision, the government merely went back to plan alternative ways to raise the revenue. This demonstration of public respect for the courts allowed Lula's government to prevent any potential alliance between the opposition and the judiciary over the financial tax issue that may have occurred had Lula's administration instead chosen to politically restrict the courts at a time when the government was politically vulnerable.

Finally, evidence shows that Brazilian governments have frequently turned to the courts for endorsement of government policies through instruments such as Declaration of Constitutionality ADCs (Taylor 2008; Alston et al. 2009). These ADCs have also been used by Brazilian governments to obtain the courts' approval for government policies, particularly when such policies were challenged by the opposition in situations where the governments' grip on office was tenuous. Lula's governing alliance, for example, frequently used ADCs to request the Supreme Court's rulings on issues as diverse as tax reform, land reform, and women's rights after these bills invited considerable political controversy and were opposed by the opposition political parties (Pinheironeto 2007, 2009; CLADEM 2009: 7; *Camara dos Deputados,* August 21, 2009).

The examples and evidence presented illustrate our causal claim that in candidate-centered democracies governments, whose survival in office is threatened by opposition parties, choose to invest in DFJI and use independent courts to serve their political ends rather than curbing their autonomy. Since the credibility of such a political strategy is conditional on the credibility of the courts themselves, ruling and opposition parties have incentives to enhance de facto judicial independence. This can be seen clearly in the substance of the judicial reform bills that have been passed in Brazil. For instance, the 2004 judicial reform bill, which became law, was designed to reduce procedural delays in the justice system.[24] The government and opposition parties in Brazil took care to ensure that this bill did not curtail the independence of the judiciary. Judge Lunardelli points this out in an interview.

> I don't believe that . . . the reforms that were done, interfered with judicial independence. There wasn't an objective of political interference (in designing the reforms).[25]

Brinks (2005: 621) reflects this view of the 2004 judicial reforms as well by pointing out the following.

> The new provisions appear to strike a defensible combination of lower court autonomy and political responsiveness without necessarily eroding judicial independence by fostering overtly partisan conduct.

While these specific examples illustrate the validity of our causal arguments about the politics about the politics of judicial independence in Brazil, our claim is also supported more broadly by a simple empirical analysis of constitutional amendments and statutory bills proposed and approved in Brazil's National Congress from 1988 to 2005. To conduct this empirical analysis, we first gathered annual data on all constitutional amendments and statutory bills that were proposed and approved or rejected by Brazil's Congress from 1988 to 2005. This data was compiled from several primary and secondary sources.[26] A broad examination of this legislative data from Brazil shows that a total of 105 constitutional amendments and 2,961 complementary plus ordinary statutory bills were proposed between 1988 and

2005. Additionally, as reported in table 6.1, 1,344 of these constitutional amendments and bills were approved by the legislature during the 1988–2005 time period.

We then used the information from this legislative data to categorize the issue area covered by each amendment and statutory bill across issue areas such as taxes, fiscal policy, privatization, the judicial system, education, housing, and so on. After classifying the issue area covered by each amendment or bill, we found that as many as 43 amendments and bills that dealt exclusively with Brazil's judicial system have been approved by the Brazilian Congress from 1988 to 2005. Building on this analysis, we then checked whether each of the approved amendments and bills that pertain to Brazil's judicial system contained any one of the five main provisions listed shortly that promote the de facto autonomy of the judicial system within countries according to a recent report by the United Nations.[27] This includes provisions that

- Direct the government to undertake steps to increase the financial autonomy of the judiciary or allow the courts to control their budgets.
- Ensure that the formal assignment of cases to judges is done on a purely legal basis without intervention from any external source.

TABLE 6.1. Constitutional Amendments and Statutory Bills in Brazil from 1988 to 2005

	Number of Bills	Median	Minimum	Maximum
Panel A				
Type				
Constitutional amendment	105	964	11	4,629
Complementary	137	713	20	5,630
Ordinary	2,855	1,498	2	5,777
Total	3,097			
Panel B				
Outcome				
Approved	1,344			
Rejected	416			
Other termination	394			

Note: The numbers in the table include censored and noncensored cases. The median, minimum, and maximum figures in the table express the descriptive values of the number of days (i.e., the time) that amendments and bills spent in both houses of the national legislature in Brazil.

- Provide guidelines to the government to institutionalize laws that formally restricts the executive from interfering with the rendering of judicial decisions or the enforcement thereof.
- Formally prevents legislators from attempting to contradict or undermine previous judicial rulings.
- Guarantees that judicial tenure is secured without threat of reduction or restriction while in service.

Table 6.2 briefly describes a couple of these constitutional amendments and statutory bills that deal with Brazil's judicial system and that also contain at least one of the five main types of provisions just listed.

The information gathered by carefully studying the provisions from each of these approved amendments and bills relating to the judiciary leads to two interesting and relevant empirical findings. First, we found that 31 out of a total of 43 (that is, 72 percent) of approved amendments and bills

TABLE 6.2. Some Amendments and Bills That Increased the Judiciary's de facto Autonomy in Brazil

Amendments/Bills	Brief Description
Constitutional Amendment 19 (1998)	Legislated a package of administrative reforms of the civil service and set new rules for the process of setting judicial salaries. Measures maintained judiciary autonomy and preserved the rule that judicial salaries were irreducible. Furthermore, the authority of the judiciary to control internal promotions was reaffirmed. Both measures preserved the judiciary's independence.
Constitutional Amendment 45 (2004)	Legislated many changes to the judicial system. Three measures were especially important. (a) Establishing a National Judicial Council (CNJ) in response to public demands that the courts needed political accountability. Despite public demands for more political accountability of "excessively" independent courts, this bill created a council that maintained a clear majority of 9 judges in a body of 15 rather than stacking it with external political appointees. (b) The establishment of súmula vinculante, binding precedent of Supreme Court decisions over lower courts if approved by a two-thirds quorum. This increased the power of the higher courts over the judicial system. (c) General Admissibility of Extraordinary Appeal. This allowed the Supreme Court more control over its docket of cases by giving it the right to refuse to review appeals by a two-thirds quorum.

about the judiciary between 1988 and 2005 contains at least one of the five main types of provisions listed above. Thus, 72 percent of these legislative instruments clearly increase de facto judicial independence. Second, consider the illustration in fig. 6.2, which is derived from our hazard rate measure of governments in Brazil and legislative data of amendments plus bills on the Brazilian judiciary from 1988 to 2005. This figure shows that the number of approved amendments plus bills that enhance the courts' autonomy increased, particularly when the hazard rate of governments in office in Brazil was high.

Specifically, the figure indicates that as many as three amendments and bills that increased the courts' de facto autonomy were approved in 1991 when the Collor government's hazard rate in office increased sharply as Collor was embroiled in a financial scandal at this time. It similarly shows that the number of approved amendments and bills enhancing the autonomy of Brazil's judiciary increased in the years in which the hazard rates of Cardoso and Lula's governments increased substantially. Thus, the illustration in fig. 6.2 provides some support for our argument that politicians in candidate-centered democracies like Brazil have incentives to initiate legislation to enhance judicial autonomy in the context of high hazard rates in office. This brief analysis of the legislative data thus suggests that politicians in Brazil prefer to tie their hands to an autonomous judiciary since they use the courts to bolster the credibility of their political strategy. What is the effect of such party strategies in dealing with the judiciary on de facto judicial independence in Brazil? We turn to answer this question in the next section.

De Facto Judicial Autonomy in Brazil

In the previous section, we discussed examples and analyzed some legislative data that reveals that politicians in Brazil have taken concrete policy actions to maintain or enhance judicial independence, particularly when their hazard rate in office was high. Have these policies translated to higher levels of de facto independence of the courts in Brazil? As an answer to this question, scholars have suggested that actions taken by incumbents to increase the autonomy of Brazilian courts has indeed led to an outcome in which the judiciary in Brazil is one of the most independent in the developing world (Hammergren 2007; Kapiszweski 2007; Rios-Figueroa and Taylor

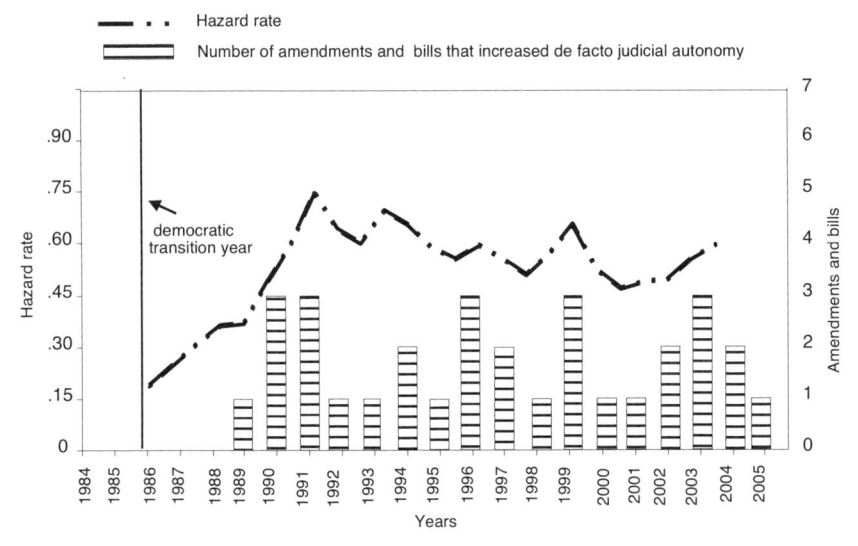

Fig. 6.2. Approved amendments and bills that increased de facto judicial autonomy in Brazil

2006; Brinks 2005; Prilliman 2000). For instance, Santiso (2003: 3) states that

> By any standard, the Brazilian judiciary enjoys extraordinarily high levels of independence. Judicial independence is both nominal, enshrined in extensive constitutional guarantees, and substantive, in terms of the powers granted to the courts and the willingness of judges to exercise them.[28]

Santiso's (2003) view is supported by Taylor (2008:), who claims that

> Brazil's federal courts are strongly independent of the elected branches. Judicial decisions are made without undue concern for the executive or legislative branches reaction; compliance with court decision by public bureaucracies is largely expected; and recent history suggests that no retaliation is to be expected in terms of court budgets or general administrative freedom.

Civil-society groups share this assessment and consider the judicial system to be genuinely "an independent institution" (Interview, Transparencia Brasil, August 18, 2010) that enjoys independence from the political establishment in general, and from political parties in particular.[29] Practicing judges at the state and federal level also share the scholarly viewpoint that the judicial system's powers, appointments process, and internal operations in Brazil are free of political interference.[30] As Judge Lunardelli observes, "There is judicial independence. There is not a direct relationship between the judicial system and the political system." He observes further that the political branch "has little influence [on the judicial branch]. I don't see a political influence . . . I don't see a submission of the judiciary to the desire of the government" (Project interview conducted August 25, 2010). Likewise, in an interview, Judge Lourenco stated the following.

> I think the political relationship [between political parties and groups and, the judiciary] is minimal. It is truly minimal. (Project interview conducted August 25, 2010)

The views held by the two judges, Lunardelli and Louernco, is also echoed by Judge Nascimento, who observes that even though judges in Brazil may be subject to various contextual influences, each judge in the country "decides in accordance with his or her conscience," and that the institutional and political system in country gives practicing judges "conditions, all the guarantees not to feel pressured" (Project interview conducted August 27, 2010).

The claims put forth about judicial autonomy in Brazil by scholars and judges—as previously posited—is also corroborated by the relevant time-series data from Brazil for the two ordinal measures of de facto judicial independence (that range from 0 for no DFJI to 2 for high DFJI) described in chapter 5.[31] In particular, we find that the moving average of the de facto judicial independence measure increased from 1.3 in 1987 to 1.6 by 2004, and likewise, the moving average of the *de facto judicial autonomy* measure increases from 1.2 to 1.57 in the same time period. Furthermore, as discussed in more detail in the following chapter, the level of de facto independence of the judiciary in Brazil's candidate-centered system is significantly higher than the courts' de facto autonomy in Indonesia's party-centered democracy.

Importantly, all the judges and civil-society groups interviewed for this project emphasized the increased role of the judiciary in resolving political and policy disputes as one of the main sources of increased independence of the Brazilian judiciary. Judge Lunardelli, for example, notes the increasingly prominent use of the legal system by political parties as part of their political tactics.

> Parties, as well as the ones of the opposition, are able to frequently sue, in particular in front of the STF, against decisions of the government. And they can sue against Congress too . . . its common and frequent . . . Every day (the judiciary) is assuming a role of greater importance . . . for sure in the definition of public politics, it is a relevant actor now today. (Project interview conducted August 25, 2010)

Judge Nascimento similarly observes

> When we look in the papers and see the political conflicts, more each day, they are involving the participation of the judiciary in the political game . . . the Supreme Court has not only a judiciary role but a political role. (Project interview conducted August 25, 2010)

He further notes that the independence of the judiciary has been increasing as a result of such democratic tensions. Additionally, as Judge Lunardelli notes, "All that is relevant, involving the environment, the consumer, that involves the big questions, passes to the judiciary. So, these questions are not only decided by the Executive, nor the Congress." Melo, Mueller, and Pereirra similarly note that "legislative and executive activities transpire 'in the shadow of the courts'" (2009: 128). This ability of the judiciary to rule on policy decisions made by the executive and the Congress, have made it an especially potent political tool for opposition and coalition parties to challenge government policy. This has made it an important political source of policy influence, and hence, an important political ally for all parties. As a result, the judiciary has been able to not just consolidate but increase its independence from the political establishment over time. In short, our in-depth analysis of the Brazil case here supports our causal story that when governments in Brazil face low time horizons in office, they increase the de facto independence of the judiciary.

While the Brazil case is useful, we turn to analyze the politics of de facto judicial independence in another prominent developing democracy that also has a candidate-centered electoral system: India. We start with a brief description of India's electoral rule and show how it produces a candidate-centered system with weak parties. We then discuss the hazard rate of governments in office in India. Finally, we explore how the interaction between the hazard rate of Indian governments and the candidate-centered nature of the country's electoral system affects de facto judicial independence.

Brief Background on India's Economy, Polity, and the Judicial System

Since its independence in 1947, India has maintained itself as a federal democracy with a central government at the national level and a directly elected state government for each of its 29 states. Key democratic institutions—including the separation of powers, and regular occurrence of elections at both the national and state level—have become firmly entrenched, creating one of the most stable democracies in the developing world (Lijphart 1996; Kohli 2001; Ganguly et al. 2007). Unlike Brazil and Indonesia, India is a parliamentary democracy. However, its political system has many political features that are common to Brazil and Indonesia— including a party system characterized by multiple parties and a high degree of party fragmentation (Yadav 2000, 2004; Chhibber and Nooruddin 2000; Chhibber and Kollman 2004).

Representatives to the Indian parliament are elected via another electoral rule common among democracies—the single-member-district plurality electoral rule where party leaders do not control access to ballots or ranks (Chhibber and Kollman 2004; Gill 2005). Following existing analyses of the Indian electoral system,[32] we suggest in the next section that like Brazil, but unlike Indonesia, India's electoral rule has, in recent decades, generated weak political parties with low levels of intraparty unity. Consequently, the control that party leaders are able to exert over individual members from their own party has declined considerably, and the country has shifted to a candidate-centered system (Sridharan 2002; Kapur 2005). The economy of India is the twelfth-largest economy in the world in nominal GDP terms and the fourth largest by purchasing power parity (PPP).[33] In terms of nominal GDP, the size of Brazil and India's economy is similar, and Brazil, India, and Indonesia are key players in the G20 group of nations.[34]

Finally, India's judicial system consists of the Supreme Court, high courts, and state and local courts. The courts in India have been constitutionally granted high levels of de jure autonomy, and, moreover, the judiciary has the power of full and explicit judicial review.[35] Judges typically belong to the higher Hindu castes, are from economically well-off families, and assume judicial posts after having spent extensive time practicing as private lawyers.[36] Supreme Court judges are more commonly drawn from the front ranks of prominent lawyers in regional courts rather than lower court judges (Gadbois 2011: 377). The careful attention to regional representation, combined with the extremely high linguistic and cultural diversity in India, has been blamed for creating a lack of espirit de corps among Supreme Court judges, who feel they have little in common despite being from similar social and economic backgrounds (Gadbois 2011: 355). Finally, almost a quarter of Supreme Court judges have some experience in politics as holders of elected office, failed candidates for legislative office at the state level, as officials in labor movements, or as party workers. However, these experiences did not directly precede their appointments to the Supreme Court and is not believed to have affected their choice as nominees.

In chapter 2, we argued that governments in highly particularistic candidate-centered developing countries' democracies have incentives to maintain and enhance the de facto independence of the judiciary in the context of high hazard rates or equivalently low time horizons in office. Brazil provided an example of the dynamics that led to this outcome in a highly particularistic system created by one specific type of electoral rule—the open-list PR system. We now examine how another highly particularistic electoral system—the SMD plurality rule—facilitates a similar outcome of high DFJI in the context of low time horizons by examining the case of India. We begin by describing India's electoral rule and its effect on intraparty unity in the country, and the hazard rate of governments in office in India.

India's Candidate-Centered Democracy and the Hazard Rate of Indian Governments

In India's SMD plurality system, voters choose individual candidates on their ballot, and the candidates with most votes in a district wins that seat.[37] As stated by Hix (2004: 197), these rules provide candidates with some incentives to cultivate a personal vote.

> In the middle of the spectrum, single-member—simple-plurality (SMSP) (that is, first-past-the-post) systems ... promote a mixture of partisan and

candidate appeals. In these systems voters choose individual candidates rather than lists of candidates from each party, an approach that encourages candidates to develop personal recognition and support in their district.

Because Indian candidates have some incentives to develop their personal reputations, party leaders do not have complete control over the actions of their party members. Additionally, since voters vote for individual candidates from each party, the political capital that candidates bring to the ticket is considerable, and voter identification with individual candidates is high. This is emphasized by Gallagher and Holliday (2003: 114), who suggest that in India

> the small district magnitude (of SMD plurality systems) means that all candidates have a strong incentive to ensure that the voters know them personally... In consequence, voters are always de facto choosing between familiar individuals, and while the party label is still important, each candidate will try their best to cultivate their particularistic personal votes... they have good reason to believe that establishing their personal popularity will assist their chances of re-election.

Since the value of the party label in SMD plurality systems where voters vote for individual candidates and where party leaders do not control access to ballots or rank is low, it therefore follows that the degree of control that party leaders can exert over party members will be low as well (Randall 2007; Punett 1994). The fact that party leaders in India have little or no control over their party members is clearly observable in India's polity during the last three decades or so.

To see this more clearly, first observe that election campaigns in India often focus more on the charisma and reputation of each candidate rather than the manifesto of the candidate's party. As suggested by Chaba (2007: 1), in India, "people don't simply vote on the basis of party programs. They follow their hearts. A stray look at the poll results over the decades shows how candidates have won seats mainly on the basis of their personal charisma." Likewise, Keefer and Khemani (2008: 2) point out that in India, "parties and individual candidates benefit from charisma: parties may have individual candidates and prominent candidates... whose individual charisma attract votes independent of the services they deliver." Keefer and Khemani's (2008) claim is also confirmed in a recent report released by India's Election Commission, which emphasized the personalist nature of Indian politics.[38] In fact, the high value given to individual candidates by voters in their voting decisions has further eroded the value of the party label for candidates and has made election campaigns more personalist in nature (Manor 1990; Chaba 2007).

An important consequence of the increasingly personal nature of Indian election campaigns is that it has exacerbated the lack of control that party leaders have over their rank-and-file party members. The clearest demonstration of this is provided by the once-dominant Congress party. Even though Indian politics and office was dominated by a single party—the Congress Party—in the immediate decades after WWII, party discipline and the control that the party leadership traditionally had over party members has declined significantly within the party in the last 30–40 years (Sisson and Wolpert 1998; Suri 2003). The lack of intraparty discipline and the inability of party leaders to credibly exert leverage over party members in the Congress (I) Party have spread to other political parties. This is suggested by Suri (2003: 24), who points out that within parties in contemporary India:

> The loyalty of party workers is . . . not to the party . . . in parties, factions are allowed and encouraged, fierce competition for patronage and power goes on . . . Look at the TDP, DMK, ADMK, Shiv Sena, SAD, Trinamool, BJD, AIMIM, and National Conference, INLD or any such party. Thus, we see most parties . . . with weak organization. Secondly, we find in recent years, a decline in party organizations: most parties revolve around Ministers, people's representatives, and others who hold positions of power in government.

The inability to exert sufficient control over party members by party leaders in India has also been exacerbated by the increased fragmentation of the party system in India and the "birth" of several new political parties in the last three decades (Sridharan 2008; Chibber and Kollman 2004). This can be seen clearly for example, in the Laakso-Taagepera index of the effective number of electoral parties in India. This index—which is a standard proxy for the fragmentation of the party system[39]—increased from 2.7 in 1987 to as much as 8.4 by 2004 for India.[40] The rapid fragmentation of the party system has not only engendered a series of unstable coalition governments in India since 1989 but has also created a situation where individual party members are prone to "shopping" between governing coalitions and opposition parties in order to maximize their material and political payoffs (NCRWC 2001; Sridharan 2002, 2006; Kapur 2005; Mehta 2002; Arora 2002). This phenomenon is emphasized by Kapur (2005: 32), who states the following.

> With political parties serving as vehicles of individual ambition rather than ideological or programmatic goals, the resulting political promiscuity has led to a landscape in which Indian political parties form a constantly shifting kaleidoscope of fission and fusion.

The increased ability of party members to "shop" between governing coalitions and opposition parties has increased their bargaining leverage within their party and consequently their political autonomy vis-à-vis party leaders (Randall 2007; Arora 2002). Dissatisfied MPs have also frequently split to form new parties based on their personal following (Arora 2002; Kashyap 2003, 2006; Kapur 2005; Sridharan 2002). These behaviors have served to further reduce the leverage of party leaders over their party members. They have also forced the executive to build a consensus within and outside the government to obtain political backing for critical policies (Kapur 2005: 44). Thus, the low leverage of party leaders and the low level of intraparty unity in India have led to an outcome where the country has shifted to a candidate-centered system. We find that the mean level of political *particularism* in India during the last three decades is almost as high as 10 on Wallack et al.'s (2006) particularism index, which ranges from a minimum value of 0 to a maximum of 13.

A second feature of the political landscape that is important for our theoretical framework is the time horizon—or, equivalently, the hazard rate governments have faced in office. A careful examination of the hazard rate of all governments in India from 1984 to 2004, which is illustrated in fig. 6.1, reveals that Indian governments have faced high hazard rates, and thus low time horizons, in office in India across this period.[41] The moving average of the hazard rate of these governments is equal to 0.62, which is marginally higher than the predicted probability of government failure in Indonesia, but slightly lower than that in Brazil.

The hazard rates of different governments in office in India can be traced clearly in this figure. For example, since a stable single-party majority government (i.e., the Congress (I) government) was in office from 1985 to 1989, the hazard rate of the executive was low in this time period. However, as shown in fig. 6.1, the government's hazard rate increased dramatically in India from 1989 to 1990 as two consecutive coalition governments ruled the country during this time period, and each of these multiparty coalitions were extremely unstable.[42] The hazard rate of the Narasimha Rao government in 1991–1993 is also high—this is shown in fig. 6.1—which is intuitive, considering that this was a minority coalition government that faced multiple votes of confidence to remove it from office. Similarly, we observe an increase in the hazard rate of the executive in India between 1996 and 1998 when India was headed by an unstable multiparty coalition (the "United Front") from 1996 to 1998, and then a minority BJP-led coalition government from 1998 to 1999. Both governments failed to complete their tenures in office.

Every single government in India since 1989 has been a coalition government. While lack of concentrated voter support for any single party is undoubtedly the prime reason for coalition governments, the rapid surge in the effective number of parties has also exacerbated the low time horizons that governing elites face in office by multiplying the possible coalitions that opposition parties can devise to bring down the current government (Sridharan 2002; Kashyap 2002). Consequently, each coalition government has undergone considerable changes in its composition through its years in office, and almost never has a coalition been ideologically compatible (Randall 2007; Sridharan 2002). These factors have combined to raise the uncertainty of tenure that governing parties face and have, thus consequently reduced their expected time horizons in office considerably.

In short, India is primarily a candidate-centered system in which the hazard rate of governments in office is fairly high. Based on our theoretical story, we therefore expect that governments in India will enhance the de facto independence of the judiciary. In the next section, we examine in detail how the political dynamics generated by the interaction of these factors lead to this outcome of high DFJI.

Political Parties, Time Horizons, and De Facto Judicial Independence in India

In order to show how the interaction between the judiciary, successive governments, and the opposition parties in India's candidate-centered system in the past two–three decades corroborates the causal story posited in chapter 2 and observed in Brazil, we first discuss the political and legal events involving rights to the Babri Mosque in 1991–1992, and the related S. R. Bommai and the Sunderlal Patwa case regarding the rights of central governments to dismiss state governments in 1993–1994. In order to assess the extent to which the dynamics underlying high DFJI are observed generally in India beyond this specific political issue, we then study all the legislative bills—including those related to the judiciary—that were considered by the Indian parliament between 1985 and 2005 and assess their influence on de facto judicial independence in India.

The Babri Mosque and S. R. Bommai Case and Judicial Autonomy

The first example we consider relates to the political and legal events surrounding a sixteenth-century mosque in Ayodhya, in the state of Uttar Pradesh, in 1991–1994. During this period, Narasimha Rao of the Congress (I) Party led a shaky alliance of multiple parties to form a minority government. It was, therefore, politically vulnerable, and the government's existence was potentially susceptible to the right strategic moves. Hence, the Rao Congress-led government in 1991–1992 faced the possibility of being removed from office via a vote of no-confidence several times, and thus its hazard rate was quite high (Venkatesan 2005; Ghosh 1996).[43] As suggested by our theory, the main opposition party—the Bharatiya Janata Party (hereafter BJP)—took full advantage of the fragile political status of the Rao government and challenged it politically using political and legal tactics (Udayakumar 2004, 2005; Varshney 1998, 2002). It did so by intensifying its challenge to the government on one of the most politically sensitive issues of the time—the controversy regarding the Ayodhya Mosque.

The opposition, the BJP, controversially claimed that the existing sixteenth-century mosque in Ayodhya had been built on the exact site where an important Hindu god, Ram, had been born in ancient times. The single most politically important issue on the BJP's agenda at this time was to build a temple at the exact site of the existing Babri Mosque structure. Sensing the government's political weakness at this time, the BJP launched a highly publicized march called the *Rath Yatra* to the Babri Mosque site, with the ostensible objective of building a temple at this site (Udayakumar 2004; Varshney 2002). This march was both a brazen political challenge to the Rao government and a political strategy that was meant to hasten the dissolution of this government (Varshney 2002; Venkatesan 2005). It is important to note here that the BJP was initially reluctant to involve the courts in the Babri Mosque dispute.[44] Subsequently, however, it did a U-turn, and—as suggested by our causal arguments—sought legal validation for its temple-building agenda. To this end, the BJP declared in its national executive resolution at Jaipur in 1991 that "the nature of the Babri Masjid and Ram Janambhoomi controversy is such that it needs to be sorted out by the court of law."[45] The BJP's decision to appeal to the courts was not driven by normative concerns about preserving the rule of law but rather by political considerations (Udayakumar 2004; Basu et al. 1993; Chanchreek and Prasad 1993). In particular, the BJP realized that it would be unable to obtain sufficient political support in the legislature for its temple-building agenda. As stated by Udayakumar (2004: 5):

> Mindful of the fact that the party had neither the capability to bring the parties to a negotiated settlement, nor the necessary parliamentary strength to push through any legislation, the BJP had to feign a newfound faith in the judicial process.

Given its "newfound faith in the judicial process," the BJP Party pursued three strategies to promote its agenda and politically challenge the fragile Rao government in 1991–1992.

First, legal counsels and senior party members from the BJP filed writ petitions to the Allahabad high court in the state of Uttar Pradesh seeking permission for devotees from the majority Hindu community to "perform worship and other religious rites at the disputed site" (Udayakumar 2004: 5). Second, party leaders and extremist elements in the BJP publicly stated that they were willing to support the rule of law and accept the courts' verdict on the Babri Mosque issue (Udayakumar 2004; Mukhia 1992). For instance, K. Sudarshan, a right-wing ideologue in the party, pointed out to a journalist in response to the latter's question that "there is no denying the fact that in a democratic society we all have to accept the judicial verdict."[46] Third, the government of the state of Uttar Pradesh, in 1991, which was incidentally a BJP-led state government, repeatedly provided assurances to the judiciary in late 1991 and early 1992 that it would not destroy the Babri Mosque structure at Ayodhya (Noorani 2000). At the same time, the BJP Party also appealed to the Supreme Court and the Allahabad high court (in the state of Uttar Pradesh) to come up with an amicable solution for the Babri Mosque issue that met the interests of the majority Hindu and the minority Muslim community (Chanchreek and Prasad 1993; Ludden 1996). This was emphasized more than a decade later by the law and justice minister of the BJP, Arun Jaitley, who stated that, "the judiciary was approached because we (the BJP) are committed to expeditious resolution of the Ayodhya issue . . . the issue is alive and existing."[47]

The BJP's threefold strategy, which involved soliciting the courts support for their agenda, was politically crucial for the BJP. Party stalwarts in the BJP calculated that appealing to the courts would (1) help them to establish the credibility and legitimacy of their agenda, and (2) solidify their support from moderate elements in the majority Hindu community in India if the courts accepted the party's appeal (Udayakumar 2004; Chanchreek and Prasad 1993). This is indicated clearly in a statement made by the president of the BJP, Murli Manohar Joshi, in early 1992.

> The BJP respects the rule of law and the decisions taken by Indian courts . . . we believe that the Babri Masjid issue that our party espouses is a just cause. Therefore, we do not hesitate to appeal to the courts because we have no doubt that the courts will rule in our favor . . . this will establish the legal basis for our cause and also help the BJP because it will show to the people of India that the BJP is a law-abiding party.[48]

The fact that BJP leaders appealed to the courts to bolster the credibility of their agenda at a time when the Rao government's grip in office was tenuous illustrates our theoretical claim that opposition parties in highly particularistic systems like India have incentives to solicit the judiciary's support to challenge and weaken the government when the latter's hazard rate in office is high.

The BJP's actions, including the strategic decision to seek the courts' support, succeeded in severely threatening the political survival of the fragile Rao government in Delhi (Noorani 2000; Chanchreek and Prasad 1993). Sensing the serious threat to its political survival, the Rao government decided to take some steps to neutralize the BJP's political challenge. In the spring and summer of 1992, the government initially mulled over the possibility of enacting legislative statutes that would lead to the introduction of president's rule in the state of Uttar Pradesh, where the Babri Mosque was located (Venkatesan 2005; Noorani 2000). Initiating president's rule in Uttar Pradesh would lead to the suspension of the legislature in this state, which was ruled by the BJP. It would also curtail the courts' (including the Supreme Court's) authority to undertake any legal action at the site of the Babri Mosque structure in Ayodhya, Uttar Pradesh.[49] Moreover, president's rule would give the president, and, by extension, the government (since the president of India is nominated by the government) the power to administer the state of Uttar Pradesh, and thus the Babri Mosque.

However, the Rao cabinet recognized in the summer of 1992 that it was unlikely to obtain the political and legislative support necessary for establishing president's rule in Uttar Pradesh (Venkatesan 2005; Udayakumar 2005). More importantly, as predicted by our theory, party leaders in the Congress-led government, including Prime Minister Narasimha Rao, realized ex ante that they did not have enough leverage over their party members and coalition partners to get them to publicly support the government's decision to initiate president's rule in Uttar Pradesh. As stated by Venkatesan (2005):

> Narasimha Rao, however, placed before the Liberhan Commission . . . an elaborate rationalization of his actions as Prime Minister . . . He told the Commission that he was *not* given sufficient political and legal backing for any firm measures that he might have contemplated. The imposition of President's Rule in Uttar Pradesh, he suggested, was ruled out by the National Integration Council, which had met before the demolition, and the Supreme Court had refused to countenance his plea that the Central government should be empowered as a "receiver" . . . in the state.[50]

Hence, the Rao government, whose time horizon (hazard rate) in office seemed to be shrinking (increasing) rapidly by early 1992 itself, initially gave up the idea of establishing president's rule in the state of Uttar Pradesh in the spring and later in the summer of 1992 (Noorani 2000; Venkatesan 2005). This turned out to be a costly political error. The BJP and the other right-wing extremist entities[51] in the Indian polity perceived the Rao's government inability to implement president's rule in spring/summer 1992 as an act of weakness, and thus were emboldened to launch yet another highly publicized march to the Babri Mosque in order to pressure the Rao government to resolve the issue (Udayakumar 2005; Basu et al. 1993). Unfortunately, the *Rath Yatra,* launched by the BJP, led to the worst religious riots witnessed in India since its independence (Noorani 2000; Varshney 2002;

Ludden 1996). Moreover, the *Rath Yatra* was perceived by both Prime Minister Rao and his cabinet as a direct political challenge to the government's grip on office (Noorani 2000; Ludden 1996).

The Rao government responded to the opposition's (i.e., the BJP's) challenge by dismissing governments in 1992–1993 in six states, including those of Uttar Pradesh, Madhya Pradesh, Rajasthan, and Himachal Pradesh, that were either ruled by BJP-led governments or by parties allied to the BJP on the grounds that they faced severe threats to public order (Sathe 2001; Das 2001; Arora 2002; Udayakumar 2004). Despite the fact that the death toll from religious riots in states headed by the Congress (I) Party was worse than the death toll from the riots in states ruled by the BJP, these Congress-led state governments were allowed to remain in power. This led credence to the view that these government dismissals were not done to protect law and order per se but rather to weaken the onslaught of the BJP's political challenge.

The BJP responded by deciding to challenge the Rao's government dismissal of all the six state governments in court. Each of the BJP-run state governments filed a writ petition in the high court of their respective state and to the Supreme Court to challenge the legality of the action taken by the Narasimha Rao government (Tummala 1994; Das 2001; Arora 2002). For example, Sunderlal Patwa, chief minister of Madhya Pradesh, challenged the dismissal of his government claiming that it "had nothing to do with the events in Ayodhya in Uttar Pradesh, except that his government also belonged to the opposition BJP" (Tummala 1996: 381). The Madhya Pradesh High Court subsequently ruled in his favor. Additionally, the BJP enthusiastically and publicly endorsed S. R. Bommai in the ongoing S. R. Bommai v. Union of India case—this case, which was initiated by former chief minister of Karntaka, S. R. Bommai, requested the Supreme Court to "sharply limit the constitutional power vested in the Central Government to dismiss a State government" (Arora and Goyal 1996: 12). The Supreme Court passed a judgment that supported S. R. Bommai's appeal as well.

It is absolutely critical to note here that even though its hazard rate in office was high at the time, the Rao government did not—in response to the BJP's tactic described in the preceding paragraph—threaten to restrict the courts' de facto autonomy (Arora and Goyal 1996). Rather than choosing to curtail the judiciary's independence to discourage courts from passing a judgment on this issue, the Rao government took a conscious decision to seek the Supreme Court and the Madhya Pradesh high court's support for the S. R. Bommai and Patwa cases, respectively. It adopted this tactic because it felt that appealing its case to the courts was necessary to seek legal validation for its act of dismissing some state governments on the premise that they posed serious threats to the stability of the Indian polity (Arora and Goyal 1996; Tummala 1994, 1996). The Rao government therefore publicly stated that it would accept both the Madhya Pradesh high court's decision for the Sunderlal Patwa case and the Supreme Court's judgment for the S. R. Bommai case. When these judgments went against the government, as emphasized by Arora and Goyal (1996: 202), the "Narasimha Rao government was quick to grasp the legal validity of the S. R. Bommai and the Sunderlal Patwa case . . . this encouraged Prime Minister Rao to not question the judiciary's intervention in these two cases." The government chose to accept the courts' rulings.

Indeed, not only did it accept these adverse legal rulings—it went even further to suggest that it would enact legislative statutes that would allow the judiciary to check the constitutional validity of future decisions relating to the dismissal of state governments by the government at the center—a move that was endorsed by the opposition parties as well (Reddy and Joseph 2006; Tummala 1994). In other words, the Rao government and the opposition in effect agreed to increase the de facto autonomy of the judiciary by allowing it to directly intervene in the often contentious issue of dismissal of state governments by the ruling party at the center in New Delhi (Thumala 1994; Noorani 2000).

Why did the Rao government turn to the judiciary to defend the legality of its action of dismissing some state governments in response to the opposition parties' attempt to challenge this decision taken by the Rao administration? Indeed, why did the Rao government choose to not constrain the courts to preempt it from intervening in the S. R. Bommai case? Why did it also commit itself to increase the court's de facto autonomy along the lines described in the preceding paragraph? Two reasons provide an answer to these questions.

First, similar to the political drama that occurred with respect to establishing president's rule over the Babri Mosque issue, the Rao administration realized that it lacked the political capacity to enact legislation that would restrict the courts autonomy and thus prevent it from passing a judgment on the S. R. Bommai and S. Patwa case. The ruling Congress (I) Party, which constituted the Rao government, lacked *intraparty unity* and was not as centralized as political parties in Indonesia's party-centered democracy

(Parikh 1993; Suri 2003). Consequently, Prime Minister Narasimha Rao, in the Congress (I) government, could neither exert sufficient leverage over rank-and-file party members nor obtain sufficient political backing from within the party itself for taking any action against the judiciary. This is suggested by Malik (1998), who points out that the divisiveness within the Rao government, and thus the incumbent's inability to influence individual party members, made it impossible for Rao to obtain adequate support from members in the government for a coherent plan to act against the judiciary if it chose to do so. Specifically, Malik (1998: 129) observes that in Rao's government, the

> rampant divisiveness at the highest level of government, where ministers and leaders.... [were] inclined to follow their own agenda rather than pursuing a collective vision made it impossible for Rao's cabinet to devise an effective strategy that may prevent either the judiciary from reversing the government's decision to dismiss the BJP-run state governments or prevent the opposition parties from using the courts to score political points.

The awareness of their political inability to ensure the passage of legislation led the Rao government to drop any ideas about restraining the judiciary to preempt it from intervening in these two cases (Malik 1998; Gagrani 2010). Instead, as predicted by our theory, its inability to act against the court provided the Rao government with a powerful incentive to obtain legal validation from the courts for its decision to dismiss some state governments. As suggested by Arora and Goyal (1996: 211):

> it was clear to Rao's cabinet that political support for blocking the courts ruling on the Bommai and the Patwa case would not be forthcoming ... instead it would be prudent to appeal the government's case to the judiciary.

Second, key members of Rao's cabinet also felt that obtaining the judiciary's endorsement for its decision to dismiss some state governments could also weaken the opposition's case with the court. This, in turn, would blunt the opposition's tactic of using the Supreme Court as a tool to first challenge the Narasimha Rao government and then to remove it from office. This is suggested quite explicitly in an op-ed article of the *Navbharat Times* in March 1993, which states the following.

The Narasimha Rao government chose to pre-empt the BJP's tactics of bringing it down through legal challenges by seeking the court's opinion itself on a multiplicity of issues including the Babri Masjid dispute and the appeals to the courts by BJP-run state governments to challenge Rao's decision to dismiss them from office.[52]

Thus, put together, the interaction between the government, the opposition (mainly the BJP), and the judiciary over the Babri Mosque issue and the subsequent Bommai/Patwa case corroborates our causal claims about the politics of de facto judicial independence in a candidate-centered system like India that exhibits high levels of particularism. The Babri Mosque issue and the Bommai and Patwa cases also illustrate how the lack of intraparty unity within the Congress (I) government induced party leaders in the Congress (I) Party to use the judiciary and enhance the courts' de facto autonomy to facilitate the government's objective of curtailing the credibility of the opposition's political challenge. Yet as we discuss later, the government's and opposition's behaviors and tactics regarding the judiciary during the Babri Mosque dispute and the Bommai and Patwa cases are neither rare nor unique.

Legislative Bills and Judicial Independence in India

Extant research also confirms our claim that the increasing political weakness and inability of ruling parties to act against the courts in India's highly particularist (i.e., candidate-centered) democracy encourages different incumbents to (1) avoid reducing the courts' independence, and (2) even increase the political autonomy of the judicial system. Kapur and Ramamurti (2005: 19), for example, suggest that the instability engendered by the rise of unstable coalitions in India since the late 1980s, which has contributed to the high hazard rate of governments in the country, fosters judicial independence.

> The 1980s and 1990s witnessed a shift in power away from the legislative and executive arms of government toward the judicial branch, in part because of erosion of the other two institutions and in part because of macropolitical changes that caused greater political instability.

Similarly, Gowda and Sridharan (2007) argue that the government's inability to dominate the court or other domestic institutions—which results from the instability and the high hazard rate of multiparty coalition governments in India's candidate-centered system—has led to an outcome where the independence of the judiciary has actually increased. Specifically, they state the following.

> The emergence of national multiparty coalitions has weakened the influence of the executive branch and hence the governing parties' ability to dominate other organs of *horizontal accountability* such as the Election Commission, the courts, and the legislative opposition. All these institutions of horizontal accountability have become notably more independent. (Gowda and Sridharan 2007: 20; italics in original)

These observations that the independence of various institutions in India, including the courts, has increased is not surprising from our perspective since India has been characterized by low time horizons in the context of a highly particularistic electoral system.

In chapter 2, we argued that these conditions provide ruling and opposition parties with incentives to adopt constitutional amendments and bills to maintain and promote the de facto judicial independence. We now conduct a brief analysis of constitutional amendments plus statutory bills proposed and approved (or rejected) in India's national legislature from 1985 to 2005 to see whether these causal links can in fact be observed there. In order to conduct this analysis, we first gathered annual data on all constitutional amendments and statutory bills that were proposed and approved or rejected by India's parliament (Lok Sabha and Rajya Sabha) from 1985 to 2005. This data was compiled from several primary and secondary sources.[53] Based on the information from these primary and secondary sources, we categorized and listed the issue area covered by each amendment or statutory bill—this includes issue areas such as taxes and fiscal policy, privatization, the judicial system, and so on.[54]

A concise analysis of this legislative data shows that a total of 328 amendments and statutory bills were proposed between January 1985 and December 2005. As reported in table 6.3, 192 of these amendment and bills were approved by the legislature during the 1985 and 2005 time period, while the remaining were either rejected or are pending. Additionally, table 6.4 reports that 28 amendments and statutory bills that dealt strictly with

TABLE 6.3. Constitutional Amendments and Statutory Bills in India from 1985 to 2005

	Number of Bills	Median	Minimum	Maximum
Type				
Constitutional amendment	31	86	5	1,060
Statutory bills	299	119	3	1,721
Total	329			
Outcome				
Approved	192			
Rejected	85			
Pending	51			

Note: The numbers in the table include censored and noncensored cases. The median, minimum, and maximum figures in the table express the descriptive values of the number of days (i.e., the time) that amendments and bills spent in both houses of the national legislature (the Rajya Sabha and the Lok Sabha).

TABLE 6.4. Approved Amendments and Bills by Issue-Area in India, 1985–2005

Issue-Areas	Number of Approved Amendments and Bills	Percentage of All Proposed Amendments and Bills Approved
Pensions	2	1.03
Public/state institutions	12	6.2
Taxes and fiscal policy	51	26.4
Public infrastructure	10	5.1
Labor legislation	6	3.1
Housing	2	1.03
Education	4	2.07
Defense	5	2.6
Farming and agriculture	21	10.9
Trade and industry	14	7.25
Political and civil rights	2	1.03
Penal legislation	6	3.1
State properties	3	1.55
National budget	14	7.25
Health	4	2.07
Judicial system	29	15.02
Other	8	4.14
Total	193	

India's judicial system were approved in the legislature between 1985 and 2005.

More specifically, as was done in the Brazil case, we checked whether each of the approved amendments or bills that pertain to the Indian judicial system contains any one of the five provisions identified by the United Nations and listed earlier as measures that promote the de facto autonomy of the judicial system within countries.[55] Table 6.5 briefly describes a few constitutional amendments and statutory bills about the Indian judicial system that have not only been approved by the legislature but which also contain at least one of the five main types of provisions listed by the UN.

The information gathered from checking the provisions from each approved amendment or bill that apply to the judicial system between 1985 and 2005 provide two key empirical insights. First, we found that as many as 21 out of 29 approved amendments and bills about the judiciary contain at least one of the five main types of provisions previously listed that fosters judicial independence. That is, 72.4 percent of all approved amendments and bills that deal with the Indian judiciary from 1985 to 2005 were implemented to enhance the de facto independence of the country's judicial system. Second, the illustration in fig. 6.3—which is derived from our legisla-

TABLE 6.5. Some Amendments and Bills That Increased the Judiciary's de facto Autonomy in India

Amendments/Bills	Brief Description
The Judges (Protection) Act, 1985	Prevented any court from considering any civil or criminal lawsuits against a judge based on his actions in pursuit of judicial duties or related matters
The High Court and Supreme Court Judges (Salaries and Conditions of Service) Amendment Act, 2002	Increased the salary and pension benefits of judges. Additionally the amount of the pension benefits that the families of the judges were entitled to was increased considerably.
The Administrative Tribunals (Amendment) Act, 2006	Required that the president appoint the chairman and all members of the Central Administrative Tribunal only after consultation with the chief justice of India

Source: Data from India Code Database, Government of India, http://indiacode.nic.in, accessed August 31, 2010; Chronology of Central Acts, Law Ministry, http://lawmin.nic.in/Legis.htm, accessed August 31, 2010.

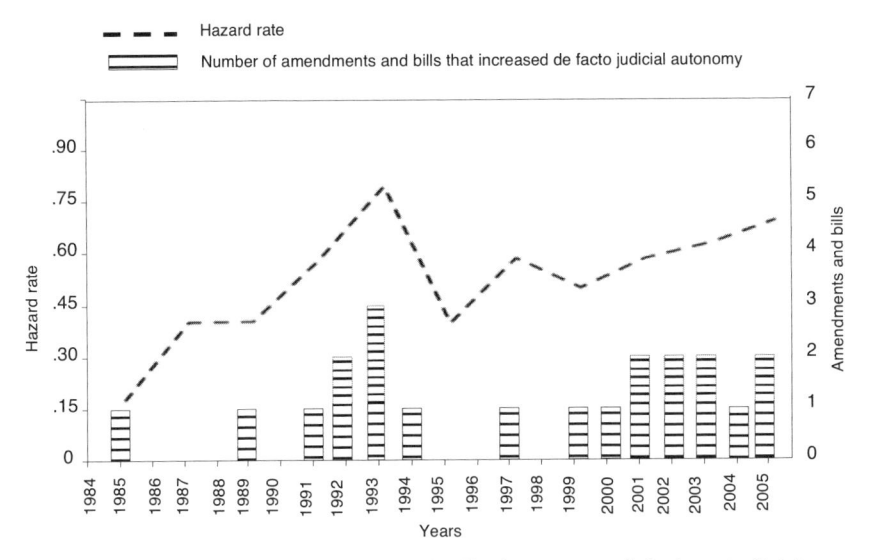

Fig. 6.3. Approved amendments and bills that increased de facto judicial autonomy in India

tive data of amendments and bills on the Indian judiciary from 1985 to 2005—reveals that the number of amendments and bills that were approved in order to enhance the courts' autonomy increased particularly when the hazard rate of governments in office in India was high.

Indeed, fig. 6.3 shows that the number of amendments and bills increasing the courts' de facto autonomy that were approved by the legislature reached its peaked in 1993 when the Rao government's hazard rate in office was as high as 0.75. We also find in the figure that amendments and bills that were targeted toward increasing the courts' de facto autonomy increased in the years (for example, 2001) when the NDA-led government's hazard rate in office increased. Thus, put together, the analysis of the annual number of approved amendments and bills on the judiciary in India, and the examples described earlier, indicate that politicians in India's highly personalist system have consistently adopted policies that consolidate and enhance de facto judicial independence. These policies have had the following three effects on the interaction between the courts and the government in India, and on the de facto independence of the judiciary.

First, consistent adoption of policies that sustain and enhance the courts' de facto autonomy have led to an outcome where the political establishment has voluntarily adhered to the norms and practices of preserving the independence of judicial institutions. Furthermore, the government and the opposition in India are almost completely deferential to the decisions taken by the courts. As observed by Mehta (2005: 111), some

> Court decisions may infuriate Parliament. . . . but Parliament thinks that they cannot simply be ignored. . . . This deference has ensured that even constitutional amendments have not been able to alter the basic structure of the Constitution and the *formal* allocation of powers within it.

Despite the consequences for the government's agenda and the political clout of the parties involved, judges in India are thus able to take decisions without political interference from politicians. More importantly, governing parties have also routinely respected judicial decisions that have either scuttled entirely, significantly modified, or delayed the implementation of important high-profile government policies. For example, when the government passed a bill that mandated setting up dedicated tribunals to speed up the debt-recovery process for banks, private firms filed a case challenging the constitutional basis of these provisions, thus challenging a key part of the government's plan for reforming the financial system program.[56] This bill had the backing of the politically powerful domestic-banking sector. However, the courts stayed its implementation and required substantial changes to be made before finally approving it in 2003.

Second, implementation of policies that foster the courts' autonomy has engendered a highly independent judicial system in de facto terms in India (Baxi 2000; Galanter 1989; Sathe 2001; Chopra 2006; Jalan 2007; Mehta 2007). Therefore, not surprisingly, experts on the Indian judicial system characterize the judiciary as "one of the most powerful courts in the world" (Shankar and Mehta 2008: 148), "a fiercely independent judiciary" (Hazra and Debroy 2007: 17), and "a relatively well-functioning and independent judiciary" (World Economic Forum 2009: 13). Moreover, Mehta (2005: 111) concludes that, "the courts have not only exercised their power of judicial review but have also managed to place limits on the power of Parliament to amend the Constitution." These claims about India's highly independent judiciary are also supported by the relevant data.

Indeed, consider the main ordinal measure of de facto judicial independence employed for our quantitative tests in chapter 5. India scores 1.7 on this DFJI index with a low of 0 and a maximum of 2; this indicates an extremely high level of DFJI. We also find in our data that the moving average of de facto judicial independence increased steadily from 1.1 to 1.7 on the 0 (low) to 2 (high) ordinal scale during the 1993–2004 time period in India. Finally, as discussed in the next chapter, the de facto independence of the judiciary in a candidate-centered system like India is much higher than the courts' de facto autonomy in Indonesia's party-centered democracy.

Conclusion

In chapter 2, we hypothesized that the degree of political particularism in developing countries' democracies plays a crucial role in shaping the incentives and strategic behavior of politicians when interacting with the judiciary. When faced with high hazard rates, and thus low time horizons in office, we predicted that governments will curtail de facto judicial independence in party-centered developing democracies (low particularism), but will do the opposite in candidate-centered systems (high particularism). In chapter 4, we tested this claim on a sample of 103 developing countries' democracies over the period 1985–2004 and we found strong support for it.

In this chapter, we analyzed within-country data and qualitative evidence from Brazil and India—two highly particularistic candidate-centered systems—to illustrate the underlying causal mechanism that leads to the prediction in hypothesis 2. We showed that when governments in Brazil and India face high hazard rates in office it heightens the value of an independent judiciary for these governments precisely because of the internal weakness and low unity of parties in these states. As a result, incumbents in these two states had strong political incentives to enhance the courts' autonomy when their survival in office is seriously threatened and thus acted to invest in their judiciaries' autonomy. These findings from Brazil and India have two main implications for understanding the future of de facto judicial independence in developing democracies.

First, at a broader level, this chapter suggests that governments in democracies that are characterized by high levels of particularism are more likely to at least maintain an independent judiciary in de facto terms if their hazard rates in office are high. At a more specific level, we learn that the de facto autonomy of the judiciary is also likely to remain high in Brazil and India in the near future as the hazard rate of governments in these two states will continue to remain high in the future. Second, it is plausible that the high de facto autonomy of the courts in the Brazil and India may engender greater judicial activism by the courts in these two states. This is a crucial observation since legal scholars in India and Brazil have questioned whether or not the level of judicial activism may increase, decrease, or retain the status quo in these countries.[57] We conjecture from our analysis that judicial activism is most likely to increase in Brazil and India even in the near future.

Notwithstanding the lessons that we learn from the Brazil and India case presented in this chapter, our evaluation of the causal mechanisms underlying the politics of de facto judicial independence in developing countries' democracies is not complete as yet. Stated more bluntly, we still need to assess whether and why politicians in developing democracies that are more party centered are likely to curtail the de facto independence of the judiciary when their hazard rate in office is high. To answer this question, we thus turn to the next chapter, where we explore the politics of de facto judicial impendence in the following developing country's democracy where the degree of political particularism is low: Indonesia.

CHAPTER 7

De Facto Judicial Independence in Party-Centered Systems

Post–Suharto Indonesia

In sharp contrast to the high levels of de facto autonomy enjoyed by the judiciary in Brazil and India, the Indonesian judiciary has often been described as an institution that lacks de facto autonomy (see, for example, Lev 2004; Butt 2007). What accounts for such striking differences in judicial autonomy across these three countries that face similar development challenges? The analysis in the previous chapter illustrated the argument we presented in hypothesis 2 that the *candidate-centered* nature of Brazil and India's electoral systems was crucial in inducing incumbents in these two countries to increase the de facto independence of the judiciary in the context of short time horizons due to high hazard rates in office. In this chapter, we use the Indonesian case to illustrate the causal dynamics, which explain why incumbents in some countries make the opposite choice when they face short time horizons in office—to curb de facto judicial independence (DFJI). As argued in the corollary to hypothesis 2, if governments facing short time horizons are operating in electoral systems that create party-centered democracies, such as Indonesia, they have strong incentives to reduce rather than increase DFJI.

Recall from the previous chapter that similar to incumbents in Brazil and India, the hazard rates Indonesian incumbents face are also high, which implies that the time horizons they face are also low. However, unlike Brazil and India, Indonesia employed a closed-list Proportional Representation (hereafter closed-list PR) electoral system for several years after the country made a transition to democracy in 1999. This gave party leaders ballot control over candidate nominations and pooled votes across all candidates in party lists. Consequently, in contrast to Brazil and India, the degree of political particularism in Indonesia was low and the country's political landscape was dominated by strong, centralized political parties. This allows us to use Indonesia to illustrate the causal claim in chapter 2, which posits that policymakers in party-centered developing democracies have both the incentives and the political capacity to curb the de facto independence of the judiciary when their survival in office is threatened.

Furthermore, from a substantive perspective, the Indonesia case allows us to demonstrate why time horizons created by levels of political competition alone are insufficient to explain variation in de facto judicial independence (DFJI) across countries. Collectively, the analyses of these three cases—Brazil and India representing candidate-centered electoral systems and Indonesia representing party-centered electoral systems—demonstrate that the incentives to increase or decrease DFJI created by political competition are conditioned by the nature of political competition political elites face as a result of the degree of particularism electoral rules create.

The remainder of this chapter is organized into the following sections. We begin with a brief background of the choice of Indonesia's electoral rule in the post–democratic transition period—especially 1999 to 2004—and show that it engendered low levels of particularism and (thus) gave rise to highly centralized political parties.[1] This is followed by a description of the hazard rate of successive Indonesian governments after the country made the transition to democracy in 1999. In section three, we explore how the presence of strong and highly centralized political parties in Indonesia played a critical role in inducing leaders from the ruling party to capture the judiciary and how the Indonesian judiciary's responded to the government's attempt to curb its independence. We then show in section four that leaders in Indonesia's party-centered system curtailed the courts' autonomy when their hazard rates in office became high. In section five, we examine some within-country legislative data that show how governments in Indonesia's party-centered democracy successfully passed legislative statutes and bills that essentially eroded the courts' de facto autonomy. We end the chapter with a brief conclusion.

Indonesia: Party-Centered Democracy and the Hazard Rate of Governments

As we discussed in chapter 2, a rich literature on institutions suggests that the constituent elements of electoral rules—such as the formula for translating votes into seats, the way electoral districts are drawn, and the structure of the ballot—exert an independent influence on the degree to which a given electoral system is personalist in nature. The fact that electoral rules determine the strength (or lack thereof) of political parties and thus the extent to which parties are personalistic was recognized by political leaders as well as by the seven-member team of "experts"—the *Tim Tujuh*—set up to study alternatives and then recommend an appropriate electoral system for Indonesia in 1998 (McBeth 1998; Suryadinata 2002; Reilly 2006). However, the proposals for a single-member district plurality voting system (first past the post, FPTP) put forth by the *Tim Tujuh* were rejected by Indonesia's political parties, who were concerned about the consequences of choosing such a highly particularistic system.[2] Instead, after the transition to democracy in 1999, the parties succeeded in establishing the closed-list (i.e., party-list) PR system as the main rule for electing representatives to the *Dewan Perwakilan Rakyat* (Croissant et al. 2002; Reilly 2006; Shin 2010).

The adoption of the closed-list PR rule was, in part, driven by the need to maintain cohesive and centralized parties in Indonesia. For instance, the most prominent political party during the period of democratization—the Golkar Party—"feared the loss of power that would occur if they could no longer determine the order of candidates" (King 2003: 61) in a non-closed list PR institution such as the FPTP system. Since the closed-list PR electoral system gives parties control over nominations and pools votes across candidates on the party list, it promotes both party discipline and centralization of the decision-making and nomination process within political parties. As Hix (2004: 196) notes these features, "allows party leaders to exert a high degree of control over their legislators." Thus, this electoral system seemed like the right choice for party leaders concerned about loss of control over rank-and-file members. Political leaders from the other main political parties—the PDI-P, PKB, PPP and the PAN[3]—took full advantage of the closed-list PR electoral rule to set up strong, centralized and unified parties in which party leaders exerted complete control over rank-and-file party members (Johnson Tan 2006; Ufen 2006; Croissant et al. 2002).[4] Indeed, as predicted by the theoretical literature,[5] on adoption in 1999, it ensured that Indonesia did not develop into a highly particularistic, or, in other words, a candidate-centered democracy (Johnson Tan 2006; Ufen 2006; King 2003). Rather, as emphasized by Ufen (2006: 19):

> The whole system of party-list proportional representation strengthens the hold of central party leaderships . . . crucial decisions such as the nomina-

tion of candidates are made by some core executive members who are usually loyal to one charismatic leader. The decision-making process is almost fully oriented from the top down to the branches.

Likewise, Johnson Tan (2006: 110) suggests that in Indonesia, "the closed-list proportional representation strengthens the parties and the party central leaderships particularly." By late 1999, Indonesia clearly emerged as a party-centered democracy (Johnson Tan 2006; Ufen 2006; Croissant et al. 2002). Given these high levels of intraparty centralization and sufficient control of individual party members by party leaders in Indonesia in the initial post–transition years, the Indonesian polity was characterized by a low particularism level of 2.5 in the 1 (minimum) to 13 (maximum) Wallack et al. (2005) ordinal scale of electoral particularism.

Apart from promoting the strength plus centralization of political parties, the low level of particularism engendered by the country's closed-list PR electoral rule has also provided party leaders with an opportunity to ban individual party candidates or chastise recalcitrant party members by terminating their party membership and replacing them with individuals that are more "loyal" to the party.[6] As a result, Ufen (2006) emphasizes that intraparty opposition has been consistently marginalized in the PDI-P, the PKB, and the PPP, which are the main political parties that constituted the government in Indonesia's party-centered democracy from 2000 to 2004. The marginalization of intraparty opposition has allowed party leaders to further augment their control over individual party members. For example, in 2003, prominent members of the ruling PDI-P party such as Sophan Sophiaan, Indira Damayanti Sugondo, Arifin Panigoro, and Haryanto Taslam, who opposed some official party statutes, were forced to resign from their party posts by President Megawati.[7] Likewise, in another mainstream political party, the PKB, prominent party members including Alwi Shibab and Syaifullah Yusuf were sacked by Abdurrahman Wahid (the chief executive of the PKB party) in 2004 after they opposed the choice of Wahid's nephew, Mujamin Iskandar, for the post of party chairman.[8] These two examples illustrate how extensive the control that Indonesian party leaders have over their party members really is. As discussed earlier, scholars attribute this high degree of party control at this time to the presence of closed list PR electoral rules in Indonesia during this period.

Although Indonesia firmly remained a party-centered democracy from 1999 to 2004, the lack of democratic accountability led to the introduction of the open-list PR electoral rule for electing representatives to the *Dewan Perwakilan Rakyat* from 2005 onwards (Reynolds et al. 2005; Reilly 2006). Scholars of Indonesian politics debate whether or not the adoption of the open-list PR rule has improved democratic accountability in Indonesia (Johnson Tan 2006; Reilly 2006). They, however, generally share the opinion that the open-list PR system has served to weaken the control that Indonesian party leaders had over their party members in the first four–five post–democratic-transition years (see, for example, Buehler 2009; Sherlock 2009). Thus, with respect to Indonesia's electoral system, we observe a clear distinction between the two periods: 2005 to 2010, and the 1999 to 2004 period. From 1999 to 2004, Indonesia is visibly a strong party-centered democracy. But during the 2005 to 2010 period, the country slowly (but not fully) shifted to a candidate-centered system.

Recall that our theoretical story predicts that in party-centered developing democracies, politicians are more likely to reduce the de facto autonomy of the judiciary when their time horizons (hazard rate) in office are low (high). Thus to directly test the causal mechanism underlying this prediction, we focus on analyzing judicial independence in Indonesia during the years in which it is strictly observed as a closed-list PR and thus party-centered democracy, but not after 2004 when its electoral rule changed to open-list PR. In particular, to save space in this chapter, we do not explore judicial politics in depth in Indonesia after 2004 because the theoretical case it represents how candidate-centered systems affect de facto judicial autonomy in developing democracies has already been extensively analyzed in the previous chapter using the Brazil and India cases.

Before we turn to explore de facto judicial independence in Indonesia, it is worth noting that since Indonesia's electoral rule promoted strong political parties (which include the ruling party) in the early years of the previous decade, one would logically expect greater government stability and consequently higher time horizons of governments in office. This is because in a party-centered democracy, the relatively high levels of intraparty discipline curtails the practice of party-switching by ruling party members which decreases the likelihood of government dissolution (Mainwaring 1990; Kitschelt 2000; Owens 2004). However, a careful examination of the hazard rate of successive governments in office in Indonesia from 1999 to 2004, which (as described in chapter 5) is computed by deriving the predicted probability of failure of each government,[9] reveals that incumbents in Indonesia generally have a low time horizon in office and correspond-

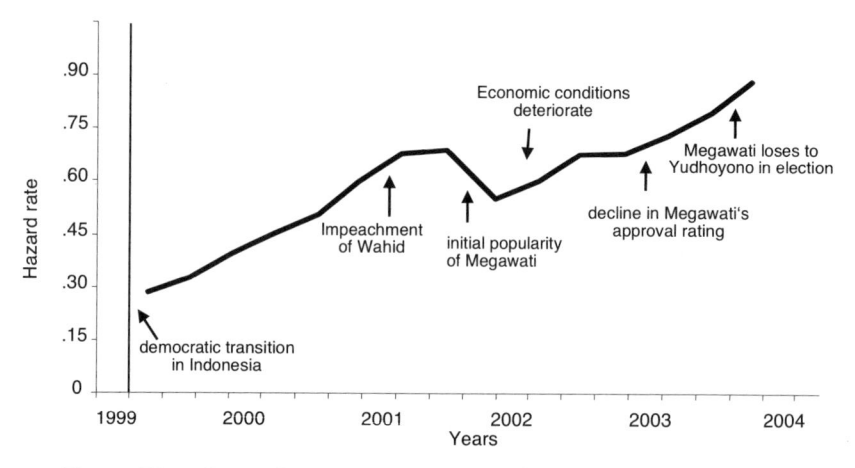

Fig. 7.1. Hazard rate of governments in post-Suharto democratic Indonesia

ingly a high hazard rate. To see this, consider fig. 7.1, which illustrates the hazard rate measure of all governments across time in post–Suharto democratic Indonesia from the year of the country's democratic transition, 1999, to 2004.

The illustration in fig. 7.1 provides two insights. First, it indicates that the hazard rate of governments in office in Indonesia has been volatile between 1999 and 2004. The volatility of the hazard rate, and, therefore, the time horizons of governments in Indonesia in the figure, reflect the country's recent political history. For instance, we find that the government's hazard rate increased quite sharply from the last half of 2003 to the middle of 2004. This is not surprising given that in the immediate months preceding the election date of July 5, 2004, the government, headed by President Megawati Sukarnopoutri, anticipated that it may be defeated by the opposition party, the *Partai Demokrat,* with a fairly high probability in the upcoming July 2004 election.[10] In sharp contrast, we find that the government's hazard rate between early 2002 and the first quarter of 2003 is low and stable. This is because the approval rating of Megawati Sukarnoputri, who was nominated as the country's president in July 2002, was considerably high in this time period,[11] and as noted by observers, "her grip on power was rock-solid."[12]

Second, fig. 7.1 and calculations derived from the predicted probability of government failure in Indonesia reveal that the moving average of the hazard rate of governments in Indonesia between 1999 and 2004 is 0.61—this is quite high. Stated differently, this implies that the probability with which successive governments in Indonesia anticipated ex ante to be removed from office in the aforementioned time period mentioned was on average as high as 0.6. Thus, governing elites could expect their tenures in office to be fairly short. Why was the hazard rate of governments in post–Suharto democratic Indonesia so high? Three reasons provide an answer to this question.

To begin with, as shown in table 7.1, none of the four major political parties in Indonesia—the PKP, the PDI-P, the PPP, and the Golkar Party—won the country's first post–democratic transition election in 1999 with a clear majority. Therefore, the head of the PKB, Abdurrahman Wahid (designated as the country's president in 1999 by the House of Representatives) formed a grand coalition and "national unity cabinet" with the other major political parties listed in table 7.1 in October 1999 (Johnson Tan 2006; Slater 2006; Ufen 2006).[13] From the very outset, this grand coalition was marred by interparty conflict even though each party in the coalition was characterized by high levels of *intraparty unity* and discipline (Imawan

TABLE 7.1. Legislative Seats Held by Eleven Largest Indonesian Political Parties

1999 Election			2004 Election		
Political Parties	Legislative Seats (N)	Percentage of Legislative Seats	Political Parties	Legislative Seats (N)	Percentage of Legislative Seats
PDI-P	153	33.1	PDI-P	109	19.8
Golkar	120	26	Golkar	128	23.3
PKB	51	11	PKB	52	9.5
PPP	58	12.6	PPP	58	10.5
PKS	7	1.5	PKS	45	8.2
PAN	34	7.4	PAN	52	9.5
Partai Demokrat	n/a	n/a	Partai Demokrat	57	10.4
PBR	n/a	n/a	PBR	13	2.4
PBB	13	2.8	PBB	11	2.0
PDS	n/a	n/a	PDS	12	2.2
PKPI	4	0.9	PKPI	1	0.2

Source: Data from Electionworld.org, "Elections in Indonesia," http://www.electionworld.org/indonesia.htm; "Perhitungan Perolehan Kursi DPR RI, KPU Indonesia, http://www.kpu.go.id/dprkursi.php.

Note: The full names of the parties are as follows: Golkar = Partai Golkar; PDI-P = Partai Demokrasi Indonesia-Perjuangan; PKB = Partai Kebangkitan Bangsa; PPP = Partai Persatuan Pembangunan; PKS = Partai Keadilan Sejahtera; PAN = Partai Amanat Nasional; PBR = Partai Bintang Reformasi; PBB = Partai Bulan Bintang; PDS = Partai Damai Sejahtera; PKPI = Partai Kesatuan dan Persatuan Indonesia. n/a = not applicable.

2004; Johnson Tan 2006; Ufen 2006). To exacerbate matters, President Wahid managed to alienate not only most of his own supporters by repeatedly sacking members of his "national unity cabinet" but also members of parliament (Sherlock 2001; Johnson Tan 2006; Fukuyama 2005).

President Wahid's deteriorating relationship with parliament finally came to a crisis when parliament formally voted him out of office on July 23, 2001 (Sherlock 2001; Fukuyama 2005). Megawati Sukarnoputri was then unanimously supported by members of parliament to take the office of president (Sherlock 2001; Ufen 2006). The instability of Indonesia's first post–Suharto democratic government owing to the absence of cooperation between (not within) the parties in government and the impeachment of President Wahid thus explains why the hazard rate of the government was high from 1999 to 2001, as shown in fig. 7.1.

However, the emergence of Megawati Sukarnoputri as Indonesia's new president did not result in higher government stability either. In fact, the second reason driving the high hazard rate of governments in Indonesia in the early years of this decade was Megawati's failure to politically and economically stabilize Indonesia. Initially, Megawati's impressively high approval ratings in 2002 during her initial months as president helped her to restore some degree of political and economic stability after the tumult of the 1999–2001 period (Johnson Tan 2006: 94; Slater 2006). However, as suggested by Johnson Tan (2006: 95), these proved to be transitory as President Megawati failed to find

> solutions to the country's many problems: corruption, rising prices, sluggish growth, little foreign investment, and unemployment. Further, the president was singularly incapable of communicating to the public what efforts the government was in fact taking in these areas.

Megawati's inability to handle the country's pressing problems made her unpopular among voters and prompted them to vote her and her party (the PDI-P) out of office in 2004 (Tomaglo 2004; Imawan 2004; Jonhson Tan 2006). As shown in table 7.1, the share of votes obtained by her PDI-P declined from 33.7 percent in the 1999 election to as low as 18.5 percent in the 2004 election. Megawati's increasing unpopularity from 2003 and eventual exit from office certainly contributed to the high levels of the hazard rate of Indonesia's governments in the initial years of this decade.

Third, the effective number of legislative parties (ENLP) in Indonesia increased from 6 in 1999 to 8.5 in 2004.[14] As suggested by Johnson Tan (2006: 93), "the effective number of parties after the 2004 elections was 8.55, up strongly from 6.1 after 1999, confirming the dilution of the party system from 1999 to 2004." An increase in the number of effective parties in the legislature tends to reduce the vote share of the major parties, including the ruling party, and thus weakens the degree of the ruling party (or parties) political support in the electorate (Merlo 1998; Martin 1999). This, in turn, has also served to decrease (increase) the time horizons (hazard rate) of incumbents in office. These political trends, which are fairly typical political phenomenon in developing country democracies, made tenure in office a highly uncertain prospect in Indonesia.

We suggested in chapter 2 that when the hazard rate of governments in office is high in party-centered developing country democracies, they will curtail de facto independence of the judiciary. We now examine how political elites and courts responded to the incentives created by these two conditions of strong parties due to low particularism and short time horizons, and how their behaviors affected DFJI in Indonesia.

Judicial Capture in the Indonesian Polity

Recall from chapter 2 that we proposed a three-step theoretical argument to account for the politics of de facto judicial independence in party-centered developing democracies where the level of particularism is low. First, we emphasized that when the ruling party (or parties) that constitute the government is strong and centralized, which occurs in party-centered systems, the government will not relinquish the management and administration of the judicial system to the judiciary. Rather, it will attempt to capture the judiciary to impose its agenda on the courts. We then suggested that if the hazard rate of the government in a party-centered democracy becomes high, the Supreme Court will exploit the government's vulnerability by openly resisting judicial capture and threatening to ally with the opposition to politically challenge the incumbent. Third, to preempt further political challenges from the court when the government's grip on office becomes tenuous (owing to a high hazard rate), we argued that party leaders from the government in a party-centered system will exercise their control over party legislators to pass legislative bills that curtail the de facto independence of the judiciary. The Indonesian case, as discussed shortly, corroborates and illustrates each of the three causal claims elucidated earlier.

To start with, a careful analysis of Indonesia's political history indicates that the government indeed attempted to control the judiciary, as suggested by the first step of our theoretical argument. After Indonesia made the transition to democracy, a working committee was set up in 1999 to study and formulate strategies for the implementation of immediate separation of the judicial and executive functions of the government, which formed the genesis of the "one-roof system."[15] To implement the working committee's recommendation, bureaucrats from the Ministry of Justice in President Abdurrahman Wahid's government designed law 35 and law 43 of 1999, which were developed to establish the one-roof system and change the status of subordinate court judges from that of civil servants to state officeholders (Lindsey 2002; Bedner 2003; Assegaf 2007).

On the surface, the development of law 35 and law 43 under the Wahid administration signaled to the public that the executive (specifically, the government led by Wahid) keenly supported efforts to reform the judicial system. In reality, however, concrete steps to implement laws 35 and 43 were specifically avoided by both the Wahid administration and his successor, President Megawati Sukarnoputri.[16] Consequently, the power of managing the judiciary was not transferred from the executive to the Supreme Court as envisaged by the one-roof system.[17] Instead, the Megawati government in Indonesia's party-centered democracy deliberately blocked the implementation of the one-roof system. As bluntly stated by Assegaf (2007: 16) who is a well-known constitutional lawyer in Indonesia:

> many observers were of the opinion that the real reason for the delay in establishing the one-roof system was the Megawati government's unwillingness to give up control over the courts and to eliminate a source of departmental funding.

Moreover, Assegaf (2007: 40–41) emphasizes that

> There were a number of reasons that are believed to have led to the delay. First, the possibility of gaining benefit from wielding administrative power over the courts . . . Second, the Department of Justice could use funding allocated to the courts to make up for funding deficiencies in other sections

of the Department. Third, the Minister did not believe that the Supreme Court would be able to better administer its affairs than the Department.

Assegaf's (2007) insight is interesting since it supports our theoretical claim that incumbents in party-centered systems (where the degree of particularism is low) like Indonesia are reluctant to relinquish the management and administration of the judicial system to the courts. This consequently serves to curtail the courts' de facto autonomy as well.

Apart from resisting implementation of the one-roof system that could potentially enhance the courts' de facto autonomy, successive incumbents in Indonesia's party-centered democracy have avoided granting financial autonomy to the courts (Susetio 2008; McLeod 2008). In fact, after she assumed the presidency, the Megawati administration publicly reaffirmed Article 5(2) of Indonesia's 1945 constitution, which states that

> the organizational, administrative and financial management of the courts will be effected by the Ministry of Justice.[18]

Through these tactics the Megawati government ensured that the task of financial management of the courts stayed with a government body (the Ministry of Justice), and no significant changes to dilute this arrangement were. In fact, till date, the courts completely depend on the state for revenue (Susetio 2008; Pompe 2005; Lev 2004).

Moreover, despite stiff opposition from the Judges Association (IKAHUI), the Wahid government proposed and the Megawati administration created the Supreme Audit Board—that is, the *Badan Pemeriksa Keuangan* (hereafter BPK)—to audit the finances of the Supreme Court, the high courts, and the state courts (Susetio 2008; Von Lubeke 2010).[19] The BPK was ostensibly set up to act as a check on judicial corruption in Indonesia, which was alleged to be widespread in the country's judiciary (Smith et al. 2003; World Bank 2006; Transparency International Report 2007). However, by controlling the substance and passage of Article 23(f) of the third amendment to Indonesia's Constitution, which set the procedures and organization of the BPK, Megawati's government ensured that the BPK's members would be selected by the president and the House of Representatives).[20] Through these appointments, Megawati's government was able to control the formal development and institutionalization of the BPK, which, in turn, allowed it to increase its financial grip over the judicial system

(Pompe 2005; Susetio 2008). Strengthening her administration's financial grip over the judiciary soon allowed it to effectively keep the courts' de facto autonomy in check (Pompe 2005; Susetio 2008). Thus from the very outset, it is quite clear that political elites in Indonesia's closed-list PR party-centered democracy resisted the implementation of any concrete arrangements that could enhance the judiciary's autonomy.

Megawati often publicly expressed her opinion that the courts had too much independence and lacked oversight. This independence posed a political problem for her administration since the judiciary could prove to be an obstacle in her government's goal of implementing their political and policy agenda. Therefore, in order to address this political problem, her government adopted three additional strategies, which capitalized on the discipline of her party to capture the judicial system and impose its agenda on the judiciary. First, even though her predecessor, President Wahid, had promised that he or his successor would transfer the authority of administering the judicial system to the Supreme Court, her administration consciously chose to not transfer the authority to administer high courts and state courts in the country to the Supreme Court.[21] The political motivation behind these tactics was pointed out by Assegaf (2007: 28), who states that under President Megawati:

> the government, through the then Minister of Justice, Yusril Mahendra, appeared to drag its heels on transferring authority over court administration to the Supreme Court. This gave rise to charges that the executive was intent on strengthening its control over the courts, and maintaining the tradition of intervention in judicial affairs.

Second, in 2002, the Ministry of Justice in Megawati's government successfully passed the "Judicial Commission Law" in the House of Representatives. This law, which was initially introduced in the third amendment to Indonesia's constitution, granted the Judicial Commission the power to propose the selection of justices to the Supreme and High Courts, and the administrative "authority to maintain and ensure the honor, dignity and behavior of judges" (Rositawati 2010; Butt 2007).[22] Although the Judicial Commission was publicized as an independent institution[23] that would act as a check on Indonesia's courts, this institution (much like the BPK) is, in effect, a government organization as "the members of the Judicial Commission . . . are appointed to, and dismissed from their position by the President" (Cumaraswamy 2006: 33). Through control over appointments to the Judicial Commission, Megawati's government was able to influence appointments and dismissals to positions throughout the judiciary, thus directly extending its control over the judiciary. Thus, the Judicial Commission also provided the government with a legal instrument to curb the judiciary's ability to be politically autonomous in de facto terms (Assegaf 2007; Butt 2007).

Third, even though the Judicial Commission can propose justices for the Supreme and High Courts, the discretion to approve justices preselected by the Judicial Commission rests on the president of Indonesia and the House of Representatives (*Dewan Perwakilan Rakyat*). This is stated explicitly in Article 24(a) of the third constitutional amendment, which was also written into law by the Megawati administration:[24]

> Candidate justices of the Supreme Court shall be proposed by the Judicial Commission to the *Dewan Perwakilan Rakyat* for approval and shall subsequently be formally appointed to office by the President.[25]

The ruling PDI-P party, led by President Megawati, which was the main ruling party in government from 2001–2004, leveraged the president's discretionary power to approve justices for the Supreme Court to "hand-pick" its "favorite" nominees to serve as justices in the Supreme Court (Assegaf 2005; Pompe 2005).[26] This tactic is emphasized in an interview by Todung Mulya Lubis, a prominent Indonesian lawyer, who mentioned that in Indonesia:

> an independent judiciary is just a myth . . . the pre-selection of justice candidates ultimately fall to the President and the House of Representatives . . . this is where the political transaction occurs. The elected justices, who will ultimately serve on the Supreme and High courts, are products of political dealings.[27]

The aforementioned discussion highlights how the Megawati government was able to capitalize on its party discipline in the legislature to successfully pass bills and amendments that enhanced its control over the judiciary and allowed it to capture the courts. These tactics corroborate our theoretical claims that incumbents in party-centered developing democracies like Indonesia (from 1999 to 2004) will not only be motivated to capture the judiciary but will also successfully take concrete steps to act on these motivations. This, of course, has the effect of reducing the judiciary's de facto autonomy.

The motivation to capture the judiciary in the first place however comes from the potential to use a captive judiciary to enhance the legitimacy of the government's political and policy agenda, to minimize opposition success in resisting it, and to prevent legal challenges to its design and implementation. After successfully amending the constitution to centralize various appointment and financial powers in the hands of government agencies, the PDI-P Party-led government under Megawati used these powers to "pack" the Supreme Court with some judges that favored its political and economic agenda.[28] This particular tactic subsequently proved immensely useful to the PDI-P in promoting and implementing key policies on its agenda. These political incentives to capture the judiciary and the payoffs from doing so can be seen clearly in the following two policy battles that President Megawati's government engaged in during her tenure.

The first issue involved a battle to govern Indonesia according to Sharia law, which implied rejection of the notion of separation between the state and religion, and potentially threatened freedom of religion in a multiethnic democracy like Indonesia (Klemb 2007; Assyaukanie 2007; Salim 2008). The PDI-P staunchly opposed the creation of an Islamic state in Indonesia and was adamant that the state should be built on the principles of *Pancasila*,[29] which envisaged, among other factors, a secular state for Indonesia where its citizens have the freedom to practice any religion and a complete separation of state and religion (Hadiwinata 2003; Indrayana 2008; Platzdasch 2008). This position was opposed by other political parties and Islamic leaders termed the "Islamic caucus" (Ichwan 2005; Indrayana 2008).[30] Hence, when the PDI-P proposed an amendment to article 29 of the Indonesian constitution, which would make it mandatory for governments in Indonesia to strictly follow the principles of *Pancasila* rather than allow the country to evolve into an Islamic state (Ichwan 2005; Diederich 2004; Indrayana 2008), it was determinedly opposed by the Islamic caucus. They demanded instead that the amendment to article 29 should include the following seven words: "dengan kewajiban menjalankan syari'at Islam bagi para pemeluknya" (with the obligation for adherents of the faith to carry out Islamic sharia), which would facilitate the implementation of Sharia law in the country.[31]

The contrasting preference between the ruling PDI-P Party and the Islamic caucus on the *Pancasila* versus *Sharia* law issue generated heated debate between these two sides on the legislative floor and increased the potential for conflict (Diederich 2004; Indrayana 2008). Given the high stakes in this issue and the PDI-P Party's determination to constitutionally reaffirm the implementation of *Pancasila,* the PDI-P turned to pro-Megawati justices in the Supreme Court—who were nominated by her cabinet and the Ministry of Justice in the first place—to obtain public statements of support from these justices for the principle of *Pancasila* (Assyaukanie 2007; Salim 2008). In response, the pro-Megawati justices not only endorsed the PDI-P's position on the aforementioned issue but also publicly stated that the Indonesian constitution should

> embrace the two sacrosanct principles of the country: the Pancasila state ideology and the unitary state of the Republic of Indonesia . . . and it is the duty of the government of Indonesia to ensure that new rules or laws do not violate these two principles.[32]

The public endorsement of the PDI-P Party's preference for resisting the creation of an Islamic state by pro-Megawati justices sympathetic to her party's agenda substantially enhanced the legal credibility of the party's position on the *Pancasila* issue in the eyes of the electorate and helped to minimize the political costs of the required legislative actions (Indrayana 2008). Her administration then used the endorsement of these hand-picked Supreme Court justices in order to legitimize the introduction of a modification to article 29 of the fourth amendment to Indonesia's constitution and to successfully pass it. This modification rejected the call for establishing Sharia law and has made it mandatory in constitutional terms for every government in Indonesia to respect the freedom of worship and allow the country's citizens to practice any religion.[33] In short, this example illustrates how the government used its legislative ability to capture the judiciary by changing judicial appointment rules, used the new rules to place pro-government judges in the Supreme and High Courts, and then subsequently used the captive courts to implement one of its key objectives, *Pancasila*. This example therefore clearly illustrates the causal mechanism proposed in our theoretical framework in practice in Indonesia.

A second example of the dynamic motivating judicial capture and its subsequent payoffs in party-centered systems can be seen in the policy fight over increasing welfare spending on key demographic groups during Megawati led PDI-P's tenure in office. The Megawati-led government proposed sharp increases in targeted spending on welfare that was directly primarily toward the PDI-P Party's key constituency—the *wong cilik,* which largely constitutes the urban and rural poor in Indonesia.[34] Instead of merely instituting a government program to enact this policy, her government proposed to amend article 33 in the fourth amendment to Indonesia's constitution such that it obliged her cabinet and future governments in Indonesia to (1) create an economic structure that takes care of Indonesia's citizens, particularly the poor, as a "family"; and (2) follow policies—for example, spending policies—that enhance social justice, equity, and national economic unity. This is stated in a rather grandiose manner in article 33, part 4, of the fourth amendment to Indonesia's constitution:

> the organization of the national economy shall be conducted on the basis of economic democracy upholding the principles of togetherness, efficiency with justice, continuity, environmental perspective, self-sufficiency, and keeping a balance in the progress and unity of the national economy.[35]

This proposal drew sharp criticism from the media and some opposition party members who perceived such targeted spending policies as blatant partisan politics by the executive. For instance, the editorial page of an Indonesian newspaper, the *Suratkabar,* bluntly pointed out in late 2003 that

> President Megawati's decision to drastically increase welfare spending to improve the livelihood of under-privileged sections of Indonesia's may seem like a noble act . . . but it is really a disguise for cheap populism. Indonesia can ill-afford to increase public spending when the country's fiscal situation is still in the doldrums.[36]

Facing such widespread criticism, the government needed to shore up the legitimacy of its position and the credentials of the program as benefitting Indonesians rather than as a populist partisan gambit to buy electoral support. In order to accomplish this goal, Megawati's cabinet again used its leverage over its hand-picked judges in the Supreme and High Courts to get them to endorse the government's stand on the welfare-spending issue and legitimize this policy agenda. This tactic worked well. The proposed amendment to article 33 was indeed supported by public statements made by judges that were picked to serve as Supreme Court justices by her government's Ministry of Justice. These public endorsements were effective in providing a veneer of legal legitimacy to her cabinet's actions and smoothed the legislative of the amendment to aforementioned article 33.[37] Once the Megawati administration obtained the required legislative support, it used article 33 as "political cover" to implement targeted spending policies that favored its main constituency: the *wong cilik* (Sebastian 2004; Aspinall 2005). The partisan motivation of the government in promoting this policy and the key role of the judiciary if facilitating its passage and implementation despite its partisan goal is indicated in the editorial page of *Suara Pembaruan*, which pointed out that

> it comes as no surprise that Supreme Court judges who depend on the goodwill of Megawati's government . . . will not question but instead support amendments to the country's constitution presented by the PDI-P even though these amendment only serve to perpetuate the PDI-P's ideological goals and helps the party to pursue economic policies that favors their vote-bank.[38]

Therefore, the second example previously described shows—as predicted by our theory—that governments in party-centered systems like Indonesia will take legislative and informal steps to exert greater control over the judiciary in order to use this control to impose their partisan agenda in the polity.

Although Megawati's government made strides toward controlling the judiciary, its grip on office became increasingly tenuous from 2003, raising the hazard rate of her government in office considerably. We now analyze how the judiciary responded to the opportunity this presented them in order to defend their institutional interests.

The Government's Hazard Rate and the Judiciary's Response

We saw in the previous section that Megawati's administration successfully adopted some tactics to exert greater control over the judiciary. But it was far less successful in dealing with the country's economic problems (Johnson Tan 2006; Schuman 2004; Dowling and Yap 2004). Consequently, Megawati's support in the electorate declined from late 2003 onwards, while the popularity of the main opposition party, *Partai Demokrat* (Democratic

Party), led by the charismatic Susilo Bambang Yudhoyono, increased dramatically during the same time period. Pessimism about Megawati's electoral prospects was suggested as early as January 2004 by a popular Jakarta-based weekly, *Laksamana,* which stated that

> an opinion poll shows Susilo Bambang Yudhoyono with 41% support compared to 11.2% for incumbent President Megawati Sukarnoputri and 10% for Wiranto, the Golkar candidate . . . whether Megawati, who trails badly in the opinion polls, is prepared to lose remains to be seen.[39]

The fact that Megawati's poll ratings were significantly behind those of the main opposition candidate, Susilo Bambang Yudhoyono, was a clear sign that her government's hazard rate was increasing and that its tenure in office was likely to be short-lived. As we argued in chapter 2, this created a political opportunity for the judiciary to fight for its institutional interests by challenging government tactics and by allying with a resurgent opposition. As we discuss shortly, the Indonesian judiciary did indeed take advantage of the increasingly precarious position of Megawati by openly (1) rejecting the tactics used by her government to control the judiciary, and (2) endorsing the policy positions of the main opposition party (the *Partai Demokrat*) to challenge the political legitimacy of her government.

Recall that the Megawati administration chose to enact the Judicial Commission Law, which would give the Judicial Commission, and, by extension, the government oversight over the judicial system. In early 2004, when the Megawati government's political weakness had become apparent, the judiciary acted to challenge this government tactic to undermine their DFJI. Numerous justices from the Supreme and High Courts—who were not selected by the Ministry of Justice under Megawati but were selected before her reign in office—challenged the constitutionality of the Judicial Commission Law in the Constitutional Court (*Mahkamah Konstitusi*). Importantly, they did so precisely when the Megawati's government grip on power became tenuous (Assegaf 2007; Lindsey 2008; Harijanti and Lindsey 2006).[40] As pointed out by Assegaf (2007: 31), this overt challenge against the government's tactic was accepted by the *Mahkamah Konstitusi* since

> the Constitutional Court held that the Judicial Commission had engaged in courses of action that had violated the principle of judicial independence, and were therefore in violation of the Constitution. Accordingly, the Court

struck down the offending provisions of the Judicial Commission Law allowing for oversight of the judiciary by the Commission, and recommended that the House of Representatives and government take immediate steps to amend the legislation.

In addition to challenging the government's tactics vis-à-vis the judiciary, the judiciary also acted to undermine the legitimacy of the government's policy agenda by taking populist positions on key policies in the guise of guarding the constitution. A prominent target was the government's high profile privatization policies. In the aftermath of the 1997–98 financial crisis in Indonesia, the IMF, the World Bank, and the Asian Development Bank (ADB) made loans contingent upon Indonesia's attempts at deregulation and liberalization, including in the electricity and water industries (Suhud 2005: 6; Walhi 2003). As a result, the Abdurrahman Wahid government, and later, the Megawati government, committed itself to liberalize and privatize the electricity sector by

> (i) establishing the legal and regulatory framework to create a competitive electricity market; (ii) adjusting electricity tariffs; and (iv) rationalizing power purchases from private sector power projects.[41]

The Megawati government, in particular, made it a top priority to privatize the electricity industry to follow through on its commitment to the IMF and to also signal to foreign investors that Indonesia favored economic liberalization and was receptive to foreign investment (Tomasa 2006; Butt 2007). Modifying article 33(2) of the constitution was absolutely critical in this privatization effort for the government since it stated that the "branches of production that . . . affect the public's necessities of life," including the utilities industry such as electricity, "are to be controlled by the state" (Butt 2007; Rositawati 2010).[42] To facilitate its privatization drive, the Megawati government attempted to enact a legislative statute in 2004 that sought to amend article 33(2) of the Indonesia's constitution.

However, sensing that President Megawati was politically weak owing to her declining pro popularity, the judiciary seized the opportunity in the first quarter of 2004 to first prevent the few—Megawati justices in the court from airing opinions that would support her cabinet's privatization goals (Indriastuti 2006; Harun 2004; Stockmann 2007). The courts then openly challenged the legality of the government's decision to amend article 33(2) in the Constitutional Court to facilitate privatization of the electric industry. This challenge was also accepted by the *Mahkamah Konstitusi* since it "rejected most of the government's arguments in favor of privatization of the electric industry" (Butt and Lindsey 2009: 11). Additionally, it declared the entire statute aimed at privatizing the electric industry as

> invalid on the grounds that it was not in line with 'the soul and spirit' of article 33(2) of the constitution, which, according to the court, 'forms the basis of the Indonesian economy'. The (constitutional) court argued that it had no choice but to do this, because it believed that to amend only a small part of the Law would 'cause chaos that would lead to legal uncertainty' in the Law's application . . . the court also held that the state's obligation to ensure public prosperity would not necessarily be fulfilled by allowing competition, because the private sector would give priority to its own profits and would concentrate on established markets.[43]

Finally, in addition to challenging the government's privatization policies, the courts also started publicly questioning the political legitimacy of Megawati's government by adopting two tactics. For one, it supported the corruption charges leveled against Megawati's ministers by the main opposition party, the *Partai Demokrat* (Kenward 2004; Marks 2004). To this end, observe that by 2004 there were serious concerns that President Megawati had failed to reduce corruption and that it had become even more pervasive under her rule. This is reflected in a report published by *Time* magazine on April 26, 2004.

> Another common complaint is that Megawati has done little to tame the corruption that saps Indonesia's economic vitality. In a survey of businessmen and academics conducted last year by Berlin-based watchdog Transparency International, Indonesia ranked as the world's 12th most corrupt country, worse than economic basket cases such as Sierra Leone, Papua New Guinea and the Congo.[44]

Given concerns about widespread corruption in the Megawati government, the main opposition party, the *Partai Demokrat,* consistently issued a series of allegations of "large-scale" corruption carried out by ministers in Megawati's cabinet while campaigning for the 2004 election (Marks 2004; Davidson et al. 2006). For instance, Susilo Bambang Yudhoyono, the leader of the *Partai Demokrat,* alleged that corruption in the Megawati government has "bought suffering to the people and has damaged the morality of the nation," and that Megawati "does not consider corruption as a serious crime."[45] These allegations were clearly strategic as the *Partai Demokrat* employed its insinuations of corruption by Megawati's ministers as a political tool to weaken the President's support among the *wong cilik* (Murphy 2005).[46]

More crucially however, the courts supported the allegations of corruption put forth by the *Partai Demokrat.* For example, after Susilo Bambang Yudhoyono, the leader of the *Partai Demokrat,* "requested" the judiciary to check the party's charges of corruption against the Megawati government in January 2004,[47] the Supreme Court (for example) issued a series of statements that it was willing to pursue Susilo Bambang Yudhoyono's request.[48] There is little doubt that the public show of support by the court for the *Partai Demokrat's* corruption charges badly damaged the reputation of key ministers in Megawati's—a fact that did not go unnoticed by the Megawati administration (Hafild 2004; Davidson et al. 2006).

With respect to the second tactic, the courts endorsed the manifesto of the *Partai Demokrat* in the months prior to the July 2004 election, which criticized the economic policies and human rights practices of the government.[49] Specifically, in its manifesto, the *Partai Demokrat* criticized the Megawati's administration plan to privatize the utilities industry such as electricity and emphasized that the government should maintain state ownership of the electric industry as it was obligated to do so under article 33(2) of Indonesia's constitution (Dhakidae 2004; Mujani 2005). The judiciary publicly endorsed the *Partai Demokrat's* position of opposing the Megawati government's privatization plan. It also lauded the party for upholding the "letter and spirit of article 33(2) of the Constitution"[50] as the "court held that the increased transparency and reduced corruption that privatization was presumed to bring were outweighed by the importance of the state fulfilling its obligations under article 33" (Butt and Lindsey 2009: 11).

Apart from corruption charges, the *Partai Demokrat's* manifesto alleged that the Megawati government's human-rights practices were extremely poor, as it threatened human rights NGOs in the country and unfairly jailed political dissidents (Wall 2004; Nujani 2005; Trotter 2006); the judiciary also endorsed the *Partai Demokrat's* stance on this issue (Kompa 2004; Suryadinata 2004). To this end, it issued, along with some prominent scholars, the following joint statement to the Megawati government:

Strengthening the spirit of democracy, promoting transparency, and upholding human rights and freedom of expression are things that make us proud to be Indonesians. We should not allow these to be derailed.[51]

The court's endorsement of the *Partai Demokrat*'s manifesto was perceived by Megawati's ruling PDI-P Party as overt political support by the court for the opposition's goal of defeating Megawati in the 2004 election (Indrayana 2004; Sherlock 2004).

Some ruling PDI-P Party members also perceived the court's behavior as an attempt to forge a de facto alliance with the main opposition party, which was arguably what the court wanted to signal to the Megawati government.[52] Last but not the least, because the Megawati's government grip on office was looking increasingly fragile from late 2003 to early 2004 (owing to its high hazard rate in office), many members from her government also felt that further criticism of the government's policies and support for the oppositions' program by the court would irreversibly damage the government's electoral prospects in the upcoming 2004 election (Wanandi 2004; Pribadi 2005). This sentiment was expressed, for example, by the Minister of Justice in Megawati's cabinet, Yusril Mahendra, who stated the following.

> The decision taken by the justices to support Susilo Bambang Yudhoyono's unfounded allegations is regrettable as it weakens the government and unnecessarily creates political instability which Indonesia cannot afford.... It also unfairly hurts the government's reputation in the eyes of citizens which is inappropriate in an election year.[53]

How did the Megawati government respond to the perceived threat to its political survival from the court and the opposition—at a time when the government's grip on office was tenuous—as indicated by Yusril Mahendra? We turn to answer this question in the next section.

Restricting the Courts' De Facto Autonomy

To rationally preempt the threat to its political survival from the court and the opposition parties when its hazard rate in office was high, the Megawati administration in Indonesia's party-centered democracy (where the level of particularism is low) took—as predicted by the third step of our theoretical argument delineated earlier—two main steps in the first few months of 2004 to restrict the courts' judicial autonomy. The objective underlying these two steps, as stated in an interview by Andi Mallarangeng (member of Partai Demokrat's central board), was to "prevent interference in politics by the courts as it makes the country less secure, poorer, and undermines the government's effectiveness and legitimacy."[54]

The first step taken by Megawati was to introduce a legislative bill in early 2004 that completely delegated the authority to transfer and discipline judges in the country's high courts, state courts, and Supreme Court to the Ministry of Justice. This bill granted the Ministry of Justice the "authority to transfer and discipline judges that failed to maintain their honor, dignity and integrity based on the guidelines of the Judicial Commission."[55] According to Cumaraswamy (2006: 35), it ensured that the "proposals for transfer of judges originate from the Ministry of Justice . . . [also] the final decision on transfer rests with the Ministry of Justice." Delegating the responsibility of managing judges to the Justice ministry provided the government with more maneuvering room to directly interfere in the transfer of judges within all courts in the Indonesian judicial system as the Ministry of Justice is a part of the government. This is emphasized by Cumaraswamy (2006: 35, 40), who states that during Megawati's tenure as president

> the Ministry of Justice exercised excessive power in the appointment, transfer and discipline of judges, increasing the likelihood that of making judges beholden to the ministry . . . the practice of transferring judges for misconduct to other courts instead of bringing them to a more formal disciplinary process was inappropriate and harmful to the interests of the public and the consumers of justice.

The government's action of introducing a legislative bill that (as described earlier), delegated the responsibility of managing judges to the Justice Ministry was a direct attack on the de jure independence of Indonesian courts. Yet, note that the aforementioned action also provided an opportunity for Megawati's ministers to curb the de facto autonomy of the courts. This is because direct interference by the state in the supervision of judges via the Ministry of Justice induced judges in Indonesia's courts to placate the Ministry of Justice owing to their "career-concerns." And since judges in Indonesia's courts have career incentives to appease the Ministry of Justice, it allowed the Indonesian government to influence decisions taken by the judges for any given case that affects the government's interests (Cumaraswamy 2006; Pompe 2005). This, in turn, has served to reduce the de facto independence of the judiciary.

For the second step, Megawati's cabinet designed and enacted another legislative bill that shifted the final court of appeal for commercial verdicts from the Supreme and High Courts to the country's Commercial Court (*Pengadilan Niaga*).[56] Initially, the Commercial Court, which was established in 1998, was merely tasked to handle bankruptcy and insolvency applications. However, once the Supreme Court successfully blocked Megawati's attempt to privatize the electric industry, officials in her cabinet felt that the precedent set by the court with respect to obfuscating the government's privatization effort was too costly for the Indonesian economy (Bey 2004; Harding and Nicholson 2009). They also perceived the court's interference in the government's attempt to privatize the utilities sector as a direct challenge to the administration's political ability to implement policies (Bey 2004; Basri and Van Der Eng 2004; Harding and Nicholson 2009). Finally, they feared that the court's intervention in the issue area of privatization policies would reduce economic growth which would further damage the government's declining electoral prospects (Sulistiyanto 2004; Harding and Nicholson 2009).

Given the concerns held by Megawati's officials about the effect of the judiciary's activism in the realm of economic policy-making on the government's political future, it is hardly surprising that they chose to curb the court's ability to intervene on privatization issues by delegating final authority over commercial and economic cases to the Commercial Court. This was done by introducing a bill that bluntly proposed that the Commercial Court "will have the final power of decision in reviewing and judging commercial cases."[57] Transferring authority on commercial cases from the Supreme and High Courts to the Commercial Court was politically rational from the viewpoint of Megawati's government. Yet, it is not difficult to discern that this action taken by the Megawati cabinet was a direct attack on judicial independence as it curtailed the de facto ability of the judiciary to have a final say over commercial matters. More importantly, delegating final authority on commercial cases to the Commercial Court effectively transferred the authority over decision-making on commercial and economic cases to the executive since the Commercial Court, whose nominees are selected and approved by the attorney general's office, is controlled by the party (or parties) in power.[58]

These two main steps taken by the Megawati cabinet to clip the wings of the Supreme and High Courts—when the government's time horizons in office was low—clearly demonstrated its intent to curb the courts' de facto judicial independence. It is important to emphasize here, however, that it was not merely intent but rather the Megawati administration's political capacity to successfully obtain legislative support for the bills previously described that helped it to reduce the de facto autonomy of the courts in Indonesia. In particular, given that the parties were strong and centralized in Indonesia during the 2001 to 2004 period (due to its party-centered electoral rules), party leaders from the three main parties in the Megawati government (the PDI-P, the PPP, and the PKB) exerted significant control over their individual party members. They exercised their leverage to credibly threaten party members with expulsion from the party if they voted against the legislative bills that were, as discussed earlier, designed to curb the courts' autonomy.[59] The ability of the party leaders in the Megawati government to credibly threaten their party members with expulsion and the government's majority status in the legislature[60] helped Megawati's cabinet to garner sufficient legislative support to successfully ratify each of the two bills described earlier on the legislative floor.[61] The political dynamics underlying the passage of the bills previously described is nicely summarized in an interview by the previous chairman of the Indonesian Corruption Watch, Danang Widoyoko, who points out that

> The proposed legislation by Megawati's government, which was undoubtedly an attack on the judiciary's autonomy, was passed with ease in the DPR. . . . Megawati and Hamzi Haz used their discretion to convince and coerce their party members to vote for the legislation. This works well in a country where party members do as they are told by their party leaders.[62]

It is worth noting here, however, that the government's political capacity to pass legislation to curb the courts' autonomy did not just stop at the successful passage of the two aforementioned bills. Rather, as we discuss later, a brief analysis of constitutional amendment and statutory bills proposed and approved in Indonesia's party-centered democracy from June 1999 to December 2004 reveals that incumbents in the country have often successfully introduced and passed legislation to "tie the hands" of the courts, particularly when their hazard rate of office was high.

In order to examine the links between the government's hazard rate and bills or amendments that affects the de facto independence of the judicial system in Indonesia, we gathered data on all constitutional amendments and statutory bills that were proposed and then approved or rejected by Indonesia's parliament from mid-1999 to late 2004, when Indonesia is strictly observed as a party-centered democracy. This data was collected from numerous primary and secondary sources.[63] We then analyzed this data to study the timing and content of approved legislation affecting the judiciary.

Using these primary and secondary sources, we recorded the following information from each amendment or statutory bill: (1) the time (in days) it spent in the *Dewan Perwakilan Rakyat;* (2) its final outcome (approved, rejected, or pending); and (3) the issue area covered by the bill (e.g., pensions, taxes and fiscal policy, judicial system, etc).[64] As shown in table 7.2, a total of 195 amendments and bills were proposed between June 1999 and March 2006, and 128 of these amendment and bills were approved by the legislature during the same time period. As table 7.3 reports, 19 out of the total of 128 amendments and bills approved from mid-1999 to early 2006 pertained to the justice system.

Second, we checked the content of each of these 19 approved bills that deal with Indonesia's judicial system. In particular, we checked the language and provisions in each of these 19 approved bills to assess whether the pro-

TABLE 7.2. Constitutional Amendments and Statutory Bills in Indonesia from 1999 to 2005

	Number of Bills	Median	Minimum	Maximum
Type				
Constitutional amendment	29	64	2	932
Statutory bills	166	103	9	1,277
Total	195			
Outcome				
Approved	128			
Rejected	41			
Pending	26			

Note: The figures in the table include censored and noncensored cases. The median, minimum, and maximum figures in the table express the descriptive values of the number of days (i.e., the time) that amendments and bills spent in the national legislature.

TABLE 7.3. Approved Amendments and Bills by Issue-Area in Indonesia (1999–2005)

Issue-Areas	Number of Approved Amendments and Bills	Percentage of All Proposed Amendments and Bills Approved
Pensions	2	1.56
Public institutions	7	5.46
Taxes and fiscal policy	24	18.75
Public infrastructure	3	2.34
Labor legislation	6	4.68
Housing	1	0.78
Education	3	2.34
Defense	5	3.90
Farming	8	6.25
Trade and industry	21	16.40
Political and civil rights	3	2.34
State properties	6	4.68
National budget	6	4.68
Health	2	1.56
Judicial system	19	14.84
Other	12	9.37
Total	128	

TABLE 7.4. Examples of Amendments and Bills That Curtail the Judiciary's de facto Autonomy

Amendments/Bills	Brief Description
Article 24A (3) of the Third Amendment to Indonesia's Constitution, 2001–2	Appointment of judges to the Supreme Court follows a "fit and proper test" conducted by the Dewan Perwakilan Rakyat (the lower house of the national legislature). More specifically, candidate justices need to be approved by the Dewan Perwakilan Rakyat and are subsequently formally appointed to office by the president.
Article 39 of Law 27/2002 (confirmation of Article 20 of Law 2/1986)	Proposals for transfer of judges originate from the Ministry of Justice. Additionally, the final decision on transfer rests with the Ministry of Justice.

visions curb the court's de facto autonomy by creating formal avenues for the executive to (1) administer the courts either directly or indirectly (via government bodies/agencies, for example), (2) control the transfer of judges either, and (3) influence or interfere in the judicial decisions taken by courts in the country. Table 7.4 provides a brief description of a few amendments and statutory bills that meet any of the three aforementioned criteria.

After conducting the exercise described in the preceding paragraph, we found that as many as 16 amendments and bills contain provisions that satisfy any of the three criteria delineated above and thus directly curb the de facto independence of the courts. In other words, an astounding 84.21 percent of all approved amendments and bills that dealt exclusively with the Indonesian judiciary from 1999 onwards were designed and implemented with the objective of curtailing the de facto independence of the judiciary. Moreover, as fig. 7.2 illustrates, 15 out of the total of 16 court-curbing amendments and bills were approved when the hazard rate of the two governments in Indonesia's party-centered system (i.e., the Wahid and the Megawati governments), was increasing or already high. In fact, as fig. 7.2 shows, the most dramatic increase in the number of bills reducing judicial independence occurred in 2003 and 2004, which are precisely the years in which the hazard rate of the Megawati government in Indonesia was high. Hence, the preliminary analysis of the relevant legislative data from Indonesia provides some evidence for our claim that governments in party-centered developing democracies tend to pass legislation to restrict the judiciary's independence, especially when their political survival in office is under threat.

In contrast, after Indonesia shifted to an open-list PR system in 2005, a total of just one bill reducing the judiciary's independence was passed in the legislature for the first two years (2005 and 2006) under Yudhoyono's presidency, even though the moving average hazard rate of his government in office was quite high during these two years.[65] This is not surprising given that we anticipated theoretically in chapter 2 that governments in more candidate-centered systems (typically produced by the open-list PR rule) will not reduce but rather maintain or enhance de facto judicial autonomy when their hazard rate in office is high. More importantly, however, the preliminary analysis of the relevant legislative data from Indonesia provides some evidence for our claim that governments in closed-list PR democracies tend to pass legislation to restrict the judiciary's independence, especially when their political survival in office is under threat.

DFJI in Party-Centered Systems   255

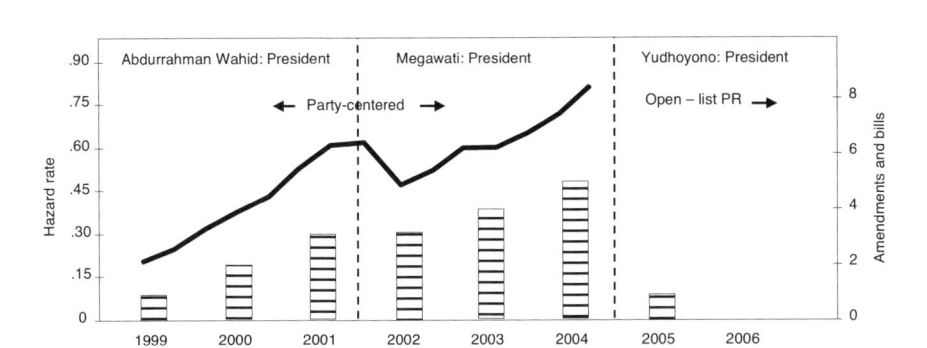

Fig. 7.2. Approved amendments and bills that curtail judicial autonomy Indonesia, 1999–2004

The capacity of the Megawati government (and her predecessor, Wahid) to successfully design and pass legislative bills that constrained the court's autonomy had three deleterious consequences on de facto judicial independence in Indonesia. First, as suggested by our theoretical argument, the actions taken by Megawati's ministers almost immediately curtailed the de facto independence of the Indonesian judiciary, which was not too high to begin with. As stated by Ikrar Nusa Bhakti (a political expert from the Indonesian Institute of Sciences) in an interview, the actions taken by the Megawati government and her predecessor, President Wahid, led to an outcome where

> the current judiciary rated only slightly higher than that of the New Order government led by the former dictator, Suharto, who ruled the judiciary ... our judiciary is still subject to political intervention despite the clear separation of the legislative, executive and judicial institutions.[66]

Moreover, in his analysis of the judicial system in Indonesia, Frans Hendra Winarta, ex-chairman of the Indonesian Advocates Association, suggests that delegating the authority of transferring judges to the Ministry of Justice (which was reaffirmed by the Megawati administration) adversely affects the de facto autonomy of Indonesia's judiciary.

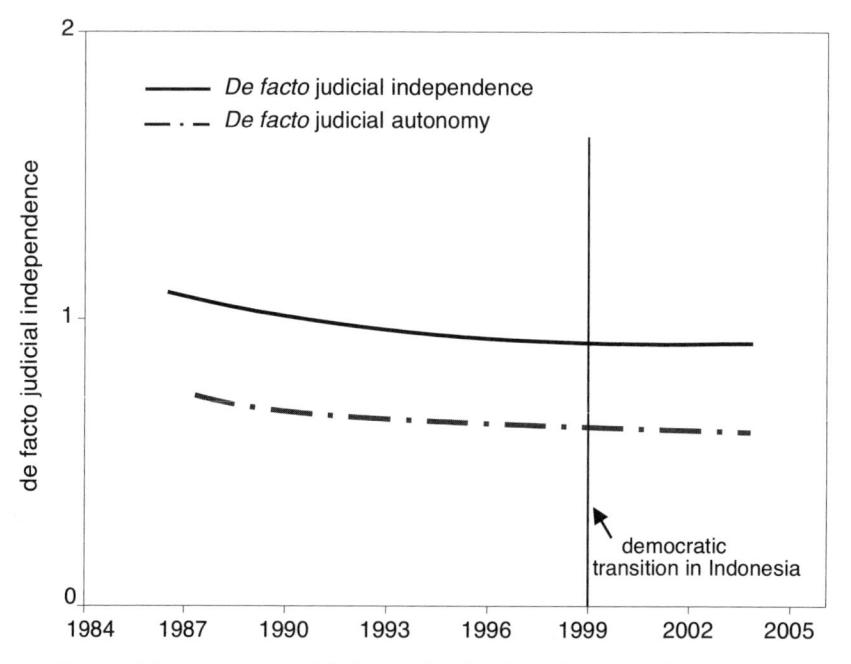

Fig. 7.3. Moving average of *de facto judicial independence* in Indonesia. (The dark solid line is the 0–2 ordinal measure of *de facto judicial independence* described in chapter 4 that is based on the measure developed by Tate and Keith [2007]. The dark dotted line is the 0–2 ordinal measure *de facto judicial autonomy* developed by Cingranelli and Richards [2008].)

> Only one thing matters in the end: can the judiciary ever be independent if judges are dependent on the goodwill of Ministry of Justice officials? The answer is an emphatic no![67]

The two statements about the lack of independence of the judiciary in Indonesia are confirmed by the illustration in fig. 7.3, which shows that the moving average of each of the two measures of de facto judicial independence employed for our quantitative tests in chapter 5 has (1) not changed from the autocratic Suharto era (years) to the democratic Megawati era (years), and (2) even marginally reduced during the years (2002–2004) in which Indonesia is firmly observed as a party-centered system characterized by low levels of particularism.[68]

Second, the decision to capture the judicial system and curb the judiciary's independence, which was taken by the Megawati and Wahid's cabinets, has adversely affected the rule of law in Indonesia (Cumaraswamy 2006; EIU 2008; Buehler 2009). This is emphatically suggested without any ambiguity by the Hong Kong-based Political and Economic Risk Consultancy (PERC), which ranked Indonesia's judiciary last among 12 other Asian countries in 2004. It also noted that the judiciary "is one of Indonesia's weakest and most controversial institution and many consider the poor enforcement of laws to be the country's number one problem."[69] Finally, the decrease in the de facto independence of the courts in Indonesia unfortunately encouraged the political harassment of judges or other personnel in the judicial system through informal channels during the Megawati era. Government officials did little or nothing to prevent such harassment. As suggested by Cumaraswamy (2006: 42), the "harassment and intimidation of judges, prosecutors and lawyers, particularly those handling human rights-related cases, is a matter of grave concern . . . the governmental authorities have failed in their duty to protect these judges, prosecutors and lawyers in areas of conflict."

Conclusion

In the previous chapter, the Brazil and India cases allowed us to assess the causal mechanism that we proposed to explain why incumbents in candidate-centered developing democracies (characterized by high levels of particularism) choose to enhance the courts' de facto autonomy when their probability of survival in office is low. We found strong statistical support for this claim in a sample of 103 developing country democracies over the period from 1985 to 2004. That said, we also suggested in the corollary to hypothesis 2 that when faced with high hazard rates in office, governments in party-centered democracies (characterized by low particularism) will curtail de facto judicial independence.

Hence, in this chapter, we examined the politics of de facto judicial independence in Indonesia, which is observed as a party-centered democracy, particularly from late 2001 to 2004. We did so since Indonesia is representative of a category of developing country democracies that exhibit a low level of political particularism in our most similar design for comparative case analysis. Therefore, the Indonesia case helps us to assess the prediction stated in the corollary to hypothesis 2, as well as the causal mechanisms underlying this prediction.

A careful analysis of the Indonesian case first revealed that the presence of strong and centralized ruling parties in government, engendered by the country's closed-list PR party-centered electoral rule, drove party leaders in the government (in this case, Megawati) to capture the judiciary. However, when the hazard rate of the Megawati government in office became high, the courts started openly rejecting the state's attempt to capture the judiciary. The judiciary also politically challenged the Megawati government by supporting the main opposition party, the *Partai Demokrat*'s, policy program and its allegations of corruption against Megawati's administration. Faced with an already fragile government, the Megawati cabinet reacted by passing and implementing statutes and bills to curb the de facto independence of the judiciary as a preemptive strategy to counter further threats from the court to the government's likelihood of political survival in office. Moreover, party leaders in the Megawati-led government exercised their leverage over party members in Indonesia to ensure that the aforementioned bills were successfully passed in the legislature. This political dynamic is also confirmed by our descriptive analysis of within-country data of legislative bills, which shows that the number of bills approved in the legislature that curtail the courts' independence increased significantly during Megawati's tenure as president when her survival in office was threatened.[70]

The evidence presented in this chapter has numerous implications. First, the Indonesia case in this chapter confirms our intuition that the extent of intraparty centralization, which determined by electoral rules, indeed explain why politicians in some developing country democracies are more likely to reduce de facto judicial independence when their time horizons in office shrink. The analysis presented in this chapter shows that the presence of a closed-list PR electoral system, with its pooled votes and party-controlled ballots in Indonesia from early 1999 to late 2004, led to strong, centralized parties, which provided political elites with both incentives and the capacity to undertake actions to restrict the court's independence. Second, the evidence presented in the preceding sections also has some specific implications for Indonesia. In particular, we can arguably infer from the analysis in this chapter that the prospects for judicial reform in Indonesia that would potentially enhance the de facto independence of the judicial system looks bleak. This is because the presence of strong political parties that still exist in Indonesia despite recent electoral reforms will continue to provide incentives for politicians to constrain the courts' autonomy. Our pessimism in this regard has also been expressed in a report in a recent *Asia Times* article, which states that

> Proposed legislation which does not directly serve the legislators' interests is often pigeonholed. Bills on a judicial . . . and administrative reform have all fallen into a *Dewan Perwakilan Rakyat* black hole. Laws relating directly to political parties, such as campaign finance, however, are given more attention and arguably decided for the legislators' own benefit rather than the larger interests of the nation.[71]

Additionally, greater politicization of the judiciary and increased state intervention in judicial decision-making exacerbates, rather than ameliorates, the problem of judicial corruption in Indonesia. This is suggested in an interview by Asep Rahmat Fajar, head of the Indonesian Judicial Monitoring Society, who states that repeated attempts by politicians to influence judicial decisions in Indonesia has led to a situations where politically "influencing court verdicts has been a systematic and organized crime in the country's legal system. It involves people from the highest levels, such as high court judges, down to the lowest levels, such as administrative staff in the Supreme Court."[72] Thus, unlike Brazil and India, we essentially learn from the Indonesia case that Indonesia elites arguably have low political incentives to invest in an independent judiciary.

In the next chapter, we discuss how the findings in this chapter and in chapters 2–6 help explain in a much more generalizable context the politics and challenge of both de jure, as well as de facto, judicial independence in developing countries. We consider how these findings contribute toward the big picture of understanding the success or failure of some developing democracies to establish or maintain independent judiciaries. We then explore how judicial independence affects corruption, economic reforms, and human rights practices by governments in developing states. Finally, we conclude by considering the implications of our findings for the debate on the benefits of judicial independence.

CHAPTER 8
Conclusion

Almost two decades ago, the collapse of the Soviet Union dramatically expanded the global breadth of the "third wave" of democratization across the developing world.[1] The third wave spread of democratization started in Latin America and then spread to central and Eastern Europe, parts of Asia, and eventually to Africa. The emergence of democracy enhanced the individual freedom for millions of citizens in developing states. It also led political leaders in new democracies to design institutions that could protect the rule of law, enforce the new constitution, and preserve the principles of democracy. A key institution that, in fact, became the focal point with respect to institutional design in many new democracies was the judicial branch (see, for example, Larkins 1996; O'Donnell 2001; Chavez 2004; Hammergren 2007b; World Bank 1998, 2010).

One of the most important judicial powers whose adoption was widely advocated was that of judicial review—the ability of courts to review laws and decrees passed by the executive and the legislature. The political rationale for granting courts review powers was that it would allow the judiciary to legally mediate conflicts between political actors and prevent the arbitrary exercise of government power by incumbents.[2] This, in turn, would allow societies to achieve the normatively important goals of protecting the rule of law and preserving democracy. However, the flip side of constitutionalizing judicial review is that it also provides judges with the opportunity and the ability to veto the policies preferred by the executive and the legislature (e.g., see Hazama 2009; Whittington 2006: 283–84; Ginsburg 2003, 2008; Vanberg 2008; Figuereido et al. 2006; Rios-Figueroa and Staton 2009; Hirschl 2003; Stephenson 2003). Given these political benefits and costs, it is perhaps not surprising as emphasized in the introduction, that there exists remarkable variation in the adoption of de jure judicial review by political elites in new democracies across the developing world.

Furthermore, as judges have discovered, the constitutionalization of de jure review powers does not necessarily imply that courts have the practical ability to exercise these powers. While governments in some established and "newly consolidated" democracies across the developing world have respected and enhanced the constitutionally-granted independence of the judiciary in practice, others have chosen to interfere with judicial decisions and operations in active bids to curtail the courts' de facto independence. Understanding the determinants of judicial empowerment in the developing world therefore requires an understanding of the foundations of both de jure and de facto independence.

In this book, we have addressed both dimensions of judicial empowerment by developing theoretical frameworks that explain why some governments but not others choose to adopt an important de jure judicial power—the power of judicial review—and why some governments but not others choose to respect the de facto independence of their courts. We have tested the validity of our explanations using a multi-methods approach by combining statistical analysis of comprehensive TSCS data sets with in-depth case studies of selected comparative cases. In this chapter, we first summarize the main theoretical and empirical contributions of this book and then discuss some key implications that emerge from its findings. We then identify some of the questions regarding the issues of democracy and judicial independence in developing countries that these findings highlight that remain unanswered. We conclude by discussing some preliminary thoughts on how democratic politics in developing countries is likely to affect this future path of judicial independence in the developing world.

Summary and Main Contributions

Scholars have invested substantial effort towards understanding how democracy affects de jure judicial independence in developing and developed states. For instance, Ginsburg (2003) uses the logic of "electoral markets" and "political insurance" to explain when elites in new democracies are more likely to adopt judicial review. According to this thesis, the decision by elites to empower the judiciary via judicial review in the post–transition period correlates with the degree of competitiveness in the polity: when political competition is intense (weak) and incumbents in new democracies have low (high) expectations of winning future elections, they are more (less) likely to introduce constitutional provisions for judicial review to "insure" their political future.

Ginsburg's (2003) thesis is reflected in the work of other scholars who also claim that politicians in democracies offer independent courts when political competition is substantial and incumbents cannot expect to win elections indefinitely (McCubbins and Schwartz 1984; Ramseyer 1994; Weingast 1997; Ferejohn 1999; Stephenson 2003; Finkel 2008).[3] Unlike the "electoral market" logic posited earlier, Hirschl (2003, 2004) suggests that the adoption of constitutional rules such as judicial review that enhance de jure judicial autonomy resulted in democracies from "a deliberate strategy undertaken by hegemonic, yet threatened political elites—in association with economic and judicial elites—who found strategic disadvantages in adhering to democratic decision-making processes."[4] Hirschl's (2003, 2004) theoretical explanation for de jure judicial empowerment is clearly distinct from the electoral market and political insurance logic of judicial independence proposed by other scholars. Yet a common thread ties together Hirschl's thesis and the electoral market, as well as the political insurance claim. This common thread is the central idea that it is the political interests of elites in democracies—particularly their interest to retain office and preserve their power—that affects the prospects for constitutionalization of judicial autonomy in these states.

A growing body of research has sought to explain this variation in the decision to constitutionalize judicial review powers by broadly examining how the ruling party's anticipation of retaining office—which is influenced by the degree of political competition it experiences—affects the incumbent's incentives to grant judicial review to the courts (McCubbins and Schwartz 1984; Weingast 1989; Gely and Spiller 1990; Ramseyer 1994; Ginsburg 2003, 2008; Stephenson 2003). Our analysis builds on this body of work by examining how the extent to which the ruling party captures and controls the legislature in a new democracy affects the design of judicial review. That said, we part company with the previous literature in that we provide a more nuanced argument which explores how public trust in the judiciary affects the goals which the incumbent government tries to achieve with its strong legislative capacity.

We incorporate insights from the judicial behavior literatures to investigate how strategic judicial behavior directly affects political calculations regarding the adoption of de jure judicial review powers. We argue that public trust in the judiciary can modify the political threat the judiciary potentially poses to governments and their agendas, and how seriously political elites take this potential threat. High public trust in the judiciary provides judges with reservoirs of diffuse public support and thus poses a considerable political threat to a government's agenda if the judiciary has the constitutional right to overturn its laws and decrees. Thus, we hypothesize that after the transition to democracy, ruling parties in new democracies that successfully capture the legislature are less likely to adopt de jure judicial review if the level of public trust in the judiciary is sufficiently high during the post–transition period. This prediction is supported by the large-n empirical tests and the Brazilian and Indonesian case studies examined in this book.

Developing a theoretical story that examines how the ruling party's (parties') decision to constitutionally adopt judicial review in a new democracy is conditional on the level of public trust in the judiciary is substantively important for two reasons. First and foremost, it explicitly identifies the precise conditions—low legislative concentration and low public trust in judiciary—under which incumbents in a new democracy will be more likely to adopt constitutional provisions that provide courts with the authority of full judicial review. This provides us with substantial empirical leverage to account for observed variation in the adoption of judicial review by leaders in new democratic states during the post–transition period.

Second, whereas extant studies on judicial autonomy tend to focus on how the extent of public support and awareness of judicial power affects the effectiveness of existing judicial power, we show the significant but counterproductive effect of public support on the constitutional establishment of new judicial powers during the initial post–transition period.[5] While we employ these causal mechanisms to develop a theoretical framework that explains the politics of de jure judicial review in new democracies, it is also plausible that this theoretical account may also explain when leaders in new democratic regimes are likely to adopt constitutional provisions for other components of de jure judicial independence such as constitutionally establishing the finality of judicial decisions. Whether this claim is valid or farfetched is a matter for future research.

Our theoretical and empirical findings about variation in de facto judicial independence across developing democracies contribute to the literatures in both judicial politics and comparative institutions in two main ways. First, while numerous studies have analyzed political competition in the electoral market as a determinant of political preferences regarding

DFJI, to the best of our knowledge relatively little attention has been paid to the effect electoral institutions may have on these preferences, despite their fundamental role in shaping political competition.

Studies that employ the logic of electoral markets have implicitly suggested that the time horizons of democratic incumbents in office, which is determined by their expectation of winning or losing future elections, influences their decision to increase or curtail judicial independence (e.g., Ramseyer 1994; Ramseyer and Rasmusen 2003; Stephenson 2003; Popova 2010). Helmke (2005) notes the incentives judges have to defect strategically from a strategy of subservience to the government, when they observe that the government's time horizons are short. However, extant studies do not account for the varying nature of political competition created by the electoral rules governing electoral competition.[6] A substantial institutional literature argues that by affecting intraparty unity, electoral particularism fundamentally shapes political behaviors on both political and policy issues (e.g., Hickens and Simmons 2008; Hallerberg and Marnier 2004; Crisp et al. 2004; Cox and McCubbins 2001; Carey and Shugart 1995). Yet, its effects on the incentives of political elites to support or undermine DFJI remain unexplored.

We build on both these literatures and suggest that both time horizons (i.e., hazard rate) of democratic incumbents in office, as well as the degree to which electoral institutions create incentives for political elites to cultivate a personal vote, gives them incentives to manipulate the de facto judicial independence of courts. The central insight from our theoretical story is that we claim that the decision by incumbents to act on the incentives created by short time horizons is mediated by the institutional context in which political elites and judges operate, particularly the level of electoral particularism created by that country's electoral institutions. Specifically, we argue that in the context of high (and increasing) hazard rates in office—or equivalently low time horizons in office—incumbents in highly personalist (that is, particularistic) systems will increase the de facto autonomy of the courts. Conversely, when faced with high hazard rates in office, governments in party-centered developing democracies, which by construction are characterized by low levels of particularism, will curtail de facto judicial independence. Our statistical tests and our case-study analyses of Brazil, India, and Indonesia support this claim. This book therefore takes an important step forward by providing a parsimonious theoretical account of how variation in political particularism created by electoral rules can explain when and why governments in some developing democracies, but not others, strategically choose to enhance the de facto independence of the judiciary.

The second contribution of our analysis of de facto judicial independence is primarily empirical in that we develop a detailed measure of the time horizons of each government in office in our sample of developing democracies. This measure is derived from the hazard rate of these governments in office and is characterized by substantial cross-sectional and temporal variation. Importantly, it also accurately captures the relevant strategic time frame—the ex ante time horizons—of each incumbent in the developing democracies sample. This measure may be vital for empirical research because causal arguments in the judicial politics literature often use the logic of electoral markets or political insurance that implicitly or explicitly analyze the influence that the time horizons of incumbents have matter on judicial independence (Stephenson 2003; Ramseyer and Rasmussen 2003; Ginsburg 2003; Hirschl 2004; Finkel 2008; Popova 2010). Yet the difficulties associated with developing an accurate measure or proxy for the time horizons of incumbents makes it extremely difficult for scholars to statistically evaluate causal arguments that examine the effect of time horizons of incumbents on judicial autonomy. Thus the measure of the time-horizons of incumbents that we have developed may be useful for researchers to closely test theoretical arguments that rely on the thesis of electoral markets and political insurance.

Research Implications

The issue of compatibility between democracy and judicial independence, which is a necessary condition for the rule of law, has been extensively debated in extant research.[7] Some scholars, for instance, claim that the conceptual affinity between democracy, judicial independence and the rule of law is strong (O'Donnell 2001). Other scholars, however, suggest that democratic institutions may not always be compatible with higher levels of judicial independence in developing nations (Helmke and Rosenbluth 2009; Staton 2010). Our findings highlight how complex the relationship between democracy and judicial independence in developing states is. The nuanced relationship between democracy and judicial independence suggested by our main theoretical and empirical results has important substantive implications for several issue-areas Here we briefly discuss their implications for two issues: (1) the analysis of corruption; and (2) institutional design.

Existing studies of corruption have found that the degree of corruption varies significantly across democracies in the developed and developing world (Treisman 2000; Chang and Golden 2007; Yadav 2011). Political scientists have thus conducted extensive research to analyze how institutional variables can potentially account for the cross-national variation in corruption mentioned earlier (Treisman 2000; Lederman et al. 2004; Chang and Golden 2007; Tavits 2007; Gerring et al. 2009). This research particularly focuses on the effect of veto players, parliamentary systems, political particularism, legislative institutions, and federalism on cross-national measures of corruption, including the Transparency International and the ICRG index of corruption (Chang 2005; Chang and Golden 2007; Tavits 2007; Gerring et al. 2009). However, political scientists have paid relatively less attention to the potential effect that judicial independence may have on corruption in developing country democracies.[8] This is surprising to some extent considering that institutions such as the World Bank and some scholars have suggested in the past that higher levels of de facto judicial autonomy in developing states may help to curb corruption in these countries (World Bank 1999; Rose-Ackerman 2007; Rios-Figueroa 2006).

Given that political particularism affects corruption in developing democracies (as suggested in the literature) and the possibility that de facto judicial independence could matter for corruption as well, we evaluated the combined effect of these two factors on corruption. We did so by conducting a simple empirical exercise: specifically, we estimated the interactive effect of the Wallack et al. (2005) particularism index (described in chapter 4) and the Cingranelli and Richards (2008) measure of de facto judicial independence on Transparency International's 0 (high corruption) to 10 (low corruption) index of corruption[9] in a panel of 79 developing country democracies from 1994 to 2007.[10] We inverted the Transparency International scale such that 0 indicates the lowest level of corruption, while 10 denotes the highest level of corruption in the index. The results obtained from conducting this exercise is illustrated in fig. 8.1, which plots the marginal effect of the interaction term *particularism × de facto judicial independence* on *TI corruption*, where TI stands for "Transparency International."

This figure shows that the interactive effect of particularism and de facto judicial independence on *TI corruption* is negative; the impact of the interaction term mentioned above is also statistically significant at the 95 per-

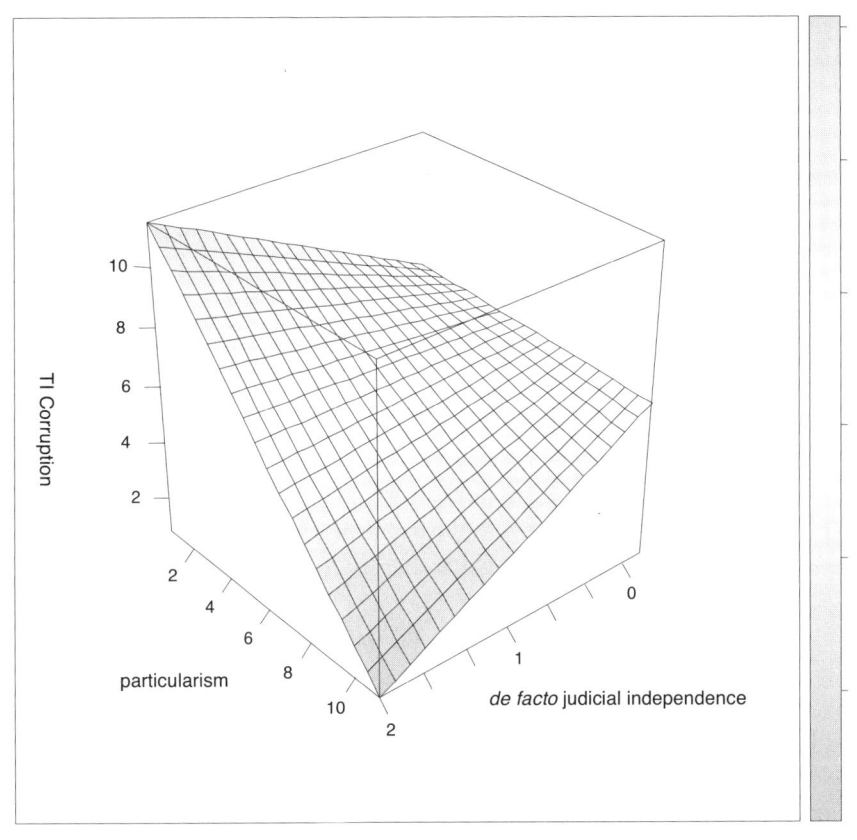

Fig. 8.1. Effect of *particularism* × *de facto judicial independence* on corruption. (Data sources employed to operationalize the de facto judicial independence and particularism measure employed for this figure are listed in chapter 5.)

cent confidence level. This means that an increase in political particularism (which implies a shift to a candidate-centered democracy) has a negative and statistically significant effect on corruption in developing democracies only when the existing degree of de facto judicial independence in these states is sufficiently high. Furthermore, with respect to the individual components of the interaction term previously mentioned, we found (but do not report to save space) that the individual estimate of *particularism* is positive and significant at the 10 percent level, while *de facto judicial independence* is insignificant. It is worth noting here that the statistically negative effect of *particularism × de facto judicial independence* on *TI corruption* has two substantive implications.

First, we learn from the illustration in fig. 8.1 that incumbents in candidate-centered democracies in the developing world may actually have incentives to curb corruption if the prevailing level of de facto judicial independence in their polity is substantial. This is an interesting and novel empirical result given that extant studies on corruption suggest that incumbents in candidate-centered developing democracies tend to engage in higher levels of corruption in office (Chang 2005; Hicken 2006; Chang and Golden 2007). We believe that this empirical result can be used as a foundation to develop a more refined and comprehensive theory of how judicial independence can combine with political institutions (in this case, electoral particularism) to influence corruption.

Second, in recent years, economists and political scientists have started to explore the impact of both de jure and de facto judicial autonomy on economic growth (Feld 2003; Feld and Voigt 2003; Klerman 2005). The results that emerge from these studies are largely inconclusive. This is because some scholars find that higher levels of de facto judicial independence have a statistically positive effect on economic growth,[11] while other researchers report that the influence of judicial independence on growth is statistically insignificant.[12] We suspect that these "mixed" and "inconclusive" results probably stem from the fact that the aforementioned studies listed focus on the direct effect of judicial independence on economic growth.

However, we can use the result in fig. 8.1 to conjecture if de facto judicial independence has an indirect but positive effect on economic growth in developing states. As shown in the figure, de facto judicial independence helps to curtail corruption in developing country democracies conditional on the nature of the electoral system in these states. Thus, it is plausible that the degree of de facto judicial autonomy may have a statistically meaningful and consistent effect on economic outcomes such as growth in the context of certain domestic political institutions. If so, then scholars may need to invest more effort toward developing and evaluating theories why de facto judicial independence may influence economic growth in developing states under certain institutional conditions but not others.

The final implication that emerges from our research, which is essentially a policy implication, speaks to the issue of institutional design. Specifically, as mentioned in chapter 1, international institutions and governments from advanced democracies have invested substantial amounts of aid to promote independent courts in the developing world. In cooperation with other international organizations, the World Bank, for instance, has spent over $7 billion over a 20-year period supporting projects that are directed toward creating and strengthening independent judiciaries in developing states (World Bank 1995, 1998, 2010). For instance, in cooperation with the Inter-American Development Bank (IDB), the World Bank attempted to encourage the Venezuelan government in 2001 to increase judicial independence by approving a "$75 million loan to improve the criminal justice system and . . . in order to effectively direct judicial reform that increases the judiciary's political autonomy."[13] Similarly, after the cessation of the civil war in Sudan and the negotiation of the Comprehensive Peace Agreement (CPA), the World Bank invested $13 million between 2006 and 2009 in a project to build judicial capacity there, noting in its project report that:

> In order to implement the CPA and effectuate the mandate of the INC (Interim National Constitution)—including the establishment of the National Judicial Service Commission (NJSC)—significant work must be done to embolden the judiciary's legal, technical, and operational competence. To that end, the objective of this project is to strengthen the capacity of the judiciary to enhance its independence; build the knowledge base of judges; and, empower the judiciary to effectively and fairly apply the law and deliver justice. (World Bank Africa Report 2008)

Similarly, both the U.S. government and the European Union often provide aid to developing states on the condition that incumbents in these states empower their judiciary and respect the political autonomy of domestic courts (Anderson and Gray 2006; Perez Linan 2007). A significant share of the aid that is invested to promote judicial independence in developing nations is directed toward building technical training facilities or providing financial assistance that funds the training of lawyers in developing states (World Bank 1995, 1998). Unfortunately, scholars and even the World Bank have emphasized that the use of foreign aid by donors to promote judicial independence in developing countries has not been successful (Gloppen et al. 2010; Hammergren 2007b; World Bank 2004).

We argue here that the strategy of promoting judicial autonomy in developing countries by building training facilities for legal programs in these states is unlikely to yield the desired results in the future. Instead, given our finding that political institutions (particularly particularism) matter considerably for the de facto independence of the courts in developing democracies, we believe that aid will help to engender greater judicial autonomy if it is directed toward encouraging developing states to design political institutions that are positively associated with judicial independence. In particular, donors that provide aid to promote judicial autonomy in developing countries should encourage these states to adopt electoral institutions such as the open-list PR system or plurality which create high levels of particularism. In short, a key policy lesson that this study offers is that inducing governments in developing nations to adopt certain electoral institutions will, in all likelihood, effectively help to promote the goal of judicial independence within these countries.

Extensions and Areas for Future Research

Similar to extant social-science theories that employ the logic of strategic interaction, our parsimonious theoretical framework is highly simplified. To focus on the causal mechanisms that we believe are important for explaining the politics of de jure judicial review and de facto judicial independence in developing country democracies, we abstracted from many details as well as other potentially important causal stories. This means that certain questions have been left unanswered and some issues have also been left unresolved, which present ample opportunities for further research. We, therefore, briefly discuss below four key important areas in which more theoretical and empirical work can and should be done to make more progress in the study of democracy and judicial independence in the developing world.

First, our theoretical framework has exclusively concentrated on how specific domestic political factors and institutions influence the adoption of judicial review and the degree of de facto judicial independence. Yet, in reality, we know that international institutions such as the World Bank and the International Monetary Fund, as well as governments from advanced democracies, employ a variety of methods (e.g., offering aid) to either induce or coerce developing countries to increase the de jure and de facto autonomy of their courts. New and established developing democracies that rely heavily on foreign aid, investment, and loans are likely to bow to inducements or pressure from international institutions and leading Western democracies to promote the rule of law by emulating the constitutional fundamentals of Western democracies. Providing constitutional provisions such as judicial review to the courts and maintaining the de facto autonomy of their domestic courts may also signal a developing state's willingness to accept the required legal standards for joining international economic institutions. Thus, to develop a more comprehensive theory of the political conditions that drive governments in new and established developing democracies to adopt judicial review and enhance de facto judicial autonomy, we need to extend our theoretical story into a "two-level" framework. This two-level framework should account for the influence of both systemic and domestic factors on de jure and de facto judicial independence in developing democracies. While developing a two-level theoretical account along the aforementioned described lines will be extremely challenging, pursuing this research agenda may yield richer and more nuanced theoretical insights about the politics of judicial independence in developing countries.

Second, the analysis in this book does not examine the effects of either de jure judicial review or de facto judicial independence on the politics of judicial activism in developing states. It is beyond the scope of this book to study whether and to what extent judicial independence drives judges to engage in political activism or "excessively" intervene in policy-making. However, given that some legal scholars have suggested that the incidence of judicial activism is increasing in developing democracies, scholars of judicial politics may obtain new insights by studying the relationship between judicial independence and judicial activism in a comparative (i.e., cross-national) context. In particular, the mechanism through which this relationship works requires theoretical elucidation and empirical confirmation. Assessing the link between judicial independence and judicial activism (that is, if this link exists) will also permit scholars to develop policy instruments that may be needed to curb excessive judicial activism.

Third, this book is about democratic politics and judicial independence in the developing world. However, it is an inescapable fact that many autocracies continue to exist in the developing world. The relationship between dictators and the courts in autocracies like China and Zimbabwe possibly directly affects the rights and physical integrity of millions of citizens in these states, and it may also affect the prospects of democratization in these autocracies. Some scholars have recently conducted research on the politics of judicial autonomy (or lack thereof) in autocracies: (Helmke 2002; Magaloni 2006; Epperly 2010). Additionally, in chapter 2, we conducted a bare-bones analysis of how the interests of dictators in autocratic states may influence the constitutional design of judicial review in these states. This bare-bones analysis is clearly not sufficient. Hence, building on extant studies of the judiciary in autocracies and some of the research presented here, it may be important for scholars to develop theories that can explain how specific institutional features that vary across autocracies may account for potential variation in de jure and de facto judicial independence across dictatorial regimes.

Fourth, notwithstanding the exhaustive statistical tests and comparative case-study research conducted in this book, the empirical research presented in this book can be developed further into two main directions. For one, the temporal range of our sample of developing countries, which dates from 1987 to 2005, needs to be extended further back to the 1970s or earlier. This may be difficult to do given the paucity of publicly available and reliable data on judicial independence across developing countries before 1987. Yet, it may be fruitful to substantially extend the temporal range of the sample used here if possible, since doing so may enhance the empirical generalizability of our reported results if the estimates that we obtain in the expanded sample corroborate our theoretical claims.

Second, with respect to our case-study analysis, we focused on the assessing the validity of our causal stories across three prominent and large democracies across the developing world: Brazil, India, and Indonesia. Although examining these three cases in detail was extremely useful from a methodological perspective, it may also be necessary for us or other researchers to check whether our causal arguments also apply to economically smaller developing democracies such as Colombia, Romania, Sri Lanka, and Uruguay. Examining the validity of the causal claims presented here in other smaller developing democracies will increase our confidence in the empirical generalizability and robustness of our claims especially if the historical evidence from these other cases corroborate our causal mechanisms.

The Future of Democracy and Judicial Independence in Developing States

Offering predictions about how judicial independence will evolve in the future, particularly in developing countries that have made a transition to democracy in the past two to three decades, is a difficult task. However, based on our theoretical claims and the evidence presented in this book, we can make some broad projections about the effect that democratic politics in developing states may have on juridical independence in the next decade or so. With respect to extant debates on democracy and judicial independence, we mentioned earlier that some researchers are sanguine and optimistic about the idea that the emergence of democracy in the developing world promotes the political autonomy of the judiciary in these states (Larkins 1996; O'Donnell 2001). However, others have found that de facto autonomy has taken a beating in many democracies after an initial period of period of increased judicial independence (Helmke and Staton 2011; Helmke 2010).

We partly (but not fully) subscribe this optimism expressed in the literature on democracy and judicial independence for the following reason. It is well known that the number of democracies in the developing world has increased from just 16 countries in 1975 to 95 countries by 2000s (Milner and Kubota 2005; Diamond 2000), and that 85 percent of the developing countries that made a transition to democracy in the last three decades have successfully consolidated democratic rule (Papaioannou and Siourounis 2008; Milner et al. 2011). It is not widely known, however, that more than two-thirds of the developing states listed in table 1.1 (see chapter 1) that made a transition to democracy in the last three decades have adopted the either the open-list Proportional Representation (PR); the single-transferable vote (STV) electoral system; block-vote systems; and the multiple-member, multiple-seats plurality system.[14] This is an important trend since all of these electoral systems engender higher levels of political particularism (Carey and Shugart 1995; Hix 2004; Hicken 2006). As shown in this book, incumbents in democracies characterized by higher levels of particularism have incentives to enhance the de facto autonomy of the judiciary. Thus, we anticipate an upward trend in de facto judicial independence across new democracies in the future as most of these states have adopted electoral systems that are conducive for judicial independence.

Notwithstanding our optimistic expectation that judicial independence will increase across developing democracies in the near future, there are two potential roadblocks that may hinder the progress of judicial empowerment. First, legal scholars have noted that the steady increase in judicial autonomy across developing country democracies has also led to more "judicial activism" in these countries. Indeed, a recent analysis of judicial activism emphasizes that judges in developing democracies often believe that they should

> go beyond their traditional role as interpreters of the Constitution and laws in order to assume a role as independent trustees on behalf of society. The reason for widespread acceptance of this view among judges is that in these countries the executive and legislature have failed to ensure good governance and provide a fair deal to their citizens.[15]

There are many examples to support the thesis that judicial activism has increased in developing democracies. For instance, India's Supreme Court has consistently intervened and passed legal judgment on various economic, privatization, and environmental policies that have been initiated by successive governments in the last 10 to 15 years (Bhagwati 2005; Saha 2008). Studies have also shown that judicial activism has increased in developing democracies as diverse as Colombia, India, Pakistan, Brazil, and the Philippines (Dakolias 1999; Landau 2010; Saha 2008).

Although judicial activism may arguably be beneficial to society to some extent, it is possible that politicians in developing democracies may take concrete steps to shield themselves against policy activism by the judiciary. Excessive intervention in the policy-making arena by judges may, for instance, induce democratic incumbents to actively curtail the autonomy of the court. Doing so may reduce the scope and opportunity for judicial activism by the courts and consequently help politicians to protect their policy-making authority. Therefore, we believe that if the frequency of judicial activism increases in democratic countries, then it may perverse effect of reducing the autonomy of the judiciary in developing democracies in the long run.

Second, some journalists and policy analysts have suggested that the extent of judicial corruption has increased in many democracies across the developing world (Buscaglia and Langseth 2002; UNDP 2003; Transparency International 2007). For instance, a report released by the United Nations Development Programme (UNDP) in 2003, which analyzes the causes and consequences of judicial corruption in new and established developing democracies, emphasizes that there is "widespread judicial corruption in many transitional and developing countries,"[16] and that this "has led to a decrease of public confidence in the judiciary."[17] It is difficult to accurately infer whether higher levels of judicial autonomy leads to more judicial cor-

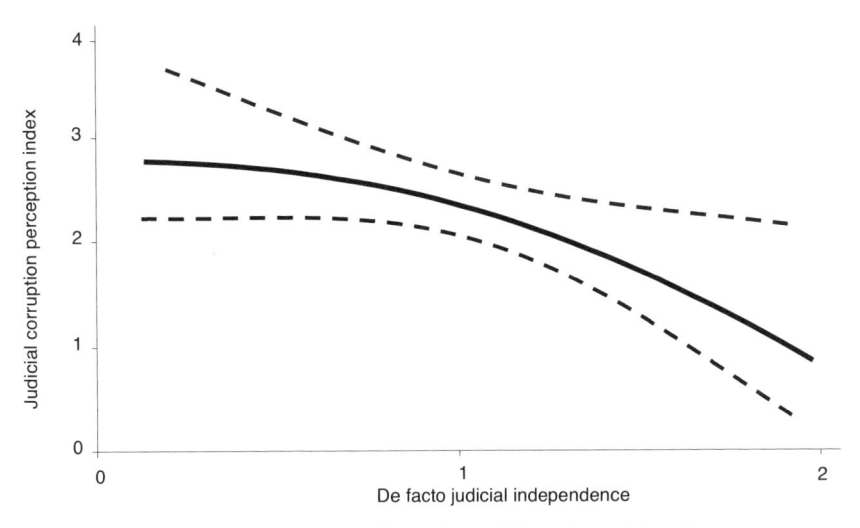

Fig. 8.2. Effect of de facto judicial independence on perception of judicial corruption. (Data sources employed to operationalize the 0–2 ordinal de facto judicial independence measure are listed in chapter 5.)

ruption since corruption in the judiciary is, by definition, unobservable. However, estimating the effect of Cingranelli and Richards' measure of *de facto judicial independence* on a 2002–2004 panel survey of *perceptions* of judicial corruption held by firms (measured on a 0 to 4 scale)[18] across 53 developing country democracies reveals, as illustrated in fig. 8.2, that greater de facto judicial independence has a statistically negative effect on perceived levels of judicial corruption.

Although greater judicial independence has a negative effect on perceived levels of judicial corruption, it is important to note that an increase in judicial corruption provides an opportunity for politicians in developing democracies to actively curb the judiciary's autonomy. For example, the UNDP's report on judicial independence in transitional countries points out that:

> There is (public) perception of the existence of a high rate of corruption among judges and judicial officers in the transitional and developing countries ... In an attempt to fight judicial corruption, Ukraine has removed the judicial immunity clause. Russia also tried to hold judges more accountable

by preparing a reform to reduce the lifetime tenure of judges to a 12-year term.

The aforementioned examples of Russia and Ukraine are interesting because they indicate that politicians in developing democracies may actually believe that curtailing judicial autonomy may be politically popular among their citizens, especially if the courts are perceived as being corrupt. This creates the opportunity for strategic politicians to reduce de jure and de facto judicial independence under the guise of curbing corruption without drawing public ire for attacking the judiciary. While it is difficult to generalize from the cases of Russia and the Ukraine, it does suggest that an increase in judicial corruption in democracies across the developing world may adversely affect the independence of the judiciary in these countries.

In sum, the brief analysis and claims in the preceding paragraphs lead to the following question: will the upward trend in judicial independence continue in the near future in developing democracies? Based on the discussion in this concluding chapter, our answer to this question is that it depends on both electoral institutions and the behavior of the judiciary. As mentioned earlier, we believe that the institutional context in which politicians in most (if not all) developing country democracies operate provides them with incentives to maintain and enhance de facto judicial autonomy under certain conditions. Yet higher levels of judicial independence will only be sustainable in developing democracies over time if the judiciaries in these countries do not engage in "excessive" judicial activism and if the courts do not resort to corrupt practices. We suggest here that judges have a rational interest to neither excessively intervene in the policymaking functions of the state nor consistently engage in rent-seeking. That said, it might be important for governments in developing country democracies to introduce rules or regulations that enhance judicial accountability and efficiency. This will serve to promote the interests of society and political actors and eventually ensure greater compatibility between democracy and judicial independence.

APPENDIX

Chapter 3

The Sample Selection Ordered Probit (S-OP) Model

Recall from the text that the S-OP statistical model consists of two stages and is defined (after dropping subscript t for time for notational convenience) as

$$d_i^* = \alpha' z_i + u_i \tag{A3.1}$$

$$d_i = \begin{cases} 1 & \text{if } d_i^* > 0 \\ 0 & \text{otherwise} \end{cases}$$

$$y_i^* = \beta' x_i + \varepsilon_i \tag{A3.2}$$

$$y_i = j \text{ if } \mu_{j-1} < y_i^* \leq \mu_j$$

$$(\varepsilon_i, u_i) \sim N_2(0,0,1,1,\rho)$$

Since y_i, x_i is observed when d_i is equal to 1, the underlying latent variable y_i^* for y_i is thus also given by the following ordered probit (i.e., outcome) equation in the second stage of the S-OP model:

$$y_i^* = \beta' x_i + \theta d_i + \varepsilon_i \tag{A3.3}$$

$$y_i = j \text{ if } \mu_{j-1} < y_i^* \leq \mu_j$$

where $(\varepsilon_i, u_i) \sim N_2(0,0,1,1,\rho)$ and $d_i \in (0,1)$ is a dichotomous variable with $d_i = 1$ indicating a new democratic regime that is realized from the nonrandom occurrence of a democratic transition. Conditional on $d_i = 1$, y_i is related to the latent variable y_i^* in (A3.1) and a boundary or cut-off parameter μ as follows:

$$y_i = \begin{cases} -1 & \text{if } y_i^* \leq 0 \text{ and } d_i = 1 \\ 0 & \text{if } y_i^* \leq 0 \text{ and } d_i = 1 \\ 1 & \text{if } 0 < y_i^* \leq \mu_1 \text{ and } d_i = 1 \\ 2 & \text{if } \mu_1 < y_i^* \leq \mu_2 \text{ and } d_{it} = 1 \\ \ldots \\ \ldots \\ J & \text{if } \mu_{J-1} < y_i^* \leq \mu_J \text{ and } d_i = 1 \end{cases} \quad (A3.4)$$

The log likelihood function of the S-OP statistical is, according to Greene and Hensher (2010), defined as

$$\log L = \sum_{d_i=0} \log \Phi(-\alpha' \mathbf{z}_i) \quad (A3.5)$$
$$+ \sum_{d_i=0} \sum_{d_i=0}^{J} m_{ij} \log[\Phi_2(\mu_j - \beta' \mathbf{x}_i, \alpha' \mathbf{z}_i, \rho) - \Phi_2 \\ \times (\mu_{j-1} - \beta' \mathbf{x}_i, \alpha' \mathbf{z}_i, \rho)]$$

where $\Phi(.)$ is the standard normal multivariate distribution. We estimate the log likelihood function in (A3.5) with random effects. Note that maximizing the log likelihood function in (A3.5) on a time-series cross section data set (which is precisely the kind of data that we are using) requires calculating normal multidimensional distribution integrals, the dimension of which grows with T where T denotes time. Since evaluating multidimensional integrals of the likelihood presented above is computationally intensive, we use simulation methods—specifically, the Geweke-Hajivassiliou-Keane (GHK) smooth recursive conditioning simulator—to maximize the log likelihood function in (A3.5). The GHK maximum simulated likelihood (MSL) method is often used by econometricians (see, e.g., Hajivassiliou and McFadden 1990; Train 2003) to evaluate the likelihood in (A3.5) as it is used to calculate multivariate normal probabilities, which is required for MSL estimation. The GHK method leads to a simulated log likelihood function, which we maximize with respect to the parameter vectors $\mathbf{x}_i$, $\mathbf{z}_i$, μ_J and the covariance matrix Ω by using the Broyden-Fletcher-Goldfarb-Shanno (BFGS) numerical optimization method (see Train 2003). Once we obtain the estimates, the variance-covariance matrix is directly derived by inverting the Hessian evaluated in the obtained maximum likelihood estimators. The estimation of the ordered probit and the S-OP model has been done by using **R**.

Calculation of Interaction Effect: Recall that the ordered probit model (and also the ordered outcome equation of the S-OP model) is given by $y_i^* = \beta'\mathbf{x} + \varepsilon$ where y_i is related to y_i^* as

$$y_i = J \text{ if } \mu_{J-1} < y_i^* \leq \mu_J \tag{A3.6}$$

where $j = 0, 1, 2 \ldots J$ is the discrete ordered outcome and the μ's are the $(J-1)$ unknown parameters known as the boundary or cut-off parameters. Assume without loss of generality that there are only three covariates (x_1, x_2, and x_3) in the $\mathbf{x}$ vector of the ordered probit equation in (A3.2) where x_2 and x_3 are interacted while x_1 is not. This implies that $\beta'\mathbf{x} = \beta_1 x_1 + \beta_2 x_2 + \beta_3 x_3 + \beta_{23}(x_2 * x_3)$. Suppose further that x_2 is the continuous independent variable (legislative) *concentration* in new democracies and x_3 is the continuous independent variable (judiciary) *trust* in new democracies, and the interaction of these two variables is $x_2 x_3 = x_2 * x_3$. The μ's and $\beta' = (\beta_1, \beta_2, \beta_3, \beta_{23})$ are jointly estimated by the GHK MSL method (mentioned above). Suppose that $\varepsilon \sim N(0,1)$; then the probability for the jth outcome is given by

$$prob(y_i = j) = \Phi(\mu_j - \beta'\mathbf{x}) - \Phi(\mu_{j-1} - \beta'\mathbf{x}) \tag{A3.7}$$

where Φ is the cumulative standard normal distribution function, which is continuous and twice differentiable. The marginal effect of the continuous variable x_2 (*concentration*) on the probability of the jth outcome in the ordered probit model, according to Mallick (2009, 4), is given by

$$\delta_{2,j} = \frac{\partial prob[y_i = j | \mathbf{x}]}{\partial x_2} = \varphi_{j-1}(.)[\beta_2 + \beta_{23} x_3] - \varphi_j(.)[\beta_2 + \beta_{23} x_3] \tag{A3.8}$$

where $\phi(.)$ is the standard normal density function, $\phi_{j-1}(.) = \phi(\mu_{j-1} - \beta'\mathbf{x})$, and $\phi_j(.) = \phi(\mu_j - \beta'\mathbf{x})$. The marginal effect of x_3 is similar to (A3.8) and will hence not be repeated here. Note that the formula in (A3.8) accounts for the fact that the impact of x_2 is also dependent on its combined effect of x_2 and x_3 on the dependent variable. Following Mallick (2009, 4), the magnitude of the interaction effect of $x_2 x_3$ on the probability of the jth outcome is obtained by computing the partial derivative of (A3.8) with respect to x_3, which leads to

$$\delta_{23,j} = \frac{\partial^2 prob[y_i = j | x]}{\partial x_2 \partial x_3} = [\varphi_{j-1}(.) - \varphi_j(.)]\beta_{23} - [\beta_2 + \beta_{23} x_3] \\ \times [\beta_3 + \beta_{23} x_2][\varphi'_{j-1}(.) - \varphi'_j(.)] \quad (A3.9)$$

where $\varphi'_j(.)$ is the first derivative of the density function with respect to its argument. Observe that the expression in (A3.9) is different from the marginal effect formula of interaction terms in ordered probit models in standard software packages, where it is simply calculated as

$$\frac{\partial prob[y_i = j | x]}{\partial(x_2 * x_3)} = [\varphi_{j-1}(.) - \varphi_j(.)]\beta_{23}.$$

To understand the asymptotic properties of the interaction effect in (A3.12) and calculate its standard error, we first need to rewrite equation (A3.7) as $prob(y_i = j) = F_j(x, \beta)$. Then the estimated value of the marginal effect of x_2 and x_3 can be computed as

$$\hat{\delta}_{23,j} = \frac{\partial^2 F_j(x, \hat{\beta})}{\partial x_2 \partial x_3} \quad (A3.10)$$

where $\hat{\beta}$ is the consistent estimator of β that is estimated via the GHK MSL method. The consistency of $\hat{\delta}_{23,j}$ is ensured by the continuity of F_j and the consistency of $\hat{\beta}$. We can compute the standard error of the above interaction effect by applying the delta method, which is given by

$$\hat{\sigma}_{23,j} = \frac{\partial}{\partial \beta} \cdot \left\{ \frac{\partial^2 F(x, \hat{\beta})}{\partial x_2 \partial x_3} \right\} \hat{\Omega}_\beta \frac{\partial}{\partial \beta} \left\{ \frac{\partial^2 F(x, \hat{\beta})}{\partial x_2 \partial x_3} \right\} \quad (A3.11)$$

In the expressions for $\sigma_{32,j}$ and $\hat{\sigma}_{32,j}$ where $\hat{\Omega}_\beta$ is the consistent covariance estimator of $\hat{\beta}$ and $\hat{\delta}_{23,j} \sim N(\delta_{23,j}, \sigma^2_{23,j})$ for all $j = 0, 1, 2 \ldots J$. Note that the delta method estimates the variance using a first-order Taylor approximation. Since a first-order Taylor approximation may provide a poor approximation in nonlinear functions (such as the ordered probit function), we follow Spanos (1999, 493–94) and use a second-order approximation by replacing the normal distribution with the chi-square distribution. Finally, observe that the *t-statistic* that tests the null that the interaction effect is zero is $t = \hat{\sigma}_{23,j} / \hat{\delta}_{23,j}$.

Chapter 5

Log-Likelihood of Bivariate Ordered Probit Model

The bivariate ordered probit model (described in equations (5.4) and (5.5) in the text) can be written more comprehensively (after dropping the subscript *t* for time for notational convenience) as

$$y^*_{i,1} = \beta'_1 \mathbf{x}_{i,1} + \varepsilon_{i,1} \tag{A5.1}$$

$$y_{i,1} = j \text{ if } \mu_{j-1} < y^*_{i,1} \leq \mu_j, \; j=0,\ldots,J_1$$

$$y^*_{i,2} = \beta'_2 \mathbf{x}_{i,2} + \varepsilon_{i,2} \tag{A5.2}$$

$$y_{i,2} = j \text{ if } \delta_{j-1} < y^*_{i,2} \leq \delta_j, \; j=0,\ldots,J_2$$

$$\begin{pmatrix} \varepsilon_{i,1} \\ \varepsilon_{i,2} \end{pmatrix} \sim N \left[\begin{pmatrix} 0 \\ 0 \end{pmatrix}, \begin{pmatrix} 1 & \rho \\ \rho & 1 \end{pmatrix} \right]$$

Thus the joint probability for $y_{i,1} = j$ and $y_{i,2} = k$ is according to Greene and Hensher (2010, 223) given by

$$prob(y_{i,1} = j, y_{i,2} = k \mid \mathbf{x}_{i,1}, \mathbf{x}_{i,2}) = \begin{bmatrix} \Phi_2[(\mu_j - \beta'_1 \mathbf{x}_{i,1}), (\delta_k - \beta'_1 \mathbf{x}_{i,2}), \rho] \\ -\Phi_2[(\mu_{j-1} - \beta'_1 \mathbf{x}_{i,1}), (\delta_k - \beta'_1 \mathbf{x}_{i,2}), \rho] \end{bmatrix} \tag{A5.3}$$

$$- \begin{bmatrix} \Phi_2[(\mu_j - \beta'_1 \mathbf{x}_{i,1}), (\delta_{k-1} - \beta'_1 \mathbf{x}_{i,2}), \rho] \\ -\Phi_2[(\mu_{j-1} - \beta'_1 \mathbf{x}_{i,1}), (\delta_{k-1} - \beta'_1 \mathbf{x}_{i,2}), \rho] \end{bmatrix}$$

Using the information from (A5.1)–(A5.3), the log likelihood function of the bivariate ordered probit model can be defined as

$$LL = \prod_{i=1}^{N} \sum_{j=0}^{J_1} \sum_{k=0}^{J_2} m_{i,j} n_{i,k} \begin{bmatrix} \Phi_2[(\mu_j - \beta_1'\mathbf{x}_{i,1}),(\delta_k - \beta_1'\mathbf{x}_{i,2}),\rho] \\ -\Phi_2[(\mu_{j-1} - \beta_1'\mathbf{x}_{i,1}),(\delta_k - \beta_1'\mathbf{x}_{i,2}),\rho] \end{bmatrix} \quad (A5.4)$$

$$-\begin{bmatrix} \Phi_2[(\mu_j - \beta_1'\mathbf{x}_{i,1}),(\delta_{k-1} - \beta_1'\mathbf{x}_{i,2}),\rho] \\ -\Phi_2[(\mu_{j-1} - \beta_1'\mathbf{x}_{i,1}),(\delta_{k-1} - \beta_1'\mathbf{x}_{i,2}),\rho] \end{bmatrix}$$

where $m_{i,j} = 1$ if $y_{i,1} = j$ and is 0 otherwise and likewise, $n_{i,k} = 1$ if $y_{i,2} = k$ and is 0 otherwise. We estimate the log likelihood function in (A5.4) with random effects. Maximizing the log likelihood function in (A5.4) on a TSCS data set requires calculating normal multidimensional distribution integrals, the dimension of which grows with T where T denotes time. Evaluating multidimensional integrals of the likelihood presented above is computationally intensive. Thus we use simulation methods—specifically, the GHK smooth recursive conditioning simulator—to maximize the log likelihood function in (A5.4). The GHK MSL method is often used by econometricians (e.g., Train 2003) to evaluate the likelihood in (A5.4) as it is used to calculate multivariate normal probabilities, which is required for MSL estimation. The GHK method leads to a simulated log likelihood function, which we maximize with respect to the parameter vectors $\mathbf{x}_i$, δ_k, $\mathbf{z}_i$, μ_j, and the covariance matrix Ω by using the BFGS numerical optimization method. After obtaining the estimates, the variance-covariance matrix is directly derived by inverting the Hessian evaluated in the obtained maximum likelihood estimators.

NOTES

Chapter 1

1. Shapiro 1996, 1999, 2000; Larkins 1996; Ginsburg 2003; Stephenson 2003; Hirschl 2004; Chavez 2004; Finkel 2005, 2008; Helmke and Rosenbluth 2009; Smithey-Ishiyama and Ishiyama 2000, 2002.

2. The term "new democracies," as employed in this book, refers to developing states that experienced a transition to democracy and retained their status as democracies for at least the first four post–transition years.

3. See, for example, Epp 1998; Burbank and Friedman 2002; Magaloni 2003; Ginsburg 2003; Chavez 2004; Vanberg 2008; Staton and Rios-Figueroa 2009; Helmke and Rios-Figueroa 2011.

4. The democratic-transition year for each country in table 1.1 is identified using the Przeworski et al. 2000 data set and the Polity indicator of the year of democratic transition.

5. Figs. 1.1 and 1.2 are drawn from constitutional data on each *de jure* judicial independence component listed above. This data—described in chapter 3—is available for 63 newly democratized developing states in table 1.1.

6. Following Ferejohn, Rosenbluth, and Shipan (2007) and Carrubba et al. (2008), we define "full judicial review" here and throughout this book broadly. It includes the review by courts (not only constitutional courts) of statutes, constitutional provisions, legislative bills, amendments, and government acts. In fig. 1.2, we distinguish full judicial review from a situation where the courts do not have any judicial review authority.

7. Studies of *de jure* judicial independence in new democracies that focus, for example, on Latin America include Helmke and Rios-Figueroa 2011; Brinks and Blass 2010; Hilbink 2007, Kapiszewski 2007, Kapiszewski and Taylor 2008.

8. For this, see, for example, Burbank and Friedman 2002; Hayo and Voigt 2003; Carrubba 2009; Chavez 2008; Vanberg 2008; Rodriguez and McCubbins 2008; Helmke and Rosenbluth 2009; Rios-Figueroa and Staton 2009.

9. Rosenn 1987; Vyas 1999; Widner 2001; Russell and O'Brien 2001; Herron and Randazzo 2003; Hayo and Voigt 2007; Chavez 2008; Vanberg 2008; Rios-Figueroa and Staton 2009; Woods and Hilbink 2009.

10. For the Argentina case see, for instance, Helmke 2005; Kapiszewski 2007. For the Ukraine case, see Smithey-Ishiyama and Ishiyama 2002; Open Society Institute 2001, 2003; Popova 2010.

11. Chapter 5 describes this *de facto* judicial independence measure and the sources used to operationalize this measure. The list of these 103 newly consolidated and established developing country democracies is provided in chapter 5, table 5.1.

12. We discuss in detail later and in chapter 2, various studies that examine how other factors including the existence of separation of powers, political competition, civil society actors, judicial culture, and economic globalization influence de facto judicial independence.

13. See Ramseyer 1994; Stephenson 2003; Whittington 2003; Hansen 2004; Beer 2006; McCubbins et al. 2006 and Ferejohn et al. 2007 for both theoretical discussions and empirical analyses.

14. The predicted probability of failure (hazard rate) of governments across 103 developing democracies in table 1.2—which is a proxy for their time horizons in office—is derived from estimating discrete-time hazard models of government survival. This measure and the data used to derive this measure are described in chapter 5.

15. For further discussions of the conceptual differences between *de jure* and *de facto* institutional characteristics and their effects see Hagger 1982; Taylor 1992; Burbank and Friedman 2002; Herron and Randazzo 2003; Norris 2003; Hayo and Voigt 2007; Vanberg 2008; Chavez 2008; Rios-Figueroa and Staton 2009.

16. For detailed discussions of *de jure* institutional characteristics see McCubbins and Rodriguez 2008; Thabane 2006; Gourevitch 2005; Norris 2003; Taylor 1992; Hagger 1982.

17. These relationships are discussed in more detail later in this chapter. See Becker 1970; Herron and Randazzo 2003; Vanberg 2008 for arguments relating specific institutional rules to higher levels of de jure independence.

18. See Shapiro 1981, 2002; Russell and O'Brien 2001; Ginsburg 2003, 2008; Herron and Randazzo 2003; Vanberg 2001, 2005; Tushnet 2008 for further discussion.

19. Scholars also differentiate between abstract review, which allows review prior to passage of legislation and concrete review, which can only be requested post legislation. Full judicial review refers to systems with both powers.

20. Currently countries that have review powers are almost evenly divided between the two arrangements (Ginsburg 2008).

21. Rogers and Vanberg 2000; Stone Sweet 2000; Vanberg 2001; Shapiro 2002.

22. See Larkins 1996; World Bank 2004; Feld and Voigt 2003; Hayo and Voigt 2007; Vanberg 2008; Kapiszewski and Taylor 2008; McCubbins and Rodriguez 2008 for further discussions of various widely used definitions of judicial independence.

23. For definitions and discussions of de facto and de jure differences see Rios-Figueroa and Staton 2009; Feld and Voigt 2003; Hayo and Voigt 2007; Burbank and Friedman 2002; Cameroon 2002.

24. For the effect of judicial independence on economic growth see Hayo and Voigt 2007; Sill 2009: on democratic consolidation see Larkins 1996; Stone Sweet 2000; Gibler and Randazzo 2011.

25. Some scholars suggest that the judiciary reflects elite interests and thus hin-

ders democracy (e.g., Tsebelis 2002), while others argue that autonomous courts fosters democratic consolidation (Larkins 1996). The empirical evidence is mixed. Staton et al. (2010) find that the effect of judicial independence on democratic stability is either negligible, or, at most, indirect. Gibler and Randazzo (2011) find that independent courts promote stability of democracies if they are established, but not when the courts are not properly consolidated.

26. Feld and Voigt 2003; Sill 2010 find that DFJI helps to promote economic growth. Yamanishi 2000, however, finds that the effect of judicial independence on growth is statistically insignificant.

27. For thorough literature reviews on the politics of judicial independence, see for example, Vanberg 2008; Helmke and Rosenbluth 2009; Hazama 2009; Woods and Hilbink 2009. We discuss this literature in chapter 2.

28. See Woods and Hilbink 2009; Vanberg 2008; McCubbins and Rodriguez 2008; Chavez 2008; Helmke and Rosenbluth 2007; Kapiszewski and Taylor 2006; Hayo and Voigt 2007; La Porta, Lopez-de-Silanes, Shleifer, and Vishny 1999; Stephenson 2003; Burbank and Friedman 2002 for excellent updated and classic overviews of various theoretical perspectives in this vast literature. See Stephenson 2003; Hayo and Voigt 2007 for empirical studies. For judicial review see Ginsburg 2008; Tushnet 2006; Shapiro 2002.

29. Other scholars have not analyzed cultural ideas as the primary driver of judicial review choices. Rather, they have integrated cultural factors into strategic models where the decision to adopt constitutional rules is modeled as an outcome of the strategic interaction between courts and political elites in the executive and the legislature (Stephenson 2003; Finkel 2004). In these models, the net payoffs the courts and political actors receive from taking different actions, reflects the cultural values and preferences of that society.

30. As discussed in the previous section, current research shows that courts have the advantage that they can use many procedural tactics such as selection of dockets, timing of decisions, framing of judicial decisions in constitutional and procedural terms to enact their own policy preferences and cater to popular preferences without undermining their own legitimacy.

31. See Woods and Hilbink 2009; Vanberg 2008; McCubbins and Rodriguez 2008; Chavez 2008; Helmke and Rosenbluth 2007; Kapiszewski and Taylor 2006; Hayo and Voigt 2007; La Porta, Lopez-de-Silanes, Shleifer, and Vishny 1999; Stephenson 2003; Burbank and Friedman 2002 for excellent updated and classic overviews of various theoretical perspectives in this vast literature.

32. See Woods and Hilbink 2009; Hilbink 2009, 2007; Sieder 2003 for recent overviews of this rich literature.

33. See, for example, Stephenson 2003; Ginsburg 2003; Hayo and Voigt 2007; Finkel 2008; Vanberg 2008.

34. See Tate and Haynie 1993; Haynie 1994; Melone 1996; Ramseyer and Rasmusen 2001; Solomon 2002; Helmke 2003, 2005; Magaloni 2006; among many, others for single country studies. See Ishiyama-Smithey and Ishiyama 2002; Popova 2010 for work on Eastern and central Europe, and Helmke and Rios-Figueroa 2011; Fin-

kel 2008; Kapiszewski and Taylor 2007; Prilliman 2000 on Latin America; Ginsburg 2003 on Asia; and Hirschl 2004 for cross-regional work. See Stephenson 2003; Herron and Randazzo 2003; Abbasi 2007; Staton 2010 for large-n analyses of various de facto arguments.

35. See Shapiro 1981; McNollgast 1995; Vanberg 2000; Whittington 2003; Friedman 2004; Hayo and Voigt 2007 for discussions of and empirical evidence for these arguments in presidential and parliamentary systems.

36. Murphy 1964; Ferejohn and Shipan 1990; Epstein and Knight 1998; Ferejohn 1999; Ramseyer and Rasmusen 2001; Rogers 2001; Smithey and Ishiyama 2002; Iaryczower, Spiller, and Tommasi 2002; Herron and Randazzo 2003; Stephenson 2003; Carruba 2005, 2008; Helmke 2005 and Rios-Figueroa 2006.

37. See Epstein, Knight, and Shvetsova 2001; Stephenson 2003; Andrews and Montinola 2004; Helmke 2005; Rios-Figueroa 2006; Staton 2010.

38. See Andrews and Montinola 2004; Helmke 2005; Rios-Figueroa 2006.

39. This extensive literature includes Carey and Shugart 1995; Cox and Thies 1998; Samuels 1999; Cox and McCubbins 2001; Milesi-Ferretti et al. 2002; Hix 2004; Chang 2005; Wallack et al. 2006; Hicken 2006.

40. Recall that procedural tactics and constitutional rhetoric allows the judiciary to manipulate legal decisions for political impact without giving the public appearance of being overtly political (Epstein, Knight, and Shvetsova 2001; Couso 2003).

41. The transition to democracy in Brazil occurred in 1985–86, while Indonesia experienced its transition to democracy in 1998–99. Brazil is thus observed in the data as a new democratic regime from 1985 to 1990, while Indonesia is observed as a new democracy from 1998 to 2003.

42. Przeworski et al.'s (2000) criteria are: (1) the chief executive and legislature must be directly elected, (2) there must be more than one party in the legislature, and (3) incumbents must allow a lawful alternation of office if defeated in elections.

43. All three countries, for example, have colonial histories and are large, ethnically diverse countries that are seen as key emerging markets in the global economy and are federal, multiparty political systems. Their hazard rates are 0.65 in Indonesia between 1999 and 2004 (the years in the data in which Indonesia is observed as a democracy), 0.65 in Brazil from 1986 to 2004, and .62 in India between 1984 and 2004.

44. Although India has been an established democracy since 1947 (except for 1976–78), we calculate the hazard rate of governments in India between 1984 and 2004. This is because: (1) data to operationalize this variable for India is only available from 1984, and (2) it facilitates comparison with the hazard rate of governments in the other two cases which is calculated from 1986 to 2004 in Brazil and 1998–2004 in Indonesia.

Chapter 2

1. As mentioned in chapter 1, full judicial review authority implies an outcome where constitutional provisions allow the courts (not just constitutional courts) to

review statutes, constitutional provisions, legislative bills, amendments, and government acts (Ferejohn et al. 2007; Carrubba et al. 2011).

2. See, for example, O'Donnell 1998; Geddes 1999. The data that we employ for testing our claims about judicial review, which is described in chapter 3, also reveals that the first post–authoritarian election occurred within the first six to nine months for over 90 percent of the developing states listed in table 1.1 (see chapter 1) that experienced a transition to democracy during the last three decades.

3. For more details on the first post–transition government attempting to exert its hegemony over the legislature after obtaining a legislative majority in (1) Bangladesh, see Ahmed 2005; (2) Indonesia and Philippines, see Johnson Tan 2006; Case 2011; and (3) Malawi, see Kalipeni 1996.

4. The PDI-P and the Golkar party successfully co-opted members from two opposition parties—the PAN and the PKB parties—into the ruling coalition. As a result, the share of the seats in the national legislature that were controlled by Indonesia's first post–transition government increased from 56 percent to 75 percent (Liddle 2000).

5. In contrast to this perspective, Hirschl (2004) argues that political elites in new democracies may carry out judicial empowerment through constitutionalization to preserve their influence in the judiciary. The end result in this scenario is that the judiciary is likely to be deferential to the executive rather than acting as an effective check on the incumbent.

6. As discussed in the previous section, current research shows that courts have the advantage that they can use many procedural tactics such as selection of dockets, timing of decisions, framing of judicial decisions in constitutional and procedural terms to enact their own policy preferences, and cater to popular preferences without undermining their own legitimacy.

7. One reason for this is because more public trust and support for the judiciary makes it harder for the executive to ignore, infringe upon, or disrespect judicial rulings. As a result, this helps the judiciary to act as a credible check on the government. Extant studies have theoretically and empirically examined the link between the legitimacy of courts (driven by public support in the courts) and the compliance they receive in the United States (see Gibson, Caldeira, and Spence 2003, 2005), and in Germany (see Vanberg 2005).

8. Vanberg (2005: 20).

9. Recall that full judicial review authority implies a situation where constitutional rules allow the courts (not just constitutional courts) to review statutes, constitutional provisions, legislative bills, amendments and government acts (see for example, Carrubba et al. 2011).

10. D. G. Palguna, 2007. *Constitutional Court in Transitional Democracy in Indonesia*, 127.

11. Studies show that cabinet members from the post–transition government in Indonesia were deeply concerned that the judiciary's opposition to the executive would not only hurt the government's reputation but also its political legitimacy and power in the national legislature. For this particular analysis for Indonesia see

Wiratna 2000; Mahfud 2007. We analyze the Indonesia case in much more detail in chapter 4.

12. Malawi's transition to democracy occurred in 1994. Extant studies reveal that public trust in the judiciary during the initial post–transition years (1994 to 1996–97) indicates that it grew from approximate 39 percent in to as high as 61 percent by late 1996–early 1997 (Kalipeni 1996; Ellett 2008).

13. Ngongola (2001, 114).

14. Studies show that cabinet members from the post–transition government in Malawi were deeply concerned as well that the judiciary's opposition to the executive would not only hurt the government's reputation but also its political legitimacy and power in the national legislature. For this particular analysis for Malawi see Von Doepp 2002; Svåsand and Patel 2007.

15. Tanchev (2001: 307).

16. Cited from *Sinar Harapan* online, July 6, 2001.

17. The rationale underlying this claim is drawn from the "electoral market logic" developed by Landes and Posner (1975) and extended by Ramseyer (1994) and Rasmussen and Ramseyer (2003).

18. For more details about the history and politics of judicial review in (1) Bulgaria, see Ganev 2004; and (2) Latvia, see Sabaliunas 1996.

19. This extensive literature includes Carey and Shugart 1995; Cox and Thies 1998; Samuels 1999; Cox and McCubbins 2001; Milesi-Ferretti et al. 2002; Hix 2004; Chang 2005; Wallack et al. (2006); Hicken (2006).

20. For a flavor of these arguments, see Stokes 2005, 2008; Carothers 2006; Kitschelt and Wilkinson 2007; Mainwaring and Torcal 2007; Magaloni, Diaz-Cayeros, and Estévez (2006); Hagopian (2009).

21. See, for example, Rose-Ackerman 1999; Carothers 2006; Kunicova 2006; Golden and Chang 2007; Gerring and Thacker 2008; Yadav 2011.

22. Carey and Shugart 1995; Cox and Thies 1998; Cox and McCubbins 2001; Hix 2004.

23. This discussion is drawn from a large literature including, for example, Carey and Shugart 1995; Samuels 1999; Cox and McCubbins 2001; Chang 2005; Wallack et al. 2006; Hicken 2007.

24. For example, in Bulgaria, when governments were changing dramatically in the 1990s, the judiciary became central to political disputes and was subject to several constitutional attacks. It responded by taking advantage of the public's attention to publicize and confront government efforts to undermine its independence during this period. As a result of their increased awareness of blatant government efforts to capture the courts and the court's efforts to resist political capture, the judiciary won increased support from its citizens who now saw it as the "last bulwark against an ominous, large-scale, campaign of re-communization." The precariousness of government's political strength therefore allowed courts to increase the reservoir of popular support for their institution. Evidence from Slovenia (Open Society Institute 2001) and Mexico (Staton 2010; Domingo 2000) also shows active use of publicity by courts for similar purposes.

25. In Costa Rica, for instance, the bar association spearheaded an organized effort to collect opinions and evaluations on judicial reforms from various stakeholders and experts, then analyze and publicize the results through NGOs, media outlets, academia, and directly to the national assembly itself (Gramont and Salazar 2007: 119–20). These reports then exercised considerable influence on subsequent judicial reforms to increase DFJI there. In Mexico (Domingo 2004; Staton 2004), Argentina (Chavez 2004; Transparency International 2007), and Guatemala (Sieder 2003; Salazar and Gramont 2007) as well we find numerous examples where courts and nongovernmental organizations including business and civic organizations were key allies of the courts in pushing for appropriate judicial reform.

26. For this claim see Carey and Shugart 1995; Hicken 2006; Cox and Thies 1998; Samuels 1999; Hix 2004; Chang 2005; Wallack et al. 2006.

27. For example, in Brazil (a developing democracy with a personalist electoral system), several legislators and a judge in Rio de Janeiro were arrested when the police raided judicial offices and found evidence of that they were colluding to raise money by abusing their powers (Transparency International 2007). Such schemes have, however, been in successful operation in many courts in India where pliable judges have been supported and protected by pliable police (Jalan 2007; Transparency International 2007).

28. For instance, consider Malawi, which is characterized by a high electoral particularism since it employs the single-member district plurality rule in which party leaders do not control access to ballot and ranks (Chingaipe 2005). In Malawi, civil society groups teamed up with foreign donors and international organizations to successfully reverse a politically motivated attempt to impeach of three judges by the president's party (Gloppen and Kanyongolo 2006). The judges were able to benefit from such deep support because the judiciary in Malawi had managed to establish itself in public opinion as a committed impartial guardian of the constitution (Gloppen et al. 2010, 101).

29. For instance, in Malawi and Colombia (which is also highly particularistic as Colombia employs the open-list PR rule), courts have been crucial in ensuring that elections are held under fair conditions and offered all sides an even playing field. To this end, during the 1999 campaign, the courts ordered the Malawi Broadcasting Corporation to provide a balanced coverage of government and opposition campaigns, while during the 2004 campaigns they postponed Election Day in order to enable officials to check the validity of voter rolls (Gloppen et al. 2010, 102). In Colombia, courts reinterpreted legislation to ensure the opposition faced an even election process (Calleros 2009: 183). Likewise, in 2001 in Hungary—which is also characterized by a high level of electoral particularism—when the government failed to pay the Christian Democrats (KDNP) party its share of public funds, the KDNP was able to successfully sue them and obtain its fair share of public campaign funds (Open Society Institute 2001: 268–69).

30. In chapter 6 of this book, we demonstrate that India has a particularistic electoral system.

31. For instance, in 2001 in Bulgaria, which has a strongly party-centered elec-

toral system, the ruling coalition was under considerable political threat from a new emerging party, the National Movement Simeon II (NMSV). Facing elections, the government pressured the Supreme Court to confirm a lower court decision to refuse registration to the NMSV party. Menem's party reaped a similar electoral dividend in Argentina (a well-known party-centered democracy) when a judge appointed by him ruled that the ruling party had not violated campaign financing laws because the party could not be held responsible of funding of which "they were unaware" (Transparency International 2007). The decision was widely seen as a political choice by the judge. The shorter the time horizons of incumbent governments in party-centered systems, the higher the immediate value of such capabilities to influence elections will be.

32. Cooter and Ginsburg (1996) argue that disciplined parties who are dominant and expect to remain so, will be able to provide policy guarantees and will see an independent judiciary as an obstacle to providing such guarantees. Our argument here is that parties will have the same incentives even if they have short time horizons in office as the benefits of a subservient judiciary provides are high for their expected short tenure in office.

33. Numerous examples broadly provide support for the claims posited earlier. For instance, retired judges reported ruling parties in Romania (a party-centered democracy) used judges to protect their financial and commercial donors in various types of legal cases (Open Society Institute 2002, 495–96). In Indonesia (another party-centered democracy), IMF efforts to create independent bankruptcy courts suffered serious setbacks when ruling parties literally coerced politically "dependent" courts to negotiate firm debt with firms in exchange for funds (Lev 2005; Ogada 2004). In Argentina (a well-known party-centered system), a judge was fired after he refused to drop a case against an important donor and replaced with a more pliant one (Transparency International 2007, 2009). Similar examples are found in other party-centered countries such as the Czech Republic and Slovenia as well (Transparency International 2007; Open Society Institute 2002).

Chapter 3

1. An analysis of the relevant primary sources revealed that constitutional data on each component of de jure judicial autonomy explored in this chapter is available for a truly global sample of developing states—that is from developing states across all possible regions around the globe—primarily from 1985 onwards. Prior to the mid-1980s, constitutional data on difference components of de jure judicial independence, including the components examined in this book, is limited to a small cross-sectional sample of less than 50 developing countries (see, for example, Greenberg et al. 1993; Cross 1999). Since an "n" of less than 50 developing states does not constitute a fully representative sample for quantitative tests, we code and use the available data for various components of de jure judicial independence starting from 1985. Doing so helps us to avoid "selecting" a relatively sample of developing nations for our tests and also allows us to enhance the empirical generalizability of our obtained results as much as possible.

2. Studies that employ an ordinal measure of judicial review include Sill 2010; Finkel et al. 2007; Lijphart 1999.

3. Data from the Democracy Assistance Project (University of Pittsburgh) can be obtained from http://www.pitt.edu/~politics/democracy/democracy.html.

4. This can be purchased from Heinonline.org.

5. These primary and secondary sources are listed in table 3.3.

6. For this, see Boix 2003; Boix and Stokes 2003; and Przeworski et al. 2000.

7. In most cases of democratization, the adoption of a new constitution and elections occur within a year after the transition to democracy.

8. Hence, for example, given that Poland made a transition to democracy in 1990, it is classified as being a new democratic regime in 1990 and in 1991, 1992, 1993, and 1994; it is however classified as an autocracy for the years preceding 1990 and the years following 1994.

9. Studies that have used the Hirschman-Herfindahl index of concentration of legislative seats held by the government or opposition to explore the impact of this concentration on economic or political outcomes include, for instance, Brock 2003; Caroll et al. 2007; Stein et al. 1998; Chhibber 2004.

10. This includes the lead party as well as its coalition partners.

11. The data sources employed to compute the *legislative concentration* measure are listed in table 3.3.

12. The mean level of the *legislative concentration* measure is .236 (on a 0 to 1 scale), while the standard deviation is .196; this indicates that there exists significant variation in *legislative concentration*.

13. Responses to this question by survey respondents have, for example, been gathered over time across several countries in the World Values Survey, Latin American Public Opinion Project (LAPOP), the Afrobarometer, and the Asian Barometer.

14. This measure of the degree of public trust in the judiciary is also available for many other developing countries in our sample that are listed in table 3.1.

15. Some existing studies of the determinants of judicial independence do not carefully distinguish between de jure and de facto measures of judicial independence including judicial review; for this point, see Rios-Figueroa and Staton 2009. However, the control variables that we include in our empirical models (where judicial review is the dependent variable) is drawn from theoretical and empirical studies that focus on the determinants of de jure judicial review either explicitly or implicitly.

16. For this, see Abbasi 2007; Vanberg 2008; Schapiro 1981; Whittington 2003.

17. Downloaded from the Polity IV data archive at http://www.systemicpeace.org/polity/polity4.htm.

18. Specifically, the coding of the *competition* measure (i.e., PARCOMP) is as follows: 0 = unregulated political competition, 1 = suppressed (no significant oppositional activity is permitted outside the ranks of the regime and ruling party), 2 = restricted/transitional (some organized, political competition occurs outside government, without serious factionalism, but the regime sharply limits its form, extent, or both in ways that exclude substantial groups from participation), 3 = fac-

tional (shows factional or factional/ restricted patterns of competition), 4 = transitional (any transitional arrangements from restricted or factional patterns to fully competitive patterns, or vice versa), and 5 = competitive (there are relatively stable and enduring political groups that regularly compete for political influence at the national level; competition among them seldom causes widespread violence or disruption).

19. Cheibub et al.'s (2010) threefold criteria for a democracy are as follows: (1) the chief executive and legislature must be directly elected; (2) there must be more than one party in the legislature; and (3) incumbents must allow a lawful alternation of office if defeated in elections. We calculated the number of years that every country in our sample that is observed as a democracy according to this three-fold criteria; this measure constitutes our democracy age variable as previously mentioned.

20. The bivariate correlation between the *new democracy* dummy and *democracy level* in our sample is weak (.181) and statistically insignificant, therein mitigating any concerns about collinearity between these two variables.

21. Hayo and Voigt 2007; Ferejohn et al. 2004; Herron and Randazzo 2003.

22. The results reported below remain robust when we use foreign aid flows as percentage of GDP rather than just the volume of foreign aid flows mentioned earlier in the text.

23. The results presented in the next subsection remain robust when we use FDI flows as percentage of GDP rather than just the volume of FDI flows mentioned earlier.

24. Political scientists often use the degree of trade openness as a proxy for economic globalization. For this, see Milner and Mukherjee 2009; Li and Reuveny 2004; Kayser 2007; Iverson 2001.

25. The results reported below remain robust when the ordered probit model is estimated with country fixed effects. However, as shown by Bester and Hansen (2009) and Carro and Traferri (2009), incorporating fixed effects in an ordered probit model that is estimated on finite samples leads to an incidental parameters problem that engenders inconsistent and inefficient estimates. Therefore, we choose to present the results from the ordered probit models that are estimated with random effects.

26. The results reported later in this chapter also remain robust when we include a cubic polynomial (see Carter and Signorino 2010) or splines in the specification to account for temporal dependence in the data.

27. For details on this particular selection bias problem see, for example, Przeworski et al. 2000; Boix 2003.

28. A country is coded as democratic regime = 1 if it satisfies the Cheibub et al. (2010) criteria for a democracy that was described in note 19 to this chapter.

29. See Przeworski et al. 2000; Boix 2003.

30. μ_{j-1} and μ_j denote the threshold parameters in the second stage—that is, in the ordered probit outcome equation, of the S-OP model. Stated more technically,

the error terms of the S-OP model (ε_i and u_i) are assumed to be bivariate normal distributed with correlation coefficient ρ with mean zero and variance one each: $(\varepsilon_i, u_i) \sim N_2(0,0,1,1,\rho)$.

31. We use simulation methods—specifically, the Geweke-Hajivassiliou-Keane (GHK) smooth recursive conditioning simulator—to evaluate the log likelihood function of the sample-selection ordered probit (S-OP) model. The technical details of the procedure are described in the appendix.

32. The estimated coefficient of the interaction term is statistically significant only when the upper and lower bounds are both above or below the zero line.

33. Criterion for low trust and low concentration.

34. Following Fearon and Laitin 2003, "elf" is computed as 1 minus the Herfindahl index of ethnolinguistic group shares. The elf measure is calculated for the developing states in our sample and is updated till 2004.

35. We thank an anonymous reviewer for this suggestion.

36. According to Przeworski et al. (2000), an authoritarian regime satisfies the following three criteria: (1) the chief-executive is not elected; (2) the legislature is not elected; and (3) there is no more than one political party or there has been no alternation in power.

37. The data for operationalizing *democracy transition sum* and *authoritarian transition sum* is drawn from Przeworski et al. (2000) and Cheibub et al. (2010).

38. Countries that use the German legal system are treated as the reference category.

39. Some researchers have suggested that bicameralism may increase the prospects for more judicial independence including judicial review; see, for example Vanberg 2008; Fortin 2008; Roy et al. 2006.

40. Veto players is drawn from World Bank's (2008) DPI. A couple of studies suggest that the presence of more veto players promotes greater de jure and de facto judicial independence (see Hayo and Voigt 2007; Stephenson 2003; Sousa 2006).

41. See, for example, Dargent 2009; Burbank and Friedman 2002; Elkins 2010.

42. The selection equation estimates from the S-OP model in this case is reported in table 3.5, column B.

43. The largest and mean VIF value in the models is less than 10 and greater than 1 respectively; thus multicollinearity is not a problem. To assess for serial correlation, we first plotted the correlograms and partial correlograms of the residuals from each estimated model; we also checked the p-values of the autocorrelation function and partial autocorrelation function for first lag as well as several additional lags of the residuals from of each estimated model. Results from this exercise reveal that the residuals do not suffer from serial correlation. Further, the Breusch-Godfrey LM test failed to reject the null of no serial correlation in the outcome and selection equations respectively. The RESET test shows that there is no omitted variable bias problem; the Jarque-Bera test shows that the residuals are distributed normally.

44. See, for example, Ginsburg 2003; Larkins 1996; Curry 2008.

Chapter 4

1. For a thorough descriptive analysis of the politics of democratization in Indonesia see Uhlin 1997; Tomasa 2008. For studies on the political causes of democratization in Brazil, see for example Mainwaring 1987 and Myers 1991.

2. For this see Clarke 2003; Omara 2008; Croissant 2011.

3. For instance, the moving average of the Hirschmann-Herfindahl index of the effective number of legislative parties is approximately 6.9 in Indonesia from the country's first year of transition to democracy 1999 to 2004, 6.8 in India, and 7.5 Brazil, respectively, during the 1999 to 2004 time period.

4. The size of Brazil and India's economy in 2009 is U.S. $1.6 trillion and U.S. $1.3 trillion, respectively (International Monetary Fund 2010).

5. As discussed in the Brazil case, many of these features are common to the Brazilian judiciary as well.

6. For instance, even after democratization, the government continues to exert significant control over judicial appointments to the Supreme and High Courts, and, moreover, the tenure of judges is limited. This serves to reduce the political autonomy of the judiciary (Susanti 2002; Hadiz 2004; Assegaf 2005).

7. A detailed historical analysis of the origins of Indonesia's Constitutional court is provided, for example, in Harun 2004; Venning 2005; Stockmann 2007.

8. Recall that this ordinal de jure judicial review measure operationalizes the extent to which constitutions explicitly grant the courts the authority of judicial review.

9. The data used to compute this concentration index value for Indonesia is drawn from (1): Johnson Tan 2006; (2) Electionworld.org, "Elections in Indonesia," http://www.electionworld.org/indonesia.htm; (3) CIA World Factbook (1999–2004); and (4) "Perhitungan Perolehan Kursi DPR RI, KPU Indonesia, http://www.kpu.go.id/dprkursi.php.

10. As described later, the moving average of the concentration of legislative seats held by governments in Brazil between 1986 and 1990—the years in which Brazil is observed as a new democracy—drops to less than 0.4 by 1989. Data for calculating this measure for Indonesia and Brazil are listed below figures 4.2 and 4.3, respectively.

11. The abbreviation PPP stands for "Partai Persatuan Pembangunan," which roughly translates to United Development Party.

12. See Ufen (2006: 25); Manning and Van Diermen 2000.

13. This cite is taken from Susardi's interview published in "PDIP Mempelajari Pembentukan Komisi Konstitusi," *Kompas,* September 1, 2001.

14. Ufen 2006; Wood 2001; Manning and Van Diermen 2000.

15. This cite is taken from Sambuaga's interview published in "Amandemen UUD 1945 tidak Konsisten dengan Tuntutan Reformasi," *Suara Pembaruan* (Jakarta), July 27, 2000.

16. Interview with Permadi, June 20, 2010.

17. This was suggested repeatedly in interviews given by Sri Somemantri (profes-

sor of constitutional law at Padjajaran University), Chusnul Mariyah (political observer and journalist at *Kompas*), and Mochtar Pabottingi (KOKB member). For this claim, also see Jyranki 2000.

18. The *Koalisi Ornop untuk Konstitusi Baru*—literally translated as "NGO Coalition for a New Constitution"—was a prominent nongovernmental organization in Indonesia formed by lawyers, political activists, and journalists. The KOKB publicly campaigned both the Wahid and (later) the Megawati government to introduce significant changes to the first, second, and third amendments to the constitution in order to increase political accountability of the state and promote judicial independence.

19. *Koalisi Ornop untuk Konstitusi Baru*, "Kertas kerja Koalisi Ornop untuk Konstitusi Baru," Unpublished working paper, KOKB: Jakarta, 2001, 9.

20. See Transparency International (Indonesia), "Measuring Corruption in Indonesia: Indonesia Corruption Perception Index 2008 and Bribery Index," 2008, 22–23. This report can be downloaded from http://www.ti.or.id/media/documents/2010/11/09/i/p/ipk-english_final.pdf.

21. For this, see Partnership for Governance Reform, *The TOR Annual Report* (Memacu Pembaruan Tata Pemerintah), Jakarta, 2000, 137.

22. Partnership for Governance Reform, *The TOR Annual Report* (Memacu Pembaruan Tata Pemerintah), Jakarta, 2002, 112.

23. GIR survey 2001; ADIA survey 2001.

24. WBES 2003; WVS 2002; Carino 2007.

25. As described earlier, in the Asian Barometer Survey (ABS) and the Global Integrity (GI) Survey in 1999 for Indonesia, just 49 percent (47 percent) of the respondents in the ABS (GI) survey expressed "trust and confidence" in the Indonesian judiciary. By 2001 this increased to 62 percent (GI survey) and 63 percent (ABS survey), respectively. For more details, see, for example, Carino 2007.

26. Taken from Sambuaga's interview published in "Amandemen UUD 1945 tidak Konsisten dengan Tuntutan Reformasi," *Suara Pembaruan* (Jakarta), July 27, 2000.

27. The amendment in Article 24(B)(3) to Indonesia's constitution states that the "Judicial Commission shall be appointed and dismissed by the President with the approval of the *Dewan Perwakilan Rakyat*." This indicates that Judicial Commission in Indonesia is completely controlled by the government. The section of the text of Article 24(B)(3) cited earlier is drawn from "Indonesia Constitution Third Amendment"; see http://confinder.richmond.edu/admin/docs/Indonesia_third_amend.pdf.

28. This section of the text of Article 24(B)(1) cited earlier is taken from "Indonesia Constitution Third Amendment"; see http://confinder.richmond.edu/admin/docs/Indonesia_third_amend.pdf.

29. This data is drawn the Risalah Rapat (the minutes of meeting) of the People's Consultative Assembly; more specifically, it is drawn from: (1) Minutes of the 1st–12th (continued) Plenary Meetings, General Session, the People's Consultative Assembly of Republic of Indonesia, October 1–19, 1999; and (2) Minutes of the 1st–

2nd Meetings of Commission C, General Session of the People's Consultative Assembly of Republic of Indonesia, October 17–18, 1999. It is also partially taken from Indrayana 2008.

30. See Susanti 2001; Tobing 2001; and sources listed in note 29.

31. Cited from *Sinar Harapan* online, November 8, 2001. Yusuf was a member of the Golkar Party, which was part of the multiparty coalition government from 1999 to 2003.

32. Taken from *Sinar Harapan* online, July 6, 2001.

33. For this see Wiratma 2000; Piliang 2000 and Indrayana 2008.

34. This is taken from Fallakh (2002: 29).

35. Fallakh (2002: 30).

36. Fallakh (2002: 30).

37. Cabinet members in Wahid and (later) Megawati's government such as Akbar Tanjung and Amien Rais shared this view. For more details of their perspective on this issue see Mahfud 2007.

38. See interview of Amien Rais published in "Indonesia: Proposed Constitutional Reforms Under Fire," *Radio Australia*, August 2, 2002.

39. Alex Litaay, "Untuk Apa UUD '45 Diamandemen," *Republika*, May 10, 2001.

40. Policy speech of Megawati Soekarnoputri, July 29, 1999. The translation of her speech is drawn from *The People's Victory in the 1999 Election* (August 1999) by Van Zorge, Heffernan & Associates.

41. Kansil et al. (2001: 36).

42. Croissant (2011: 13).

43. Data drawn from the Risalah Rapat (the minutes of meeting) of the People's Consultative Assembly; specifically: (1) Second Book Volume 8A: Minutes of the 36th–39th Meeting of the Ad Hoc Committee I of Working Body, Annual Session of the People's Consultative Assembly of Republic of Indonesia, September 26, 2001–October 22, 2001; (2) Third Book Volume 1: Minutes of the 1st–3rd Plenary Meeting (continued), Annual Session of the People's Consultative Assembly of Republic of Indonesia, November 1, 2001–November 2, 2001; and (3) Third Book Volume 3: Minutes of the 7th (continued)—8th Plenary Meeting, Annual Session of the People's Consultative Assembly of Republic of Indonesia, November 9, 2001.

44. Ibid. Also see Susanti 2001; Tobing 2001.

45. Interview with Mochtar Pabottingi, member of the Coalition for a New Constitution, July 3, 2003.

46. We pointed out in the previous chapter that the size of Brazil's nominal GDP in 2008 was $1.5 trillion, which makes it the tenth largest economy in the world.

47. See Power (1990) and Skidmore (1997) for more details. From 1985 to 1989—the period during which Brazil is defined as a new democracy according to our five-year post–transition standard—the country held elections for the federal congress in 1986 and for president and a new congress in 1990.

48. See Oliveira 1993 for details in Portuguese, and Ames and Power 1990; Reich 2007, for summaries in English.

49. The Chamber of Deputies is the lower house of Brazil's national legislature.

50. The data to calculate the index value in this case is drawn from Kingstone and Power 2008; Neto 2000; CPDOC (n.d.), Ministros de Estado da República, Rio de Janeiro, Fundação Getúlio Vargas.

51. Seat-share data for the entire discussion has been drawn from Mainwaring and Pérez-Lĩnán (1997); Santos and Vilarouca (2008); and from the Ames and Power (1990) database provided very kindly by them to the authors.

52. Details on the chronology and functional structure of the constitutional process in this section are drawn from various reports authored by Oliveria (1993) and published by the Subsecretaria de Edições Técnicas, Senado Federal, Brasil.

53. Cited in Shirley (1987, 11).

54. In 1985 a group of human-rights activists spearheaded by the church in Sao Paolo researched and published a report, *Brasil: Nunca Mais,* which detailed the arrests, detention, and torture perpetrated by over 9,000 military personnel during the military regime (Pereira 2003: 5; Weschler 1998: 75; Skidmore 1988: 268, 395). Among the terms of its support for the transition to democracy, the military establishment had negotiated government adherence to a 1979 amnesty, which allowed the perpetrators of these crimes to go free (Calleros 2009, 119; Pereira 2000; Gillespie 1989: 101; Skidmore 1988: 217–19). The prosecution of the perpetrators of these crimes was therefore not taken up by the government and most of the accused retained their positions (Weschler 1998: 76). The legality of this amnesty was challenged in the courts by survivors and their relatives after the release of a 1985 report detailing these crimes (Pereira 2003: 225; Weschler 1998: 75). These cases demanded information on missing people as well as compensation for their losses.

55. The report stayed on the best-seller list in Brazil for 26 straight weeks (Weschler 1998: 94).

56. This lack of access was also a function of lack of government investment in facilities and rural states and regions especially suffered from acute shortages of judges and courts (Calleros 2009: 169).

57. CEPAC-IBOPE poll conducted in 1989. Cited in Linz and Stepan (2001: 176). 3,600 respondents were asked the following question about the justice system "In Brazil the justice system only functions to help the powerful," only 7.6 percent disagreed partially or completely, 58 percent agreed completely, and 26 percent agreed partially.

58. The exact quote in Portuguese is *"hoje, o Poder Judiciário—digo isso com grande tristeza aos meus colegas que estão na Mesa, porque sou um homem do Poder Judiciário, filho de um homem do Poder Judiciário—seja um poder desacreditado junto à população brasileira."* Translation by Chad Evans.

59. CEDI 1993, Volume 1, Mapa 1, Parte 2, 95–97.

60. CEDI 1993, Volume 1, Mapa 1, Parte 2, 95–97.

61. CEDI 1993, Volume 1, Mapa 1, Parte 2, 96.

62. Quoted in Prilliman (2000: 83).

63. This ordinal *judicial review* measure and the sources employed to develop this measure is described in chapter 3. Recall that this measure operationalizes the

extent to which constitutions explicitly grant the courts the authority of judicial review.

64. See, for example, Larkins 1996; Dung 2003; Kis and Dworkin 2004.

65. For examples of this perspective see Rottman and Tomkins 1999; CCPIO Report 2010.

Chapter 5

1. Democracies in the developing world that exhibit higher levels of electoral particularism are largely, as mentioned earlier, candidate-centered systems where the level of intraparty unity and centralization is low (Ames 1995; Mainwaring 1998; Hix 2004; Johnson and Wallack 2006; Hicken 2009).

2. Developing democracies characterized by low levels of particularism are primarily party-centered systems where (1) intra-party unity within political parties is high, and (2) political parties are highly centralized. For this, see Hix 2004; Hankla 2006; Hicken 2007; Eaton 2009.

3. The main results presented in this chapter hold if countries are coded as democracies when their Polity score is 6 or greater than 6 in −10 (full autocracy) to +10 (full democracy) scale. Scholars that have used this Polity-based criterion to classify states as democracies include, for example, Mansfield et al. 2000; Hankla 2006.

4. Tate and Keith 2007; Cingranelli and Richards 2008; Rios-Figueroa and Staton 2009.

5. Operationalizing the dependent variable from several primary and secondary sources helps us maximize the number of observations and employ the entire temporal range of the sample being examined here.

6. For example, see Solomon 2008; Popova 2010 for Russia; Open Society Institute 2003, 2002, 2001 for Russia, Slovakia, and Hungary; Sajo for Hungary; Staton 2010 and Rios-Figueroa and Taylor 2006 for Mexico; Hammergren 2007b for Bolivia, Costa Rica, and Mexico; Gloppen et al. 2010 for Costa Rica, Mali, and Malawi; and Mollah 2006 for Bangladesh.

7. See, for instance, Rios-Figueroa and Staton 2009; Haggard et al. 2008; Tiede 2008.

8. See, for example, Alesina et al. 1996; Przeworski et al. 2000; Crain and Tollison 1993.

9. A handful of studies have used the predicted probability of failure to operationalize the hazard rate of governments; see Persson and Tabellini 2005; Wright 2008.

10. Beck, Katz, and Tucker (1998) show that the hazard rate of a discrete hazard model with a logit specification and temporal dummies is similar to the hazard rate in the Cox duration model.

11. A large number of studies have statistically evaluated the effect of difference covariates on the likelihood of government failure in democracies. Early studies that empirically assessed the determinants of government failure by employing haz-

ard/duration models include Diermeier and Stevenson 1999; King et al. 1990; Warwick 1992, 1994; Martin 1999. More recent studies that have statistically estimated the impact of various economic and political variables on the probability of government failure in developing democracies include Kang 2008; Jackle 2009; Kapstein and Converse 2009. The variables that we include in our discrete time hazard model of government failure are drawn from these studies.

12. This variable is drawn from the World Bank's (2008) *Database of Political Institutions*. It is operationalized in the World Bank's DPI database as the maximum distance between the chief executive's value of party ideology and the values (party ideology) of the three largest government parties and the largest opposition party.

13. Following standard convention (see, for example, Bawn and Rosenbluth 2006), ENLP is operationalized as the reciprocal of the sum of squared seats shares across all parties represented in the legislature.

14. We include the Pedersen (1983) index of electoral volatility which is commonly used by scholars to operationalize electoral volatility (Mainwaring and Scully 1995; Roberts and Wibbels 1999; Mozaffar 2005).

15. The *electoral risk* variable captures the possibility that leaders may voluntarily dissolve their government and call for elections as the end of the constitutionally defined interelection period approaches. We include this variable in the discrete time hazard model since scholars have shown that as the end of constitutionally defined inter-election period approaches particularly (but not only) in parliamentary democracies, the risk that leaders may voluntarily dissolve their government and call for elections increases significantly which, in turn, increases the hazard rate of these governments (Smith 2003; Kayser 2006; Cheibub et al. 2004). Since developing democracies have different constitutionally mandated election periods—(i.e., 36, 48, 60, or 84 months)—we operationalize *electoral risk* as:

$$1 - \frac{\text{Number of Months Remaining in CIEP when leader dissolves government}}{\text{Constitutional Electoral Period}},$$

where CIEP denotes "constitutionally defined inter-election period." The electoral risk variable, which is bounded between 0 and 1, has several advantages. First, it captures Smith's (2003) empirical finding the likelihood of government dissolution increases the longer the government has been in office. For instance, using the formula just described, we find that the electoral risk for an incumbent that dissolves his government after being in office for 45 out of 48 months is 0.93, while the electoral risk for an incumbent that dissolves his or her government after being in office for 20 out of 48 months is 0.41. Second, the electoral risk variable captures how voluntary dissolution by incumbents affects the duration of their government in the hazard model. Third, it also accounts for how different constitutionally mandated election periods influence the duration and thus the hazard rate of each government.

16. We include a dummy variable for parliamentary democracies as researchers have extensively debated whether the hazard rate of governments in parliamentary democracies is higher or lower than governments in presidential democracies

(Warwick 1994; Maeda and Nishikawa 2006; Cheibub and Limongi 2002; Mainwaring and Scully 1995). Likewise, we add a dummy variable for minority governments in the data since scholars have suggested that the probability of survival (failure) of minority governments in office is low (high) relative to majority governments in both developed and developing democracies; for this, see Somer-Topcu and Williams 2008; Warwick 1992; Roozendaal 1997.

17. See Beck and Katz (1998) for a discussion of duration dependence in models of regime survival.

18. For a discussion of the causes of democratic transition in South Africa and the year (i.e., 1994) in which South Africa experienced a transition to democracy, see Tordoff 2002; Jung and Shapiro 1995.

19. For instance, in 1989, a small set of minor political parties in India called the Janata Dal joined with the Hindu-nationalist Bharatiya Janata Party (BJP) on the right and the Communists on the left to form an unstable multiparty coalition government. This loose coalition collapsed in November 1990, and the Janata Dal, supported by the main opposition party, the Congress-I, came to power for a short period, with Chandra Shekhar as prime minister. That alliance also collapsed, resulting in national elections in June 1991. Between 1996 and 1999, India was headed either by unstable multiparty coalitions, including the United Front (between 1996 and 1998) or a the minority BJP-led government; the United Front government and the minority BJP-led government eventually collapsed and failed to complete their tenure in office.

20. A number of reports in the newspapers and magazines in South Africa in 1997 and 1998 suggested that the ANC may not win the general elections that were expected to occur in 1999. For examples of these reports, see Jovial Rantao, "Will Ramaphosa Make a Comeback to Challenge for ANC Deputy President," *Star,* October 18, 1997; and Ramotena Mabote, "Youth League's Backing of Phosa Could Send Shivers through the ANC," *Star,* April 4, 1997. Some scholars argued in 2003 that the ANC's poor economic performance in office may cost them the upcoming election in 2004; for this see Lodge 2003.

21. Studies of the determinants of de facto judicial independence across countries include controls such as *log GDP per capita,* (political) *competition, judiciary trust,* and *press freedom* in their empirical specifications. These variables are often included in empirical models of de jure judicial independence. For this, see Hayo and Voigt 2007; Feld and Voigt 2003; Rios-Figueroa and Staton 2009; Abbasi 2007.

22. For example, Berggren (2003) and Wolf (1997) suggest that higher levels of trade openness increases economic growth and per-capita income that, in turn, generates incentives for developing states to design independent institutions including an autonomous judiciary.

23. As described in chapter 3, the *competition* (PARCOMP) measure is coded on an increasing 0–5 scale.

24. Note that the Finkel et al.'s (2007) de jure judicial independence also accounts for separation of powers; we, however, dropped this component from the index as we explicitly control for separation of powers in the specification.

25. The results reported below remain robust when the ordered probit model is estimated with country fixed effects. Since incorporating fixed effects in an ordered probit model leads to an incidental parameters problem that engenders inconsistent and inefficient estimates (Carro and Traferri 2009), we focus on presenting the results from the ordered probit models estimated with random effects.

26. The results also remain robust when we include a cubic polynomial or splines in the specification to account for temporal dependence.

27. See, for example, Greene and Hensher 2009; Biswas and Das 2002.

28. See, for example, Carey and Shugart 1995; Schneier 2006; Morena 2004; Shugart and Wattenberg 2003; Mainwaring and Shugart 1997; Hix 2004; Hicken 2007.

29. Desposato (2006) and Shin (2010) claim that in less developed countries or districts where the majority of voters are poor and less educated, personalistic parties—whose members are more likely to vote against party lines and to switch parties in order to provide voters with those particularistic benefits—are more likely to flourish. However, we are more likely to observe the opposite in countries with higher levels of per-capita income.

30. For this, see Carey and Shugart 1995; Hicken 2002, 2007; Hix 2004.

31. The reference category in this case includes democracies with an open-list PR system.

32. Hix 2004; Hicken 2007; Shin 2010.

33. Shin (2010: 46).

34. μ_{j-1} and μ_j denote the threshold parameters in the first stage, that is the ordered probit selection equation, of the bivariate ordered probit model; δ_{j-1} and δ_j denote the respective threshold parameters in the second stage—that is, the ordered probit outcome equation, of the bivariate ordered probit model. Put more technically, the error terms from the selection and outcome equation of the BVOP model are assumed to be bivariate normal distributed with correlation coefficient ρ with mean zero and variance one each: $(\varepsilon_{i1}, \varepsilon_{i2}) \sim N_2(0,0,1,1,\rho)$.

35. The coefficients are statistically significant when the upper and lower bounds are both above or below the zero line.

36. The fact that Brazil is a candidate-centered system is well-known and is suggested by scholars such as Mainwaring 1999; Samuels 2004; Ames and Power 2007. We show in chapter 7 that India is also primarily candidate-centered rather than party-centered system as suggested by researchers such as Keefer and Khemani (2009) and Chaba (2007), for example.

37. Both Benin and Romania employ a closed-list PR electoral system and are thus characterized by low levels of electoral particularism (Shin 2010).

38. Following Fearon and Laitin (2003), "elf" is computed as 1 minus the Herfindahl index of ethnolinguistic group shares. The elf measure is calculated for all the developing democracies in our sample and is updated until 2004.

39. See, for example, Guarnieri 2001; Halmai 2000.

40. Countries that use the German legal system are treated as the reference category.

41. The ordered probit model in column 5 and the BVOP model that includes the outcome equation in column 6 are estimated with random effects.

42. Some researchers have suggested that bicameralism may increase the prospects for more judicial independence including judicial review; see, for example Vanberg 2008; Fortin 2008; Roy et al. 2006.

43. The veto players' variable is drawn from World Bank's (2008) *Database of Political Institutions*. A couple of studies suggest that the presence of more veto players promotes greater de jure and de facto judicial independence (see Hayo and Voigt 2007; Stephenson 2003; Sousa 2006).

44. A handful of recent studies have suggested the possibility of diffusion of judicial independence which is potentially generated by states attempting to emulate either the level of judicial independence or particular features of the judicial system that prevails in neighboring states. For this claim, see Garoupa and Ginsburg 2008; Feldbrugge 2006; Ginsburg 2008.

45. The largest and mean VIF value in the models is less than 10 and greater than 1, respectively; thus multicollinearity is not a problem. To check for the possibility of serial correlation, we first plotted the correlograms and partial correlograms of the residuals from each estimated model; we also checked the *p*-values of the autocorrelation function and partial autocorrelation function for first lag as well as several additional lags of the residuals from of each estimated model. Results from this exercise reveal that the residuals do not suffer from serial correlation. Further, the Breusch-Godfrey LM test failed to reject the null of no serial correlation in the outcome and selection equations respectively. The RESET test shows that there is no omitted variable bias problem; the Jarque-Bera test shows that the residuals are distributed normally.

Chapter 6

1. See, for example, Carey and Shugart 1995; Hix 2004; Hicken 2007, 2009; Mainwaring 1999.

2. Reilly 2006; Ellis 2008.

3. For instance, the moving average of the Hirschmann-Herfindahl index of the effective number of legislative parties is approximately 6.9 in Indonesia from the country's first year of transition to democracy 1999 to 2004, 6.8 in India, and 7.5 Brazil, respectively, during the 1999 to 2004 time period.

4. As estimated by the IMF in 2009, the size of Brazil's economy in nominal GDP terms is approximately U.S. $1.6 trillion dollars, while the size of India's economy is U.S. $1.3 trillion dollars.

5. We calculate the mean hazard rate of governments in Brazil between 1986 and 2004 as Brazil made a transition to a full-fledged democracy in 1986 and (as described in chapter 4) because the relevant data that we have to calculate the hazard rate of governments in Brazil is available until 2004.

6. Although India has been an established democracy since 1947 (except for 1976–78, when the country experienced emergency rule), we calculate the hazard

rate of governments in India between 1984 and 2004. This is because (1) data to operationalize this variable for India is only available from 1984, and (2) it facilitates comparison with the hazard rate of governments in the other two cases which is calculated from 1986 to 2004 in Brazil and 1999 to 2004 in Indonesia.

7. A large literature on electoral systems in political science claims and finds that the open-list PR electoral rule promotes a candidate-centered system. For this, see Shugart and Carey 1992, 1995; Cox and Rosenbluth 1995; Samuels 1999, 2000, 2001.

8. For example, based on their measure of the degree to which electoral systems are personalist/candidate-centered Carey and Shugart (1995: 428) find that in Brazil, party "leaders have no formal sanctions to encourage cooperation and maintaining party reputations. The value of personal reputation is thus high."

9. There is a stream of literature which disagrees with this assessment of Brazilian parties as weak (Figuerido and Limongi 2000; Limongi and Cheibub 2002; Santos Vilaroucas 2008; Lyne 2008). Figueirido and Limongi (1995, 2000) argue that legislative centralization neutralizes the party-weakening incentives of OLPR rules and present analysis of roll-call data to support their arguments. However, roll-call analyses suffer from many problems of selection bias (Carruba et al. 2008). Political considerations that influence which bills reach the floor agenda and, the voting stage and, the price and probability of their success are not accounted for (Ames 2002; Desposato 2004; Samuels 2004; Zucco 2009; Yadav 2011). For these reasons, we agree with the assessment of scholars that Brazilian parties are weak political actors.

10. Despite party appeals to voters to cast a party vote rather than vote or an individual, only 18 percent in 1990, 8 percent in 1994, 14 percent in 1998, and 10 percent in 2002 of all votes credited to a party came from votes cast as a party vote rather than chose to cast their votes for parties (Nicolau 2007, 12).

11. As discussed in chapter 5, we derived the predicted probability of failure of each government in our sample—which provides a useful and accurate proxy for their ex ante hazard rate in office—from estimating discrete-time hazard models. The data that we used to calculate the hazard rate of governments in Brazil from 1986 to 2004 are drawn from Schmitt 2000; Banks 2003; Dabene 2003; Nicolau, J. *Dados eleitorais do Brasil* (1982–86).

12. We used the standard formula of the Hirschmann-Herfindahl index, which equals the sum of squared seat shares of the parties, to calculate the effective number of parties in Brazil's case. The data for computing this measure is drawn from: (1) Rogério Schmitt (2000) Partidos Políticos no Brasil (1945–2000), Rio de Janeiro, Jorge Zahar; (2) Dabene 2003; (3) the TSE's website (http://www.tse.gov.br/partidos); and (4) W. G. dos Santos, *Almanaque de dados eleitorais: Brasil e outros países.*

13. At this time, 95 percent of all electrical power consumed in Brazil came from hydroelectric sources (Economic Intelligence Unit 2001).

14. More recently, the PPB party has changed its name to PP—*Partido Progressista.*

15. In 1990, President Collor first issued an executive decree freezing bank ac-

counts and then preemptively issued another decree placing restrictions on the judiciary's ability to rule on injunctions against this policy (Santiso 2003: 6). While this ensured that the Supreme Court did not overturn this particular government policy outright, it antagonized the courts and assured opposition parties of a more friendly court when they did file lawsuits against this policy and against the government generally. The decree also failed to prevent hostile judges from ruling in ways that undermined the bank freeze policy itself without actually overturning it. It also failed to discourage judges from ruling against the government on the myriad other cases in their jurisdiction. Additionally, the judiciary gained public support due to the government's actions while the government looked authoritarian and undemocratic (Santiso 2003: 7).

16. This is also illustrated in fig. 6.1, where we find that the hazard rate of the Cardoso government starts steadily increasing from 2001 onwards.

17. For example Itamar Franco of the PMDB, then governor of Minas Gerais and ex-president of Brazil, stated publicly that he would not implement the policy in his state unless the courts declared it to be constitutional (Taylor 2008: 68).

18. Translation from the original Portuguese quoted in Taylor (2008: 80); insertions in brackets added.

19. ADINs (also known as the Declaration of Unconstitutionality of Policies) are one of several specific forms of legal constitutional challenges allowed under the Brazilian legal system. Opposition parties have often used ADINs as a legal tool to challenge government policies (Taylor 2008).

20. While ADINs can only be filed by those with the legal standing to do so, *acao popular* are instruments that can be filed by anyone. See Taylor (2008); Rios-Figueroa and Taylor (2006) for more details.

21. President Cardoso was elected with the support of a heterodox alliance that included his own Social Democratic Party, the PSDB, and two right-wing parties: the Liberal Front Party (PFL) and the Brazilian Labor Party (PTB). Brazil's largest party—the centrist Party of the Brazilian Democratic Movement (PMDB)—joined Cardoso's governing coalition after the election, as did the right-wing PPB, the Brazilian Progressive Party, in 1996.

22. Interview with Claudio Abramo Weber, Director Transparencia Brasil, conducted on August 18, 2010.

23. This is illustrated in fig. 6.1, where we find that the hazard rate of Lula's coalition government increased quite sharply almost immediately after he assumed office in early 2003.

24. For more details on this, see Taylor (2008: 29–31).

25. Interview of Judge Lunardelli, conducted on August 19, 2010.

26. These sources include: (1) Câmara dos Deputados (various years), *Projetos de lei e outras proposições* [Bills of law and other propositions], http://www2.camara.gov.br/proposicoes; (2) Senado Federal (various years), *Constituição da República Federativa do Brasil* [Constitution of the Federative Republic of Brazil], Brasilia, Brazil; (3) Senado Federal (various years), *Atividade legislativa* [Legislative activity], http://www.senado.gov.br/sf/atividade/Materia/pesqAvancada.asp; (4) Vianna

et al. 1999; (5) Senado Federal (various issues), Relatório da Presidência [Report from the Presiding Office] Brasilia, Brazil; (6) Taylor 2008.

27. United Nations, *Basic Principles on the Independence of the Judiciary*, 1986, adopted by the Seventh United Nations Congress on the Prevention of Crime and the Treatment of Offenders, held at Milan from August 26 to September 6, 1985, and endorsed by General Assembly resolutions 40/32 of November 29, 1985, and 40/146 of December 13, 1985. U.N Doc. A/CONF.121/22/Rev.1.

28. Concerns about the independence of judges stemming from its authoritarian past ensured that the 1988 constitution contained provisions granting the judiciary many de jure powers. De jure powers including wide jurisdictions, finality of decisions, and a limited form of judicial review, as well as insulation from political interference in appointments and budgeting procedures were constitutionally mandated (Taylor 2006, 2008; Rios-Figueroa 2006; Pereira 2003; Prilliman 2000). However, as previous analysis suggested, these de jure rules may influence the realization of de facto independence but they do not guarantee it.

29. Interview with Claudio Weber Abramo, director, Transparência Brasil (August 18, 2010), Judges for Democracy (August 12, 2010), and Association of Federal Judges of Brazil (AJUFE)—SP (August 25, 2010).

30. Interviews with Judge Felippe (August 12, 2010), Judge Nascimento (August 25, 2010), Judge Lunardelli (August 25, 2010), and Judge Lourenco (August 25, 2010).

31. The two de facto judicial independence measures that we employ are Cingranelli and Richards (2008), and Keith and Tate's (2007) measure. These two measures were described in detail in chapter 4.

32. See, for example, Arora 2004; Sridharan 2002; Kapur 2005.

33. CIA—World Factbook—Rank Order—GDP (purchasing power parity)," https://www.cia.gov/library/publications/the-world-factbook/rankorder/2009rank.html.

34. For a discussion of the growing role of these three countries in the G20 group of nations, see Guebert 2009.

35. See Mehta 2008 for details.

36. See Gadbois 2011 for these and further details.

37. A more detailed description of India's electoral rule where voters choose individual candidates on their ballot, see Election Commission of India, "System of Selection," in India, http://eci.nic.in/eci_main/ElectoralSystem/the_function.asp.

38. See Election Commission of India 2006, *Political Parties–Organisation Election, Contribution Reports, Expense Reports,* ECI, Government of India, New Delhi.

39. For this, see Hicken and Stoll 2010; Hankla 2007; Chibber and Kollman 2004.

40. We use the standard Hirschman-Herfindahl index—which equals to the sum of squared seat shares of the parties—to calculate the effective number of legislative parties in India.

41. As described in chapter 4, the hazard rate of governments in India is given by the predicted probability of failure of each government in the sample that is derived from estimating discrete-time hazard models. The data that we used to calculate the

hazard rate of Indian governments are drawn from Election Results by the Central Election Commission (various years), Government of India; Banks 2003; Sridharan 2004; Nikolenyi 2009.

42. More specifically, in 1989, a small set of minor political parties in India called the Janata Dal joined with the Hindu-nationalist Bharatiya Janata Party (BJP) on the right and the Communists on the left to form an unstable multiparty coalition government. This loose coalition collapsed in November 1990. After the collapse, the multiparty coalition Janata Dal government, supported by the main opposition party, the Congress-I, came to power for a short period, with Chandra Shekhar as prime minister. That alliance also collapsed, resulting in national elections in June 1991.

43. In fact, the Rao government did face a parliamentary vote of confidence in 1993, which it won by a margin of just two votes. Rao was later convicted of bribing opposition MPs to vote for his government in order to win the no-confidence vote (Mitra 1998).

44. Party leaders in the BJP were initially against involving the courts in the dispute because religious fundamentalists in the party opposed judicial intervention on the Babri Masjid issue. For example, Ramchandradas Paramahans, a right-wing extremist element in the BJP, emphatically stated on December 12, 1991, that "law is not bigger than the faith. If supporters of the Ram temple movement unite, the law will have to take a back seat," cited from Jay Dubashi, "Hindutva's Challenge to India's Constitution," *Hindustan Times,* December 12, 1991. Notwithstanding such provocative rhetoric, moderate elements in the BJP prevailed and eventually chose to appeal to the courts to intervene in the Babri Masjid issue. For more details on the BJP's strategy in dealing with the courts in 1991–1992 over the Ayodhya dispute, see Tapan Basu et al. 1993; Mukhia 1992; Engineer and Nayak 1993.

45. Cited from the BJP's *National Executive Resolution*—1991, New Delhi: BJP Central Office, 36; this resolutions was released at the 5th National Convention of the BJP at Jaipur, India.

46. Manoj Kurien, "The RSS, the Babri Masjid Dispute and Indian Law," *Malyalam Manorama,* March 19, 1992.

47. Taken from the *Hindustan Times,* February 7, 2003.

48. Cited from "BJP, the Ayodhya Dispute and Indian Law," *Dainik Jagran,* translated from Hindi to English by the authors.

49. President's rule (or central rule) in any state in India occurs when the state legislature is dissolved or suspended and the state is placed under direct federal rule by the central government. More specifically, president's rule is enabled by article 356 of the Indian constitution, which gives wide powers to the central government to assert its complete authority over the administration and judicial system of a state if civil unrest occurs in that state; consequently, this allows the central government to limit the intervention by the courts in the political affairs of a state when it is under President's rule. For more details on president's rule in India, see for example, Sethy 2003.

50. V. Venkatesan, "A Scholar and a Politician," *Frontline,* January 1–14, 2005, http://www.hinduonnet.com/fline/fl2201/stories/20050114008013000.htm.

51. The right-wing extremist entities in India's polity that envisage the creation of a polity built on the religious principles of Hindutva rather than secularism include the Vishwa Hindu Parishad (VHP) and the Rashtriya Swayamsevak Sangh (RSS). For more details on these two organizations see Jaffrelot (1996, 2003); Varshney 2002.

52. Cited from "Narasimha Rao and the SR Bommai Case," *Navbharat Times*, March 11, 1993; translated from Hindi to English by the authors.

53. These sources include: (1) Lok and Rajya Sabha, Parliamentary Bills Information System, Government of India, http://164.100.47.4/newlsbios_search/in tsessionreport3.aspx; (2) S. C. Kashyap, *History of the Parliament of India, Vols. I-VI* (New Delhi: Shirpa, 1997–2000); (3) http://www.ipu.org/parline/re ports/2145.htm; (4) G.C. Malhotra, *Fifty Years of Indian Parliament* (New Delhi: Lok Sabha Secretariat, 2002); (5) B. Goswami, *Parliament and Administration* (New Delhi: Rawat, 2002); (6) S. C. Kashyap, *Parliamentary Procedure Law Privilege Practice and Precedents* (New Delhi: Universal Law, 2006); (7) Chari Gururaja, *Supreme Court Rules, Practice & Procedure Vols. 1 and 2*. New Delhi: Wadhwa Publishers & Distributors, 2005); (8) D. Sunder Ram, ed., *Parliamentary Institutions in India: Development or Decay* (Jaipur: National Publishing House, 1998).

54. Our analysis of all the amendments and bills from India in the 1985 to 2005 period showed that in terms of issue area, these bills or amendments can be classified into 16 different categories. These 16 categories are listed in table 6.4.

55. As mentioned earlier, this includes provisions that: (1) direct the government to undertake steps to increase the judiciary's financial autonomy; (2) ensure that the formal assignment of cases to judges is done without intervention from any external source; (3) instructs the government to institutionalize laws that restricts the executive from interfering in judicial decisions; (4) formally prevents legislators from contradicting judicial rulings; and (5) guarantees that judicial tenure is secured without threat of reduction. United Nations, *Basic Principles on the Independence of the Judiciary*, 1986, adopted by the Seventh United Nations Congress on the Prevention of Crime and the Treatment of Offenders, held at Milan from August 26 to September 6, 1985, and endorsed by General Assembly resolutions 40/32 of November 29, 1985, and 40/146 of December 13, 1985. U.N Doc. A/CONF.121/22/Rev.1.

56. This was "The Recovery of Debts Due to Banks and Financial Institutions Act," which was approved by Parliament in 1993 (Armour and Lele 2008: 16).

57. For debates on judicial activism in (1) India, see, for example, Khosla 2008; Baxi 2007; and (2) Brazil, see Brinks (2005); Taylor (2008).

Chapter 7

1. As mentioned in the earlier chapters, existing theoretical studies suggest that the party-centered electoral rules engenders strong and centralized political parties that are characterized by high levels of intraparty unity; for this, see, for example, Hix 2004; Eaton 2009; Hicken 2007.

2. The seven-member *Tim Tujuh* team was headed by Ryaas Rasyid, who was the head of the Institut Ilmu Pemerintahan (Institute of Government Studies), the government bureaucracy's largest training school (Woodward 2002). As emphasized by Shin (2010: 16), this seven-member team, in fact, "proposed a single-member district plurality voting system (first past the post, FPTP)" for Indonesia in 1998–99.

3. The complete name of these parties are as follows: the Partai Demokrasi Indonesia-Perjuangan (Indonesian Democracy Party-Struggle, or PDI-P), Partai Golkar (Functional Group Party, or Golkar), the Partai Kebangkitan Bangsa (National Awakening Party, or PKB), the Partai Persatuan Pembangunan (United Development Party, or PPP), and the Partai Amanat Nasional (National Mandate Party, or PAN).

4. The four party leaders that have, in particular, benefitted from Indonesia's closed-list PR electoral rule (1999–2004) in order to consolidate their control over individual members in their party include Megawati Sukarnoputri (head of the PDI-P), Abdurrahman Wahid (founder and chief executive of the PKB), Hamzah Haz (head of the PPP), Amien Rais (party leader of PAN), and Aburizal Bakrie (chairman of Golkar party).

5. See, for example, Hix 2004; Eaton 2009; Hicken 2007.

6. In Indonesia's closed-list PR electoral system, party members who are elected as legislative members can be dismissed from the legislative body if they lose their membership in the respective political parties (Ufen 2006; Hadiz 2004). Party leaders in the country have exploited this rule to credibly threaten to expel party members from the legislature if they fail to toe the party line. This has helped them to further strengthen their control over rank-and-file party members (for this, see Teehankee 2006; Ufen 2006).

7. For this, see Hadiz 2004; Johnson Tan 2004.

8. Hadiz 2004.

9. As discussed in detail in chapter 4, we derived the predicted probability of failure of each government in our sample—which provides a useful and accurate proxy for their ex ante hazard rate in office—from estimating discrete-time hazard models. The data that we used to calculate the hazard rate of governments in Indonesia from 1999 to 2004 are drawn from Banks 2003; Electionworld.org, "Elections in Indonesia"; and "Perhitungan Perolehan Kursi DPR RI," KPU Indonesia, http://www.kpu.go.id/dprkursi.php.

10. For this claim see King et al. 2005; Liddle and Mujani 2005. Note that Megawati's poll ratings in the 2004 presidential election declined from 14 percent in January 2004 to 11 percent in June 2004, while the poll rating of the main opposition leader, Susilo Bambang Yudhoyono increased from just 9.1 percent in January 2004 to as much as 45 percent by June 2004. These poll rating figures are taken from *International Foundation of Electoral Systems* (2006).

11. On average, President Megawati's approval rating was around 59 percent between early 2002 and the first months of 2003; see Thornton and Thornton (2008: 77).

12. Bill Guerin, "Indonesia's First Man," *Asia Times,* August 17, 2002.

13. In particular, the post of vice president was offered to Megawati Sukarnoputri (the chief executive of the PDI-P), while the "national unity cabinet" included leaders and representatives from the PPP, the PDI-P, and the Golkar Party.

14. We use the Hirschmann-Herfindahl index formula, which equals the sum of squared seat shares of the parties, to calculate the ENLP in Indonesia's case. The data sources to calculate the ENLP index for Indonesia is drawn from Johnson Tan (2006); Electionworld.org, "Elections in Indonesia," http://www.electionworld.org/indonesia.htm; and "Perhitungan Perolehan Kursi DPR RI, KPU Indonesia, http://www.kpu.go.id/dprkursi.php.

15. This committee was established by the interim administration of President Habibie under Presidential Decree no. 21 of 1999, and had a multi-stakeholder membership composition. For more details on this see Assegaf 2007; Pompe 2005.

16. For this see Manan 2004; Witoelar 2003; Pompe 2005.

17. See Manan 2004; Witoelar 2003; Pompe 2005.

18. This quotation from Article 5(2) of the Indonesian Constitution is taken from Pompe (2005, 134).

19. A useful description of the organizational structure and functions of the BPK is provided in Aditjundro 2009; Von Lubeke 2010.

20. Article 23(f) of the third amendment to Indonesia's constitution states that "The members of the *Badan Pemeriksa Keuangan* will be chosen by the *Dewan Perwakilan Rakyat,* . . . and will be formally appointed by the President." This particular section of the text of article 23(f) is cited from "Indonesia Constitution Third Amendment." See http://confinder.richmond.edu/admin/docs/Indonesia_third_amend.pdf.

21. For Abdurrahman Wahid's "promise" on this issue, see Bedner 2003; Lindsey 2002. See Assegaf 2004; Pompe 2005 for more details on Megawati's decision to not transfer the authority to administer Indonesia's high courts and state courts to the Supreme Court.

22. More specifically, the complete relevant sentence in Article 24(b) of the third amendment to Indonesia's constitution states that "there shall be an independent Judicial Commission, which shall possess the authority to propose candidates for appointment as justices of the Supreme Court and shall possess further authority to maintain and ensure the honor, dignity and behavior of judges." This is taken from article 24(b) in "Indonesia Constitution Third Amendment"; see http://confinder.richmond.edu/admin/docs/Indonesia_third_amend.pdf.

23. This follows from the particular set of words in Article 24(b) of the third constitutional amendment, which states that "there shall be an independent Judicial Commission . . ."; see "Indonesia Constitution Third Amendment," http://confinder.richmond.edu/admin/docs/Indonesia_third_amend.pdf. Additionally, the Megawati government and the House of Representatives at the time advertised the commission as an independent and politically autonomous body even though this was (and is) not really the case; for this, see Cumaraswamy 2006; Rositawati 2010.

24. Pompe 2005; Rositawati 2010.

25. Cited from "Indonesia Constitution Third Amendment," as discussed earlier at chapter 4, note 27; available at http://confinder.richmond.edu/admin/docs/Indonesia_third_amend.pdf.

26. In 2000, the ruling PDI-P party in the governing coalition headed by President Wahid, supported the nomination of the following individuals to become chief justice of the Supreme Court: Bagir Manan and Professor Muladi. President Wahid (who led the PKB), however, refused to approve either of these two candidates. However, after once Megawati (the chief of the PDI-P party) assumed the office of president, she and her party approved the nomination of Bagir Manan as the Chief Justice of Indonesia's Supreme Court. Hence, Manan was in some sense "selected" by Megawati's party. For more details on the politics underlying the selection of the chief justice of the Supreme Court, as described earlier, see Rositawati 2010; Suseito 2008.

27. Communicated to the authors in an interview, July 27, 2010.

28. In addition to Manan, the Megawati administration selected (and approved) two additional individuals with nonjudicial backgrounds to serve as justices in the Supreme Court: Abdul Rahman Saleh and Benyamin Mangkoedilaga. Both these justices were publicly known to be sympathetic to her government's agenda (Rositawati 2010; Pompe 2005). The choice of these (and other) judges by her government was done in a nontransparent and ad hoc manner which, to exacerbate matters, was justified by administration officials on grounds of privacy. The choice of these judges and the manner in which they were picked was met with skepticism by the print media. This skepticism is, for example, expressed in an editorial from the *Indonesia Observer* of August 16, 2002, "the government's reasoning that the *ad hoc* recruitment of judges should be kept secret to protect the candidate's privacy is not acceptable."

29. A central component of *Pancasila,* as emphasized by Klemb (2007) is that "Pancasila, or Five Principles, instituted by the country's founder Sukarno, (is that) the government expressly guarantees freedom of religion." See Jurgen Klemb, "Indonesia' Secular State Under Siege," *Der Spiegel,* June 4, 2007.

30. The three main political parties that supported the inclusion of the "seven words" mentioned earlier are the Partai Bulan Bintang (PBB) [Crescent Star Party], the Perserikatan Daulat Ummat (PDU) [Union of Moslem Sovereignty], and Partai Perasatuan Pembangunan (PPP) [United Development Party]; for more details on this see Indrayana (2008, xxiii).

31. Cited from Indrayana (2008, 114).

32. Susanti (2006, 12).

33. This is stated explicitly in the modified version of article 29 of the fourth amendment to Indonesia's constitution, "The State guarantees all persons the freedom of worship, each according to his/her own religion or belief." This section of the text of article 29 is cited from, "The 1945 Constitution of the Republic of Indonesia as amended by . . . the Fourth Amendment of 2002," http://www.indonesia-ottawa.org/indonesia/constitution/fourth_amendment_const.pdf.

34. In terms of literal translation, *wong cilik* refers to "little people" in Javanese. However, in Indonesia's political landscape, it is often used to refer to the rural and urban poor. For this, see Curtin 1997.

35. This section of the text of article 33 is cited from, "The 1945 Constitution of the Republic of Indonesia As amended by . . . the Fourth Amendment of 2002," from http://www.indonesia-ottawa.org/indonesia/constitution/fourth_amendment_const.pdf.

36. "Populism or Promoting Growth," *Suratkabar*, December 15, 2003.

37. Specifically, the following four parties in the Megawati government supported article 33 in the fourth amendment: the PDI-P party (led By President Megawati), the Golkar Party, the PKB, and the PPP. The share of the legislative seats held by these four parties in the national legislature was as high as 79.4 percent (Johnson Tan 2006). The relatively high share in the proportion of seats held by these parties allowed the Megawati government to easily obtain sufficient legislative support for their proposal to modify article 33 in the fourth amendment to Indonesia's constitution.

38. "Is the Supreme Court neutral?" *Suara Pembaruan* (Memihak Kebenaran), January 9, 2004.

39. See "Review—Politics: Prepared to Lose," Laksamana, June 6, 2004; http://www.bion.cz.cc/urimesing/laksamana070604a.htm.

40. The Constitutional Court was initially set up by the People's Consultative Assembly (MPR) during the process of Indonesia's democratic transition between 1998 and 1999 (Harijanti and Lindsey 2006; Butt and Lindsey 2009). Both the Abdurrahman Wahid and the Megawati administration felt that they could use the Constitutional Court to act as a check on the Supreme Court (Pompe 2005; Suseito 2008). Subsequent events, however, showed that the Wahid and the Megawati's expectation about using the Constitutional Court to balance the Supreme Court was wrong.

41. Government of Indonesia, letter of intent to the IMF, March 16, 1999, http://www.imf.org/external/np/loi/1999/031699.htm.

42. Article 33(2) of Indonesia's 1945 Constitution cited in Butt and Lindsey (2009: 5).

43. Taken from Butt and Lindsey (2009: 12)

44. Michael Schuman. "Will Megawati be Ousted?" *Time,* April 26, 2004.

45. Cite taken from Robinson and Hadiz (2002: 114).

46. For this, also see the following articles: (1) "Megawati's Bargaining Position," *Jakarta Post,* May 26, 2004; and (2) Michael Schuman. "Will Megawati be Ousted?" *Time,* April 26, 2004.

47. A detailed discussion of some of the corruption charges made by Susilo Bambang Yudhoyono and the appeal his party's appeal to the Supreme Court to investigate alleged cases of corruption by Megawati's ministers and her husband is provided in McLeod 2005 and Davidson et al. 2006.

48. Mietzner 2005; Hafild 2004; Trotter 2006.

49. Trotter 2006.
50. Butt (2007, 114).
51. Taken from "Bukti Bukan Janji [Proof Not Promises]," *Tempo*, March 29, 2004. This statement is part of a larger declaration that was designed and issued by a set of Supreme Court judges and prominent academics such as Priyambudi Sulistiyanto, Smita Notosusanto, and Subur Budhisantosa (who later became chair of the Partai Demokrat).
52. See Indrayana 2004; Wanandi 2004; Pribadi 2005.
53. Cite taken from Badoh (2005, 12).
54. Interview with Andi Mallarangeng, member of Partai Demokrat's central board, July 19, 2010.
55. This is cited from the text of law no. 11 of 2004 that was passed by the Dewan Perwakilan Rakyat, Dewan Perwakilan Rakyat, Jakarta.
56. For more details of the history and functions of Indonesia's Commercial Court see Tabalujan 2002; International Monetary Fund 2004; Basri and Van Der Eng 2004.
57. Cited from the text of article 12(g) in law no. 17 of 2004 that was passed by the Dewan Perwakilan Rakyat, Dewan Perwakilan Rakyat, Jakarta.
58. Tabalujan 2003; Basri and Van Der Eng 2004.
59. Trotter 2006; Rositawati 2010.
60. The total share of seats held by the three main ruling parties in the Megawati government in the immediate months prior to the 2004 election was 68.79 percent; the data for this is drawn from Electionworld.org, "Elections in Indonesia", http://www.electionworld.org/indonesia.htm; "Perhitungan Perolehan Kursi DPR RI", KPU Indonesia, http://www.kpu.go.id/dprkursi.php.
61. For example, 71 percent of all legislators in the Dewan Perwakilan Rakyat voted to support the implementation of law no. 17 of 2004, which contained the article that granted the authority to transfer and discipline judges to the Ministry of Judges. For this, see Suryadinata 2005.
62. Cited in Widya Mandala, "Internal Politics in Indonesia's Political Parties," *Indonesia Observer*, January 10, 2004.
63. These sources include: (1) Dewan Perwakilan Rakyat (DPR), Laws Republik Indonesia, Government of Indonesia, http://www.dpr.go.id/en/laws-and-bills/laws; (2) Dewan Perwakilan Rakyat (DPR), Deliberated Bills, Government of Indonesia, http://www.dpr.go.id/en/laws-and-bills/bill-deliberation; (3) Dewan Perwakilan Rakyat (DPR), Approved Bills, Government of Indonesia, http://www.dpr.go.id/en/laws-and-bills/bill-deliberation; (4) http://www.hukumonline.com/; Legal Database; (5) Lindsey 2008; (6) Antara Indonesian "Legislative News" subscription service, http://www.antara.co.id/WartaPerundangan.asp; (7) PT Asiamaya Dotcom Indonesia Indonesian Legislation, http://www.asiamaya.com/hukum/index_uu.htm; (8) Austlii Indonesian Law References, http://www.austlii.edu.au/links/223.html.
64. Our examination of the amendments and bills from Indonesia showed that in terms of issue area, these bills or amendments can be classified into 14 categories. Each of these 14 categories is listed in table 7.3.
65. The moving average of the predicted probability of failure of Yudhoyono's

government in 2005 and 2006, which is computed from an estimated discrete time hazard model, is 0.71, which is undoubtedly high.

66. Interview with Ikrar Nusa Bhakti, July 22, 2010.

67. Cite taken from Indrayana (2004: 117). Note that Frans Hendra Winarta, a prominent Jakarta trial lawyer, was chairman of the Indonesian Advocates Association.

68. More specifically, the dashed line in the figure is the 0–2 ordinal measure of *de facto judicial independence* described in chapter 4, which is based on the measure developed by Keith and Tate (2007), while the solid line in the figure is the 0–2 ordinal measure *de facto judicial autonomy* developed by Cingranelli and Richards (2008).

69. Cited from Buehler (2009: 12).

70. Conversely, once Indonesia shifted to an open-list PR democracy, the incumbent did not curb the courts' de facto autonomy even though his government's hazard rate in office was high.

71. Jacqueline Hicks, "The problem with Indonesian Democracy," *Asia Times*, September 11, 2008.

72. Cited from Adnan Verity, "Skewed Justice in Indonesia's Tainted Courts," *Asia Sentinel*, August 21, 2006.

Chapter 8

1. The term "third wave" of democratization is drawn from Huntington (1991).

2. Larkins 1996; Herron and Randazzo 2003; Ginsburg 2003, 2008.

3. Other scholars, however, argue that more intense political competition in particularly the post-transition period in new democracies "*hinders* rather than *promotes* the maintenance of independent courts" (Popova 2008, 2010).

4. Cited from Ran Hirschl, 2003, "Review of *Judicial Review in New Democracies: Constitutional Courts in Asian Cases* by Tom Ginsburg, New York: Cambridge University Press."

5. For example, Staton (2006, 2010); Vanberg (2001, 2005); Carrubba 2008; Gibson and Caldeira (2009) analyze how public support (or lack thereof) for the judiciary affects the interaction between the executive and the judiciary in democracies. Other scholars, however, pay more attention to the effect of the office-motivated incumbents on the constitutionalization of judicial empowerment (Ramseyer 1994; Weingast 1997; Ferejohn et al. 2007; Stephenson 2003; Ginsburg 2003, 2008).

6. For instance, Hayo and Voigt (2003, 2007) assess the effect of political stability, different levels of democracy, and presidential systems on a 0–1 continuous measure of de facto judicial independence in a limited cross-sectional sample of 46 countries. But they do not, as mentioned earlier, examine how political particularism influences the behavior of politicians with respect to preserving or curtailing the de facto independence of the courts.

7. See, for example, Ramseyer 1994; Helmke 2002; Iaryczower et al. 2002; Vanberg 2005; Whittington 2003, 2005; Staton 2010.

8. Rios-Figueroa (2006) examines the effect of judicial independence on corruption in Latin American countries, while Rose-Ackerman (2007) theorizes about how judicial autonomy may influence bureaucratic and judicial corruption. Additionally, Ades and Di Tella (1996) and Robinson (2003) evaluate the effect of judicial independence on corruption in a limited cross-sectional sample of developed and developing states.

9. Transparency International's (TI) Corruption Perceptions Index (CPI) measures corruption as the "perceptions of the degree of corruption as seen by business people, risk analysts and the general public," and explicitly includes perceptions of political and administrative corruption as well. It computes the average of a number of different surveys that assess this perception of each country's corruption level in a given year to generate a continuous 0–10 index where a higher score means less corruption. The results that we obtain remain robust when we also use the Inter-Country Risk Guide (ICRG) index of corruption.

10. The start and end date and the number of developing country democracies in the sample are determined by the availability of data of the TI corruption measure.

11. Feld and Voigt 2003; Sill 2010.

12. Yamanishi 2000; Peretti 2003.

13. World Bank (2004: c.7).

14. This information has been calculated based on data drawn from Golder 2004; Ellis 2006.

15. Adnan Falak Sher, "Good Governance versus Judicial Activism," Quaid-E-Azam Law College, Lahore (Pakistan), 2007, 2.

16. UNDP, "Judicial Independence in Transitional Countries," UNDP: Oslo Governance Centre, 2003, 15.

17. Ibid.

18. This data on perceptions of judicial corruption is drawn from the response by individual firms to the following question on a survey (conducted by the World Business Environment Survey [WBES] from 2002–2005): "In many countries, firms are said to give unofficial, private payments or other benefits to public officials to gain advantages in the drafting of laws, decrees, regulations, and other binding government decisions. To what extent has the following practice—*private payments or other benefits to judges to affect the decisions of court cases*—had a direct impact on your business?" The response by firms to this question is operationalized on a 0 (low) to 4 (high) ordinal scale (World Business Environment Survey, World Bank, Washington, DC).

REFERENCES

Abbasi, Hossein A. 2007. "Determinants of Judicial Independence: Rules or Rulers." Unpublished manuscript. http://www.economics.uiuc.edu/docs/people/candidates/abbasi_paper.pdf.

Abraham, H. 2002. "The Pillars and Politics of Judicial Independence in the United States." In *Judicial Independence at the Crossroads: An Interdisciplinary Approach*, ed. S. Burbank and B. Friedman. Thousand Oaks, CA: Sage.

Abreu, Marcelo de Paiva, and Rogério L. F. Werneck. 2005. "The Brazilian Economy from Cardoso to Lula: An Interim View." Paper 504. Departamento De Economia. www.econ.puc-rio.br.

Ackerman, B. 1997. "The Rise of World Constitutionalism." *Virginia Law Review* 83:771–802.

Acuna, C., and C. Smulovitz. 1996. "Adjusting the Armed Forces to Democracy: Successes, Failures, and Ambiguities in the Southern Cone." In *Constructing Democracy: Human Rights, Citizenship, and Society in Latin America*, ed. E. Jelin and E. Hershberg, 14–35. Boulder: Westview Press.

Ades, A., and R. Di Tella. 1996. "The New Economics of Corruption: A Survey and Some New Results." *Political Studies* 45:496–515.

Alesina, Alberto, and Howard Rosenthal. 1996. "A Theory of Divided Government." *Econometrica* 64:1311–41.

Alston, Lee J., Edwyna Harris, and Bernardo Mueller. 2009. "De Facto and De Jure Property Rights: Land Settlement and Land Conflict on the Australian, Brazilian, and U.S. Frontiers." NBER working paper no. 15264.

Alston, Lee J., and Bernardo Mueller. 2006. "Pork for Policy: Executive and Legislative Exchange in Brazil." *Journal of Law, Economics, and Organization* 22:87–114.

Ames, Barry. 2001. *The Deadlock of Democracy in Brazil*. Ann Arbor: University of Michigan Press.

Ames, Barry, Andy Baker, and Lucio Rennó. 2008. "The Quality of Elections in Brazil: Policy, Performance, Pageantry, or Pork?" In *Democratic Brazil Revisited*, ed. P. Kingstone and T. Power. Pittsburgh: University of Pittsburgh Press.

Ames, Barry, and T. Power 2007. "Parties and Governability in Brazil." In *Party Politics in New Democracies*, ed. Paul Webb and Stephen White. New York: Oxford University Press.

Andrews, Josephine T., and Gabriella Montinola. 2004. "Veto Players and the Rule of Law in Emerging Democracies." *Comparative Political Studies* 37:55–87.

Apodaca, Clair. 2004. "The Rule of Law and Human Rights." *Judicature* 87:292–99.
Arantes, Rogerio B. 2000. "The Judiciary, Democracy, and Economic Policy in Brazil." In *Handbook of Global Legal Policy*, ed. Stuart Nagel. New York: Marcel Dekker.
Arantes, Rogerio B. 2005. "Constitutionalism, the Expansion of Justice and the Judicialization of Politics in Brazil." In *The Judicialization of Politics in Latin America*, ed. Rachel Sieder, Line Schjolden, and Alan Angell. New York: Palgrave Macmillan.
Armour, John, and Priya Lele 2008. "Law, Finance, and Politics: The Case of India." ESRC Centre for Business Research, working paper no. 361. http://www.cbr.cam.ac.uk/pdf/WP361.pdf.
Arora, Balveer. 2003. "Federalisation of India's Party System." In *Political Parties and Party Systems*, ed. Ajay K. Mehra, D. D. Khanna, and Gert W. Kueck. New Delhi: Sage.
Arora, R. K., and R. Goyal. 1996. *Indian Public Administration: Institutions and Issues*. 2nd ed. Delhi: Wishwa Prakshan Press.
Asian Development Bank. 2001. Law and Policy Reform at the Asian Development Bank. http://www.asiandevbank.org/Documents/Others/Law_ADB/.
Assegaf, Rifqi. 2005. *Dan Josi Khatarina, Membuka Ketertutupan Pengadilan*. Jakarta: LeIP.
Assegaf, Rifqi. 2007. "Judicial Reform in Indonesia: 1998–2006." IDE Discussion Papers. www.ide.go.jp/English/Publish/Download/Asedp/pdf/074_3.pdf.
Asshiddiquie, J. 2004. *Format Kelembagaan Negara dan Pergeseran Kekuasaan dalam UUD 1945*. Cet. 1. Yogyakarta, Indonesia: FH UII Press.
Assyaukanie, L. 2009. *Islam and the Secular State in Indonesia*. Singapore: Institute of Southeast Asian Studies.
Aspinall, E. 2005. *Opposing Suharto Compromise, Resistance, and Regime Change in Indonesia*. Palo Alto, CA: Stanford University Press.
Badoh, Ibrahim Fahmy. 2005. "Manipulasi dana kampanye dan politik uang pemilu; Deskripsi dan evaluasi untuk perbaikan pasal-pasal dana politik dan paket undangundang politik." Jakarta: Indonesia Corruption Watch, Position paper, Political Finance.
Baijal, Pradeep. 2002. "Privatization: Gains to Taxpayers and Employees." *Economic and Political Weekly*, April 27, 1595–98.
Baird, Vanessa A., and Amy Gangl. 2006. "Shattering the Myth of Legality: The Impact of the Media's Framing of Supreme Court Procedures on Perceptions of Fairness." *Political Psychology* 27:597–614.
Baird, Vanessa A., and Debra Javeline. 2007. "The Persuasive Power of Russian Courts." *Political Research Quarterly* 60:429–42.
Baker, Chris, and Pasuk Phongpaichit. 2005. *A History of Thailand*. New York: Cambridge University Press.
Ballard, Megan. 1999. "The Clash between Local Courts and Global Economics: The Politics of Judicial Reform in Brazil." *Berkeley Journal of International Law* 17:230–90.

Banks, A. S. 2003. Cross-National Time Series Data Archive. http://www.databanksinternational.com/53.html

Banks, A. S., and Thomas C. Muller. 2003. *Political Handbook of the World.* Binghamton: CSA Publications.

Baranha de Brito, A. 1997. *Human Rights and Democratization in Latin America: Uruguay and Chile.* New York: Oxford University Press.

Barrett, S. 2005. "Raters and Examinations." In *Applied Rasch Measurement: A Book of Exemplars,* ed. S. Alagumalai, D. D. Curtis, and N. Hungi. Dordrecht: Springer.

Basri, M. Chatib, and Pierre Van der Eng, eds. 2004. *Business in Indonesia: New Challenges, Old Problems.* Singapore: ISEAS.

Basu, Tapan, Pradip Datta, Sumit Sarkar, Tanika Sarkar, and Sambuddha Sen. 1993. *Khaki Shorts and Safron Flags: A Critique of the Hindu Right.* New Delhi: Orient Longma.

Baum, Lawrence. 2006. *Judges and Their Audiences: A Perspective on Judicial Behavior.* Princeton: Princeton University Press.

Bawn, Kathleen, and Frances Rosenbluth. 2006. "Short versus Long Coalitions: Electoral Accountability and the Size of the Public Sector." *American Journal of Political Science* 50:251–65.

Baxi, Upendra. 2000. "The Avatars of Indian Judicial Activism: Explorations in the Geographies of [In]justice." In *Fifty Years of the Supreme Court of India,* ed. S. K. Verma and Kusum. New York: Oxford University Press.

Baxi, Upendra. 2008. *The Future of Human Rights.* New York: Oxford University Press.

BBC News. 2001a. "Brazil's President Acts Over Scandal." May 3. http://news.bbc.co.uk/hi/english/world/americas/newsid_ . . . /1309764.stm.

BBC News. 2001b. "Brazil Eases Power Rationing." June 5. http://news.bbc.co.uk/2/hi/americas/1370510.stm.

Beck, Nathaniel, Jonathan N. Katz, and Richard Tucker. "Taking Time Seriously: Time-Series—Cross-Section Analysis with a Binary Dependent Variable." *American Journal of Political Science* 42:1260–88.

Becker, Theodore L. 1970. *Comparative Judicial Studies.* Chicago: Rand McNally.

Bedner, A. W. 2003. *Administrative Courts in Indonesia: A Socio-Legal Study.* London and The Hague: Kluwer Law International.

Bednar, Jenna, William N. Eskridge Jr., and John Ferejohn. 2001. "A Political Theory of Federalism." In *Constitutional Culture and Democratic Rule,* ed. John Ferejohn, Jack N. Rakove, and Jonathan Riley, 223–70. New York: Cambridge University Press.

Benomar, J. 2004. "Constitution-Making after Conflict: Lessons for Iraq." *Journal of Democracy* 15:81–95.

Berggren, Niclas, and Nils Karlson. 2003. "Constitutionalism, Division of Power and Transaction Costs." *Public Choice* 117:99–124.

Bester, Alan, and Christian Hansen. 2009. "Grouped Effects Estimators in Fixed Effects Models." http://ssrn.com/abstract=1719684.

Bey, Fachri. 2004. "Three Most Important Features Of Indonesian Legal System That Others Should Understand." Ials conference, Learning From Each Other: Enriching the Law School Curriculum In An Interrelated World.

Bhagwati, Jagdish. 2005. *In Defense of Globalization.* New York: Oxford University Press.

Bhakti, I. K. 2004. "The Transition to Democracy in Indonesia: Some Outstanding Problems." In *The Asia-Pacific: A Region in Transition,* ed. Jim Rolfe. Honolulu: Asia-Pacific Centre for Security Studies.

Billikopf, David Marshall. 1973. *The Exercise of Judicial Power: 1789–1864.* New York: Vantage Press.

Biswas, A., and K. Das. 2002. "A Bayesian Analysis of Bivariate Ordinal Data: Wisconsin Epidemiologic Study of Diabetic Retinopathy Revisited." *Statistics in Medicine* 21:549–59.

Bjornskov, Christian. 2006. "The Multiple Facets of Social Capital." *European Journal of Political Economy* 22:22–40.

Blasi, Gerard J., and David L. Cingranelli. 1996. "Do Constitutions and Institutions Help Protect Human Rights?" In *Human Rights and Developing Countries,* ed. David L. Cingranelli. Greenwich: JAI.

Blaustein, Albert P., and G. Flanz, eds. 1971–Present. *Constitutions of the Countries of the World.* Dobbs Ferry, NY: Oceana.

Boix, Carles. 2003. *Democracy and Redistribution.* Cambridge: Cambridge University Press.

Boix, Carles, and Susan Stokes. 2003. "Endogenous Democratization." *World Politics* 55:517–44.

Bond, J. L. 2007. "Judicial Independence in Transition: Revisiting the Determinants of Judicial Activism in the Constitutional Courts of Post-Communist States." Working paper, University College London.

Boquérat, Gilles. 2009. "The Democratic Transition in Pakistan Under Stress." Asie Visions no. 13, Institut Français des Relations Internationales, Paris, France.

Botero Juan Carlos, Rafael La Porta, Florencio Silanes-de-Silanes, Andrei Shleifer, and Alexander Volokh. 2003. "Judicial Reform." *World Bank Research Observer* 18:61–88.

Boudreaux, D., and A. C. Pritchard. 1994. "Reassessing the Role of the Independent Judiciary in Enforcing Interest Group Bargains." *Constitutional Political Economy* 5:1–21.

Boulanger, C. 2003. "Beyond Significant Relationships, Tolerance Intervals and Triadic Dispute Resolution: Constructing a Comparative Theory of Judicial Review in Post-Communist Societies." Presented at the Law and Society Association Meeting, June 5–8, Pittsburgh.

Brinks, Daniel. 2005. "Judicial Reform and Independence in Brazil and Argentina: The Beginning of a New Millennium?" *Texas International Law Journal* 40:595–622.

Brinks, Daniel, and Abby Blass. 2010. "New Court for New Democracies: Judicial Changes in Latin America from 1975–2009." Paper prepared for the Spring Speaker Series, Center for the Study of Law, Economics and Politics. January 25.

Bugaric, Bojan. 2001. "Courts as Policy-Makers: Lessons from Transition." *Harvard International Law Journal* 42:247–88.

Buehler, M. 2009. "Islam and Democracy in Indonesia." *Insight Turkey* 11:51–63.

Bueno de Mesquita, Bruce, James D. Morrow, Randolph M. Siverson, and Alastair Smith. 2004. "Testing Novel Implications from the Selectorate Theory of War." *World Politics* 56:363–88.

Bunsuwan, Kanin. 1999. "The Draft Bill on State Enterprise-Privatisation or Sale?" *Matichon*, 4 March.

Burbank, Stephen, Barry Friedman, and Deborah Goldberg, eds. 2002. "Introduction." In *Judicial Independence at the Crossroads: An Interdisciplinary Approach*. Thousand Oaks, CA: Sage.

Buscaglia, Edgardo. 2001. *Judicial Corruption in Developing Countries: Its Causes and Consequences*. Prepared for UN Office for Drug Control. http://www.unodc.org/pdf/crime/gpacpublications/cicp14.pdf.

Business India. 1997. "Activism's Excesses." June 2–15, 45.

Buthe, Tim, and Helen Milner. 2011. "Institutional Diversity in Trade Agreements and Foreign Direct Investment: Credibility, Commitment, and Economic Flows in the Developing World, 1971–2007." Paper presented at the Annual Convention of the ISA, Montreal.

Butt, Simon. 2007. *Judicial Review in Indonesia: Between Civil Law and Accountability? A Study of Constitutional Court Decisions* 2003–2005. PhD diss., Melbourne University.

Butt, S., and T. Lindsey. 2009. "Economic Reform When the Constitution Matters: Indonesia's Constitutional Court and Article 33 of the Constitution." Legal Studies Research Paper no. 09/29.

Caldeira, Gregory. 1986. "Neither the Purse nor the Sword: Dynamics of Public Confidence in the Supreme Court." *American Political Science Review* 80:1209–26.

Calleros, Juan Carlos. 2009. *The Unfinished Transition to Democracy in Latin America*. New York: Routledge Press.

Camara Dos Deputados 1993. *O Processo Historico Da Elabaracao Do Texto Constitucional. Assembleia Nacional Constituente 1987–1988*. Volume 1, Mapa 1, Parte 2.

Camara, Dos Deputados. 1993. *O Processo Historico Da Elabaracao Do Texto Constitucional. Assembleia Nacional Constituente 1987–1988*. Volume 2, Mapa 3.

Cameron, Charles M. 2002. "Judicial Independence: How Can You Tell It When You See It?" In *Judicial Independence at the Crossroads: An Interdisciplinary Approach*, ed. Stephen B. Burbank and Barry Friedman. Thousand Oaks, CA: Sage.

Capelletti, Mauro. 1989. *The Judicial Process in Comparative Perspective*. Oxford: Clarendon Press.

Carey, John, and Matthew Shugart. 1995. "Incentives to Cultivate a Personal Vote: A Rank Ordering of Electoral Formulas." *Electoral Studies* 14:417–39.

Caroll, R., Gary W. Cox, and Mónica Pachón. 2006. "How Parties Create Electoral Democracy, Chapter 2." *Legislative Studies Quarterly* 31:153–75.

Carothers, Thomas. 2006. *Confronting the Weakest Link: Aiding Political Parties in New Democracies*. New York: Carnegie Endowment for International Peace.

Carro, Jesus M., and Alejandra Traferri. 2009. "Correcting the Bias in the Estimation of a Dynamic Ordered Probit with Fixed Effects of Self-Assessed Health Status." UC3M working paper. Economics 09-21. http://e-archivo.uc3m.es:8080/handle/10016/5210.

Carruba, Clifford James. 2009. "A Model of the Endogenous Development of Judicial Institutions in Federal and International Systems." *Journal of Politics* 71:55-69.

Carruba, Clifford James, Matthew Gabel, and Charles Hankla. 2008. "Judicial Behavior under Political Constraints: Evidence from the European Court of Justice." *American Political Science Review* 102:435-52.

Carter, David, and Curt Signorino. 2010. "Back to the Future: Modeling Time Dependence in Binary Data." *Political Analysis* 18:271-92.

Case, William. 2011. *Executive Accountability in Southeast Asia: The Role of Legislatures in New Democracies and Under Electoral Authoritarianism*. Policy Studies No. 57. Honolulu: East-West Center.

Castro, Nivalde Jose de, and Andre Luis da Silva Leite. 2009. "Regulatory Challenges: Competition Defense in The Brazilian Electricity Sector." In *Energy Policy*, ed. Noah B. Jacobs. Hauppauge, NY: Nova. http://www.nuca.ie.ufrj.br/gesel/artigos/castro88.pdf.

Chaba, Anju A. 2007. "Where People Vote for Charisma and not Caste." Express India, February 2. http://www.expressindia.com/news/fullstory.php?newsid=80706.

Chanchreek, K. L., and Saroj Prasad, eds. 1993. *Crisis in India*. Delhi: H. K. Publishers.

Chandoke, Neera. 2003. "A Critique of the Notion of Civil Society as the 'Third Sphere.'" In *Does Civil Society Matter? Governance in Contemporary India*, ed. Rajesh Tandon and Ranjita Mohanty. New Delhi: Sage.

Chandra, Kanchan. 2008. "Ethnic Invention: A New Principle for Institutional Design in Ethnically Divided Democracies." In *Designing Democratic Government: Making Institutions Work*, ed. Margaret Levi, James Johnson, Jack Knight, and Susan Stokes. New York: Russell Sage Foundation.

Chang, Eric C. C. 2005. "Electoral Incentives for Political Corruption under Open-List Proportional Representation." *Journal of Politics* 67 (3): 716-30.

Chang, Eric C. C., and Miriam Golden. 2007. "Electoral Systems, District Magnitude and Corruption." *British Journal of Political Science* 37:115-37.

Chang, Eric, with Yun-han Chu. 2006. "Corruption and Trust: Exceptionalism in Asian Democracies?" *Journal of Politics* 68 (2): 259-71.

Chavez, Rebecca Bill. 2004. *The Rule of Law in Nascent Democracies: Judicial Politics in Argentina*. Palo Alto, CA: Stanford University Press.

Chavez, Rebecca Bill. 2008. "The Rule of Law and Courts in Democratizing Regimes." In *Oxford Handbook of Law and Politics*, ed. Gregory Caldeira, Dan Keleman, and Keith Whittington. Oxford: Oxford University Press.

Chavez, Rebecca Bill, John, Ferejohn, and Barry Weingast. 2003. "A Theory of the Politically Independent Judiciary." Paper presented at the annual meeting of the American Political Science Association, Philadelphia, August 27.

Cheibub, J.-A., and J. Gandhi. 2004. "Classifying Political Regimes: A Six-Fold Measure of Democracies and Dictatorships." Paper presented at the annual meeting of the American Political Science Association, Chicago.

Cheibub, José Antonio, and Fernando Limongi. 2002. "Modes of Government Formation and the Survival of Presidential Regimes: Presidentialism and Parliamentarism Reconsidered." *Annual Review of Political Science.*

Chhibber, Pradeep. 2004. "Do Party Systems Count? The Number of Parties and Government Performance in the Indian States." *Comparative Political Studies* 37:152–87.

Chhibber, Pradeep, and Kenneth Kollman. 2004. *The Formation of National Party Systems: Federalism and Party Competition in Britain, Canada, India, and the U.S.* Princeton: Princeton University Press.

Chhibber, Pradeep, and Irfan Nooruddin. 2000. "Party Competition and Fragmentation in Indian National Elections: 1957–1998." In *Indian Politics and the 1998 Elections: Regionalism, Hindutva, and State Politics,* ed. Ramashray Roy and Paul Wallace. New Delhi and London: Sage.

Chhokar, Jagdeep S. 2006. "Getting Electoral Reforms Implemented: Moving from Discussion to Action." In *Constitution of India: Review and Reassessment,* ed. Subhash C. Kashyap, 102–8. Delhi: Universal Law Publishing.

Chiozza, Giacomo, and Heins Goemans. 2004. "International Conflict and the Tenure of Leaders: Is War Still *Ex Post* Inefficient?" *American Journal of Political Science* 48:604–19.

Chiozza, Giacomo, and Heins Goemans. "Avoiding Diversionary Targets." *Journal of Peace Research* 41:423–43.

Chopra, Pran, ed. 2006. *The Supreme Court versus the Constitution.* New Delhi: Sage.

Cingranelli, David L., and David L. Richards. 2008. *The Cingranelli-Richards (CIRI) Human Rights Data Project Coding Manual Version 2008.3.13.* http://ciri.bing hamton.edu/documentation/ciri_coding_guide.pdf.

Clark, Tom S. 2010. *The Limits of Judicial Independence.* New York: Cambridge University Press.

Clark, Tom S. 2009. "The Separation of Powers, Court-Curbing, and Judicial Legitimacy." *American Journal of Political Science* 53:971–89.

Clarke, R. 2003. "Retrospectivity and the Constitutional Validity of the Bali Bombing and East Timor Trials." Asian Law 5:1–32.

Codato, Adriano N. 2006. *Political Transition and Democratic Consolidation: Studies on Contemporary Brazil.* Hauppauge, NY: Nova.

Collier, David. 1999. "Democracy and Dichotomies: A Pragmatic Approach to Choices about Concepts." *Annual Review of Political Science* 2:537–65.

Collier, David, and Steven Levitsky. 1996. "Democracy with Adjectives." *World Politics* 49:430–51.

Cook, T. D., and D. T. Campbell. 1979. Quasi-Experimentation: Design and Analysis for Field Settings. Chicago: Rand McNally.
Cooter, Robert, and Tom Ginsburg. 1996. "Comparative Judicial Discretion: An Empirical Test of Economic Models." *International Review of Law and Economics* 16:295–313.
Couso, J. A. 2003. "The Politics of Judicial Review in Chile in the Era of Democratic Transition, 1990–2002." *Democratization* 10:70–91.
Cox, G. 1990. "Centripetal and Centrifugal Incentives in Electoral Systems." *American Journal of Political Science* 34:903–35.
Cox, Gary W., and Mathew D. McCubbins. 2001. "The Institutional Determinants of Economic Policy." In *Presidents, Parliaments and Policy*, ed. S. Haggard and M. D. McCubbins. Cambridge: Cambridge University Press.
Cox, Gary, and Frances Rosenbluth. 1995. "The Structural Determinants of Electoral Cohesiveness: England, Japan, and the United States." In *Structure and Policy in Japan and the United States*, ed. Cowhey and McCubbins. New York: Cambridge University Press.
Cox, G., and Michael Thies. 1998. "The Cost of Intraparty Competition: SNTV and Money Politics in Japan." *Comparative Political Studies* 31:267–91.
Crain, W. M., and R. D. Tollison. 1993. "Time Inconsistency and Fiscal Policy: Empirical Analysis of US States, 1969–89." *Journal of Public Economics* 51:153–59.
Croissant, Aurel. 2011. "Provisions, Practices and Performances of Constitutional Review in Democratizing East Asia." Paper presented at the IPSA-ECPR joint conference: Whatever Happened to North-South? Sao Paulo, Brazil, February 19.
Croissant, A. 2002. "Majoritarian and Consensual Democracy, Electoral Systems and Democratic Consolidation in Asia." *Asian Perspectives* 26.
Cross, Frank. 1999. "The Relevance of Law in Human Rights Protection." *International Review of Law and Economics* 19 (1): 87–98.
Cumaraswamy, D. P. 2006. "Report on Visit to Indonesia by the UN Special Rapporteur on the Independence of Judges and Lawyers." *Article of the International Covenant of on Civil and Political Rights* 5:32–45.
Dabene, Olivier. 2003. L'Amérique latine à l'époque contemporaine. Paris: Armand Colin.
Dainik Jagran. 2000. "BJP, the Ayodhya Dispute and Indian Law." February 5.
Dambewski, Hans. 2001. *Taking the State to Court: Public Interest Litigation and the Metropolitan Public Sphere in India*. New York: Oxford University Press.
DANC. 1988. *Técnicas Fontes De Informações Sobre A Assembléia Nacional Constituinte De Quais São, Onde Buscá-Las E Como Usá-Las*. Senado Federal, Brasília.
Dargent, Eduardo. 2009. "Determinants of Judicial Independence: Lessons from Three 'Cases' of Constitutional Courts in Peru (1982–2007)." *Journal of Latin American Studies* 41:251–78.
Davidson, S., V. Juwono, and T. Timberman. 2006. "Curbing Corruption in Indonesia, 2004–2006, a Survey of National Policies and Approaches." The United

States–Indonesia Society Center for Strategic and International Studies (USINDO), Indonesia.

Desposato, Scott. 2004. "The Impact of Federalism on National Political Parties in Brazil." *Legislative Studies Quarterly* 29:259–85.

Desposato, Scott. 2006. "The Impact of Electoral Rules on Legislative Parties: Lessons from the Brazilian Senate and Chamber of Deputies." *Journal of Politics* 68:1018–30.

Dhakidae, D., ed. 2003. *Partai-Partai Politik Indonesia: Ideologi, Strategidan Program* [Indonesian Political Parties: Ideology, Strategy, and Programs]. Jakarta: Kompas.

Diamond, Larry. 2000 "Developing Democracy in Africa: African and International Imperatives." *Cambridge Review of International Affairs* 14:191–213.

Diamond, Larry, Jonathan Hartlyn, Juan J. Linz, and Seymour Martin Lipset, eds. 1999. *Democracy in Developing Countries: Latin America*. Boulder: Lynne Rienner.

Diederich, Mathias. 2004. "A Closer Look at Dakwah and Politics in Indonesia: The Partai Keadilan." *Archipel* 64:101–15.

Diermeier, D., and R. T. Stevenson. 1999. "Cabinet Survival and Competing Risks." *American Journal of Political Science* 43:1051–68.

Dimitrov, V. 2001. *Bulgaria: The Uneven Transition*. London: Routledge.

Dodson, Michael, and Donald W. Jackson. 2001. "Judicial Independence and Instability in Central America." In *Judicial Independence in the Age of Democracy: Critical Perspectives from Around the World*, ed. Peter Russell and David M. O'Brien. Charlottesville: University of Virginia Press.

Domingo, Pilar. 2000. "Judicial Independence: The Politics of the Supreme Court in Mexico." *Journal of Latin American Studies* 32:705–35.

Dowling, J. Malcolm, and Yap Chin Fang. 2008. "Indonesian Economic Development: Mirage or Miracle?" *Journal of Asian Economics* 19 (5–6): 474–85.

Dung, L. 2003. *Judicial Independence in Transitional Countries*. Oslo: United Nations Development Program.

Durant, Robert F., Daniel J. Fiorino, and Rosemary O'Leary. 2004. *Environmental Governance Reconsidered: Challenges, Choices, and Opportunities*. Cambridge, MA: MIT Press

Durr, Robert H., Andrew D. Martin, and Christina Wolbrecht. 2000. "Ideological Divergence and Public Support for the Supreme Court." *American Journal of Political Science* 44:768–76.

Dworkin, R. 2004. *From Liberal Values to Democratic Transition: Essays in Honor of Janos Kis*. Budapest: Central University Press.

Economic Intelligence Unit. 2001. *Brazil: Country Profile 2001*. London: EIU.

Edwards, Martin S., and Frank C. Thames. 2007. "District Magnitude, Personal Votes, and Government Expenditures." *Electoral Studies* 26:338–45.

Election Commission of India. 2006. *Political Parties—Organisation Election, Contribution Reports, Expense Reports*. New Delhi: ECI, Government of India.

Ellett, Rachel L. 2008. *Emerging Judicial Power in Transitional Democracies: Malawi, Tanzania, and Uganda*. PhD diss., Northeastern University.

Ellis, A. 2004. "Indonesia: Transition and Change, but Electoral System Continuity." In *Handbook of Electoral System Choice*, ed. J. Colomer. New York: Palgrave Macmillan.

Engineer, Asghar A., and Pradeep Nayak. 1993. *Communalisation of Politics and 10th Lok Sabha Elections*. New Delhi: South Asia Books.

Epp, Charles R. 1998. *The Rights Revolution: Lawyers, Activists, and Supreme Courts in Comparative Perspective*. Chicago: University of Chicago Press.

Epperly, B. 2010. "The Determinants of Judicial Independence in Non-Democracies." Paper presented at the Law and Society Association, Chicago, May 27.

Epstein, David, and Sharyn O'Halloran. 1996. "Divided Government and the Design of Administrative Procedures: A Formal Model and Empirical Test." *Journal of Politics* 58:373–97.

Epstein, Lee, and Jack Knight. 1996. "On the Struggle for Judicial Supremacy." *Law and Society Review* 30 (1): 87–130.

Epstein, Lee, Jack Knight, and Olga Shvetsova. 2001. "The Role of Constitutional Courts in the Establishment of Democratic Systems of Government." *Law and Society Review* 35:117–67.

Eskridge Jr., William N. 1991. "Reneging on History? Playing the Court/Congress/President Civil Rights Game." *California Law Review* 79:613–84.

Estadão. 2007. "Governo teme derrota na votação da CPMF no Senado." October 10. http://www.estadao.com.br/nacional/not_nac62948,0.htm.

Falaakh, Mohammad Fajrul, 2001. "Nahdlatul Ulama and Civil Society in Indonesia." In *Islam and Civil Society in Southeast Asia*, ed. Nakamura. Singapore: ISEAS.

Fausto, B. 1999. *A Concise History of Brazil*. Translated by Arthur Brakel. New York: Cambridge University Press.

Fearon, James, and David Laitin. 2003. "Ethnicity, Insurgency, and Civil War." *American Political Science Review* 97:75–90.

Fearon, James, and David Laitin 2008. "Integrating Qualitative and Quantitative Methods." In *Oxford Handbook of Political Methodology*, ed. Janet Box-Steffensmeier, Henry Brady, and David Collier. New York: Oxford University Press.

Feith, Herbert. 2006. *The Decline of Constitutional Democracy in Indonesia*. Sheffield, UK: Equinox.

Feld, Lars P., and Stefan Voigt. 2003. "Economic Growth and Judicial Independence: Cross Country Evidence Using a New Set of Indicators." *European Journal of Political Economy* 19:497–527.

Feldbrugge, F., ed. 2006. *Russia, Europe, and the Rule of Law*. Leiden: Brill.

Ferejohn, John. 1999. "Independent Judges, Dependent Judiciary: Explaining Judicial Independence." *Southern California Law Review* 72:353–84.

Ferejohn, John. 2002. "Judicializing Politics, Politicizing Law." *Law and Contemporary Problems* 41:41–68.

Ferejohn, John, and Larry D. Kramer. 2002. "Independent Judges, Dependent Judiciary: Institutionalizing Judicial Restraint." *New York University Law Review* 77:962–1039.

Ferejohn, John, Frances Rosenbluth, and Charles Shipan. 2007. "Comparative Judicial Politics." In *Oxford Handbook of Comparative Politics*, ed. Carles Boix and Susan Stokes, 727–51. New York: Oxford University Press.

Ferejohn, John, and Charles Shipan. 1990. "Congressional Influence on Bureaucracy." *Journal of Law, Economics, and Organization* 6:1–21.

Ferejohn, John, and Barry Weingast. 1992. "A Positive Theory of Statutory Interpretation." *International Review of Law and Economics* 12:263–79.

Figuerido, Argelina Cheibub. 1999. *Executivo e Legislativo na Nova Ordem Constitucional*. Rio de Janeiro: Editora FGV.

Figuerido, Argelina Cheibub, and Fernando Limongi. 2000. "Presidential Power, Legislative Organization, and Party Behavior in Brazil." *Comparative Politics* 32:151–70.

Finkel, Jodi S. 2003. "Supreme Court Decisions on Electoral Rules after Mexico's 1994 Constitutional Reform: An Empowered Court." *Journal of Latin American Studies* 35:777–99.

Finkel, Jodi S. 2005. "Judicial Reform as Insurance Policy: Mexico in the 1990s." *Latin American Politics and Society* 46:87–113.

Finkel, Jodi S. 2008. *Judicial Reform as Political Insurance: Argentina, Peru, and Mexico in the 1990s*. Notre Dame: University of Notre Dame Press.

Finkel, S. E., A. Pérez-Liñán, and M. A. Seligson. 2007. "The Effects of U.S. Foreign Assistance on Democracy Building, 1990–2003." *World Politics* 59 (3): 404–39.

Fiorina, Morris P. 1986. "Legislator Uncertainty, Legislative Control, and the Delegation of Legislative Power." *Journal of Law, Economics, and Organization* 2:33–51.

Fiss, Owen M. 1993. "The Right Degree of Independence." In *Transition to Democracy in Latin America: The Role of the Judiciary*, ed. Irwin P. Stotzky. Boulder: Westview Press.

Forrester, Geoff, and R. J. May, eds. 1998. *The Fall of Suharto*. Bathurst, Australia: Crawford House.

Fortin, Nicole. 2008. "Gender Role Attitudes and Women's Labor Market Participation: The Persistent Appeal of Housewifery." Paper presented at the 2007 meeting of the Population Association of America.

Foweraker, J., and Krznaric, R. 2002. "The Uneven Performance of the Democracies of the 3rd Wave: Electoral Politics and the Imperfect Rule of Law in Latin America." *Latin American Politics and Society* 44:29–60.

Frankel, Francine. 2004. *India's Political Economy: 1947–2004*. New York: Oxford University Press.

Friedman, Barry. 2002. "The Birth of an Academic Obsession: The History of the Countermajoritarian Difficulty, Part Five." *Yale Law Journal* 112:153–228.

Friedman, Barry. 2004. "The Importance of Being Positive: The Nature and Function of Judicial Review." *University of Cincinnati Law Review* 72:1257–1303.

Friedman, Barry. 2005. "The Politics of Judicial Review." *Texas Law Review* 84:257–337.

Friedman, Barry. 2010. *The Will of the People: How Public Opinion Has Influenced the Supreme Court and Shaped the Meaning of the Constitution*. New York: Farrar, Straus and Giroux.

Fukuyama, Francis. 2005. "Facing the Perils of Presidentialism?" *Journal of Democracy* 16:102–16.

Gadbois Jr., George H. 2011. *Judges of the Supreme Court of India, 1950–1989*. New York: Oxford University Press.

Gagrani, H. 2010. "Appointment or Disappointment: Historical Backdrop and Present Problems in the Appointment of Judges of Indian Judiciary." Working paper, National Law Institute University, Bhopal.

Galanter, Marc. 1989. *Law and Society in Modern India*. New York: Oxford University Press.

Gallagher, Michael, and Ian Holliday. 2003. "Electoral Systems, Representational Roles and Legislator Behaviour: Evidence from Hong Kong." *New Zealand Journal of Asian Studies* 5:107–20.

Ganev, V. 2004. "History, Politics and the Constitution: Ethnic Conflict and Constitutional Adjudication in Postcommunist Bulgaria." *Slavic Review* 63 (1): 66–89.

Ganguly, Sumit, Larry Diamond, and Marc F. Plattner., eds. 2007. "Introduction." In *The State of India's Democracy*. Baltimore: Johns Hopkins University Press.

Garoupa, Nuno, and Tom Ginsburg. 2009. "The Comparative Law and Economics of Judicial Councils." University of Illinois Law and Economics Research Paper no. LE08-036.

Garoupa, Nuno, Veronica Grembi, and Shirley Ching Ping Lin. 2011. "Explaining Constitutional Review in New Democracies: The Case of Taiwan." *Pacific Rim Law and Policy Journal* 20 (1): 10–45.

Geddes, Barbara. 1999. "What Do We Know About Democratization After Twenty Years?" *Annual Review of Political Science* 2:115–44.

Geddes, Barbara, and Amorim Neto. 1992. "Institutional Sources of Corruption in Brazil." *Third World Quarterly* 13:641–61.

Gely, Rafael, and Pablo T. Spiller. 1992. "The Political Economy of Supreme Court Constitutional Decisions: The Case of Roosevelt's Court-Packing Plan." *International Review of Law and Economics* 12:45–67.

George, Alexander. 1979. "Case Studies and Theory Development: The Method of Structured, Focused Comparison." In *Diplomacy: New Approaches in History, Theory, and Policy*, ed. P. G. Gordon, 43–67. New York: Free Press.

George, Alexander, and Andrew Bennett. 2005. *Case Studies and Theory Development in the Social Sciences*. Cambridge, MA: MIT Press.

Gerring, John. 2007. *Case Studies Research: Principles and Practices*. New York: Cambridge University Press.

Gerring, John, Strom C. Thacker, and Carola Moreno. 2009. "Are Parliamentary Systems Better?" *Comparative Political Studies* 42:327–49.

Ghosh, R., ed. 1996. *In Quest of a Secular Symbol: Ayodhya and After*. Perth, WA:

Indian Ocean Centre and South Asian Research Unit, Curtin University of Technology.
Ghoshal, B. 2004. "Democratic Transition and Political Development in Post-Soeharto Indonesia." *Contemporary Southeast Asia* 26:506–29.
Gibler, Douglas, and Kirk Randazzo. 2011. "Testing the Effects of Independent Judiciaries on the Likelihood of Democratic Backsliding." *American Journal of Political Science* 55 (3): 696–709.
Gibson, James L. 2006. "Judicial Institutions." In *The Oxford Handbook of Political Institutions,* ed. R. A. W. Rhodes, Sarah A. Binder, and Bert A. Rockman, 514–34. New York: Oxford University Press.
Gibson, James L. 2007. "The Legitimacy of the U.S. Supreme Court in a Polarized Polity." *Journal of Empirical Legal Studies* 4:507–38.
Gibson, James L., and V. A. Baird. 1998. "On the Legitimacy of National High Courts." *American Political Science Review* 92:343–58.
Gibson, James L., and Gregory A. Caldeira. 2007. "Supreme Court Nominations, Legitimacy Theory, and the American Public: A Dynamic Test of the Theory of Positivity Bias." Paper delivered at the 2007 annual meeting of the American Political Science Association, Chicago, August 30–September 2.
Gibson, James L., and Gregory A. Caldeira. 2009. *Citizens, Courts, and Confirmations.* Princeton: Princeton University Press.
Gibson, James L., Gregory A. Caldeira, and Lester Kenyatta Spence. 2003. "The Supreme Court and the U.S. Presidential Election of 2000: Wounds, Self-Inflicted or Otherwise?" *British Journal of Political Science* 33:535–56.
Gibson, James L., Gregory Caldeira, and Lester Spence. 2005. "Why Do People Accept Public Policies They Oppose? Testing Legitimacy Theory with a Survey-Based Experiment." *Political Research Quarterly* 58:187–201.
Gill, M. S. 2005. *The Electoral System in India.* New Delhi: Election Commission of India, Government of India Publication.
Ginsburg, Tom. 2003. *Judicial Review in New Democracies: Constitutional Courts in Asian Cases.* New York: Cambridge University Press.
Ginsburg, Tom. 2006. "Constitutional Review." In *Oxford Handbook of Comparative Politics.* New York: Oxford University Press.
Ginsburg, Tom. 2008. "The Global Spread of Constitutional Review." In *Oxford Handbook of Law and Politics,* ed. Gregory Caldeira, Dan Keleman, and Keith Whittington. New York: Oxford University Press.
Ginsburg, Tom. 2010. "Public Choice and Constitutional Design." In *Handbook in Public Choice and Public Law,* ed. Daniel Farber and Anne Joseph O'Connell. Williston: Elgar.
Ginsburg, Tom, and Tamir Moustafa, eds. 2008. *Rule by Law: The Politics of Courts in Authoritarian Regimes.* Cambridge: Cambridge University Press.
Glaeser, Edward, Rafael la Porta, Florencio Silanes-de-Lopez, and Andrei Shleifer. 2004. "Do Institutions Cause Growth?" *Journal of Economic Growth* 9:271–303.
Glaeser, Edward, and Andrei Shleifer. 2002. "Legal Origins." *Quarterly Journal of Economics* 117:1193–1229.

Global Integrity Report. 2001. Indonesia–GIR Survey. http://report.globalintegrity.org/report/2001/Indonesia.
Gloppen, Siri, Bruce Wilson, Roberto Gargarella, Elin Skaar, and Morten Kinander. 2010. *Courts and Power in Latin America and Africa*. New York: Palgrave Macmillan.
Gloppen, Siri, and Fidelis Kanyongolo. 2006. "The Role of the Judiciary in the 2004 General Elections in Malawi." *East African Journal of Peace and Human Rights* 12:279–317.
Gloppen, Siri, Roberto Gargarella, and Elin Skaar, eds. 2004. *Democratization and the Judiciary: The Accountability Function of Courts in New Democracies*. London: Frank Cass.
Goertzel, Ted. 2003. "So this is Lula?" In English at *Brazzil Magazine*, January, http://www.brazzil.com/p118jan03.htm; in Portuguese as "O legado de FHC e o Brasil de Lula," *Folha de São Paulo*, January 5, http://www1.folha.uol.com.br/folha/brasil/ult96u44443.shtml.
Golder, M. 2005. "Democratic Electoral Systems around the World, 1946–2000." *Electoral Studies* 24:103–21.
Gowda, M. V. Rajeev, and E. Sridharan. 2007. "Parties and the Party System: 1947–2006." In *The State of India's Democracy*, ed. Sumit Ganguly, Larry Diamond, and Marc F. Plattner, 3–25. Baltimore: Johns Hopkins University Press.
Graber, M. 2000. "The Problematic Establishment of Judicial Review." In *The Supreme Court in American Politics*, ed. H. Gillman and C. Clayton, 28–42. Lawrence: University Press of Kansas.
Greene, W. H., and D. A. Greene. 2010. *Modeling Ordered Choices: A Primer and Recent Developments*. Cambridge: Cambridge University Press.
Guarnieri, C. 2001. "Judicial Independence in Latin Countries of Western Europe." In *Judicial Independence in the Age of Democracy: Critical Perspectives From Around The World*, ed. Peter H. Russell and David M. O'Brien, 112–13. Charlottesville: University of Virginia Press.
Guarnieri, Carlo, and Patrizia Pederzoli. 2002. *The Power of Judges: A Comparative Study of Courts and Democracy*. New York: Oxford University Press.
Guebbert, J. 2009. "G20 Economic Summit: Plans for the Second Meeting in April 2009. Senior Researcher G20 Research Group." Unpublished paper. http://www.g20.utoronto.ca/g20plans/g20leaders081201.pdf.
Hadiwinata, Bob Seung. 2003. *The Politics of NGOs in Indonesia: Developing Democracy and Managing a Movement*. London: Routledge.
Hadiz, Vedi R. 2004. "The Failure of State Ideology in Indonesia: The Rise and Demise of Pancasila." In *Communitarian Politics in Asia*, ed. Beng Huat Chua, 148–61. London: Routledge.
Hafild, E. 2004. "Hasil Assesement Penerapan Pekta Integrasi Kabupaten Solok." Paper presented by TI–Indonesia in the Workshop Mewujudkan Sistem Pengadaan Barang dan Jasa yang Effisien dan Bebas KKN, Jakarta, August 25.
Haggard, Stephan, and Robert R. Kaufman. 1995. *The Political Economy of Democratic Transitions*. Princeton: Princeton University Press.

Hagger, Mark. 1982. "Nine Nations Make a Law: A Comparison of the Politics of the Legislative Process for Direct Elections." *Comparative Politics* 15:1–22.

Hagopian, Frances. 2009. "Parties and Voters in Emerging Democracies." In *Oxford Handbook of Comparative Politics*, ed. Carles Boix and Susan Stokes. New York: Oxford University Press.

Hajivassiliou, V. H., and D. McFadden. 1990. "The Method of Simulated Scores for the Estimation of LDV Models with an Application to External Debt Crises." Cowles Foundation Discussion Paper 967, Yale University.

Halmai, Gabor, ed. 2002. *The Constitution Found? The First Nine Years of Hungarian Constitutional Review on Fundamental Rights*. Budapest: Indok.

Hamilton, Alexander, James Madison, and John Jay. 2001 [1787]. *The Federalist: A Commentary on the Constitution of the United States*. New York: Modern Library.

Hamilton, Alexander, James Madison, and John Jay. 1787. "Federalist 78." In *The Federalist Papers*, ed. George Carey and James McClellan. Dubuque, IA: Kendall/Hunt.

Hammergren, Linn. 2007a. "Lessons Learned about Fighting Judicial Corruption." In *Global Corruption Report 2007*. New York: Cambridge University Press.

Hammergren, Linn. 2007b. *Envisioning Reform: Improving Judicial Performance in Latin America*. University Park: Penn State University Press.

Hankla, Charles. 2006. "Party Strength and International Trade: A Cross-National Analysis." *Comparative Political Studies* 39:1133–56.

Harding, A., and P. Nicholson, eds. 2010. *New Courts in Asia*. London: Routledge.

Harijanti, Susi Dwi, and Tim Lindsey. 2006. "Indonesia: General Elections Test, Constitutional Amendments, and New Constitutional Court." *International Journal of Constitutional Law* 4 (1):138–50.

Haris, Syamsuddin. 2002. "Konflik Elite Sipil dan Dilema Konsolidasi Demokrasi Pasca Orde Baru" [Conflict Among Civilian Elites and the Dilemma of Democratic Consolidation in the Post–Suharto Era]. In *Reformasi Politik dan Kekuatan Masyarakat. Kendala dan Peluang Menuju Demokrasi* [Political Reform and the Strength of the Society, Problems, and Prospects toward Democracy], ed. M. D. Maruto and W. M. K. Anwari, 3–21. Jakarta: LP3ES.

Harman, B. K. 2006. *Konfigurasi Politik dan Kekuasaan Kehakiman di Indonesia*. Jakarta: ELSAM.

Harun, Refly. 2004. "Bikin lembaga zonder KKN" [Creating an Institution without Corruption, Collusion, and Nepotism]. In *Menjaga Denyut Konstitusi; Refleksi Satu Tahun Mahkamah Konstitusi* [Guarding the Pulse of the Constitution: Reflections on One Year of the Constitutional Court], ed. Refly Harun, Zainal A. M. Husein, and Bisariyadi, 309–27. Jakarta: Konstitusi Press.

Hasan, Zoya, ed. 2002. *Parties and Party Politics in India*. New York: Oxford University Press.

Haynie, Stacia L. 1994. "Resource Inequalities and Litigation Outcomes in the Philippine Supreme Court." *Journal of Politics* 56:752–72.

Hayo, Bernd, and Stefan Voigt. 2007. "Explaining *de facto* Judicial Independence." *International Review of Law and Economics* 27:269–90.

Hazama, Yasushi. 2009. "Constitutional Review and Democratic Consolidation: A Literature Review." IDE discussion paper no. 192. http://202.244.105.132/English/Publish/Download/Dp/pdf/192.pdf.

Hazra, Arnab Kumar, and Bibek Debroy. 2007. *Judicial Reforms in India: Issues and Aspects*. New Delhi: Academic Foundation.

Heckelman, Jac. C. 2010. "The Connection between Democratic Freedoms and Growth in Transition Economies." *Applied Economic Quarterly* 56:121–46.

Helmke, Gretchen. 2002. "The Logic of Strategic Defection: Court-Executive Relations in Argentina under Democracy and Dictatorship." *American Political Science Review* 96:305–20.

Helmke, Gretchen. 2004. *Courts under Constraints: Judges, Generals, and Presidents in Argentina*. Cambridge: Cambridge University Press.

Helmke, Gretchen, and Julio Rios-Figueroa, eds. 2011. *Courts in Latin America*. New York: Cambridge University Press.

Helmke, Gretchen, and Frances Rosenbluth. 2009. "Regimes and the Rule of Law: Judicial Independence in Comparative Perspective." *Annual Review of Political Science* 12:345–66.

Helmke, Gretchen, and Jeff Staton. 2009. "Courting Conflict: A Logic of Risky Judicial Decisions in Latin America." Working paper, University of Rochester.

Helmke, Gretchen, and Jeffrey K. Staton. 2010. "The Puzzle of Judicial Politics in Latin America: A Theory of Litigation, Judicial Decisions, and Inter-Branch Conflict." In *Courts in Latin America*, ed. Gretchen Helmke and Julio Ríos-Figueroa. New York: Cambridge University Press.

Hensher, D. A., and W. H. Greene. 2009. "Valuation of Travel Time Savings in WTP and Preference Space in the Presence of Taste and Scale Heterogeneity." Working paper, Institute of Transport and Logistics Studies, University of Sydney, November.

Herron, Erik S., and Kirk A. Randazzo. 2003. "The Relationship between Independence and Judicial Review in Post-Communist Courts." *Journal of Politics* 65:422–38.

Hicken, Allen. 2006. "How Do Rules and Institutions Encourage Vote Buying?" In *Democracy for Sale: The Causes, Consequences, and Reform of Vote Buying*, ed. Frederic C. Schaffer, 47–60. Boulder: Lynne Rienner.

Hicken, Allen, and Joel Simmons. 2008. "The Personal Vote and Efficacy of Education Spending." *American Political Science Review* 52:109–24.

Hicken, Allen, and Heather Stoll 2011. "Presidents and Parties: How Presidential Elections Shape Coordination in Legislative Elections. *Comparative Political Studies* 44 (7): 854–83.

Hilbink, Lisa. 2003. "An Exception to Chilean Exceptionalism? In *What Justice? Whose Justice? Fighting for Fairness in Latin America*, ed. Susan E. Eckstein and Timothy P. Wickham-Crowley. Berkeley and Los Angeles: University of California Press.

Hilbink, Lisa. 2007. *Judges beyond Politics in Democracy and Dictatorship: Lessons from Chile*. Cambridge: Cambridge University Press.

Hindustan Times. February 7, 2003.
Hirschl, Ran. 2004. *Towards Juristocracy: The Origins and Consequences of the New Constitutionalism*. Cambridge, MA: Harvard University Press.
Hirschl, Ran. 2008. "The Judicialization of Mega-Politics and the Rise of Political Courts." In *The Oxford Handbook on Law and Politics*, ed. Keith Whittington, Daniel Kelemen, and Gregory Caldeira. New York: Oxford University Press.
Hix, Simon. 2004. "Electoral Institutions and Legislative Behavior: Explaining Voting Defection in the European Parliament." *World Politics* 56:194–223.
Holston, James, and Teresa Caldeira. 1998. "Democracy, Law and Violence: Disjunctions of Brazilian Citizenship." In *Fault Lines of Democracy in Post-Transition Latin America*, ed. Felipe Aguero and Jeffrey Stark. Miami: North-South Center Press.
Homes, Stephen. 1993. "Back to the Drawing Board: An Argument for Constitutional Postponement in Eastern Europe." *East European Constitutional Review* 2:21–25.
Honna, Jun. 2003. Military Politics and Democratization in Indonesia. New York: Routledge.
Howard, A. E. Dick. 1992. "Drafting Constitutions for the New Democracies." *Problems of Communism* 28:63–65.
Howard, A. E. Dick. 2001. "Judicial Independence in Post-Communist Central and Easter Europe." In *Judicial Independence in the Age of Democracy*, ed. Peter H. Russell and David M. O'Brien, Charlottesville: University of Virginia Press.
Howell. Katrina. 1995. "Politicized Justice? Judicial Review in Democratizing Brazil." Paper presented to the 19th International Congress of the Latin American Studies Association, September 28–30.
Hurlin, Christophe, and Baptiste Venet. 2003. "Granger Causality Tests in Panel Data Models with Fixed Coefficients." Working Paper Eurisco 2001–09, University of Paris Dauphine.
Iaryczower, Matias, Pablo Spiller, and Mariano Tomassi. 2002. "Judicial Decision-Making in Unstable Environments." *American Journal of Political Science* 46:699–716.
Ichwan, Moch Nur. 2005. "'Ulama,' State and Politics: Majelis Ulama Indonesia after Suharto." *Islamic Law and Society* 12:45–72.
Imawan, Riswandha. 2004. *"The Lonely Winners" Kompas. Siapa Mau Jadi Presiden? Debat Publik Seputar Program dan Partai Politik pada Pemilu*. Jakarta: Penerbit Buku Kompas.
Inclán, Silvia. 2004. *Judicial Reform and Democratization: Mexico in the 1990s*. PhD diss., Boston University.
Indrayana, D. 2004. "Kabinet SBY dan presidensial di Indonesia." *Kolom Tempo* 33:111–28.
Indrayana, D. 2008. *Indonesian Constitutional Reform: An Evaluation of Constitution-Making in Transition*. Jakarta: Kompas.
Indriastuti, D., M. Z. dan Wahyudi. 2010. Pemilihan elektronik: Tawaran kemudahan pemungutan suara dari Jembrana, Kompas, 5 mei, Jakarta.

International Monetary Fund. 2009. *Global Financial Statistics.* Washington, DC: Intenational Monetary Fund. (CD-ROM).

Jackle, Sebastian. 2009. "Government Termination in Parliamentary Democracies—An Event History Approach with Special Attention to Party Ideology." Paper presented ECPR workshop, Lisbon, April 14–19.

Jaffrelot, Christopher. 1996. *The Hindu Nationalist Movement in India.* New York: Columbia University Press.

Jaffrelot, Christopher. 2003. *India's Silent Revolution: The Rise of the Lower Castes in North India.* New York: Columbia University Press.

Jain, U. C. 2000. *Judiciary in India.* Jaipur: Saujanya Books.

Jain, M. P. 2008. *Outlines of Indian Legal and Constitutional History.* New Delhi: Wadhwa and Company.

Jain, R. B., and P. S. Bawa. 2003. "National Integrity Systems: Country Study Report: India." *Transparency International Annual Report* 2004.

Jalan, Bimal. 2007. *India's Politics: A View from the Backbench.* New Delhi: Penguin.

Johnson Tan, Paige. 2002. "Anti-Party Reaction in Indonesia: Causes and Implications." *Contemporary Southeast Asia* 3:484–508.

Johnson Tan, Paige. 2005. "Parties and Pestas: An Analysis of Indonesian Democratization after the 2004 Elections through the Lens of Party System Institutionalization." Paper presented to the Association for Asian Studies annual meeting. Chicago, April.

Johnson Tan, Paige. 2006. "Indonesia Seven Years after Suharto: Party System Institutionalization in a New Democracy." *Contemporary Southeast Asia* 28 (1): 88–114.

Johnson, Joel, and Jessica Wallack. 2006. *Electoral Systems and the Personal Vote.* San Diego: University of California. Available at http://dss.ucsd.edu/~jwjohnso.espv.htm (accessed July 10, 2011).

Jung, Courtney, and Ian Shapiro 1995. "South Africa's Negotiated Transition: Democracy, Opposition, and the New Constitutional Order." *Politics and Society* 23:269–308.

Jyranki, Antero, ed. 1999. *National Constitutions in the Era of Integration.* Kluwer International Law Series. London.

Kalipeni, E. 1996. "Transition to Democracy in Malawi: The Role of Internal and External Forces." *21st Century Afro-Review* 2 (2): 49–77.

Kang, G. C. 2008. "Government Formation and Termination in European. Democracies with Presidential Heads of State." PhD diss., University of Rochester.

Kansil, C. S. T., and Engeline R. Palandeng. 2001. *Konstitusi-konstitusi Indonesia Tahun 1945–2000.* Yogyakarta, Indonesia: Pustaka Sinar Harapan.

Kapiszweski, Diana. 2007. "Challenging Decisions: High Court Politics in Argentina and Brazil." PhD diss., University of California, Berkeley.

Kapiszewski, Diana, and Matthew M. Taylor. 2008. "Doing Courts Justice? Studying Judicial Politics in Latin America." *Perspectives on Politics* 6:741–67.

Kapstein, Ethan B., and Nathan Converse. 2008. *The Fate of Young Democracies.* New York: Cambridge University Press.

Kapur, Devesh. 2005. "Explaining Democratic Durability and Economic Performance: The Role of India's Institutions." In *Public Institutions in India*, ed. Devesh Kapur and Pratap Bhanu Mehta. New York: Oxford University Press.

Kapur, Devesh, and Pratap Bhanu Mehta. 2005. *Public Institutions in India: Performance and Design*. New York: Oxford University Press.

Kapur, Devesh, and R. Ramamurti. 2005. "Privatization in India: The Imperatives and Consequences of Gradualism." In *India after a Decade of Economic Reforms: Retrospect and Prospects*, ed. T. N. Srinivasan. Palo Alto, CA: Stanford University Press.

Kashyap, Subhash C. 2003. *Anti-Defection Law and Parliamentary Privileges*. New Delhi: Universal Law.

Kashyap, Subhash C. 2006. *Constitution of India: Review and Reassessment*. New Delhi: Universal Law.

Katz, R. S., and W. Crotty, eds. 2006. *Handbook of Party Politics*. Thousand Oaks, CA: Sage.

Kawamura, Koichi. 2003. "Politics of the 1945 Constitution: Democratization and Its Impact on Political Institutions in Indonesia." IDE research paper. http://papers.ssrn.com/sol3/papers.cfm?abstract_id=1742676.

Kayser, Mark A. 2007. "How Domestic Is Domestic Politics? Globalization and Elections." *Annual Review of Political Science* 10:341–62.

Keck, M. E., and K. Sikkink. 1998. *Activists Beyond Borders: Advocacy Networks in International Politics*. Ithaca: Cornell University Press.

Keefer, Philip. 2007. "Beyond Legal Origin and Checks and Balances: Political Credibility, Citizen Information, and Financial Sector Development." Policy Research Working Paper Series 4154, the World Bank. http://ideas.repec.org/p/wbk/wbrwps/4154.html#download.

Keefer, Philip, and Stuti Khemani. 2009. "When Do Legislators Pass on Pork? The Role of Political Parties in Determining Legislator Effort." *American Political Science Review* 103:99–112.

Keith, Linda Camp. 2002. "Constitutional Provisions for Individual Human Rights (1977–1996): Are They More than Mere Window Dressing?" *Political Research Quarterly* 55:111–43.

Kenward, Lloyd. 2004. "Survey of Recent Developments." *Bulletin of Indonesian Economic Studies* 40 (1): 9–35.

Khosla, Madhav. 2008 "Addressing Judicial Activism in the Indian Supreme Court: Towards an Evolved Debate." *Hastings International & Comparative Law Review* 32:55–75.

King, Dwight Y. 2003. *Half-Hearted Reform. Electoral Institutions and the Struggle for Democracy in Indonesia*. Westport, CT: Praeger.

King, Dwight Y., Anies Baswedan, and Nicolaus Harjanto. 2005. "The Relative Importance of Social-based Voting in the 2004 Indonesian Elections." Paper presented at the Association for Asian Studies Annual Meeting, Chicago.

King, Gary, James Alt, Nancy Burns, and Michael Laver. 1990. "A Unified Model of

Cabinet Dissolution in Parliamentary Democracies." *American Journal of Political Science* 34:846–71.
King, Gary, Robert Keohane, and Sidney Verba. 1994. *Designing Social Inquiry*. Princeton: Princeton University Press.
Kingsbury, Damien, and Budiman Arief. 2001. *Indonesia the Uncertain Transition*. Bathurst, Australia: Crawford Publishing.
Kingstone, Peter R. 1999. *Crafting Coalitions for Reform: Business Preferences, Political Institutions, and Neo-liberal Reform in Brazil*. University Park: Penn State University Press.
Kinzo, M. D'Alva, and Y. De Souza Carreirão. 2004. "Partidos Politicos, Preferência Partidária e Decisão Eleitoral no Brasil (1989/2002)." *Dados* 47:131–67.
Kirpal, B. N., Ashok Desai, Gopal Subramaniam, Rajeev Dhavan, and Raju Ramachandran. 2000. *Supreme But Not Fallible: Essays in the Honour of the Supreme Court of India*. New York: Oxford University Press.
Kitschelt, Herbert. 2000. "Linkages between Citizens Politicians in Democratic Polities." *Comparative Political Studies* 33:845–79.
Kitschelt, Herbert, and Steven Wilkinson, eds. 2007. "Citizen-Politician Linkages: An Introduction." In *Patrons, Clients, and Policies: Patterns of Democratic Accountability and Political Competition*. New York: Cambridge University Press.
Klemb, Jurgen. 2007. "Indonesia's Secular State under Siege." *Der Spiegel*, June 4.
Klerman, Paul G., and Daniel M. Mahoney. 2005. "The Value of Judicial Independence: Evidence from Eighteenth-Century England." *American Law and Economics Review* 7:1–27.
Klug, Heinz. 2000. *Constituting Democracy: Law, Globalism, and South Africa's Political Reconstruction*. New York: Cambridge University Press.
Kohli, Atul. 2001. *The Success of India's Democracy*. New York: Cambridge University Press.
Kommers, Donald. 1997. *The Constitutional Jurisprudence of the Federal Republic of Germany*. Durham: Duke University Press.
Kompas. 2004. *Partai-Partai Politik Indonesia: Ideologi dan Program 2004–2009*. Jakarta: Penerbit Kompas KPU. http://www.kpu.go.id/.
Kurien, Manoj. 1992. "The RSS, the Babri Masjid Dispute and Indian Law." *Malyalam Manorama*, March 19.
Lamounier, Bolivar, and Rachel Meneguello. 1986. *Partidos Políticos e Consolidação Democrática: O Caso Brasileiro*. São Paulo: Brasiliense.
Landau, Paul B. 2010. *Popular Politics in the History of South Africa, 1400–1948*. New York: Cambridge University Press.
Landes, William M., and Richard A. Posner. 1975. "Independent Judiciary in an Interest-Group Perspective." *Journal of Law and Economics* 18:875–901.
Lanti, Irman G. 2001. "Back to the (Slightly Different) Future: Continuity and Change in *Indonesian* Politics." ISEAS working paper. http://www.asia-studies.com/ISEASvr.html.
La Porta, Rafael, Florencio Lopez-de-Silanes, Christian Pop-Elches, and Andrei

Shleifer. 2004. "Judicial Checks and Balances." *Journal of Political Economy* 112:445–70.
Larkins, Christopher. 1996. "Judicial Independence and Democratization: A Theoretical and Conceptual Analysis." *American Journal of Comparative Law* 44:605–26.
Laksamana. 2004. "Review—Politics: Prepared to Lose," June 6. http://www.bion.cz.cc/urimesing/laksamana070604a.htm.
Ledivina V. Cariño. 2007. "Building Trust on Government in Southeast Asia." Working paper, East West Center, University of Hawaii.
Leonard, Meghan. E. 2011. "Institutional Legitimacy and Decision-Making on State High Courts: Examining Judicial Review." Paper prepared for presentation at the 11th annual State Politics and Policy Conference, June 3–4, Dartmouth College, Hanover, New Hampshire.
Lev, Daniel S. 2004. "Comments on the Judicial Reform Program in Indonesia." Unpublished paper, Washington, DC: International Monetary Fund.
Li, Quan, and Rafael Reuveny. 2004. "Democracy and Environmental Degradation." *International Studies Quarterly* 50:935–56.
Liddle, R. William. 2001. "Indonesia in 2000: A Shaky Start for Democracy." *Asian Survey* 41:1–12.
Liddle, R. William, and Saiful Mujani. 2005. "Comparing the 1999 and 2004 Indonesian Legislative Elections." Paper presented to the Association for Asian Studies Annual Meeting, April.
Lijphart, Arend. 1996. "The Puzzle of Indian Democracy: A Consociational Interpretation." *American Political Science Review* 90:258–68.
Lindberg, Staffan I. 2005. "Consequences of Electoral Systems in Africa: A Preliminary Inquiry." *Electoral Studies* 24:41–64.
Lindsey. Tim. 2008. "Constitutional Reform in Indonesia: Muddling Towards Democracy." In *Indonesia: Law and Society,* 2nd ed., ed. Tim Lindsey, 23–47. Sydney: Federation Press.
Linz, J., and A. Stepan. 1996. *Problems of Democratic Transition and Consolidation: Southern Europe, South America, and Post-Communist Europe.* Baltimore: Johns Hopkins University Press.
Lodge, Tom. 2003. *Politics in South Africa: From Mandela to Mbeki.* Johannesburg: Mets & Schilt.
Lora, Eduardo. 2007. *The State of State Reform in Latin America.* Palo Alto, CA: Stanford University Press.
Ludden, David E. 1996. *Contesting the Nation: Religion, Community, and the Politics of Democracy in India.* Philadelphia: University of Pennsylvania Press.
Lyne, Mona. 2008. "Personal *and* Party: Reputation Building in the Brazilian Legislature." *American Journal of Political Science* 52:290–303.
Mabote, Ramotena. 1997. "Youth League's Backing of Phosa Could Send Shivers through the ANC." *Star,* April 4.
MacCormick, Neil. 1999. "Rhetoric and the Rule of Law." In *Recrafting the Rule of*

Law: The Limits of Legal Order, ed. David Dyzenhaus, 163–77. Portland: Hart Publishing.

Maeda, Ko, and Misa Nishikawa. 2006. "Duration of Party Control in Parliamentary and Presidential Governments: A Study of 65 Democracies, 1950 to 1998." *Comparative Political Studies* 39:352–74.

Machado, Altino. 2003. "Facundo Critica Aumento aos Magistrados do Acre." *Página 20* Rio Branco, Brazil. April 30.

Maddex, R. 1995. *Constitutions of the World*. 1st ed. Thousand Oaks, CA: CQ Press.

Maddex, R. 2007. *Constitutions of the World*. 3rd ed. Thousand Oaks, CA: CQ Press.

Magalhaes, Pedro. 1999. "The Politics of Judicial Reform in Eastern Europe." *Comparative Politics* 31:43–62.

Magaloni, Beatriz. 2003. "Authoritarianism, Democracy and the Supreme Court: Horizontal Exchange and the Rule of Law in Mexico." In *Democratic Accountability in Latin America*, ed. Scott Mainwaring and Christopher Welna, 266–305. New York: Oxford University Press.

Magaloni, Beatriz. 2006. *Voting for Autocracy: Hegemonic Party Survival and Its Demise in Mexico*. Cambridge: Cambridge University Press.

Magaloni, Beatriz Magaloni, Alberto Diaz-Cayeros, and Federico Estevez. 2007. "Clientelism and Portfolio Diversification: A Model of Electoral Investment with Applications to Mexico." In *Patrons, Clients, and Policies: Patterns of Democratic Accountability and Political Competition*, ed. H. Kitschelt and S. Wilkinson. New York: Cambridge University Press.

Magaloni, Beatriz, and Arianna Sánchez. 2001. "Empowering Courts as Constitutional Veto Players: Presidential Delegation and the New Mexican Supreme Court." Paper presented at the 97th meeting of the American Political Science Association, San Francisco, August 30–September 2.

Mahfud, Mohd. 2007. *Perdebatan Hukum Tata Negara Pasca Amandemen Konstitusi* [Constitutional Law Debate Post Amendment]. Jakarta: LP3ES.

Mahfud, Mohd. 2009. "The Role of the Constitutional Court in the Development of Democracy in Indonesia." Paper presented at the World Conference on Constitutional Justice, Cape Town, January 23–24.

Mainwaring, Scott P. 1999. *Rethinking Party Systems in the Third Wave of Democratization: The Case of Brazil*. Palo Alto: Stanford University Press.

Mainwaring, Scott P., and Anibal Pérez-Liñán. 1997. "Party Discipline in the Brazilian Constitutional Congress." *Legislative Studies Quarterly* 22:452–83.

Mainwaring, Scott P., and Timothy Scully, eds. 1995. *Building Democratic Institutions: Party Systems in Latin America*. Palo Alto: Stanford University Press.

Mainwaring, Scott P., and Mariano Torcal. 2006. "Party System Institutionalization and Party System Theory after the Third Wave of Democratization." In *Handbook of Party Politics*, ed. Richard Katz and William Crotty. Thousand Oaks, CA: Sage.

Mainwaring, Scott P., and Christopher Welna, eds. 2003. *Democratic Accountability in Latin America*. New York: Oxford University Press.

Mainwaring, Scott P., and E. Zoco. 2007. "Political Sequences and the Stabilization of Interparty Competition." *Party Politics* 13 (2): 155–78.

Malik, Balwant Singh. 1998. *P. V. Narasimha Rao v. State: A Critique of Supreme Court Cases.* New Delhi: Eastern Book Co.

Mallik, D. 2009. "Microfinance and Moneylender Interest Rate: Evidence from Bangladesh." MPRA Paper 17800, University Library of Munich, Germany.

Manan, B. 2006. "Independence of the Judiciary, Indonesian Experience." (Former Chief Justice of Indonesia). Text of speech addressed to the Supreme Court of Pakistan, Lahore, Pakistan.

Manning, Chris, and Peter van Diermen, eds. 2000. *Indonesia in Transition: Social Aspects of Reformasi and Crisis.* Singapore: Institute of Southeast Asian Studies.

Manor, John. 1990. "How and Why Liberal and Representative Politics Emerged in India." *Political Studies* 38:20–38.

Mansfield, Edward, Helen Milner, and B. Peter Rosendorff. 2000. "Free to Trade: Democracies, Autocracies, and International Trade Negotiations." *American Political Science Review* 94:305–22.

Marks, Gary, and Liesbet Hooghe. 2004. "Does Identity or Economic Rationality Drive Public Opinion on European Integration?" *PS: Political Science and Politics* 37:415–20.

Martin, Lanny. 1999. "The Strategic Government Agenda in Parliamentary Democracies." Presented at the conference of the Midwest Political Science Association, Chicago, April 1–4.

Martinez-Lara, Javier. 1996. *Building Democracy in Brazil: The Politics of Constitutional Change, 1985–95.* New York: St. Martin's.

McBeth, John. 1998. "Political Update." In *Post Soeharto Indonesia: Renewal or Chaos?* ed. Geoff Forrester. Bathurst: Crawford House.

Mcguire, K., and J. Stimson. 2004. "The Least Dangerous Branch Revisited: New Evidence on Supreme Court Responsiveness to Public Preferences." *Journal of Politics* 66:1018–35.

McCubbins, Mathew, and Daniel Rodriguez. 2008. "The Judiciary and the Role of Law." In *Oxford Handbook of Political Economy,* ed. Barry Weingast and Don Wittman. New York: Oxford University Press.

McCubbins, M. D., and T. Schwartz. 1984. "Congressional Oversight Overlooked: Police Patrols versus Fire Alarms." *American Journal of Political Science* 28:165–79.

McLeod, R. 2008. "Privatisation Failures in Indonesia." Working paper, Economic Division, Indonesia Project, Australian National University.

McNollgast. 1987. "Administrative Procedures as Instruments of Political Control." *Journal of Law, Economics, and Organization* 3:243–77.

McNollgast. 1989. "Structure and Process, Politics and Policy: Administrative Arrangements and the Political Control of Agencies." *Virginia Law Review* 75:431–82.

McNollgast. 1995. "Politics and the Courts: A Positive Theory of Judicial Doctrine and the Rule of Law." *Southern California Law Review* 68:1631–83.

McNollgast. 2006. "Conditions for Judicial Independence." *Journal of Contemporary Legal Issues* 15:105–20.

Mehta, Pratap Bhanu. 2002. *Democracy and the Idea of Social Cooperation in a Common Cause.* New Delhi: Oxford University Press.

Mehta, Pratap Bhanu. 2007. "The Rise of Judicial Sovereignity." In *The State of India's Democracy,* ed. Sumit Ganguly, Larry Diamond, and Marc F. Plattner. Baltimore: Johns Hopkins University Press.

Melone, A. P. 1996. "The Struggle for Judicial Independence and the Transition toward Democracy in Bulgaria." *Communist and Post-Communist Studies* 29:231–43.

Mietzner, Marcus. 2007. "Party Financing in Post-Soeharto Indonesia: Between State Subsidies and Political Corruption." *Contemporary Southeast Asia* 29:238–63.

Milesi-Ferretti, Gian Maria, Roberto Perotti, and Massimo Rostagno. 2002. "Electoral Systems and Public Spending." *Quarterly Journal of Economics* 117:609–57.

Mill, John Stuart. 1834. *A System of Logic.* New York: Harper & Brothers.

Milner, Helen, and Keiko Kubota. 2005. "Why the Move to Free Trade? Democracy and Trade Policy in the Developing Countries." *International Organization* 59:107–44.

Milner, Helen, and Bumba Mukherjee. 2009. "Democratization and Economic Globalization." *Annual Review of Political Science* 12:163–81.

Mitra, Chandan. 1998. *The Corrupt Society.* New Delhi: Viking Penguin.

Monken, Mario Hugo. 2001. "Same as primeiras liminares contra o plano." *Folha de Sao Paulo,* May 22.

Moravcsik, Andrew. 2000. "The Origins of Human Rights Regimes." *International Organization* 54:217–52.

Morena, A. 2004. "The Effects of Negative Campaigns on Mexican Voters." In *Mexico's Pivotal Democratic Election: Candidates, Voters, and the Presidential Campaign of 2000,* ed. J. I. Dominguez and C. H. Lawson. Palo Alto: Stanford University Press.

Moreno, Erika, Brian F. Crisp, and Matthew Shugart. 2003. "The Accountability Deficit in Latin America." In *Democratic Accountability in Latin America,* ed. Scott Mainwaring and Christopher Welna. Oxford: Oxford University Press.

Mozaffar, S., J. R. Scarritt, and G. Galaich. 2003. "Electoral Institutions, Ehnopolitical Cleavages and Party Systems in Africa's Emerging Democracies." *American Political Science Review* 97:379–90.

Mukhia, Harbans. 1992. "Ayodhya Dispute: Historical Evidence and BJP's Aim." In *Politics of Confrontation: The Babri-Masjid Ramjanmabhoomi Controversy Runs Riot,* ed. Asghar A. Engineer. New Delhi: Ajanta.

Murphy, W. 1964. *Elements of Judicial Strategy.* Chicago: University of Chicago Press.

Murphy, Walter F., and Joseph Tanenhaus. 1968. "Public Opinion and the United States Supreme Court: Mapping of Some Prerequisites for Court Legitimation of Regime Changes." *Law and Society Review* 2:357–84.

Myers, David. 1991. *Regional Hegemons: Threat Perception and Strategic Response.* Boulder: Westview Press.
Myerson, Roger B. 1995. "Analysis of Democratic Institutions: Structure, Conduct, and Performance." *Journal of Economic Perspectives* 9:77–89.
Nariman, Fali. 2005. "Protect Integrity, Independence." *Indian Tribune,* September 24. http://www.tribuneindia.com/2005/specials/tribune_125/main4.htm.
National Commission to Review the Working of the Constitution. 2001. Consultation paper on Review of Election Law, Processes and Reform Options Advisory Panel, on Electoral Reforms; Standards in Political Life, Member-In-Charge—Dr. Subhash C. Kashyap, Chairperson—Shri R. K. Trivedi, January 8, Vigyan Bhavan Annexe, Parliament Of India, New Delhi.
Navbharat Times. 1993. "Narasimha Rao and the SR Bommai Case." March 11.
Navia, Patricio, and Julio Ríos-Figueroa. 2005. "The Constitutional Adjudication Mosaic of Latin America." *Comparative Political Studies* 38:189–217.
Neubauer, David W., and Stephen S. Meinhold. 2009. *Judicial Process: Law, Courts, and Politics in the United States.* 5th ed. Belmont: Wadsworth.
New Vision. 2005. "Odoki Condemns Military Presence at Court." November 18. http://www.newvision.co.ug/.
Ngongola, C. 2001. "Judicial Mediation in Electoral Politics in Malawi." In *A Democracy of Chameleons: Politics and Culture in the New Malawi,* ed. H. Englund. Uppsala: Nordiska Afrika Institutet.
Nicolau, Jairo. 2007. "The Open-List Electoral System in Brazil." *Dados* 3:1–27
Nicolau, Jairo. *Dados eleitorais do Brasil* (1982–06). Rio de Janeiro: IUPERJ.
Nikolenyi, C. 2007. "Learning to Win: Parties, Parliaments and Minority Governments in Post-Communist Democracies." Working paper, Department of Political Science, Concordia University.
Nóbrega, Mailson da. 2000. *O Brasil em Transfarmacão.* São Paulo: Editora Gente.
Noorani, A. G. 2000. *The RSS and the BJP: A Division of Labor.* New Delhi: Left World Books.
Norris, P. 2003. "Do Institutions Matter? The Consequences of Electoral Reform for Political Participation." In *Rethinking the Vote,* ed. Ann N. Crigler, Marion R. Just, and Edward J. McCaffery. Oxford: Oxford University Press.
Norris, Pippa. 2004. *Electoral Engineering: Voting Rules and Political Behavior.* Cambridge: Cambridge University Press.
O'Donnell, Guillermo A. 1998. "Horizontal Accountability in New Democracies." *Journal of Democracy* 9:112–26.
O'Donnell, Guillermo A. 2000. "The Judiciary and the Rule of Law." *Journal of Democracy* 11:25–31.
Ogada, Ceda. 2004. "Out-of-Court Corporate Debt Restructuring: The Jakarta Initiative Task Force." In *Indonesia Selected Issues,* IMF country report no. 04/189. www.imf.org/external/pubs/ft/scr/2004/cr04189.pdf.
O Globo. 1995. "O Contrôle do Judiciário." June 17.
Oliveira, Mauro Márcio. 1993. *Técnicas Fontes De Informações Sobre A Assembléia*

Nacional Constituinte De Quais São, Onde Buscá-Las E Como Usá-Las. Senado Federal, Brasília.
Omara, A. 2008. "Lessons from the Korean Constitutional Court. What Can Indonesia Learn from The Korean Constitutional Court Experience?" Working paper, Gadjah Mada University.
Open Society Institute. 2001. "Monitoring the EU Accession Process: Judicial Independence." http://www.soros.org/resources/articles_publications.
Open Society Institute. 2002. "Monitoring the EU Accession Process: Corruption and Anti-Corruption Policy." http://www.soros.org/resources/articles_publications.
Open Society Institute. 2003. "Monitoring the EU Accession Process: Judicial Independence." http://www.soros.org/resources/articles_publications.
Owens, John E. 2004. "Cohesion." *Journal of Legislative Studies* 9:12–40.
Palguna, I. D. G. 2007. *Mahkamah Konstitusi Dalam Transisi Demokrasi di Indonesia in Konstitusi dan Ketatanegaraan Indonesia Kontemporer* [Constitutional Court in Transitional Democracy in Indonesia]. Mahkamah Konstitusi RI, Jakarta, Indonesia.
Palshikar, Suhas. 2003. "The Regional Parties and Democracy: Romantic Rendezvouz or Localized Legitimation?" In *Political Parties and Party Systems*, ed. Ajay K. Mehra, D. D. Khanna, and Gert W. Kueck. New Delhi: Sage.
Panizza, F. 1995. "Human Rights in the Process of Transition and Consolidation of Democracy in Latin America." *Political Studies* 43:168–88.
Papaioannou, Elias, and Gregorios Siourounis. 2008. "Economic and Social Factors Driving the Third Wave of Democratization." *Journal of Comparative Economics* 36:365–87.
Parikh, Sunita, and Barry R. Weingast. 1993. "A Comparative Theory of Federalism: India." *Virginia Law Review* 83:1593–1615.
Pasquino, Pasquale. 2001. "One and Three: Separation of Powers and the Independence of the Judiciary in the Italian Constitution." In *Constitutional Culture and Democratic Rule*, ed. John Ferejohn, Jack N. Rakove, and Jonathan Riley, 205–22. New York: Cambridge University Press.
Payne, L. 1991. "Industrialists, Labor Relations, and the Transition to Democracy in Brazil." https://kellogg.nd.edu/publications/workingpapers/democracy.shtml.
Pedersen, Morgens N. 1983. "Changing Patterns of Electoral Volatility in European Party Systems, 1948–1977: Explorations in Explanation." In *Western European Party Systems: Continuity and Change*, ed. Hans Daalder and Peter Mair, 29–66. Beverly Hills: Sage.
Pereira, Anthony. 2000. "An Ugly Democracy: State Violence and the Rule of Law in Postauthoritarian Brazil." In *Democratic Brazil: Actors, Institutions, and Processes*, ed. Peter Kingstone and Timothy Power. Pittsburgh: University of Pittsburgh Press.
Pereira, Anthony W. 2005. *Political (In)Justice, Authoritarianism, and the Rule of Law in Brazil, Chile, and Argentina*. Pittsburgh: University of Pittsburgh Press.
Peretti, Terri. 2003. "A Normative Appraisal of Social Scientific Knowledge Regarding Judicial Independence." *Ohio State Law Journal* 64:349–66.

Persson, Torsten, and Guido Tabellini. 2005. *The Economic Effects of Constitutions.* Cambridge, MA: MIT Press.

Piliang, Indra J. 2000. "Amandemen Konstitusi dan Gerakan Mahasiswa: Sebuah Proyeksi." 4 *Analisis CSIS.*

Pinheironeto Advogados. *Taxation.* 2007. 20th ed. http:www.pinheironeto.com.br.

Pinheironeto Advogados. 2009. *Taxation.* 35th ed. http:www.pinheironeto.com.br.

Platzdasch, B. 2009. *Politics in Indonesia: Politics in the Emerging Democracy.* Singapore: Institute of Southeast Asian Studies.

Pompe, Sebastiaan. 2005. *The Indonesian Supreme Courts: A Study of Institutional Collapse.* Ithaca: Cornell University Press.

Popkin, M. 2000. *Peace without Justice: Obstacles to Building the Rule of Law in El Salvador.* University Park: Penn State University Press.

Popova, Maria. 2010. "Political Competition as an Obstacle to Judicial Independence: Evidence from Russia and Ukraine." *Comparative Political Studies* 43:1202–29.

Posner, R. 2003. "The Anti-Hero." *New Republic,* February 24.

Powell, Emilia J., and Jeffrey K. Staton. 2009. "Domestic Judicial Institutions and Human Rights Treaty Violation." *International Studies Quarterly* 53:149–74.

Power, Timothy. 2000. *The Political Right in Post-Authoritarian Brazil: Elites, Institutions, and Democratization.* University Park: Penn State University Press.

Pribadi, Airlangga. 2005. "Darwinisme Partai Politik pada Pemilu 2004" [Darwinism of Political Parties in the 2004 General Election]. *Demokrasidan HAM* 4:53–76.

Prillaman, William. 2000. *The Judiciary and Democratic Decay in Latin America: Declining Confidence in the Rule of Law* Westport, CT: Praeger.

Protsyk, Oleh, and Lupsa Marius Matichescu. 2010. "Electoral Rules and Minority Representation in Romania." *Communist and Post-Communist Studies* 43:31–41.

Przeworski, Adam, Michael Alvarez, José Antonio Cheibub, and Fernando Limongi. 2000. *Democracy and Development: Political Regimes and Economic Well-being in the World, 1950–1990.* New York: Cambridge University Press.

Przeworski, Adam, and Henry Teune. 1970. *The Logic of Comparative Inquiry.* New York: John Wiley and Sons.

Punett, R. M. 1994. *British Government and Politics.* Aldershot: Heinemann.

Ragin, Charles. 1987. *The Comparative Method: Moving Beyond Qualitative and Quantitative Strategies.* Berkeley and Los Angeles: University of California Press.

Raju, S., S. E. Corbridge, and S. Kumar, eds. 2006. *Colonial and Postcolonial Geographies of India.* New Delhi: Sage.

Rakner, Lise, and Nicholas Van De Walle. 2009. "Democratization by Elections? Opposition Weakness in Africa." *Journal of Democracy* 20:108–21.

Ramchandran, V. 2004. *Gender and Social Equity in Primary Education: Hierarchies of Access.* New Delhi: Sage.

Ramseyer, Mark J., and Eric B. Rasmusen. 2003. *Measuring Judicial Independence: The Political Economy of Judging in Japan.* Chicago: University of Chicago Press.

Rantao, Jovial. 1997. "Will Ramaphosa Make a Comeback to Challenge for ANC Deputy President." *Star,* October 18.

Randall, V. 2007. "Political Parties and Democratic Developmental States." *Development Policy Review* 25:633–52.

Rao, P. P. 2006. "The Constitution, Parliament and the Judiciary." In *The Supreme Court versus the Constitution: A Challenge to Federalism,* ed. Pran Chopra. New Delhi: Sage.

Ratliff, William, and Edgardo Buscaglia. 1997. "Judicial Reform: The Neglected Priority in Latin America." *Annals of the American Academy of Political and Social Science* 550:59–71.

Reich, Gary. 2007. "Constitutional Coordination in Unstable Party Systems: The Brazilian Constitution of 1988." *Constitutional Political Economy* 18:177–97.

Reilly, Ben. 2002. "Electoral Systems for Divided Societies." *Journal of Democracy* 13:156–70.

Reilly, B. 2006. *Democracy and Diversity: Political Engineering in the Asia-Pacific.* Oxford: Oxford University Press.

Reynal-Querol, Marta. 2002. "Ethnicity, Political Systems, and Civil Wars." *Journal of Conflict Resolution* 46:29–54.

Reynolds, A., B. Reilly, and A. Ellis. 2005. *Electoral System Design: The New International IDEA Handbook.* Stockholm: International Institute for Democracy and Electoral Assistance.

Ríos-Figueroa, Julio. 2006. *Judicial Independence: Definitions, Measurement, and its Effects on Corruption: An Analysis of Latin America.* PhD diss., New York University.

Ríos-Figueroa, Julio, and Jeffrey Staton. 2009. "Unpacking the Rule of Law: A Review of Judicial Independence Measures." http://papers.ssrn.com/sol3/papers.cfm?abstract_id=1434234.

Ríos-Figueroa, Julio, and Matthew M. Taylor. 2006. "Institutional Determinants of the Judicialization of Policy in Brazil and Mexico." *Journal of Latin American Studies* 38 (4): 739–66.

Risse, Thomas, and Stephen C. Ropp. 2010. "Introduction and Overview." In *From Commitment to Compliance: The Persistent Power of Human Rights,* ed. Thomas Risse, Stephen Ropp, and Kathryn Sikkink. New York: Cambridge University Press.

Risse, Thomas, Stephen C. Ropp, and Kathryn Sikkink. 1999. *The Power of Human Rights: International Norms and Domestic Change.* New York: Cambridge University Press.

Roberts, K. W., and E. Wibbel. 1999. "Party Systems and Electoral Volatility in Latin America: A Test of Economic, Institutional, and Structural Explanations." *American Political Science Review* 93:575–90.

Robinson, Davis R. 2003. "The Role of Politics in the Election and the Work of Judges of the International Court of Justice." *Proceedings of the Annual Meeting, American Society of International Law* 97:277–82.

Robison, Richard, and Vedi R. Hadiz. 2002. "Oligarchy and Capitalism: The Case of

Indonesia." In *East Asian Capitalism: Conflicts, Growth and Crisis*, ed. Luigi Tomba, 37–74. Milan: Fondazione Giancomo Feltrinelli.

Rogers, J. 2001. "Information and Judicial Review: A Signaling Game of Legislative-Judicial Interaction." *American Journal of Political Science* 45:84–99.

Rogers, J. 2006. "The Majoritarian Basis for Judicial Countermajoritarianism." Presented at the annual meeting of the Midwest Political Science Association, Chicago, April 3–6.

Root, Hilton J., and Karen May. 2008. "Judicial Systems and Authoritarian Transition." In *Rule by Law: The Politics of Courts in Authoritarian Regimes*, ed. Tom Ginsburg and Tamir Moustafa. New York: Cambridge University Press.

Roozendaal, Peter Van. 1997. "Government Survival in Western Multi-Party Democracies: The Effect of Credible Exit Threats via Dominance." *European Journal of Political Research* 32:71–92.

Ros, Luciano da. 2010. "Judges in the Formation of the Nation-State: Professional Experiences, Academic Background and Geographic Circulation of Members of the Supreme Courts of Brazil and the United States." *Brazilian Political Science Review* 40:102–30.

Rose-Ackerman, Susan. 2007. "Judicial Independence and Corruption." In *Global Corruption Report 2007*. New York: Cambridge University Press.

Rosenberg, Gerald N. 1992. "Judicial Independence and the Reality of Political Power." *Review of Politics* 54:369–98.

Rosenn, Keith S. 1987. "The Protection of Judicial Independence in Latin America." *Inter-American Law Review* 19:1–35.

Rositawati, D. 2000. "Judicial Review in Brazil: Developments under the 1988 Constitution." *Southwestern Journal of Law and Trade in the Americas* 7:291–319.

Rositawati, D. 2010. "The Indonesia Supreme Court: A Study of Relationship between Judicial Recruitment and Independency." Working paper, Djakarta, the Indonesian Institute for Independent Judiciary (LeIP), Indonesia.

Rosser, Andrew. 2004. "Indonesia: The Politics of Inclusion." IDS working paper no. 229.

Rottman, David B., and Alan J. Tomkins. 1999. "Public Trust and Confidence in the Courts: What Public Opinion Surveys Mean to Judges." *Court Review* (Fall): 24–31.

Rugege, Sam. 2007. "Judicial Independence in Rwanda." Paper presented at the Judicial Independence and Legal Infrastructure: Essential Partners for Economic Development conference, University of the Pacific, McGeorge School of Law, Sacramento, California, October 28, 2005.

Russell, P. 2001. "Toward a General Theory of Judicial Independence." In *Judicial Independence in the Age of Democracy: Critical Perspective from Around the World*, ed. P. Russell and D. O'Brien. Charlottesville: University of Virginia Press.

Russell, Peter H. 2004. "Adjudication and Enforcement of Laws in a Federal System." In *The Dynamics of Real Federalism: Law, Economic Development, and Indigenous Communities in Russia and Canada*, ed. P. Solomon. Toronto: CREES University of Toronto.

Russell, Peter H., and David O'Brien. 2001. *Judicial Independence in the Age of Democracy.* Charlottesville: University of Virginia Press.
Saad, P. 1997. *La Cáida de Abdalá: Un Análisis Actual.* Quito: El Conejo.
Sabaliunas, L. 1996. "Comparative Perspectives on Judicial Review in Lithuania." *Europe-Asia Studies* 48 (5): 783–95.
Sadek, Maria Tereza, and Rosângela Batista Cavalcanti. 2003. "The New Brazilian Public Prosecution: An Agent of Accountability." In *Democratic Accountability in Latin America*, ed. Scott Mainwaring and Christopher Welna. Oxford: Oxford University Press.
Saha, S. C. 2008. "Hindu-Muslim Communal Violence in India: An Analysis of Causes." http://www.pondiuni.edu.
Sajó, András. 2006. "Social Rights as Middle-Class Entitlements in Hungary: The Role of the Constitutional Court." In *Courts and Social Transformation in New Democracies: An Institutional Voice for the Poor?*, ed. Roberto Gargarella, Pilar Domingo, and Theunix Roux. Burlington: Ashgate.
Salazar, Katya, and Jacqueline de Gramont. 2007. "Civil Society's Role in Combating Judicial Corruption in Central America." In *Global Corruption Report 2007.* New York: Cambridge University Press.
Salim, Arksal. 2008. *Challenging the Secular State: The Islamization of Law in Modern Indonesia.* Honolulu: University of Hawaii Press.
Salzberger, Eli M. 1993. "A Positive Analysis of the Doctrine of Separation of Powers, or: Why Do We Have an Independent Judiciary?" *International Review of Law and Economics* 13:349–79.
Samuels, David. 1999. "Incentives to Cultivate a Party Vote in Candidate-centric Electoral Systems: Evidence from Brazil." *Comparative Political Studies* 32:487–518.
Samuels, David. 2001. "Does Money Matter? Credible Commitments and Campaign Finance in New Democracies: Theory and Evidence from Brazil." *Comparative Politics* 34:23–42.
Samuels, David. 2002. "Pork-Barrel Politics Is Not Credit-Claiming or Advertising: Campaign Finance and the Sources of the Personal Vote in Brazil." *Journal of Politics* 64:845–63.
Samuels, David. 2004. *Ambition, Federalism, and Legislative Politics in Brazil.* New York: Cambridge University Press.
Santiso, Carlos. 2003. "Economic Reform and Judicial Governance in Brazil: Balancing Independence with Accountability." *Democratization* 10:161–80.
Santiso, Carlos. 2004. "Economic Reform and Judicial Governance in Brazil: Balancing Independence with Accountability." In *Democratization and the Judiciary: The Accountability Function of Courts in New Democracies*, ed. Siri Gloppen, Robert Gargarella, and Elin Skaar. London: Frank Cass.
Santos, C., and M. G. Vilarouca. 2008. "Political Institutions and Governability from FHC to Lula." In *Democratic Brazil Revisited*, ed. P. Kingstone and T. Power. Pittsburgh: University of Pittsburgh Press.
Santos, W. dos, and Fabricia C. Guimarães. 2002. *Votos e Partidos: Almanaque de*

Dados Eleitorais: Brasil e Outros Países. Rio de Janeiro, Brazil: FGV Editora, FAPERJ.

Sathe, S. P. 2002. *Judicial Activism in India*. New York: Oxford University Press.

Sato, Miyuki. 2003. "Judicial Review in Brazil. Nominal and Real." *Global Jurist* 3:1–24.

Scartascini, Carlos. 2008. "Who's Who in the PMP: An Overview of Actors, Incentives, and the Roles They Play." In *Policymaking in Latin America How Politics Shapes Policies*, ed. Ernesto Stein and Mariano Tommasi. Washington, DC: Inter-American Development Bank.

Scheppele, Kim Lane. 2005. "Democracy by Judiciary or, Why Courts Can Be More Democratic than Parliaments." In *Rethinking the Rule of Law after Communism*, ed. Adam Czarnota, Martin Krygier, and Wojciech Sadurski. Budapest: Central European University Press.

Schmitt, Rogério. 2000. *Partidos Políticos no Brasil (1945–2000)*. Rio de Janeiro: Jorge Zahar.

Schneier, Edward V. 2006. *Crafting Constitutional Democracies: The Politics of Institutional Design*. Lanham, MD: Rowman & Littlefield.

Schuman, Michael. 2004. "Will Megawati be Ousted?" *Time*, April 26.

Schwartz, Herman. 2000. *The Struggle for Constitutional Justice in Post-Communist Europe*. Chicago: University of Chicago Press.

Scribner, D. L. 2004. "The Chilean Supreme Court: Political Isolation and Institutional Stability—Stable Judicial Tenure and Judicial Decision-Making." Presented at the Latin American Studies Association meeting, Las Vegas.

Sebastian, L. C. 2004. "The Paradox of Indonesian Democracy." *Contemporary Southeast Asia* 26:256–79.

Sethy, Rabindra K. 2003. *Political Crisis and President's Rule in an Indian State*. New Delhi: A.P.H. Publication.

Shambayati, Hootan, and Esen Kirdis. 2009. "In Pursuit of 'Contemporary Civilization': Judicial Empowerment in Turkey." *Political Research Quarterly* 30:1–13.

Shankar, Shylashri, and Pratap Bhanu Mehta. 2008. "Courts and Socioeconomic Rights in India." In *Courting Social Justice: Judicial Enforcement of Social and Economic Rights in the Developing World*, ed. Varun Gandhi and Daniel Brinks. New York: Cambridge University Press.

Shapiro, Martin. 1981. *Courts: A Comparative and Political Analysis*. Chicago: University of Chicago Press.

Shapiro, Martin. 1992. "Federalism, the Race to the Bottom and the Regulation-Averse Entrepreneur." In *North American and Comparative Federalism*, ed. H. Scheiber. Berkeley: Institute of Governmental Studies Press.

Shapiro, Martin. 1996. "The Globalization of Judicial Review." In *Legal Culture and the Legal Profession*, ed. H. Scheiber and L. Friedman. Boulder: Westview Press.

Shapiro, Martin. 1999. "The Success of Judicial Review." In *Constitutional Dialogues in Comparative Perspective*, ed. S. Kenney, W. Reisinger, and J. Reitz, 193–219. London: Macmillan.

Shapiro, Martin, and Alec Stone Sweet. 2002. *On Law, Politics, and Judicialization.* New York: Oxford University Press.

Sheehan, Reginald S., William Mishler, and Donald R. Songer. 1992. "Ideology, Status, and the Differential Success of Direct Parties Before the Supreme Court." *American Political Science Review* 86:464–71.

Sherlock, Stephen. 2001. "Indonesia's New Government: Stability at Last?" Working paper, Parliamentary Library, Government of New Zealand.

Sherlock, Stephen. 2005. *The Role of Political Parties in a Second Wave of Reformasi.* Jakarta: UNSFIR.

Sherlock, S. 2009. "The 2004 Indonesian Elections: How the System Works and What Parties Stand For." http://aceproject.org/ero-en/regions/asia/ID/Sherlock.pdf/view.

Shin, J. H. 2010. "Why Personalistic Parties? The Choice of Candidate-Centered Electoral Systems in New Democracies." Working paper, Department of Political Science, University of California, Los Angeles.

Shirley, Robert. 1987. "A Brief of Law in Brazil." *Canadian Journal of Latin American and Caribbean Studies* 23:1–14.

Sieder, R. 2003. "Renegotiating 'Law and Order': Judicial Reform and Citizen Responses in Post-War Guatemala." *Democratization* 10:137–60.

Sieder, Rachel, Line Schjolden, and Alan Angell, eds. 2005. *The Judicialization of Politics in Latin America.* New York: Palgrave Macmillan.

Silver Martins, Ives Gandra da. 1996. "Decisao foi Eminentemente Tecnica." *Folha de Sao Paolo.* April 13.

Simmons, Beth. 2008. *Globalization, Sovereignty, and Democracy: The Role of International Organizations in a Globalizing World.* Urbana: University of Illinois Press.

Simmons, Beth. 2009. *Mobilizing for Human Rights: International Law in Domestic Politics.* New York: Cambridge University Press.

Singh, M. P., and Bhagwan Dua, eds. 2003. *Indian Federalism in the 21st Century.* New Delhi: Manohar.

Sisson, Richard, and Stanley Wolpert, eds. 1988. *Congress and Indian Nationalism.* Berkeley and Los Angeles: University of California Press.

Skidmore, T. E. 1989. "Brazil's Slow Road to Democratization: 1974–1985." In *Democratizing Brazil: Problems of Transition and Consolidation,* ed. A. Stepan. New York: Oxford University Press.

Skocpol, Theda, and Margaret Somers. 1980. "The Uses of Comparative History in Macrosocial Inquiry." *Comparative Studies in Society and History* 22:174–97.

Slater, D. 2006. "The Architecture of Authoritarianism: Southeast Asia and the Regeneration of Democratization Theory." *Taiwan Journal of Democracy* 2:1–22.

Smith, A. 2004. *Election Timing.* Cambridge: Cambridge University Press.

Smithey, Shannon Ishiyama, and John Ishiyama. 2002. "Judicial Activism in Post-Communist Politics." *Law and Society Review* 36:719–42.

Solomon, Peter H. Jr., and Todd Foglesong. 2000. *Courts and Transition in Russia: The Challenge of Judicial Reform.* Boulder: Westview Press.

Somer-Topcu, Z., and L. Williams. 2008. "Survival of the Fittest? Cabinet Duration in Postcommunist Europe." *Comparative Politics* 40:313–29.

Spanos, A. 1999. *Probability Theory and Statistical Inference: Econometric Modeling with Observational Data.* Cambridge: Cambridge University Press.

Sridharan, E. 2002. "The Origins of the Electoral System: Rules, Representation, and Power-sharing in India's Democracy." In *India's Living Constitution: Ideas, Practices, Controversies,* ed. Zoya Hasan, E. Sridharan, and R. Sudarshan, 344–69. London: Anthem Press.

Sridharan, E. 2008. "Coalition Politics in India: Types, Duration, Theory and Comparison." ISAS working paper no. 50. http://www.isas.nus.edu.sg.

Staats, Joseph L., Shaun Bowler, and Jonathan T. Hiskey. 2005. "Measuring Judicial Performance in Latin America." *Latin American Politics and Society* 47:77–106.

Staton, Jeffrey. 2004. "Judicial Policy Implementation in Mexico City and Mérida." *Comparative Politics* 37:41–60.

Staton, Jeffrey. 2006. "Constitutional Review and the Selective Promotion of Case Results." *American Journal of Political Science* 50:98–112.

Staton, Jeffrey. 2010. *Judicial Power and Strategic Communication in Mexico.* New York: Cambridge University Press.

Stein, Ernesto Hugo, Ernesto Talvi, and Alejandro Grisanti. 1998. "Institutional Arrangements and Fiscal Performance: The Latin American Experience." IDB working paper no. 303.

Stein, Ernesto, and Mariano Tommasi, eds. 2008. *Policymaking in Latin America How Politics Shapes Policies.* Washington, DC: Inter-American Development Bank.

Stepan, Alfred C. 1989. *Democratizing Brazil: Problems of Transition and Consolidation.* New York: Oxford University Press.

Stephenson, Matthew C. 2003. "When the Devil Turns . . .": The Political Foundations of Independent Judicial Review." *Journal of Legal Studies* 32:59–89.

Stockmann, Petra. 2007. *The New Indonesian Constitutional Court: A Study into its Beginnings and First Years of Work.* Jakarta: Hanns Seidel Foundation.

Stokes, Susan C. 2001. *Mandates and Democracy: Neoliberalism by Surprise in Latin America.* New York: Cambridge University Press.

Stone Sweet, Alec. 1992. "Abstract Constitutional Review and Policy Making in Western Europe." In *Comparative Judicial Review and Public Policy,* ed. Donald W. Jackson and C. Neal Tate. Westport, CT: Greenwood Press.

Stone Sweet, Alec. 2000. *Governing with Judges: Constitutional Politics in Europe.* New York: Oxford University Press.

Stotzky, Irwin P., ed. 1993. *The Transition to Democracy in Latin America: The Role of the Judiciary.* Boulder: Westview Press.

Sudarshan, R. 2002. "Stateness and Democracy in India's Constitution." In *India's Living Constitution: Ideas, Practices, Controversies,* ed. Zoya Hasan, E. Sridharan, and R. Sudarshan, 159–78. London: Anthem Press.

Suhud, Muhamad. 2003. "Privatisation: A Review of the Power Sector Restructuring in Indonesia." Background paper on Privatisation INFID, International NGO forum on Indonesian development, Djakarta.

Sulistiyanto, P. 2004. "The 2004 General Elections and the Virtues of Indonesian Presidentialism." *Kasarinlan: Philippine Journal of Third World Studies* 19:4–24.

Suri, K. C. 2004. "Democracy, Economic Reforms, and Election Results in India." *Economic and Political Weekly* 39:5404–11.

Suryadinata, L. 2002. *Elections and Politics in Indonesia.* Singapore: Institute of Southeast Asian Studies.

Suryadinata, L., ed. 2004. *Ethnic Relations and Nation-Building in Southeast Asia: The Case of the Ethnic Chinese.* Singapore: Institute of Southeast Asian Studies.

Susanti, Bivitri. 2006. "The Emergence of Constitutionalism in Post-Reformasi Indonesia." Unpublished PhD diss., University of Melbourne.

Susetio, W. 2008. "Guarding Constitution of Indonesia through the Court." Unpublished paper, Universitas Indonusa Esa Unggul Indonesia. International Association of Law Schools conference on constitutional law, September 11–12. http://www.ialsnet.org/meetings/constit/papers/MasterBookletConLaw.pdf.

Tabalujan, B. S. 2002. "Why Indonesian Corporate Governance Failed—Conjectures Concerning Legal Culture." *Columbia Journal of Asian Law* 15:141–71.

Tate, C. Neal. 1992. "Comparative Judicial Review and Public Policy: Concepts and Overview." In *Comparative Judicial Review and Public Policy,* ed. Donald W. Jackson, C. Neal Tate, and Torbjörn Vallinder. New York: New York University Press.

Tate, C. Neal, and Stacia L. Haynie. 1993. "Authoritarianism and the Functions of Courts: A Time Series Analysis of the Philippine Supreme Court, 1961–1987." *Law and Society Review* 27:707–40.

Tate, C. Neal, and Linda Camp Keith. 2007. "Conceptualizing and Operationalizing Judicial Independence Globally." Paper presented at the annual meeting of the American Political Science Association, Chicago, August 30–September 1.

Tate, C. Neal, and Torbjörn Vallinder. 1995. *The Global Expansion of Judicial Power.* New York: New York University Press.

Tavits, Margit. 2007. "Clarity of Responsibility and Corruption." *American Journal of Political Science* 51:218–29.

Taylor, Matthew. 2005. "Citizens against the State: The Riddle of High-Impact, Low-Functionality Courts in Brazil." *Revista de Economia Política* 25:418–38.

Taylor, Matthew. 2006. "Veto and Voice in the Courts: Policy Implications of Institutional Design in the Brazilian Judiciary." *Comparative Politics* 38:337–56.

Taylor, Matthew. 2008. *Judging Policy: Courts and Policy Reform in Democratic Brazil.* Palo Alto: Stanford University Press.

Taylor, Michael C. 1997. "Why No Rule of Law in Mexico? Explaining the Weakness of Mexico's Judicial Branch." *New Mexico Law Review* 27:141–66.

Teehankee, J. 2006. "Consolidation or Crisis of Clientelistic Democracy? The 2004 Synchronized Elections in the Philippines." In *Between Consolidation and Crisis. Elections and Democracy in Five Nations in Southeast Asia,* ed. A. Croissant and B. Martin, 215–76. Berlin: Lit Verlag.

Thabane, Tebello. 2006. *Bridging the Gap between De Jure and De Facto Parliamentary Representation of Women in Africa: Lessons from Rwanda and South Africa.* Master's thesis, Makerere University.

Thakurta, Paranjoy Guha, and Shankar Raghuraman. 2004. *A Time of Coalitions: Divided We Stand*. New Delhi: Sage.

Tobing, Jakob. 2001. "Constitutional Amendments: A Brief Note on Indonesia's Case." Paper presented at the international symposium on Constitutional and Human Rights in a Global Age: an Asia-Pacific Perspective, Canberra, December 1-3.

Tomagola, Tamrin Amal. 2004. "Pasangan Presidensial 2004." In *Kompas. Siapa Mau Jadi Presiden? Debat Publik Seputar Program dan Partai Politik pada Pemilu*. Jakarta: Penerbit Buku Kompas.

Tomasa, Taryn Rae. 2006. "Ho'Olahui: Rebirth of a Nation." *Asian Law Journal* 5:247-63.

Tomsa, Dirk. 2008. *Party Politics and Democratization in Indonesia Golkar in the Post-Suharto Era*. New York: Routledge.

Tordoff, William. 2002. *Government and Politics in Africa*. Bloomington: Indiana University Press.

Train, K. E. 2003. *Discrete Choice Methods with Simulation*. Cambridge: Cambridge University Press.

Transparency International. 2007. *Global Corruption Report: Corruption in Judicial Systems*. New York: Cambridge University Press.

Trochev, Alexei. 2004. "Less Democracy, More Courts: A Puzzle of Judicial Review in Russia." *Law & Society Review* 38:513-46.

Trotter, L. 2006. *Islam, Women and Indonesian Politics: The PKS Challenge to Substantive Theories of Democracy*. Unpublished master's thesis, University of Sydney.

Tsebelis, George. 2002. *Veto Players: How Political Institutions Work*. Princeton: Princeton University Press.

Tummala, Krishna K. 1994. *Public Administration in India*. Singapore: Times Academic Press.

Udayakumar, S. P. 2004. "Historicizing Myth and Mythologizing History: The Ayodhya Case in India." *Social Scientist* 32 (7/8): 11-26.

Udayakumar, S. P. 2005. *Presenting the Past: Anxious History and Ancient Future in Hindutva India*. Westport, CT: Praeger.

Ufen, Andreas. 2006. "Political Parties and Party System Institutionalization in Southeast Asia. Lessons for Democratic Consolidation in Indonesia, the Philippines and Thailand." Working paper no. 37, GIGA Working Paper Series. www.giga-hamburg.de/content/publikationen/pdf/wp44_ufen.pdf.

Uhlin, Anders. 1997. *Indonesia and the "Third Wave of Democratization": The Indonesian Pro-Democracy Movement in a Changing World*. New York: St. Martin's.

Uprimmy, R. 2003. "The Constitutional Court and Control of Presidential Extraordinary Powers in Colombia." *Democratization* 10:46-69.

Ura, J. D. 2006. *The Effects of Judicial Review in American Politics*. PhD diss., University of North Carolina.

United States Agency for International Development [USAID]. 2004. *An Assessment of Corruption in Paraguay*. Alexandria, VA.

Vanberg, Georg. 1998. "Abstract Judicial Review, Legislative Bargaining, and Policy Compromise." *Journal of Theoretical Politics* 10:299-326.

Vanberg, Georg. 2000. "Establishing Judicial Independence in Germany: The Impact of Opinion Leadership and the Separation of Powers." *Comparative Politics* 32:333–53.

Vanberg, Georg. 2001. "Legislative-Judicial Relations: A Game-Theoretic Approach to Constitutional Review." *American Journal of Political Science* 45:346–61.

Vanberg, Georg. 2005. *The Politics of Constitutional Review in Germany.* New York: Cambridge University Press.

Vanberg, Georg. 2008. "Establishing and Maintaining Judicial Independence." In *Oxford Handbook of Law and Politics,* ed. Gregory Caldeira, Dan Keleman, and Keith Whittington. Oxford: Oxford University Press.

Varshney, Ashutosh. 1998. "Why Democracy Survives." *Journal of Democracy* 9:36–50.

Varshney, Ashutosh. 2002. *Muslims in India.* New Haven: Yale University Press.

Venkatesan, V. 2005. "A Scholar and a Politician." Frontline, January 1–14. http://www.hinduonnet.com/fline/fl2201/stories/20050114008013000.htm.

Verma, S. K., and K. Kusum, eds. 2000. *Fifty Year of the Supreme Court of India: Its Grasp and Reach.* New Delhi: Oxford University Press.

Vondoepp, Peter. 2006. "Politics and Judicial Assertiveness in Emerging Democracies: High Court Behavior in Malawi and Zambia." *Political Research Quarterly* 59:389–99.

Von Luebke, Christian. 2010. "The Politics of Reform: Political Scandals, Elite Resistance, and Presidential Leadership in Indonesia." *Journal of Current Southeast Asian Affairs* 29:79–94.

Vora, Rajendra, and Suhas Palshikar. 2004. Indian Democracy: Meanings and Practices. New Delhi: Sage.

Walhi (Wahana Lingkungan Hidup, Environmental Forum). 2003. "Privatisasi air Melanggar Prinsip air Sebagai Hak Asasi Rakyat" [Privatization of Water Breaches Principle of Water as a Basic Human Right of the People]. http://www.walhi.or.id/kampanye/air/privatisasi/030921_privairhak_sp/.

Wallack, Jessica Seddon, Alejandra Gaviria, Ugo Panizza, and Ernesto Stein. 2003. "Political Particularism around the World." *World Bank Economic Review* 17:133–43.

Wanandi, J. 2004. "The Indonesian General Elections 2004." *Asia-Pacific Review* 11:115–31.

Warwick, Paul. 1992. "Ideological Diversity and Government Survival in Western European Parliamentary Democracies." *Comparative Political Studies* 25:332–61.

Warwick, Paul. 1994. *Government Survival in Parliamentary Democracies.* Cambridge: Cambridge University Press.

Wattenberg, M. 1992. *The Rise of Candidate-Centered Politics: Presidential Elections of the 1980s.* Cambridge, MA: Harvard University Press.

Weaver, Kent. 2002. "A New Look at Federalism Electoral Rules and Governability." *Journal of Democracy* 13:111–25.

Weingast, Barry. 1997. "The Political Foundations of Democracy and the Rule of Law." *American Political Science Review* 91:245–63.

Werneck Vianna, Luiz, and Marcelo Burgis. 2002. "Revolucao Processual do Direito e Democracia Progressive." In *A Democracia e os Tres Poderes no Brasil*, ed. Luiz Wernerck Vianna. Belo Horizonte: Editora UFMG.
Weschler, L. 1998. *A Miracle, a Universe: Settling Accounts with Torturers*. Chicago: University of Chicago Press.
Weyland, Kurt. 2006. *Bounded Rationality and Policy Diffusion: Social Sector Reform in Latin America*. Princeton: Princeton University Press.
Whittington, K. E. 2003. "Legislative Sanctions and the Strategic Environment of Judicial Review." *International Journal of Constitutional Law* 1:446–74.
Whittington, K. E. 2005. "Interpose your Friendly Hand: Political Supports for the Exercise of Judicial Review by the United States Supreme Court." *American Political Science Review* 99:583–96.
Whittington, K. E. 2007. *Political Foundations of Judicial Supremacy: The Presidency, the Supreme Court, and Constitutional Leadership in U.S. History*. Princeton: Princeton University Press.
Widner, Jennifer. 2001. *Building the Rule of Law: Francis Nyalali and the Road to Judicial Independence in Africa*. New York: W. W. Norton.
Widner, Jennifer, and Daniel Scher. 2008. "Building Judicial Independence in Semi-Democracies: Uganda and Zimbabwe." In *Rule by Law: The Politics of Courts in Authoritarian Regimes*, ed. Tom Ginsburg and Tamir Moustafa. New York: Cambridge University Press.
Wilkinson, Steven. 2004. *Votes and Violence: Electoral Competition and Ethnic Riots in India*. New York: Cambridge University Press.
Williams, Glynn, and Emma Mawdsley. 2006. "Postcolonial Environmental Justice: Government and Governance in India." *Geoforum* 37:660–70.
Wilson, Bruce M. 2005. "Changing Dynamics: The Political Impact of Costa Rica's Constitutional Court." In *The Judicialization of Politics in Latin America*, ed. Rachel Sieder, Line Schjolden, and Alan Angell. New York: Palgrave Macmillan.
Wiratma, L. 2000. "Reformasi Konsti- tusi: Potret Demokrasi dalam Proses Pembelajaran." *Analisis CSIS* 29 (4): 401–12.
Witoelar, E. 2003. "Governance Reform in Indonesia." Paper presented at the Interim CGI meeting in Jakarta. http://www.ssronline.org/document_result.cfm?id=570.
Wolf, H. 1997. "Transition and Strategies: Choices and Outcomes." New York University, Stern Business School.
Wolfrum, Rudiger, and Rainer Grote. 1971–. *Constitutions of the Countries of the World*. Oxford and New York: Oxford University Press.
Woods, Patricia J., and Lisa Hilbink. 2009. "Comparative Sources of Judicial Empowerment: Ideas and Interests." *Political Research Quarterly* 62:745–52.
World Bank. 2003. *Judicial Systems in Transition Economies: Assessing the Part, Looking to the Future*. Washington, DC: The World Bank.
World Bank. 2004. *Initiatives in Legal and Judicial Reform*. Washington, DC: The World Bank.
World Bank. 2006. "World Development Indicators." CD-ROM.

World Bank. 2008. "World Development Report." Washington, DC: The World Bank.
World Bank. 2010. *The World Bank Annual Report: 2009: Year in Review.* Washington, DC: The World Bank.
World Business Environment Survey. 2003. http://www.gcgf.org/ifcext/economics.nsf/Content/ic-wbes.
World Economic Forum. 2009. *The Global Competitiveness Report.* Geneva: World Economic Forum.
World Values Survey. 2002. http://www.worldvaluessurvey.org/.
Wright, Joseph. 2008. "Do Authoritarian Institutions Constrain? How Legislatures Affect Economic Growth and Investment." *American Journal of Political Science* 52:322–43.
Yadav, Vineeta. 2011. *Political Parties, Business Groups, and Corruption in Developing Countries.* New York: Oxford University Press.
Yadav, Y. 2000. "Understanding the Second Democratic Upsurge: Trends of Bahujan Participation in Electoral Politics in the 1990s." In *Transforming India: Social and Political Dynamics of Democracy,* ed. Francine R. Frankel, Zoya Hasan, Rajeev Bhargava, and Balveer Arora. New Delhi: Oxford University Press.
Yadav, Y. 2004. "The Elusive Mandate of 2004." *Economic and Political Weekly* 39:5383–98.
Yamanishi, David S. 2000. "Rule of Law, Property Rights, and Human Rights: An Empirical Study of the Effects (and Non-effects) of Legal Institutions." Paper presented at annual meeting of the American Political Science Association, Washington, DC.
Yusuf, Slamet Effendy, and Umar Basalim. 2000. *Reformasi Konstitusi Indonesia: Perubahan Pertama UUD1945.* Jakarta: Pustaka Indonesia Bersatu.
Zimmerman, Augusto. 2008. "How Brazilian Judges Undermine the Rule of Law: A Critical Appraisal." *International Trade and Business Law Review* 11:179–217.
Zucco, Cesar. 2009. "Ideology or What? Legislative Behavior in Multiparty Presidential Settings." *Journal of Politics* 7:1076.

INDEX

Note: Page numbers in *italics* indicate figures and tables.

ADB (Asian Development Bank), 245
ADBIAS (Asian Development Bank Institutional Assessment Survey), 119
Ades, A., 314n8
Africa, 37, 260, 313n1. *See also specific countries*
Ames, Barry, 185, 301n36
Annual Human Rights Reports (U.S. Department of State), 151, 153
Apodaca, Clair, 78
Argentina, 4, 23, 56, 59, 289n25, 289n31, 290nn33. *See also* Latin America
Arifin, Firmansyah, 43, 122
Arora, R. K., 217, 218
Asian Development Bank (ADB), 245
Asian Development Bank Institutional Assessment Survey (ADBIAS), 119
Assegaf, Rifqi, 236–38, 244–45

Babri Mosque *(Rath Yatra)* case, 212–16, 306nn44–45, 306n49, 307n51
Ballard, Megan, 136, 144
Bangladesh, 37, 99, 152
Beck, Nathaniel, 298n10
Benin, 170–71, 301n37
Berggren, Niclas, 300n22
Bester, Alan, 292n25
Bharatiya Janata Party (BJP), 212–17, 218–19, 300n19, 306n42, 306n44
Blasi, Gerard J., 151
Blaustein, Albert P., 78
Brazil, and democratic transition in context of judicial review: overview of, 30, 108–10, 145–47, 294n4, 296n46; case selection strategy and, 110–11, 294n3; corollary to hypothesis 1 and, 29, 108–10, 128–29, 141; democratic transition for, 29, 127–28, 286n41, 296n47; full judicial review authority and, 128–30, 141–45, 297n63; hazard rates in office for, 170, 301n36; high electoral particularism with low time horizons/high hazard rates in office in context of judicial review and, 289n27; Hirschman-Herfindahl index and, 131, 134; historical context for, 127–30, 286n41, 294n5; legislative concentration and, 117, 130–38, 294n10, 296n49; ordinal measure of judicial review and, 144, 297n63; public trust in judiciary and, 138–41, 297nn54–58
Brazil, and electoral particularism in context of DFJI: overview of, 202–5, 225–26, 305n28, 305n31; candidate-centered system and, 184–87, 303nn7–10, 303n12; case selection strategy and, 181–84, 302nn3–6; constitutional amendments and statutory bills and, 199–202, *200, 201, 203;* empirical evidence for, 187–202, *200, 201, 203,* 303nn13–15, 304nn16–17, 304nn19–20, 304n21, 304n23; hazard rates in office for, 29, 185–87, *186,* 286n43, 302nn5–6, 303n9, 303n11; high electoral particularism with low time horizons/high hazard rates in office and, 185–86, *186,* 193–94, 303n11; Hirschman-Herfindahl index and, 302n3, 303n12; hypothesis 2 and, 29–30, 31, 286n43; judicial reform efforts and, 199; judicial review during energy crisis in 2001 and, *186,* 188–94, 303nn13–15, 304nn16–17; open-list PR and, 29, 182, 184–85, 196; opposition parties and, 194–99, 304nn19–20, 304n21, 304n23. *See also* Brazil, and democratic transition in context of judicial review; electoral particularism, and DFJI
Brinks, Daniel, 199
Bulgaria, 2–3, 42–43, 50, 288n24, 289n31

353

Caldeira, Gregory A., 313n5
candidate-centered systems, and DFJI: Brazil's electoral particularism in context of, 184–87, 303nn7–10, 303n12; India's electoral particularism in context of, 207–11, 301n36, 305n40, 306n42
Cardoso, Fernando Henrique, 186, *186*, 188–93, 196–98, 202, 304n16, 304n21
Carey, John, 156, 184, 303n8
Carro, Jesus M., 292n25, 301n25
Carrubba, Clifford James, 39, 283n6, 313n5
Case, William, 37
case studies (comparative case studies): overview of, 7; democratic transition in context of judicial review and, 110–11, 294n3; electoral particularism in context of DFJI and, 181–84, 302nn3–6. *See also specific countries, and case studies*
Chaba, Anju A., 208, 301n36
Cheibub, José Antonio, 89, 103, 292n19, 292n28, 293n37
China, 271
Chiozza, Giacomo, 156
Cingranelli, David L., 151–53, 266, 275, 305n31, 313n68
closed-list PR (proportional representation), and Indonesia's party-centered system, 227, 228–35, 308nn2–4, 308n6
Collor, Ferdinand, 186, 190, 202, 303n15
Colombia, 55, 272, 274, 289n29
comparative case studies (case studies). *See* case studies (comparative case studies); *and specific countries, and case studies*
competitiveness of participation (PARCOM), 88, 158, 291n18, 300n23
constitutional amendments and statutory bills, in context of DFJI: overview of, 261; Brazil's electoral particularism in context of, 199–202, *200, 201, 203;* India's electoral particularism in context of, 219–20, *221, 221*–23, *222, 223,* 307nn54–55; Indonesia's party-centered system and, 248–57, *252, 253, 255,* 312n55, 312nn60–61, 312nn64–65, 313nn67–68
control variables: for empirical evidence for electoral particularism, 157–59, *160, 161,* 300nn21–24; in empirical evidence for full judicial review authority, 88–90, 291n15, 291n18, 292nn19–20, 292nn22–24
Cooter, Robert, 23, 290n32
corollary to hypothesis 1: overview of, 46–51, 73–74, 288n17; Brazil's democratic transition in context of judicial review and, 29, 108–10, 128–29, 141; democratic transition in context of judicial review and, 100; empirical evidence for full judicial review authority and, 75, 100, 107; Indonesia's democratic transition in context of judicial review and, 108–10. *See also* hypothesis 1
corollary to hypothesis 2: overview of, 28, 72, 74, 289n31, 290nn32–33; electoral particularism in context of DFJI and, 180–82; empirical evidence for electoral particularism and, 148, 164, 167, 169–71, 177, 298n2; Indonesia's party-centered system and, 227, 257–58; party-centered system in context of DFJI and, 227. *See also* hypothesis 2
corruption levels: democracy in context of DJJI and, 10–11, 266–68, *267,* 274–76, *275,* 314nn8–10, 314n18; empirical evidence for electoral particularism and, 151–52; Indonesia's party-centered system and, 237, 246–47, 258–59; theoretical framework for DFJI and, 56–59
Costa Rica, 152, 289n25
court authority. *See* de facto judicial independence (DFJI)
Cox, G., 55, 58
Cross, Frank, 151, 153
Cumaraswamy, D. P., 249, 257

de facto judicial independence (DFJI): overview and definition of, 6–7, 8–9; case studies and, 7; democracy and judicial independence studies in context of, 9–12, 284n25, 285n26; DJJI in relation to, 9; electoral particularism and, 26–27; electoral systems and, 4–6; full judicial review authority in context of, 8–9; hazard rates in office and, 6, *7,* 264–65, 284n14; judicial review in context of variation in, 12–19, 285n29; judiciary capture and, 22, 26, 52; studies in, 51–53; theoretical framework for variations in, *7,* 12–19, 21–26, 285n29; time horizons in office and, 5–6, 26–28, 264–65; variation in, 1–6, *3, 5,* 283n5, 284nn11–12. *See also* de jure judicial independence (DJJI); full judicial review authority; judicial review; new democracies; theoretical framework, for DFJI
de facto subservient judiciary, and electoral particularism, 27

INDEX   355

de jure judicial independence (DJJI): overview and definition of, 6–7, 8; democracy and judicial independence studies in context of, 9–12, 284n25; DFJI in relation to, 9; empirical evidence for electoral particularism and, 159, 172, 174; empirical evidence for full judicial review authority and, 88, 104, 106, 290n1; Indonesia's democratic transition in context of judicial review and, 113; judicial review in context of variation in, 12–19, 285n29; new democracies and, 1, 2, 3, 4, 283n5; variations in, 1–3, 3, 12–19, 283n6, 285n29. *See also* de facto judicial independence (DFJI); democracy, and DJJI; full judicial review authority; new democracies

democracy, and DJJI: overview of, 31; corruption levels and, 10–11, 266–68, *267*, 274–76, *275*, 314nn8–10, 314n18; economic growth and, 11, *267*, 268, 285n26, 300n22; electoral systems in context of, 31, 270, 273; empirical analysis as contributions understanding and limitations of, 31, 265; future of, 272–76, *275*, 314n18; future research in, 270–72; international investments in institutional design and, 10–11, 16–18, 269–70; judicial reform efforts and, 10–11, 29–31, 269; methodological analysis as contribution to understanding and limitations of, 31, 265–70, *267*, 314nn8–10; studies on, 9–12, 261–65, 284n25, 285n26, 313n3, 313nn5–6. *See also* de jure judicial independence (DJJI); new democracies

democratic transition, in context of judicial review: overview of, 30, 108–10, 145–47; for Brazil, 29, 127–28, 286n41, 296n47; case selection strategy and, 110–11, 294n3; corollary to hypothesis 1 and, 100; for Indonesia, 29, 286n41. *See also* Brazil, and democratic transition in context of judicial review; full judicial review authority; Indonesia, and democratic transition in context of judicial review

democratic transitions, for new democracies, 1, *2*, 283nn4–5, 286n41. *See also specific new democracies*

dependent variable and sample. *See* sample and dependent variable

Desposato, Scott, 301n29

developing countries. *See* new democracies; *and specific new democracies*

DFJI (de facto judicial independence). *See* de facto judicial independence (DFJI); de jure judicial independence (DJJI); full judicial review authority; judicial review; new democracies; theoretical framework, for DFJI

Di Tella, R., 314n8

DJJI (de jure judicial independence). *See* de facto judicial independence (DFJI); de jure judicial independence (DJJI); democracy, and DJJI; full judicial review authority; new democracies

economic growth: democracy in context of DJJI and, 11, *267*, 268, 285n26, 300n22; Indonesia's democratization in context of judicial review and, 111, 250

effective number of legislative parties (ENLP), 154, 235, 299n13, 309n14

electoral particularism, and DFJI: overview of, 26–27, 31, 180–81, 225–26, 264–65; case selection strategy and, 181–84, 302nn3–6; corollary to hypothesis 2, 180–82; de facto subservient judiciary and, 27; electoral rules and, 54–57; Hirschman-Herfindahl index and, 302n3; hypothesis 2 and, 28, 29–30, 31, 68, *69*, 180–81, 286nn41–44, 286n43; judiciary capture and, 64, 67; new democracies and, 63–68. *See also* Brazil, and electoral particularism in context of DFJI; empirical evidence, for electoral particularism; India, and electoral particularism in context of DFJI; party-centered system (low electoral particularism), and DFJI

electoral rules, and electoral particularism in context of DFJI, 54–57

electoral systems (political systems): overview of, 6–7, 31, 273; democracy and judicial independence studies in context of, 11–12; democracy in context of DJJI and, 31, 270, 273; DFJI and, 4–6; judicial review in context of, 27–28, 286n40. *See also* high electoral particularism (personalistic vote electoral system); high electoral particularism with low time horizons/high hazard rates in office; party-centered system (low electoral particularism), and DFJI; *and specific types of electoral systems*

empirical evidence, for electoral particularism: overview of, 30–31, 148–49, 177–79; Brazil in context of DFJI and, 187–202, *200, 201, 203*, 303nn13–15, 304nn16–17,

empirical evidence, for electoral particularism (*continued*)
304nn19–20, 304n21, 304n23; control variables for, 157–59, *160, 161,* 300nn21–24; corollary to hypothesis 2 and, 148, 164, 167, 169–71, 177, 298n2; corruption levels and, 151–52; DJJI and, 159, 172, 174; Hirschman-Herfindahl index and, 158; hypothesis 2 and, 148–53, 155–57, 161, 164, 167–68, 170, 172–73, 298n1; independent variables for, *150,* 153–57, *156,* 298nn9–11, 299nn12–16, 300nn19–20; India in context of DFJI and, 211–19, 306nn43–45, 306n49, 307n51; log-likelihood of bivariate ordered probit model and, 163, 281–82; PARCOM and, 158, 300n23; political accountability and, 31; results report for, 164–73, *165, 166, 167, 168, 169, 170, 171,* 301nn35–37; robustness test results for, 173–74, *175–76,* 177, 301n38, 301n40, 302n41–45; sample and dependent variable for, 149, *150,* 151–53, *161,* 298n3, 298n5; statistical methodology for, 161–64, 301nn25–26, 301n29, 301n31. *See also* electoral particularism, and DFJI

empirical evidence, for full judicial review authority: overview of, 30, 31, 75–76, 105–7, 265; control variables in, 88–90, 291n15, 291n18, 292nn19–20, 292nn22–24; corollary to hypothesis 1 and, 75, 100, 107; DJJI and, 88, 104, 106, 290n1; Heckman selection and, 91; Hirschman-Herfindahl index and, 79, 86, 291n9; hypothesis 1 and, 78–88, *80–85, 87,* 90, 96, 98–100, 102, 104, 291nn5–14; independent variables in, 78–79, *80–85,* 86, *87,* 88, 291nn5–14; ordinal measure of judicial review and, 76, 78, 89–91; PARCOM and, 88, 291n18; results report for, 93–102, *94, 95–96, 97, 99, 100,* 293nn32–33; robustness test results for, *95–96,* 102–5, 293n34, 293nn36–40, 293nn42–43; sample and dependent variable in, 76, *77,* 78, 290n1, 291n2; S-OP model and, 90–94, 96–97, 100–102, *101,* 104, 277–81, 292n30, 293n31; statistical methodology for, 90–93, *91,* 292n25–26, 292nn25–26, 292n28, 292n30, 293n31. *See also* full judicial review authority

ENLP (effective number of legislative parties), 154, 235, 299n13, 309n14
European Union, 269

Fearon, James, 103, 293n34, 301n38
Feld, Lars P., 9, 285n26
Ferejohn, John, 8, 45, 283n4
Finkel, S. E., 76, 78, 86, 151, 153, 159, 291n2, 300n24
Flanz, G., 78
full judicial review authority: overview and definition of, 8, 283n6, 284nn19–20; Brazil's democratic transition and, 128–30, 141–45, 297n63; DFJI in context of, 8–9; new democracies and, 1–2, *3,* 283n6. *See also* Brazil, and democratic transition in context of judicial review; de facto judicial independence (DFJI); de jure judicial independence (DJJI); democratic transition, in context of judicial review; empirical evidence, for full judicial review authority; Indonesia, and democratic transition in context of judicial review; judicial review; ordinal measure of judicial review

Gallagher, Michael, 208
Gerring, John, 56
Gibler, Douglas, 284n25
Gibson, James L., 313n5
Ginsburg, Tom, 16, 21, 23, 49, 261–62, 290n32
GIR (Global Integrity Report), 119
Global Integrity Report (GIR), 119
Gloppen, Siri, 38, 59
Goemans, Heins, 156
Gowda, M. V. Rajeev, 220
Goyal, R., 217, 218
Greene, W. H., 91–92, 278, 281
Grote, Rainer, 78

Habibie, Jusuf, 112, 309n12
Hansen, Christian, 292n25
Hayo, Bernd, 23, 102–3, 159, 173, 313n6
hazard rates in office: for Brazil's electoral particularism in context of DFJI and, 29, 185–87, *186,* 286n43, 302nn5–6, 303n9, 303n11; DFJI in context of, 6, *7,* 264–65, 284n14; high electoral particularism with low time horizons/high hazard rates in office in context of judicial review and, 57–68, 288n24, 289n25, 289nn27–28; India's electoral particularism in context of DFJI and, 29, 155, *156,* 170, *186,* 210–11, 286nn43–44, 289n27, 300n19, 302n6, 305n41, 306n42; Indonesia's party-centered

system and, 29, 231–35, *232*, 243–48, 286n43, 302n6, 308nn9–11, 309nn13–14, 311n40, 312n51; low electoral particularism with low time horizons/high hazard rates in office with limits on DFJI and, 68–72, 289n31, 290nn32–33
Heckman (Heckit) selection, 91, 161
Helmke, Gretchen, 40, 44–45, 59
Hensher, D. A., 91–92, 278, 281
Herfindahl (Hirschman-Herfindahl) index. *See* Hirschman-Herfindahl (Herfindahl) index
Herron, Erik S., 23, 159
high electoral particularism (personalistic vote electoral system), 28, 29, 59. *See also* electoral particularism; electoral systems (political systems); hypothesis 2
high electoral particularism with low time horizons/high hazard rates in office: Brazil's electoral particularism in context of DFJI and, 185–86, *186*, 193–94, 303n11; judicial review in context of, 57–68, 288n24, 289n25, 289nn27–28. *See also* high electoral particularism (personalistic vote electoral system)
Hilbink, Lisa, 159
Hirschl, Ran, 262, 287n5
Hirschman-Herfindahl (Herfindahl) index: Brazil's democratic transition in context of judicial review and, 131, 134; Brazil's electoral particularism in context of DFJI and, 302n3, 303n12; electoral particularism in context of DFJI and, 302n3; empirical evidence for electoral particularism and, 158; empirical evidence for full judicial review authority and, 79, 86, 291n9; India's electoral particularism in context of DFJI and, 294n3, 302n3, 305n40; Indonesia's democratic transition in context of judicial review and, 116–17; Indonesia's party-centered system and, 302n3, 309n14
Hix, Simon, 207–8, 229
Holliday, Ian, 208
Howell, Katrina, 143
Hungary, 4, 152, 289n29
Huntington, Samuel P., 313n1
Hurlin, Christophe, 105, 176–77
hypothesis 1: overview of, 20, 46, *47*, *69*, 73, 75; empirical evidence for full judicial review authority and, 78–88, *80–85, 87*, 90, 96, 98–100, 102, 104, 291nn5–14; independent variables in empirical evidence for judicial review and, 78–79, *80–85*, 86, *87*, 88, 291nn5–14; Indonesia's democratic transition in context of judicial review and, 29, 108–9, 114–27, *116*; judicial review and, 20, 29, 296n41; methodology and, 29, 296n41; statistical methodology in empirical evidence for judicial review and, 90; statistical results report in empirical evidence for judicial review and, 96, 98–100, 102, 104. *See also* corollary to hypothesis 1
hypothesis 2: overview of, 28, 68, *69*, 74, 148–49, 298n1; Brazil's electoral particularism in context of DFJI and, 29–30, 31, 286n43; control variables for empirical evidence for electoral particularism and, 157; electoral particularism in context of DFJI and, 29–30, 31, 68, *69*, 180–81, 286n43; electoral systems and, 28, 29, 286nn41–44; independent variables for empirical evidence for electoral particularism and, 155–57; India's electoral particularism in context of DFJI and, 29–30, 31, 286nn43–44; methodology and, 29, 286nn41–44; results report for empirical evidence for electoral particularism and, 164, 167–68, 170, 172; robustness test results for empirical evidence for electoral particularism and, 173; sample and dependent variable for empirical evidence for electoral particularism and, 149–53; statistical methodology for empirical evidence for electoral particularism and, 161. *See also* corollary to hypothesis 2

IDB (International Development Bank), 269
IMF (International Monetary Fund), 245, 270, 302n4
independent variables: for empirical evidence for electoral particularism, *150*, 153–57, *156*, 298nn9–11, 299nn12–16, 300nn19–20; in empirical evidence for full judicial review authority, 78–79, *80–85,* 86, *87*, 88, 291nn5–14
India, and electoral particularism in context of DFJI: overview of, 23, 206–7, 223–26; Babri Mosque case and, 212–16, 306nn44–45, 306n49, 307n51; candidate-centered system and, 207–11, 301n36, 305n40, 306n42; case selection strategy and, 181–84, 302nn3–4, 302n6; constitutional amendments and statutory bills and,

India (*continued*)
219–20, *221*, 221–23, *222*, *223*, 307nn54–55; empirical evidence for electoral particularism and, 211–19, 306nn43–45, 306n49, 307n51; hazard rates in office for, 29, 155, *156*, 170, *186*, 210–11, 286nn43–44, 289n27, 300n19, 302n6, 305n41, 306n42; Hirschman-Herfindahl index and, 294n3, 302n3, 305n40; hypothesis 2 and, 29–30, 31, 286nn43–44; opposition parties and, 211–19; political accountability and, 220; SMD plurality rule and, 29, 182, 206–8; *S. R. Bommai* case and, 216–19; Sunderlal Patwa case and, 216–19. *See also* electoral particularism, and DFJI

Indonesia, and democratic transition in context of judicial review: overview of, 30, 108–10, 145–47, 294n4; case selection strategy and, 110–11, 294n3; corollary to hypothesis 1 and, 108–10; democratic transition for, 29, 286n41; DJJI and, 113; economic growth and, 111, 250; Hirschman-Herfindahl index and, 116–17; historical context for democratization in context of judicial system in, 111–14, 294nn5–6, 294n8; hypothesis 1 and, 29, 108–9, 114–27, *116*; legislative concentration and, 37, 287n4; legislative control and, 114–19, *116*, 294nn10–11, 294n17, 295n18; ordinal measure of judicial review and, 114, 294n8; public trust in judiciary and, 41–43, 119–27, 287n11, 295n25, 295nn27–29, 296n31, 296n37. *See also* Indonesia, and party-centered system

Indonesia, and party-centered system: overview of, 227–28, 307n1, 313n70; case selection strategy and, 181–83, 302n3, 302n6; closed-list PR and, 227, 228–35, 308nn2–4, 308n6; constitutional amendments and statutory bills in context of DFJI and, 248–57, *252*, *253*, *255*, 312n55, 312nn60–61, 312nn64–65, 313nn67–68; corollary to hypothesis 2 and, 227, 257–58; corruption levels and, 237, 246–47, 258–59; ENLP and, 235, 309n14; hazard rates in office for, 29, 231–35, *232*, 243–48, 286n43, 302n6, 308nn9–11, 309nn13–14, 311n40, 312n51; Hirschman-Herfindahl index and, 302n3, 309n14; judiciary capture and, 235–43, 309n15, 309n20, 309nn22–23, 310n26, 310nn28–30, 310n33, 311n34, 311n37; open-list PR and, 230–31, 254, 313n70;

Pancasila and, 240–41, 310n29; political accountability and, 146, 230–31; Sharia law and, 240–41, 310n30, 310n33; SMD plurality rule and, 229, 308n2. *See also* Indonesia, and democratic transition in context of judicial review; party-centered system (low electoral particularism), and DFJI

International Development Bank (IDB), 269
international investments, in institutional design, 10–11, 16–18, 269–70
International Monetary Fund (IMF), 245, 270, 302n4
Ishiyama, John, 14

Jaitley, Arun, 214
Johnson, Joel, 156–57
Johnson Tan, Paige, 230, 234–35, 311n37
Joshi, Murli Manohar, 214
judicial empowerment or independence. *See* de facto judicial independence (DFJI); de jure judicial independence (DJJI)
judicial reform efforts: Brazil's electoral particularism in context of DFJI and, 199; democracy in context of DJJI and, 10–11, 29–31, 269; empirical evidence for full judicial review authority and, 104; Indonesia's democratic transition in context of judicial review, 120, 126–27
judicial review: overview and definition of, 8–9, 260; during Brazil's energy crisis in 2001, *186*, 188–94, 303nn13–15, 304nn16–17; case studies and, 7; democracy and judicial independence studies in context of, 11; DFJI variation in context of, 12–19, 285n29; DJJI variation in context of, 12–19, 285n29; electoral systems in context of, 27–28, 286n40; hypothesis 1 and, 29, 296n41; new democracies and, 4, 19–20, 285n30. *See also* full judicial review authority; hypothesis 1
judiciary capture: DFJI and, 22, 26, 52; high electoral particularism and, 59; Indonesia's party-centered system and, 235–43, 309n15, 309n20, 309nn22–23, 310n26, 310nn28–30, 310n33, 311n34, 311n37; new democracies and, 20; particularism in context of DFJI and, 64, 67; public trust in judiciary and, 40

Kapur, Devesh, 210, 219
Karlson, Nils, 300n22
Katz, Jonathan N., 298n10

Keefer, Philip, 208–9, 301n36
Keith, Linda Camp, 78, 151, 153, 305n31, 313n68
Khemani, Stutti, 208–9, 301n36
Klemb, Jurgen, 310n29
Koalisi Ornop untuk Konstitusi Baru (KOKB), 118, 122, 126–27, 294n17, 295n18

Laitin, David, 103, 293n34, 301n38
Landes, William M., 288n17
Larkins, Christopher, 8–9, 284n25
Latin America, 4, 40, 44, 260, 313n1. *See also specific countries*
Latvia, 50
legislative concentration: Brazil's democratic transition in context of judicial review, 117, 130–38, 294n10, 296n49; government policy-making and, 44–51; Indonesia's democratic transition in context of judicial review and, 37, 287n4; low legislative concentration and low public trust in context of judicial review and, 46–51; in new democracies, 35–38, 287n2, 287nn4–5
legislative control, and Indonesia's democratic transition in context of judicial review, 114–19, *116*, 294nn10–11, 294n17, 295n18
Lijphart, Arend, 291n2
Linz, J., 140
Litaay, Alex, 124
log-likelihood of bivariate ordered probit model, and empirical evidence for electoral particularism, 163, 281–82
long time horizons, and DFJI, 6
low (short) time horizons: DFJI and, 5–6; low electoral particularism with low time horizons/high hazard rates in office with limits on DFJI and, 68–72, 289n31, 290nn32–33. *See also* high electoral particularism with low time horizons/high hazard rates in office; time horizons
Lubis, Todung Mulya, 239
Lula (Luiz Inácio Lula da Silva), *186,* 191, 198, 202, 304n23

Maddex, R., 78
Mainwaring, Scott P., 184–85, 301n36
Malawi, 37, 42, 59, 67, 152, 288n14, 289nn28–29
Malik, Balwant Singh, 218
McCubbins, Mathew D., 55, 58
Megawati Sukarnoputri: closed-list PR and, 230, 308n4, 309n13; constitutional amendments and statutory bills in context of DFJI and, 248–57, *252, 253, 255,* 312n55, 312nn60–61, 312nn64–65, 313nn67–68; corruption levels and, 237, 246–47, 258–59; democratic transition in Indonesia and, 112, 116; hazard rates in office for, 232, 234, 243–48, 258, 308nn10–11, 311n40, 312n51, 313n70; judiciary capture and, 236–43, 309n20, 309nn22–23, 310n26, 310nn28–30, 310n33, 311n34, 311n37; legislative control and, 295n18; public trust in judiciary and, 124
Mehta, Pratap Bhanu, 224
Melo, Marcus, 205
methodological analysis, and democracy in context of DJJI, 31, 265–70, *267,* 314nn8–10
Mexico, 152, 288n24, 289n25
Mill, John Stuart, 181–82
Mueller, Bernardo, 205
multi-methodological approach (research methodology), 28–30

Narasimha Rao (Rao government), 211–19, 306n43
new democracies: overview of, 260, 283n2; democratic-transition year for, 1, *2,* 283n4, 283nn4–5, 286n41; DJJI in, 1, *2, 3, 4,* 283n5; electoral particularism in context of DFJI and, 63–68; full judicial review authority in, 1–2, *3,* 283n6; hazard rates in office and, 6, *7,* 284n14; judicial review in context of, 4, 19–20, 285n30; judiciary capture and, 20; political accountability in, 31; "third wave" of democratization and, 260, 313n1. *See also* de facto judicial independence (DFJI); democracy; judicial review

open-list PR (proportional representation): Indonesia's party-centered system and, 230–31, 254, 270, 273, 313n70; Brazil's electoral particularism and, 29, 182, 184–85, 196; candidate-centered system and, 303n7; empirical evidence for electoral particularism and, 301n31
opposition parties: Brazil's electoral particularism in context of DFJI and, 194–99, 304nn19–20, 304n21, 304n23; India's electoral particularism in context of DFJI and, 211–19
ordinal measure of judicial review: Brazil's democratic transition in context of judicial

ordinal measure of judicial review (*continued*)
review, 144, 297n63; Brazil's electoral particularism in context of DFJI, 204; corruption levels and, *275,* 314n18; empirical evidence for electoral particularism and, 149–52, 161–64, 167, 173–74; empirical evidence for full judicial review authority and, 76, 78, 89–91; India's electoral particularism and, 224–25; Indonesia's democratic transition in context of judicial review and, 114, 294n8; Indonesia's party-centered system in context of DFJI and, 256, *256,* 313n68. *See also* full judicial review authority

Pabottingi, Mochtar, 126, 294n17
Palguna, I. D. G., 42
Pancasila, 240–41, 310n29
PARCOM (competitiveness of participation), 88, 158, 291n18, 300n23
Partnership for Governance Reform (PEGR), 119
party-centered system (low electoral particularism), and DFJI: overview of, 27, 31, 227–28, 257–59; corollary to hypothesis 2 and, 227; low time horizons/high hazard rates in office with limits on DFJI and, 68–72, 289n31, 290nn32–33. *See also* electoral particularism, and DFJI; electoral systems (political systems); Indonesia, and party-centered system
Pedersen, Morgens N., 159, 299n14
PEGR (Partnership for Governance Reform), 119
Pereira, Anthony, 139
Pereira, Carlos, 205
Permadi, 118
personalistic vote electoral system (high electoral particularism), 28, 29, 59. *See also* electoral particularism; electoral systems (political systems); hypothesis 2
Philippines, 37, 55, 274
plurality rule or SMD (single-member district) plurality rule, 29, 163, 182, 207, 229, 270, 273, 308n2
political accountability, in new democracies, 31, 36, 146, 220, 230–31
political particularism, and DFJI. *See* electoral particularism, and DFJI
political systems (electoral systems). *See* electoral systems (political systems); high electoral particularism (personalistic vote electoral system); high electoral particularism with low time horizons/high hazard rates in office; party-centered system (low electoral particularism), and DFJI; *and specific types of electoral systems*
Popova, Maria, 22
Posner, Richard A., 288n17
Power, Timothy, 185, 301n36
Prillaman, William, 140
Przeworski, Adam, 29, 103, 149, 156, 283n4, 286n42, 293nn36–37
public trust in judiciary: Brazil's democratic transition in context of judicial review and, 138–41, 297nn54–58; Indonesia's democratic transition in context of judicial review and, 41–43, 119–27, 287n11, 295n25, 295nn27–29, 296n31, 296n37; judiciary capture and, 40; theoretical framework for DFJI and, 38–44, 287nn6–7, 287n9, 288n12, 288n14

Rakner, Lise, 37
Ramamurti, R., 219
Ramseyer, Mark J., 288n17
Randazzo, Kirk (A.), 23, 159, 284n25
Rao government (Narasimha Rao), 211–19, 306n43
Rasmussen, Eric B., 288n17
Rath Yatra (Babri Mosque) case, 212–16, 306nn44–45, 306n49, 307n51
Reich, Gary, 134–37
research methodology (multi-methodological approach), 28–30
results report: for empirical evidence for electoral particularism, 164–73, *165, 166, 167, 168, 169, 170, 171,* 301nn35–37; for empirical evidence for full judicial review authority, 93–102, *94, 95–96, 97, 99, 100,* 293nn32–33
Richards, David L., 152–53, 266, 275, 305n31, 313n68
Rios-Figueroa, Julto, 9, 159, 314n8
Robinson, Davis R., 314n8
robustness test results: for empirical evidence for electoral particularism, 173–74, *175–76, 177,* 301n38, 301n40, 302n41–45; for empirical evidence for full judicial review authority, *95–96,* 102–5, 293n34, 293nn36–40, 293nn42–43
Rodrik, Dani, 79

Romania, 170–71, 272, 290n3, 301n37
Rose-Ackerman, Susan, 314n8
Rosenbluth, Frances, 8, 45, 283n4
Rosenn, Keith S., 136, 144–45, 151
Russia, 22, 40, 151–52, 275–76

Sambuaga, Theo, 117–18, 119–20
Sampaiao, Plinio Arruda, 141, 297n58
sample and dependent variable: in empirical evidence for electoral particularism, 149, *150,* 151–53, *161,* 298n3, 298n5; in empirical evidence for full judicial review authority, 76, *77,* 78, 290n1, 291n2
sample selection ordered probit (S-OP) model, 90–94, 96–97, 100–102, *101,* 104, 277–81, 292n30, 293n31
Samuels, David, 301n36
Santiso, Carlos, 140, 143–44, 203, 303n15
Sarney, Jose, 127, 130–33, 186
Sharia law, 240–41, 310n30, 310n33
Shin, J. H., 301n29, 301n37, 308n2
Shipan, Charles, 8, 45, 283n4
short (low) time horizons. *See* high electoral particularism with low time horizons/high hazard rates in office; low (short) time horizons; time horizons
Shugart, Matthew, 156, 184, 303n8
Sill, Kaitlyn, 285n26, 291n2
single-member district (SMD) plurality rule, 29, 163, 182, 207, 229, 270, 273, 308n2
Slovakia, 152
Smithey, Shannon Ishiyama, 14
S-OP (sample selection ordered probit) model, 90–94, 96–97, 100–102, *101,* 104, 277–81, 292n30, 293n31
South Africa, 23, 155–56, *156,* 300n20. *See also* Africa
S. R. Bommai v. Union of India (1994), 216–19
Sridharan, E., 220
Sri Lanka, 272
statistical methodology: for empirical evidence for electoral particularism, 161–64, 301nn25–26, 301n29, 301n31; for empirical evidence for full judicial review authority, 90–93, *91,* 292n25–26, 292nn25–26, 292n28, 292n30, 293n31
Staton, Jeffrey (K.), 9, 40, 44–45, 284n25, 313n5
Stepan, A., 140
Stephenson, Mathew C., 21, 24, 88
Stockmann, Petra, 121, 125

Sudan, 269
Sunderlal Patwa case, 216–19
Suri, K. C., 209

Tanchev, Evgeni, 43
Tate, C. Neal, 45, 151, 153, 305n31, 313n68
Taylor, Matthew, 194–95
Thacker, Strom C., 56
Thailand, 37, 49–50
theoretical framework, for DFJI: overview of, 7, 30, 32–35, 73–74, 261; corruption levels and, 56–59; DFJI studies, 51–53; electoral rules in context of electoral particularism and, 54–57; interaction between government, opposition, and judiciary and, 6–7; legislative concentration in context of government policy-making and, 44–51; legislative concentration in new democracies and, 35–38, 287n2, 287nn4–5; low electoral particularism with low time horizons/high hazard rates in office with limits on DFJI and, 68–72, 289n31, 290nn32–33; low legislative concentration and low public trust in context of judicial review and, 46–51; political accountability and, 36; public trust in judiciary and, 38–44, 287nn6–7, 287n9, 288n12, 288n14; variations in DFJI and, 7, 12–19, 21–26, 285n29. *See also* de facto judicial independence (DFJI); high electoral particularism with low time horizons/high hazard rates in office; hypothesis 1; hypothesis 2
"third wave" of democratization, 260, 313n1. *See also* new democracies
TI (Transparency International), 246, 266–67, 289n27, 289n31, 290n33, 314nn9–10
time horizons in office: DFJI in context of, 26–28, 264–65; low electoral particularism with low time horizons/high hazard rates in office with limits on DFJI and, 68–72, 289n31, 290nn32–33. *See also* high electoral particularism with low time horizons/high hazard rates in office
Traferri, Alejandra, 292n25, 301n25
Transparency International (TI), 246, 266–67, 289n27, 289n31, 290n33, 314nn9–10
Tucker, Richard, 298n10

Udayakumar, S. P., 213
Ufen, Andreas, 229–30
Ukraine, 4, 22, 275–76

United Nations Development Programme (UNDP), 274–76
United States, 40, 269, 287n7
Uruguay, 272

Vanberg, Georg, 8, 40, 57, 313n5
Van De Walle, Nicholas, 37
Venet, Baptiste, 105, 176–77
Venkatesan, V., 215
Voigt, Stefan, 9, 23, 102–3, 159, 173, 285n26, 313n6

Wacziarg, Romain, 79
Wahid, Abdurrahman: closed-list PR and, 230, 308n4; constitutional amendments and statutory bills in context of DFJI and, 254–55, *255;* democratic transition in Indonesia and, 112, 116; hazard rates in office for, 233–34, 245, 311n40; judiciary capture and, 236–38, 310n26; legislative control and, 295n18; public trust in judiciary and, 42, 116–22

Wallack, Jessica (Seddon), 156–57, 184, 210, 230, 266
WBES (World Bank Enterprise Survey), 119
Werneck Vianna, Lutz, 195
Whittington, K. E., 13, 48–49
Winarta, Frans Hendra, 255–56, 313n67
Wolf, H., 300n22
Wolfrum, Rudiger, 78
Woods, Patricia J., 159
World Bank, 10, 110, 156, 182–83, 245, 266, 269–70, 293n40, 299n12, 302n43
World Bank Enterprise Survey (WBES), 119
World Values Survey (WVS), 119

Yamanishi, David S., 285n26
Yudhoyono, Susilo Bambang, 243–44, 246–48, 254, *255,* 308n10, 311n47, 312n65
Yusuf, Slamet Effendi, 122, 296n31

Zambia, 59
Zimbabwe, 271